Regulating Development

THE CRC SERIES ON COMPETITION, REGULATION AND DEVELOPMENT

Series Editors: Paul Cook, *Professor of Economics and Development Policy* and Martin Minogue, *Senior Research Fellow, Institute for Development Policy and Management, University of Manchester, UK*

Titles in the series include:

Leading Issues in Competition, Regulation and Development
Edited by Paul Cook, Colin Kirkpatrick, Martin Minogue and David Parker

The Politics of Regulation
Institutions and Regulatory Reforms for the Age of Governance
Edited by Jacint Jordana and David Levi-Faur

Regulating Development
Evidence from Africa and Latin America
Edited by Edmund Amann

Regulating Development

Evidence from Africa and Latin America

Edited by

Edmund Amann

Senior Lecturer in Development Economics, University of Manchester, UK and Affiliate Research Associate Professor, Regional Economics Applications Laboratory, University of Illinois, Urbana-Champaign, USA

THE CRC SERIES ON COMPETITION, REGULATION AND DEVELOPMENT

Edward Elgar
Cheltenham, UK • Northampton, MA, USA

Published by
Edward Elgar Publishing Limited
Glensanda House
Montpellier Parade
Cheltenham
Glos GL50 1UA
UK

Edward Elgar Publishing, Inc.
136 West Street
Suite 202
Northampton
Massachusetts 01060
USA

A catalogue record for this book
is available from the British Library

Library of Congress Cataloguing in Publication Data

Regulating development: evidence from Africa and Latin America/edited by
    Edmund Amann.
        p.   cm. — (The CRC series on competition, regulation and development)
    Includes bibliographical references and index.
    'Chapters 3, 7, 8–10 and 12 of this book were originally presented at the Centre
    for Regulation and Competition's third international conference in Cape Town,
    South Africa during September 2004' — Acknowledgements.
    1. Trade regulation—Africa. 2. Trade regulation—Latin America. 3. Industrial
    policy—Africa. 4. Industrial policy—Latin America. 5. Africa—Economic policy.
    6. Latin America—Economic policy. 7. Africa—Economic conditions—1960– .
    8. Latin America—Economic conditions—1982– . I. Amann, Edmund. II. Series.
    HD3616.A3513R44   2006
    343'.07—dc22   2005051518

ISBN-13: 978 1 84542 499 2
ISBN-10: 1 84542 499 9

Typeset by Cambrian Typesetters, Camberley, Surrey
Printed and bound in Great Britain by MPG Books Ltd, Bodmin, Cornwall

Contents

PART III   THE AFRICAN EXPERIENCE

Figures and tables

FIGURES

TABLES

vii

Contributors

Ama Asantewah Ahene is Principal Research Assistant in the Institute of Economic and Social Statistics at the University of Accra, Ghana, a regional research partner with CRC, Manchester, UK

Oludele A. Akinboade is a Professor in the Department of Economics at the University of South Africa, Pretoria

Edmund Amann is Senior Lecturer in Development Economics at the University of Manchester UK and Affiliate Research Associate Professor at the University of Illinois Regional Economics Applications Laboratory, Urbana–Champaign, USA

Ernest Aryeetey is Professor and Deputy Director of the Institute of Economic and Social Statistics at the University of Accra, Ghana, a regional research partner with CRC, Manchester, UK

Werner Baer is Professor of Economics at the University of Illinois, Urbana–Champaign, USA

João Carlos Ferraz is Chief, Division of Production, Productivity and Management at the United Nations Economic Commission for Latin America and the Caribbean (ECLAC). He is also Associate Professor at the Federal University of Rio de Janeiro, Brazil

Andrea Goldstein is Senior Economist at the OECD Development Centre in Paris, France

Peter Holmes is Reader in Economics at the University of Sussex, Brighton, UK

Judi Hudson is Senior Researcher at the Centre for Policy Studies, Doornfontein, South Africa

Hossein Jalilian is Senior Lecturer at the Bradford Centre for International Development, University of Bradford, UK

Afeikhena Jerome is Senior Researcher at the National Institute for Economic Policy in Johannesburg, South Africa

Colin Kirkpatrick is Professor of Development Economics at IDPM, University of Manchester and Co-director of the Regulation Research Programme in CRC, Manchester, UK

Christopher May is Professor of Political Economy at the University of Lancaster, UK

David Parker is Professor of Business Economics, University of Cranfield, UK and Co-director of the Regulation Research Programme in CRC, Manchester, UK

Germano Mendes de Paula is Associate Professor of Economics at the Federal University of Uberlândia, Brazil

José Claudio Linhares Pires is an economist based at the Inter-American Development Bank, Washington, DC, USA

Fungai Sibanda is based at the Competition Commission, Pretoria, South Africa

Yin-Fang Zhang is Lecturer in Development Economics at IDPM, University of Manchester, UK and a Research Associate of CRC

Preface

The Centre on Regulation and Competition (CRC) was established in 2001 with core funding from the UK Department of International Development, to conduct research into hitherto neglected issues of competition, regulation and regulatory governance in developing countries. This Elgar Series represents one of many forms of dissemination of research findings and conceptual studies, including conferences, workshops, journal publication and policy briefs.

A particular focus in CRC's policy-related work is on the linkages between regulatory reforms, pro-poor growth, and more general structures and processes of development. This book, the third in the series, examines the impact that regulation – good or bad – can have on the development of poorer societies. The volume opens with a review of some critical general issues, including the implications of the spread of intellectual property rights legislation and the role of the World Trade Organisation (WTO). Subsequent chapters examine the regulatory experiences of three important developing economies: Brazil, Ghana and South Africa. Key regulatory themes are analysed, most notably capital markets and corporate governance regulation, the regulation of the telecommunications sector, and the use of regulatory reforms to promote the development of small and medium enterprises. Within each chapter, policy lessons are drawn whose relevance extends well beyond national or even regional boundaries. The principal contribution of the book is to show the extent to which regulation is moving increasingly to centre stage as a driver of development in Africa and Latin America.

Paul Cook
Martin Minogue
CRC, University of Manchester, UK

Acknowledgements

Chapters 3, 7, 8–10 and 12 of this book were originally presented at the Centre for Regulation and Competition's third international conference in Cape Town, South Africa during September 2004. I would like to take this opportunity to thank our South African hosts and all those who helped organize the conference. I am also grateful for the support of the UK Department for International Development (DFID), which has provided generous sponsorship for the CRC, its events and research programmes. Lastly, I wish to express my thanks to the CRC's Director, Paul Cook, the Director of its Regulatory Governance Research Programme, Martin Minogue and its administrator, Lesley Harris. Their support has been crucial at various points during the preparation of this book.

1. Introduction

Edmund Amann

The global economy is currently in the throes of far-reaching structural change. To an increasing extent, the established economic dominance of Western Europe, North America and Japan is being challenged by the rise of the Asian export-oriented economies, above all China. The apparently unstoppable rise of Asia appears to provide conclusive proof that economic catch-up among poorer societies is both possible and achievable. By the same token, though, the success of Asia serves to throw into even sharper relief the continuing difficulties encountered by the world's other key emerging regions, Africa and Latin America. Over the past two decades, policymakers throughout both regions have striven to emulate Asia's stunning economic trajectory, but with little success. For the most part, these efforts have involved the pursuit of fiscal orthodoxy and trade and market liberalization. While it is true that these policies have broadly succeeded in curtailing inflation, they have yet to stimulate the sustained year-on-year increases in per capita income necessary to close the gap with the rest of the world. As a consequence, the pursuit of economic liberalization, which appeared to have gained hegemonic status by the end of the 1990s, is now being called into question throughout Africa and Latin America. A key focus of the current wave of critical policy evaluation is the nature of economic regulation, whether of public utilities or of other sectors. It is this issue, specifically as it relates to Brazil, Ghana and South Africa, that forms the subject matter of this book.

Before highlighting the present critical debate concerning economic regulation, it is worth recalling the policy path both regions took to arrive at where they are today. During the 1980s both Africa and Latin America were faced with the urgent need to escape from the trap of indebtedness and macroeconomic instability into which they had fallen during the troubled 1970s. As private sector credit dried up, African and Latin American economies were forced to turn to the World Bank and the International Monetary Fund for financial assistance. Such assistance, when it came, was invariably associated with a comprehensive package of policy conditionality. Under the terms of this, recipient countries were obliged to pursue privatization, to deregulate domestic markets and to adopt trade liberalization. These microeconomic reforms were allied to a programme of fiscal retrenchment and a shrinking of the state.

The underlying premise of these reforms was not unreasonable. With their adoption, it was presumed, countries which had long been economic laggards would be obliged to become more competitive and closely integrated into the global trading system. This would ultimately boost productivity growth and raise export performance. In such a manner, the means of escape would be provided from a legacy of low per capita income growth and a tendency towards debt accumulation. With some, though hardly extensive variations, these policies were put into train starting in the 1980s (with Ghana) and the early 1990s (in the case of Brazil). In the case of South Africa, the end of apartheid and the election of Nelson Mandela in 1994 provided the catalyst for a series of liberalizing reforms. These were designed to promote competitiveness and to dismantle the remaining structures of import substitution industrialization. The latter had been established under apartheid as a partial response to global economic sanctions.

As was recognized in all three countries, an essential concomitant of economic liberalization was that markets be regulated effectively. Without such regulation, the benefits of freeing up markets could be lost as inefficiency and outright malpractice gained hold. Nowhere was this danger taken more seriously than in the field of privatized public utilities. As a result, a new or at least highly evolved species of government agency moved into the foreground in the 1980s and 1990s: the utilities regulator. Utilities regulators soon achieved a very high profile given their position in the vanguard of liberal reform. Not surprisingly, they also became the focus of heated political debate. Although most attention has tended to focus on utilities regulators, it should not be forgotten that liberalization also stimulated the development or strengthening of other regulatory bodies, not least in the field of competition policy. Here, the objective was to ensure that as governments vacated their role as direct producers, their private sector successors would not replicate the inefficiencies of nationalized industries. Aside from the creation of regulatory bodies, substantial attention was also paid to legislative reform. Hence initiatives were taken to break down legal barriers to competition and market entry.

Despite the enormous scale of liberalization and regulatory efforts, it seems fair to say that the early hopes of their protagonists have not been entirely borne out in reality. While growth performance in Brazil, Ghana and South Africa could not be characterized as dismal, neither could it be said that all three countries have experienced the step-change in economic performance once thought to be within reach. In all three countries, poverty and inequality remain as ingrained as ever, the product of a failure of growth to accelerate on a sustained or equitable basis. At the same time, in the case of South Africa and Brazil (the most heavily industrialized economies in their respective regions), the apparent promise held out by globalization of a move up the global value chain towards more technologically sophisticated, less commoditized exports has failed to materialize. Instead, the current tendency appears to be towards a reinforcement of the role of traditional, natural-resource-based exports. All of this is occurring at a time when, as has been pointed out, economies across Asia have been reinventing themselves and redefining their position in the international division of labour.

Against this background the central question seems clear: what can economies in Africa and Latin America do to stop the rot and close the gap with the rest of the world? This book, of course, cannot even begin to examine this complex question in totality. However, it does set out to shed light on one particularly important issue: the role that effective regulation might play in attempting to tackle some of Africa's and Latin America's most entrenched economic difficulties. This preoccupation appears especially timely given the political challenge now faced by regulators from governments, the private sector and disaffected elements of civil society. The challenge to the regulators' position stems partly from a generalized perception that globalization is failing Africa and Latin America. More specifically, however, regulators are also suffering from a perception that they may in some way be operationally deficient or that the policy framework itself may be flawed. In this connection, another function of the volume is to evaluate the performance of regulators across different sectors on both continents.

In terms of structure, this book divides into three parts. The first comprises a three-chapter review of some of the most critical regulatory issues now facing emerging market countries. In the first of these chapters, Chapter 2, Hossein Jalilian, Colin Kirkpatrick and David Parker analyse the relationship between the quality of regulation and economic performance. As suggested earlier in this introduction, the pursuit of growth and efficiency has served as a prime justification for the rise of regulatory institutions among emerging market countries. Does, however, such a justification rest on solid empirical ground? Jalilian, Kirkpatrick and Parker suggest that such a foundation exists, at least if the quality of regulatory arrangements is taken into account. The authors employ a large, multi-country data set previously used in World Bank studies. Through cross-sectional and panel data analysis, the impacts on productivity and growth of two proxies for regulatory quality are quantified. The chapter establishes that a strong link does in fact exist between the form and quality of regulation on the one hand and growth (whether in income or productivity terms) on the other. For Africa and Latin America, whose growth performance has been less than sparkling, the implications of this seem clear enough. The mere establishment of regulatory institutions and norms is not enough in itself; attention needs to be paid to quality-related issues such as transparency, predictability and swiftness of operation.

In Chapter 3 Peter Holmes adopts a qualitative rather than a quantitative approach in focusing on a key issue affecting developing economies throughout the world: the impact of the World Trade Organisation (WTO) on domestic regulatory arrangements. The chapter reveals the surprising extent to which WTO rules, designed to promote non-discriminatory behaviour in trade, intimately affect the nature and scope of a broad range of domestic regulatory activity. Two of the highest-profile areas in which WTO norms have been brought to bear on the domestic policy agenda have been in the fields of intellectual property legislation and sanitary and phytosanitary measures. As Aryeetey and Ahene note in their chapter (Chapter 11), the adoption of such standards has become a key issue in Africa, where agricultural exports remain of critical importance. Although Chapter 3 concedes that the adoption of superior external regulations may play a useful role, it nevertheless sounds a note of warning. In particular, there is concern surrounding the power of the appellate system and the ambiguous nature of some WTO rules.

The theme of external norms impinging on domestic regulation is also taken up by Christopher May in Chapter 4. The chapter focuses on the growth in international intellectual property regulation and its potential implications for poorer societies. While it is conceded that such measures as patent protection can act as a stimulus for innovation within certain countries (thanks to the ability to generate rents that they create), the recent expansion in international intellectual property rights (IPR) legislation may hold a number of dangers for emerging economies. In particular, through effectively increasing access costs to foreign technology, the ability of poorer societies to close the gap with wealthier countries has been impeded. At the same time, May is concerned at the implications of a 'one-size-fits-all' approach to international IPR legislation. This arises from an observation that the technological needs and structural characteristics of developing countries differ markedly from those of developed nations.

Shifting the focus from general to regional considerations, Part II of this volume considers the experience of Brazil, South America's largest economy and the second most populous country in the Western Hemisphere. In Chapter 5 Amann and Baer examine the rise of the regulatory state in the Brazilian context. The recent growth of regulatory institutions in Brazil is seen as the direct result of the crisis encountered by the Brazilian state in the 1980s. Faced with mounting internal and external deficits, the authorities were obliged to embark on a privatization programme and to open up certain 'strategic' sectors to foreign participation. To ensure that privatization and market liberalization delivered efficiency benefits and welfare gains, regulatory agencies were launched across a range of sectors from the public utilities to oil and gas. While Amann and Baer consider Brazil's regulatory institutions generally well designed, a number of problems are nevertheless identified. In particular, the authors are concerned at the implications of recent changes in tariff-setting policy for the long-term viability of private sector utilities' investments.

Attention is also drawn to the growing threat to the independence of regulatory agencies following the election of President Lula in 2002.

Chapter 6, by Andrea Goldstein and José Claudio Linhares Pires, also concerns itself with the rise of Brazilian regulatory institutions but focuses in particular on the electricity, oil and telecommunications sectors. The authors examine the operational track record of the various regulatory agencies, highlighting both their achievements and lingering challenges. Attention is drawn to the success of regulatory bodies in boosting investment in telecommunications and oil exploration and production. Such investment has had very favourable implications, especially in terms of lowering the cost of telecommunications services and boosting self-sufficiency in oil. Still, as the authors stress, a number of problems remain. In particular, concern is expressed as to the insufficient coordination that exists between the various agencies and the unclear definition of their competencies. Goldstein and Pires, like Amann and Baer, are troubled by threats to the independence of regulatory agencies. They also have doubts concerning the design of a mooted new Brazilian antitrust agency.

Whereas Chapters 5 and 6 are primarily concerned with regulated public utilities, Chapter 7, by Edmund Amann, João Carlos Ferraz and Germano Mendes de Paula, focuses on a more 'conventional' sector: the Brazilian steel industry. The authors suggest that, contrary to what might be expected, the privatization of the steel sector has not resulted in the exit of the state as a provider of financial resources. This is because a combination of weak corporate governance regulation allied to complexity and instability in ownership structures has discouraged minority shareholder participation. As a result, lacking a deep and liquid market in their shares, steel companies have largely eschewed equity finance. Instead, given the presence of high real interest rates in private capital markets, enterprises have been obliged to access public sector credits. Thus, as in previous chapters, evidence is offered supporting the view that more effective regulation is required if economic performance is to be improved.

Part III of the book turns its attention to a region of the world, Africa, whose economic challenges are arguably even more pressing than those of Latin America. Chapter 8, by Afeikhena Jerome, focuses on the regulatory experiences of Africa's largest economy, South Africa. As in the case of Brazil – another large, resource-rich economy emerging from a period of undemocratic rule – South Africa has embarked on a programme of privatization. Jerome emphasizes the point that privatization in South Africa has been a relatively slow process. As in Brazil, privatization has strongly divided opinion in society, and opposition to its extension has been substantial. This, incidentally, is a point echoed in Chapter 12, which examines the case of the South African telecommunications sector. Chapter 8, meanwhile, goes on to suggest that the

South African privatization programme should not be rolled back, but rather maintained in place. However, it is argued that this will only be possible if much more attention is devoted to the regulatory framework. In particular, an urgent need is identified to promote improved competition and to upgrade the transparency and accountability of regulatory arrangements.

Chapter 9, by Colin Kirkpatrick, David Parker and Yin-Fang Zhang, also focuses on the issue of privatization and its regulatory aspects. The authors examine the experience of a series of water privatizations throughout Africa, comparing the performance of private utilities with their public sector counterparts. Using data envelopment analysis and stochastic cost frontier techniques, it is established that private sector operators are associated with superior performance indicators. However, with regard to cost, no statistically significant differences were found between the public and private sector. The authors then move on to consider the difficulties that might be associated with water privatization. In particular, they highlight the existence of regulatory weaknesses as well as difficulties associated with technology and transactions costs.

The focus of Chapter 10, by Judi Hudson, contrasts with those of its predecessors in that it is concerned with the impact of regulation on small businesses – an issue also taken up in the Ghanaian context by Ernest Aryeetey and Ama Ahene. Examining the experience of South Africa, Hudson argues that small and medium enterprises have much to contribute in an emerging market context thanks to their capacity for generating local employment and – in the South African context at least – for empowering previously oppressed racial groups. This potential, so Hudson argues, can only be fully realized given the existence of a sympathetic regulatory framework. In South Africa, it is contended that such a framework does not yet exist. Consequently, the chapter calls for a number of regulatory reforms. In particular a lighter regulatory touch is argued for along with simplified rules and, where possible and desirable, the adoption of non-regulatory alternatives.

In a similar vein, Chapter 11, by Ernest Aryeetey and Ama Asantewah Ahene, argues for the development potential of small- and medium-sized enterprises (SMEs). Analysing the case of Ghana with the aid of a large sample survey, the authors investigate the impact of regulation on SME growth. While the importance of the regulatory framework is not discounted, it is contended that other factors may be of greater significance as obstacles to enterprise growth. In particular, the authors highlight the lack of cost-effective access to external sources of finance and limited ambition among entrepreneurs to pursue growth-oriented business strategies. Of course, regarding the former issue, it could be argued that regulatory reform in financial markets might have favourable consequences for the availability of funds.

In Chapter 12, the final chapter, the focus switches away from the low-technology and capital-starved SME sector back towards public utilities. Examining the case of Telkom, a high-technology, capital-intensive South African telecommunications utility, Oludele Akinboade and Fungai Sibanda chart the regulatory challenges currently faced by the authorities. The Telkom case represents an interesting contrast to the Brazilian experience since the South African utility has only been part-privatized and the market in which it operates subjected to only limited liberalization. As a result of this regulatory compromise, the authors argue that Telkom has entrenched its market position and continues to benefit from a monopoly in regard to long-distance and international calls. Partly due to political obstacles, the arrival of competition in these segments has been delayed. As a result, while Telkom's financial and operational performance has been creditable, consumers have yet to realize the full benefits. Against this background, the authors call for prudent regulation accompanied by progressive market liberalization. Such liberalization would be expected to benefit consumer welfare while imparting a much-needed competitive fillip to the South African economy.

Diverse as Brazil, Ghana and South Africa may be, this book demonstrates that a common challenge will need to be faced if economic performance is to significantly improve. While country- and sector-specific issues will need to be confronted, all the evidence within the following chapters suggests that better growth prospects are fundamentally tied to the implementation of predictable, transparent and technically competent regulation. One key question remains, therefore: can the necessary political will and financial resources be amassed to meet this challenge?

PART I

General Considerations

2. Creating the conditions for international business expansion: the impact of regulation on economic growth in developing countries – a cross-country analysis

Hossein Jalilian, Colin Kirkpatrick and David Parker

1. INTRODUCTION

The role of an effective regulatory regime in promoting economic growth and development has generated considerable interest among researchers and practitioners in recent years. State regulation is the means by which the state attempts to affect private sector behaviour; but the particular meaning attached to regulation and its translation into public policy has shifted over time, as a result of theoretical reasoning, new evidence and changes in political ideology (Hood, 1994). This evolving 'force of ideas' is particularly evident in the changing focus of regulatory policy in developing countries. Economic regulation by government is associated with righting 'market failures', including ameliorating the adverse distributional effects of private enterprise. From the 1960s to the 1980s, market failure was used to legitimize direct government involvement in productive activities in developing countries, by promoting industrialization through import substitution, investing directly in industry and agriculture, and by extending public ownership of enterprises.

However, following the apparent success of market liberalization programmes in developed countries, and the evidence of the failure of state-led economic planning in developing ones (World Bank, 1995), the role of state regulation was redefined and narrowed to that of ensuring a 'level playing field' and an 'undistorted' policy environment in which markets could operate. Deregulation was widely adopted, often as part of structural adjustment programmes, with the aim of reducing the 'regulatory burden' on the market economy. At the same time, however, the wave of infrastructure privatization that spread throughout the developing world in the 1990s – 121 developing countries introduced private investment in infrastructure schemes in the public utilities during that decade (Gray, 2001: 2) – has led to the creation of new regulatory bodies.

Privatization and the more general process of economic liberalization in developing countries have produced their own problems and failures. While economic assessments of the effects of privatization on economic welfare in developing countries have generally been positive (Cook and Kirkpatrick, 2003), evidence of political mismanagement and corruption, together with perceptions of negative effects on employment, income distribution and the poor, have led to growing criticism of privatization (Birdsall and Nellis, 2002; Chong and Lopez-de-Silanes, 2002). General dissatisfaction with the experience of privatization has focused the attention of policymakers on the need for an effective regulatory framework, particularly in the utilities infrastructure field, where natural monopoly conditions can often prevent the emergence of competitive markets (Parker, 2002).

The results of some economic liberalization programmes in developing countries have also been disappointing, with economic performance at the macro and sectoral levels failing to show a significant and sustained improvement, as compared to the pre-reform period. In seeking to explain the 'failure' of structural adjustment and economic liberalization in the developing world, analysts have sought to show that weaknesses in public policy have contributed significantly to the limited impact of the reforms (Burnside and Dollar, 1997; de Castro et al., 2002).

Since the 1960s, therefore, regulation policy in developing countries has shifted from the model of a positive or interventionist state to a deregulation, state-reduction model, to the current focus on the regulatory state (Majone, 1994, 1997). The regulatory state model implies leaving production to the private sector where competitive markets work well and using government regulation where significant market failure exists (World Bank, 2001: 1). Arguably, however, the performance of the new regulatory state remains under-researched, especially in the context of developing countries with their own peculiar economic and social problems and institutional characteristics. Building effective regulatory structures in developing countries is not simply an issue of the technical design of the regulatory instruments; it is also concerned with the quality of supporting regulatory institutions and capacity (World Bank, 2002: 152). Many of the institutions that support markets are publicly provided, and the effectiveness of these regulatory institutions will be an important determinant of how well markets function. The quality of regulatory governance will affect regulatory outcomes, which in turn can be expected to impact on economic growth.

This chapter explores the role of regulatory governance in affecting economic growth using an econometric model. More precisely, it assesses through econometric modelling the impact of variations in the quality of regulation on economic performance. Although earlier studies have looked at governance as a cause of cross-country productivity or income differences (Olson et al., 1998; Kaufmann and Kraay, 2002), this chapter differs in concentrating on regulation rather than wider governance issues. The subject discussed is of real importance to international business because of the effects of regulation on the economic environment that firms face internationally, with consequent implications for trade flows and foreign investment. Regulatory quality, as reflected in economic growth performance, contributes to the market environment faced by firms internationally. The results confirm that 'good' regulation is associated with higher economic growth, which in turn is conducive to the expansion of international business.

The rest of the chapter is organized as follows. Section 2 reviews issues in the economics literature pertinent to the debate on the role of regulation in economic growth, before turning to regulatory measures and proxies for regulatory governance. In Section 3 the models used are presented. Section 4 deals with a descriptive analysis of the data used and reports the regression results. Finally, Section 5 provides conclusions and the implications for development policy. The results confirm that the quality of state regulation impacts on economic growth.

2. ECONOMIC REGULATION: A BRIEF LITERATURE REVIEW

The theory of economic regulation developed from the nineteenth century and the literature is now vast (for recent reviews, see Laffont and Tirole, 1993, 2000; Levy and Spiller, 1994; Newbery, 1999). The case for economic regulation is premised on the existence of significant market failure resulting from economies of scale and scope in production, from information imperfections in market transactions, from the existence of incomplete markets and externalities, and from resulting income and wealth distribution effects. It has been suggested that market failures may be more pronounced, and therefore the case for public regulation is stronger, in developing countries (Stern, 1991; Stiglitz, 1998). However, regulation of markets may not result in a welfare improvement as compared to the economic outcome under imperfect market conditions. The economics of regulation literature has identified various circumstances where the regulation of markets might reduce rather than increase economic welfare. The seminal study by Averch and Johnson (1962) demonstrated how regulation of a firm's rate of return could lead to incentives to over-invest. Following publication of Averch and Johnson's paper, studies highlighted other potential inefficiencies that could be introduced by rate-of-return regulation, notably distorted service quality and higher operating costs (e.g. Bailey, 1973).

Information asymmetries may also contribute to imperfect regulation. The regulator and the regulated can be expected to have different levels of information about such matters as costs, revenues and demand. The regulated company holds the information that the regulator needs to regulate optimally and the regulator must establish rules and incentive mechanisms to coax this information from the private sector. Given that it is highly unlikely that the regulator will receive all of the information required to regulate optimally to maximize social welfare, the results of regulation, in terms of outputs and prices, remain 'second best' to those of a perfectly competitive market. Shapiro and Willig (1990) argue that state ownership provides more information to regulators than private ownership, so contracting should be less problematic when the state both owns and regulates. However, state ownership is associated with inadequate incentives to gather and use this information to maximize economic welfare (Hayek, 1945). In other words, there tends to be a trade-off between state ownership reducing the information asymmetries and hence transaction costs of regulation and the relative incentives under state control and private ownership for agents to maximize economic efficiency (Grossman and Hart, 1986; Sappington and Stiglitz, 1987; Shapiro and Willig, 1990; Yarrow, 1999).

Welfare-improving regulation assumes that the regulatory authority's actions are motivated by the public interest. This has been criticized by public choice theorists, who argue that individuals are essentially self-interested in or out of the public arena and it is necessary, therefore, to analyse the regulatory process as the product of relationships between different groups (Buchanan, 1972; Baldwin and Cave, 1999: chapter 3). This has been refined in the concept of 'regulatory capture', which involves the regulatory process becoming biased in favour of particular interests. In the extreme case, the regulatory capture literature concludes that regulation *always* leads to socially suboptimal outcomes because of 'inefficient bargaining between interest groups over potential utility rents' (Newbery, 1999: 134; also Laffont, 1999). In the Chicago tradition of regulatory capture (Stigler, 1971; Peltzman, 1976) regulators are presumed to favour producer interests because of the concentration of regulatory benefits and diffusion of regulatory costs, which enhances the power of lobbying groups as rent seekers (Reagan, 1987).

Regulation is also subject to 'political capture'; indeed, political capture may be a much greater threat than capture by producer groups outside the political system. Where political capture occurs, the regulatory goals are distorted to pursue political ends. Under political capture, regulation becomes a tool of self-interest within government or the ruling elite (Stiglitz, 1998). More generally, it is to be expected that both the process and outcomes of a regulatory regime will be determined by the specific institutional context of an economy, as reflected in its formal and informal rules of economic transacting (North, 1990).

By setting the 'rules of the game', institutions impact on economic development (World Bank, 2002). Economic development is seen not simply as a matter of amassing economic resources in the form of physical and human capital, but as a matter of 'institution building' so as to reduce information imperfections, maximize economic incentives and reduce transaction costs. Included in this institution building are the laws and political and social rules and conventions that are the basis for successful market production and exchange. In particular, relevant modes of conduct in the context of the regulatory state might include probity in public administration, independence of the courts, low corruption and cronyism, and traditions of civic responsibility. 'Institution building', including building a 'good' regulatory regime, is one of the most difficult problems facing developing countries and the transition economies at the present time (Kirkpatrick and Parker, 2004).

'Good' Regulation, Regulatory Governance and Development Outcomes

To decide whether a system of economic regulation is 'good', or in need of reform, it is necessary to identify the criteria for assessing regulatory quality. Regulation quality can be judged in terms of two main criteria – the quality of the outcomes and the processes of regulation.

The outcome of a regulatory system can be assessed against the yardsticks of effectiveness and efficiency. Effective regulation achieves the social welfare goals set down by the government for the regulatory authority. In developing countries the social welfare objectives of regulation are likely to be not simply concerned with the pursuit of economic efficiency but with wider goals to promote sustainable development and poverty reduction. Efficient regulation achieves the social welfare goals at minimum economic costs. The economic costs of regulation can take two broad forms: (1) the costs of directly administering the regulatory system, which are internalized within government and reflected in the budget appropriations of the regulatory bodies; and (2) the compliance costs of regulation, which are external to the regulatory agency and fall on consumers and producers in terms of the economic costs of conforming with the regulations and of avoiding and evading them (Guasch and Hahn, 1999).

The criteria for assessing the quality of regulatory processes will be derived from the arguments that are commonly used to 'legitimate' regulation (Baldwin and Cave, 1999: 77). Parker (1999: 224) argues that a well-functioning regulatory system is one that balances accountability, transparency and consistency. Accountability requires the regulatory agencies to be accountable for the consequences of their actions, to operate within their legal powers, and to observe the rules of due process when arriving at their decisions (e.g. to ensure that proper consultation occurs). Transparency relates to regulatory decisions being reached in a way that is revealed to the interested parties. The third process which provides regulatory legitimacy is consistency. Inconsistent regulatory decisions undermine public confidence in a regulatory system. Inconsistency leads to uncertainty for investors, which raises the cost of capital and may seriously damage the willingness to invest. Since political intervention tends to undermine regulatory consistency, and politicians may be prone to alter the regulatory rules of the game for short-term political advantage, consistency is a primary argument for some kind of 'independent' regulator.

This discussion suggests that the capacity of the state to provide strong regulatory institutions will be an important determinant of how well markets perform. An economy with a developed institutional capacity is more likely to be able to design and implement effective regulation, which should contribute to improved economic growth. Good governance is 'epitomized by predictable, open and enlightened policy making; a bureaucracy imbued with a professional ethos; an executive arm of government accountable for its actions; a strong civil society participating in public affairs, and all behaving under the rule of law' (World Bank, 1997). Weaknesses in institutional capacity to deliver 'good governance' may be predicted to affect adversely economic development (World Bank, 2002).

Regulatory institutions are a relatively recent addition to the institutional structure in developing countries and evidence on the quality of regulation is therefore limited. The evidence that is available, however, suggests that the results of post-privatization regulation have been disappointing. Where research has occurred, it has exposed a number of regulatory failures. A study of 12 infrastructure industries across six developing Asian economies found much variation in practices and a considerable shortfall from regulatory best practice, as understood in the UK and USA (Stern and Holder, 1999). Cook (1999), based on case studies of utility sector reforms in developing countries, concludes that creating effective regulation and a competitive environment is at best a difficult and slow process. In the context of Africa, it was found that 'regulation is being examined as part of individual sector initiatives, but these efforts are uncoordinated, and implementation is being left to follow privatization instead of being put in place concurrently' (Campbell-White and Bhatia, 1998: 5).

Water sector reforms in a number of countries have been associated with second-best outcomes and inefficiencies brought on by the institutional context within which reform has been attempted, especially a failure of the government machinery (Dinar, 2000; Estache and Kouassi, 2002). In India, regulatory structures are associated with acute failures in institution building and with a bureaucratic approach that curtails enterprise (Lanyi, 2000). South Africa's proliferation of regulatory bodies is associated with a lack of clarity about roles and responsibilities and with the adoption of policy-making roles independent of government (Schwella, 2002: 3). In Malawi, the electricity industry regulator remains closely connected to the state electricity industry, compromising any notion of real regulatory independence and encouraging capture.[1] In Sri Lanka, the policies governing the regulatory process are judged to have been *ad hoc* and based on short-term political interests, with deficiencies apparent at each stage of the process (Knight-John, 2002). Experiences in the transitional economies also demonstrate much variability in the performance of the newly established regulatory institutions (Cave and Stern, 1998).

In the financial sector, limited regulatory capacity contributed to the instability of the financial sector during the 1997 Asian crisis (Brownbridge and Kirkpatrick, 2000). Similarly, liberalization of the financial sector in sub-Saharan African economies has exposed the weakness of financial regulation and has resulted in widespread bank failure and systemic weaknesses (Maimbo, 2002; Brownbridge and Kirkpatrick, 2002). In recognition that not all is well, the World Bank (2001: v) has stressed the importance of 'improving regulatory regimes and building institutions and capacity effectively to supervise the private sector'. The Asian Development Bank (2000: 18) has also emphasized the need for improved regulation.

Several papers have identified the causal effects of better governance on higher per capita incomes in the long run, using regressions with instrumental variables on a cross-section of countries (Barro, 1997; Hall and Jones, 1999; Kaufmann and Kraay, 2002). The causal chain between governance and economic outcome has also been examined. Some studies find that the quality of governance and institutions is important in explaining rates of investment, suggesting that one way in which better governance can improve economic performance is by improving the climate for capital creation (Clague et al., 1995; Keefer and Knack, 1995; Mauro, 1995; World Bank, 2003). Olson et al. (1998) find that productivity growth is higher in countries with better institutions and quality of governance. Kaufmann and Kraay (2002) reinforce these findings, relating the quality of governance to economic outcomes using a data set covering 175 countries for the period 2000–2001.

Measures of Regulatory Governance

The literature suggests, therefore, that the ability of the state to provide effective regulatory institutions will be an important determinant of how an economy performs. The major variable of interest is the quality of regulatory governance. Other researchers have operationalized the broad concept of governance using two different groups of variables. The International Country Risk Guide (ICRG) is produced by a private company for sale to firms and portfolio managers who are considering foreign investments. The ICRG data set is produced annually and covers three aspects of government – bureaucratic quality, law and order and corruption (Political Risk Services, 2002; King and Zeng, 2000 for ICRG data covering 1989–95). Each variable is measured on a points scale, with higher points denoting better performance with respect to the variable concerned. The assessment is based on expert analysis from an international network and is subject to peer review. The ICRG variables have been used as proxies for the quality of governance (Neumayer, 2002; Olson et al., 1998).

The second set of governance variables comprises a set of six aggregate indicators developed by the World Bank and drawn from 194 different measures (Kaufmann and Kraay, 2002). These indicators are based on several different sources (including international organizations, political and business risk rating agencies, think tanks and non-governmental bodies) and a linear unobserved components model is used to aggregate these various sources into one aggregate indicator.[2] The indicators are normalized, with higher values denoting better governance. The six indicators provide a subjective assessment of the following aspects of a country's quality of governance:

- Voice and accountability: respect for political rights and civil liberties, public participation in the process of electing policymakers, independence of media, accountability and transparency of government decisions.
- Political instability: political and social tension and unrest, instability of government.
- Government effectiveness: perceptions of the quality of public provision, quality of bureaucracy, competence of civil servants and their independence from political pressure, and the credibility of government decisions.
- Regulatory quality: burden on business via quantitative regulations, price controls and other interventions in the economy.
- Rule of law: respect for law and order, predictability and effectiveness of the judiciary system, enforceability of contracts.
- Control of corruption: perceptions of the exercise of public power for private gain.

In this study we focus on the regulatory quality and government effectiveness variables in the World Bank data set, which is more suitable than ICRG data for our purposes. These two variables are the closest to capturing the nature of the aspects of regulatory governance discussed above, which can be summarized under the headings of regulatory quality and process. Regulatory quality is taken as a proxy for the quality of the outcomes of applying regulatory instruments. Government effectiveness proxies the process dimensions (consistency, accountability, transparency) of regulatory governance. All six World Bank indicators, however, are closely related, as indicated by the extent of the bivariate correlation between them shown in Table 2.1.

The objective of the empirical analysis reported below is to test for a causal link between regulation and economic performance. The approach adopts a growth accounting framework, where economic growth is used as the measure of economic performance and regulation is entered as an input in the production function.

Neoclassical growth modelling began with the work of Solow (1956), who employed a neoclassical production function to explain economic growth in the USA during the first half of the twentieth century. Important assumptions of this approach are constant returns to scale and diminishing returns to investment, which imply that for a given rate of saving and population growth economies move towards their steady-state growth path. This can be extended to differences in income levels between countries, to argue that in the long run income per capita levels will converge. A lack of empirical support for convergence and the presence of a large, unexplained 'residual' factor in the function estimates have presented a major challenge to these models.

The endogenous growth theory put forward by Romer (1986) and Lucas (1988) led to renewed interest in economic growth analysis. An important advantage of endogenous over traditional growth models is that, through the assumption of constant or increasing returns to a factor input, in particular human capital, it is possible to explain a lack of growth and income convergence

Table 2.1   The correlation coefficients between the institutional indicators

Variables	GE	Graft	PI	RQ	RL	VA
Government effectiveness (GE)	1.00					
Control of corruption (Graft)	0.94	1.00				
Political instability (PI)	0.81	0.78	1.00			
Regulatory quality (RQ)	0.69	0.64	0.71	1.00		
Rule of law (RL)	0.90	0.90	0.90	0.70	1.00	
Voice and accountability (VA)	0.75	0.76	0.73	0.70	0.75	1.00

Notes:
The variable listings vertically define the listings horizontally.
See text for a brief explanation of each of these variables; for fuller details and information on their construction see Kaufmann and Kraay (2002).

between countries and helps account more fully for the residual factor in Solow-type analyses. The 'growth accounting' exercises, popularized by Barro and others (Barro, 1991, 2000; Barro and Sala-i-Martin, 1999), fall within the generalized Solow-type growth model. An important characteristic of this approach is the inclusion of various indicators of economic structure.

Most empirical research using this approach has found evidence of 'conditional' convergence, where convergence is conditional on the level or availability of complementary forms of investment, including human capital and a supportive policy environment. This suggests that the failure of developing countries to converge on the income levels of developed countries may be attributed, at least in part, to institutional factors.[3] The importance of institutional capacity to design and implement effective economic policy has been demonstrated in various empirical studies of cross-country growth, for example Sachs and Warner (1995) and Barro (2000). A similar approach is adopted in this study to examine the role of regulatory institutional capacity in accounting for cross-country variations in economic growth.

An issue that needed to be addressed at the outset is causality. It could be argued that instead of regulatory quality determining economic growth, regulatory quality could be determined by the economy's growth rate. Economies that grow faster are able to generate higher levels of income and are therefore able to support the development of better institutions. Or, alternatively, there may be a level of simultaneity, in the sense that institutional quality generates more sustained economic growth, which in turn supports more and better regulatory institutions.

The Granger causality test is commonly used in empirical work to establish the direction of causation. However, this test is sensitive to the length of lags of variables used and therefore requires a relatively long time-series dimension to be able to select the right length of lag and to be relatively confident about the conclusion drawn. The problem we face is that the time dimension of most variables in our data set is rather limited; in the case of regulatory governance we only have one observation per country. We were therefore unable to apply the Granger causality test. Instead, and less formally, we note that the existing literature is consistent with institutional change leading to economic growth. For example, Olson et al. (1998) argue that causation runs from institutional change to economic change using the examples of China, Korea, Taiwan, Indonesia and Chile. They conclude that 'Simultaneity bias appears to be a theoretical, but not a realistic, possibility' (p. 33). Kaufmann and Kraay (2002) implement an empirical procedure for testing for causation, which leads to the identification of strong positive causal effects running from better governance to higher per capita incomes, but weak and even negative causation in the opposite direction from per capita incomes to governance. The latter result, they argue, may be the consequence of elites with rising incomes using laws and regulations for their own rather than the social benefit. We proceed, therefore, on the assumption that the causation is from regulatory quality to economic performance.

3. THE MODELLING

The approach used in the modelling is to assume that each country's production possibility set, in common with most literature in this area, is described by a Cobb–Douglas production function:

$$Y_{it} = A_{it} K_{it}^{\alpha} L_{it}^{\beta}, \tag{2.1}$$

where Y is the output level; A, level of productivity; K, stock of capital; and L, stock of labour – i and t stand for country and time respectively. Assuming that the production function exhibits constant return to scale with respect to physical inputs, (2.2) can be written in per capita terms as:

$$y_{it} = A_{it} k_{it}^{\alpha}, \tag{2.2}$$

where small letters refer to per capita units. Assume a simple Keynesian capital accumulation rule according to the following specification:

$$dk/dt = sy - (n + \delta)k, \tag{2.3}$$

where dk/dt is the rate of change of the per capita capital stock, which is assumed to be equal to the flow of saving (equal to investment) minus capital depreciation and the growth of the labour force. In this equation s is the share of gross saving in output per capita, δ is the depreciation of capital and n the rate of growth of population as a proxy for the growth of the labour force. Setting (2.3) equal to zero gives us the steady-state solution for the stock of per capita capital; $k = sy/(n + \delta)$. Taking the logarithm of both sides of equation (2.2) and replacing the steady-state solution for k from above into (2.2) gives the steady-state solution for output per capita, which is as follows:

$$\ln (y_{it}^{*}) = [1/(1 - \alpha)][\ln A_{it} + \alpha \ln (s_{it}/(n_{it} + \delta_{it})], \tag{2.4}$$

where * above the variable signifies the steady-state solution.

We adopt the Mankiw et al. (1992) assumption that economies move towards their steady-state solution according to the following approximation:

$$\ln y_{it} - \ln y_{i0} = \lambda(\ln y_{it}^{*} - \ln y_{i0}), \tag{2.5}$$

where y_0 stands for the initial level of per capita income, and $\lambda = (1 - e^{-\eta t})$ is the adjustment dynamic towards steady state, where η is the speed of convergence. From (2.5) we can solve for the growth of per capita output, which is as follows:

$$g_{it} = (\lambda/t)(\ln y_{it}^* - \ln y_{i0}). \tag{2.6}$$

Replacing $(\ln y_{it}^*)$ with its equivalent from (2.4) gives us a relationship for actual growth of per capita output:

$$g_{it} = (\lambda/t(1-\alpha))[\ln A_{it} + \alpha \ln(s_{it}/(n_{it} + \delta_{it})] - (\lambda/t)\ln y_{i0}. \tag{2.7}$$

As far as total factor productivity growth is concerned, we assume that its dynamic takes the following form:

$$A_{it} = A_{i0}e^{\gamma_i t}, \tag{2.8}$$

where A_{i0} specifies the initial level of productivity and γ its rate of growth per period. Substituting for A from (2.8) into (2.7), per capita growth of output (g) is represented by the following relationship:

$$g - \phi_1 \ln A_{i0} + \phi_2 \gamma_i + \phi_3 \ln(s_{it}/(n_{it} + \delta_{it})) - \phi_4 \ln y_{i0}, \tag{2.9}$$

where $\phi_1 = \lambda/t(1-\alpha)$, $\phi_2 = \lambda/(1-\alpha)$, $\phi_3 = \lambda\alpha/t(1-\alpha)$, and $\phi_4 = \lambda/t$. Adding some control and qualitative variables as well as a stochastic term to (2.9) provides the model which we use to assess the role that regulatory quality plays in economic growth.

In this model differences in total factor productivity growth rates are related to regulatory quality and control variables. Variables added to equation (2.9) broadly follow the growth empirics literature, such as Barro (1991, 2000), Mankiw et al. (1992) and Islam (1995). Amongst the control variables included in most empirical research are initial conditions, in terms of both the level of development (as proxied by GDP per capita) and human capital and institutions. Most also include proxies for the macroeconomic environment such as inflation, trade openness and the government's involvement in economic activities. Qualitative variables can also be added to account for specific events in a country, as well as data heterogeneity when panel data are used. In our analysis, depending on the nature of data set constructed, we make use of all or some of these variables to make sure that our regressions are fully specified.

Total productivity growth, γ, is expected to play an important role in total growth within an economy. In the context of our specification in (2.9) we make the additional assumption, drawing on the literature relating to regulation in developing countries reviewed earlier, that productivity growth γ directly varies with the quality of regulatory institutions in the country. Those countries with good institutions in place can design and implement policies that allow them to continue with their future growth. If instead the country in question lacks or has a weak institutional structure, its growth potential is likely to be diminished because the design and implementation of appropriate policies are then adversely affected. In the case of developing countries, in particular, to be able to benefit from being a latecomer in terms of industrialization and grow at a high speed to 'catch up', it is important that institutional supports are present to realize the potential for income convergence.

We assume that γ in (2.9) varies directly with institutional quality. In the absence of better information about the initial institutional quality, we adopted educational attainment as a proxy variable. At first blush this may seem an unusual choice, but our proxy, secondary school enrolment, is highly correlated with the regulatory governance variables we are using (see Table 2.3 below), supporting its choice as a sound proxy for initial institutional quality in general.[4] The finding that education is highly correlated with our regulatory variables is an interesting finding in itself and one worthy of further exploration in future research. We do not pursue it further here.

We apply two methods of estimation to the model specified by equation (2.9). One is based on cross-section analysis, in which we attempt to measure *directly* any possible impact that regulation has on economic growth. The second is based on panel data, in which we *indirectly* estimate the growth contribution of regulation. The reason for applying different estimation procedures is due to our data on the indexes of regulation; we have only one observation per country. Therefore, for the cross-section regression we average the relevant data over the period 1980–99 and combine the result with the regulation data. This allows a direct measure of the possible role that regulation plays in growth, using equation (2.9) as a base to estimate ϕ_2.

In the second method we adopt a variant of the one applied by Olson et al. (1998) and apply the fixed effects technique to the panel data constructed.[5] This data set combines cross-section and time-series data for the countries included in the first data set. This procedure, which essentially involves including a dummy for every country in the estimated equation, produces consistent estimates even where data are not available for some time-invariant factors that affect growth. The fixed effects estimator does require, however, that each included variable varies significantly within countries. Clearly, even if available, the regulatory variables may not satisfy this requirement since institutions usually change slowly. The estimation procedure, therefore, involves two stages. We first regress GDP per capita growth in each country per period g_{it} on $\ln(s_{it}/n_{it} + \delta_{it}))$ plus a set of country dummies. The coefficient on the country dummies reflects the effect on growth of all the time-invariant variables, including regulatory institutions. In the second stage we use the coefficients of the country dummy as the dependent variable and regress them on the measures of regulatory quality and control variables. The coefficients on the measures of regulatory quality in the second stage-regression reflect the impact of regulation on GDP per capita growth after controlling for capital accumulation and certain other variables.

4. THE DATA AND REGRESSION RESULTS

Data for the regulatory quality measures were set out in Kaufmann and Kraay (2002) and are available for downloading on the World Bank website.[6] As discussed earlier, the two regulation indicators used from this study are regulatory quality and government effectiveness measures (the other regulation indicators included in Kaufmann and Kraay being highly correlated with these two). Other data required for the regression analysis were taken from the World Bank's *World Development Indicators.*

The data set used in the analysis covers 84 countries for the cross-section regression and 80 for the panel version of the regression (for a full list of the countries see the Appendix). Although the main focus of the study is the impact of 'good' regulation on economic performance in developing countries, a heterogeneous data set was used, including some transitional and advanced countries as well as developing ones. The reason for including some non-developing countries was to improve the statistical reliability of the results by including more countries with regional dummies used to capture the differing levels of economic development. As information on regulatory governance is only available for one period, as referred to earlier, in the cross-section model all other variables were converted into one period by averaging for 1980–99. Initial effect variables relate to 1980. For the panel version, the data cover the period 1980–99. However, the time-series dimension is not complete for a number of the countries in the data set and therefore the panel data are unbalanced, containing 313 observations.

Tables 2.2 and 2.3 provide summary statistics and the correlation coefficient matrix respectively for the key variables used in the study. The first data column in Table 2.3 shows the simple correlation coefficients between the dependent variable, GDP growth per capita, and possible explanatory variables. The correlation coefficients have the expected signs, including a slight suggestion that lower government consumption expenditure is associated with higher GDP growth but not with improved regulation. The correlation coefficients between the indicators of regulatory governance, namely government effectiveness and regulatory quality, and GDP per capita growth have the

Table 2.2 Summary statistics

Variable*	GDP per capita	GE	RQ	Log NFCF	Log initial GDP per capita	Log schooling	Trade	Inflation	Government expenditure
Maximum	8.62	2.08	1.24	2.27	9.59	99.70	306.11	4010.70	29.10
Minimum	-8.28	-1.77	-2.34	0.81	5.91	2.70	2.46	0.51	4.53
Mean	1.40	0.12	0.29	1.53	7.77	47.85	35.59	95.39	14.12
Std deviation	2.30	0.90	0.65	0.35	1.05	28.87	44.56	460.75	4.98
Skewness	-0.71	0.41	-1.24	-0.11	-0.01	0.17	4.00	7.60	0.65
Kurtosis -3	3.39	-0.56	2.37	-0.66	-1.06	-1.23	19.01	60.86	0.25
Coefficient of variation	1.64	7.63	2.27	0.23	0.13	0.60	1.25	4.83	0.35

Notes:
GDP per capita = GDP per capita growth (% per annum).
GE = Government effectiveness.
RQ = Regulatory quality.
Log NFCF = Logarithm of net fixed capital formation as a percentage of GDP.
Log initial GDP per capita = Logarithm of initial (1980) GDP per capita.
Log schooling = Initial (1980) secondary school enrolment (%).
Trade = Exports + imports as a percentage of GDP.
Inflation = Rate of inflation using country GDP deflators.
Government expenditure = General government consumption expenditure as a percentage of GDP.

Value figures were standardized to US$ valuations using purchasing power parities.

Table 2.3   Correlation coefficient matrix

Variable*	GDP per capita	GE	RQ	Log NFCF	Log initial GDP per capita	Log schooling	Trade	Inflation	Government expenditure
GDP per capita	1.00								
GE	0.38	1.00							
RQ	0.44	0.69	1.00						
Log NFCF	0.31	0.35	0.25	1.00					
Log initial GDP per capita	0.13	0.73	0.66	0.33	1.00				
Log schooling	0.15	0.71	0.59	0.55	0.81	1.00			
Trade	0.18	0.54	0.40	0.30	0.40	0.38	1.00		
Inflation	-0.48	-0.26	-0.43	-0.14	-0.06	-0.09	-0.12	1.00	
Government exp.	-0.05	0.45	0.26	0.17	0.42	0.47	0.16	-0.05	1.00

Notes:
GDP per capita = GDP per capita growth (% per annum).
GE = Government effectiveness.
RQ = Regulatory quality.
Log NFCF = Logarithm of net fixed capital formation as a percentage of GDP.
Log initial GDP per capita = Logarithm of initial (1980) GDP per capita.
Log schooling = Logarithm of initial (1980) secondary school enrolment (5%).
Trade = Exports + imports as a percentage of GDP.
Inflation = Rate of inflation using country GDP deflators.
Government expenditure = General government consumption expenditure as a percentage of GDP.

expected positive sign. The bivariate correlations between inflation and the regulatory proxies used are negative, supporting the proposition that economies with better regulatory governance are also better able to design macroeconomic policies that stabilize the economy and control inflation.

There is also a high correlation between the logarithm of initial GDP per capita and initial secondary school education, both of which are in turn correlated with the various proxies for regulatory governance.[7] This suggests that, included in the same regression, parameter estimates for these variables may not be individually reliable, due to multicollinearity. This is also the case with the two regulatory proxies that we intend to use in the analysis, namely government effectiveness (GE) and regulatory quality (RQ). These two are highly correlated and therefore cannot be included in the same regression in order to estimate each variable's contribution. For this reason we considered first the contribution of each of these proxies to growth in separate regressions, and then combined them by addition to form a composite regulation variable (RQGE).

The results reported in Table 2.4 are based on the model specified in equation (2.9) using OLS (ordinary least squares) and cross-country data, as detailed above. Table 2.4 reports eight regressions containing different combinations of the independent variables from our data set. The economic variables in the full set of regressions tested included the variables derived from the model itself, as specified in equation (2.9), and measures for general inflation, trade, government expenditure, as well as the regional dummies.

The regional dummies are used to test the hypothesis that different regions may have characteristics that affect growth differently. This is validated with respect to Asia and Latin America, indicating that these two regions had, on average, performed better with respect to economic growth than other regions. A dummy for Africa was found to be statistically insignificant, whereas the one covering other countries, principally developed and transition economies, was statistically significant and negative.[8] The initial level of GDP per capita has a negative sign and usually is statistically significant at the 5 per cent level, confirming 'conditional' convergence. Other studies, including Barro (2000), Islam (1995) and Mankiw et al. (1992), also confirm conditional convergence. Amongst other variables included in the full set of regressions were proxies for government expenditure, openness of the economy (trade), as well as inflation. Except for inflation, which we found to be negative and statistically significant, these other variables were found to be statistically insignificant at the 10 per cent level or better and are therefore not reported here.

We also included the initial level of human capital as a proxy for the initial level of 'institutions'. This variable, as indicated in Table 2.3, is highly correlated with initial GDP per capita. When the two appear in the same regression (column 7 in Table 2.4), the level of significance and magnitude of the initial

Table 2.4 Cross-country analysis of the determinants of economic growth (dependent variable is growth of GDP per capita)

Variables	1	2	3	4	5	6	7	8
C	4.10**	5.03**	7.52*	5.27**	5.59**	3.90**	0.87	-1.87*
	(1.71)	(1.98)	(3.12)	(1.67)	(2.67)	(1.87)	(0.36)	(2.16)
Schooling							-0.03*	-0.03*
							(2.28)	(3.60)
RQ	2.15*							
	(3.14)							
GE		1.44*						
		(3.91)						
RQGE			1.22*	1.20*	1.19*	0.91*	1.02*	0.90*
			(5.43)	(6.00)	(6.11)	(4.29)	(4.82)	(4.81)
Log NFCF	1.87*	1.54*	1.53*	2.01*	2.00*	1.93*	2.58*	2.68*
	(2.17)	(2.22)	(2.38)	(3.29)	(3.31)	(3.35)	(4.10)	(4.28)
Log initial GDP per capita	-0.79*	-0.79*	-1.15*	-1.05*	-1.08*	-0.82*	-0.39	
	(2.25)	(2.52)	(3.74)	(3.03)	(4.00)	(2.97)	(1.21)	
Inflation						-0.001*	-0.001*	-0.001*
						(2.88)	(2.68)	(2.99)
Africa				0.13				
				(0.14)				
Asia				2.16*	2.08*	1.96*	1.99*	2.03*
				(2.75)	(4.38)	(4.30)	(4.49)	(4.58)

	(1)	(2)	(3)	(4)	(5)	(6)	(7)	(8)
Latin America				1.45*	1.38*	1.31*	1.26*	1.17*
				(2.07)	(3.10)	(3.07)	(3.05)	(2.86)
Others				−1.91**	−1.98*	−2.14*	−1.99*	−2.02*
				(1.88)	(2.23)	(2.51)	(2.39)	(2.42)
No. of observations	84	84	84	84	84	84	84	84
Adjusted R^2	0.28	0.22	0.32	0.50	0.51	0.55	0.57	0.57

Notes:
C is the intercept term.
Schooling = Initial (1980) secondary school enrolment (%).
RQ = Regulatory quality.
GE = Government effectiveness.
RQGE = Combined regulatory variable (GE + RQ).
Log NFCF = Logarithm of net fixed capital formation as a percentage of GDP.
Log initial GDP per capita = Logarithm of initial (1980) GDP per capita.
Inflation = Rate of inflation using country GDP deflators.
Africa, Asia, Latin America and Others (other regions) are regional dummies.

Values in parenthesis are *t*-ratios.
*   Statistically significant at 5% significance level.
**   Statistically significant at 10% significance level.

GDP per capita variable are adversely affected, which is a symptom of multi-collinearity. The initial level of human capital, as proxied by secondary schooling, has the expected negative sign and is statistically significant. This again confirms the conditional convergence hypothesis.

The regulatory variables are correctly signed and statistically significant in all cases. The sign and level of significance of the parameter estimates for these regulatory proxies indicate that they have a statistically significant and positive effect on growth. Based on the estimates for the combined regulatory variable (RQGE), a unit change in the quality and effectiveness of regulation is, on average, associated with approximately a unit increase in growth, everything else remaining equal.

Table 2.5   Alternative cross-country analysis of the determinants of economic growth (dependent variable is estimate of country dummies)

Variables	1	2	3
C	−0.90*	−2.55*	−1.24**
	(3.98)	(5.66)	(1.76)
RQGE		0.41*	0.21*
		(4.87)	(2.16)
Inflation			0.001*
			(2.97)
Africa			−1.18*
			(2.11)
Asia			1.40*
			(2.62)
Latin America			−0.65
			(1.18)
Others			−0.52
			(0.62)
No. of observations	80	80	80
Adjusted R^2	0.13	0.22	0.45

Notes:
C is the intercept term.
RQGE = Combined regulatory variable (GE + RQ).
Inflation = Rate of inflation using country GDP deflators.
Africa, Asia, Latin America and Others (other regions) are regional dummies.

Values in parenthesis are *t*-ratios.
*   Statistically significant at 5% significance level.
**   Statistically significant at 10% significance level.

Table 2.5 reports results based on the second method of estimation, which, as discussed earlier, involves two stages. In the first stage, by applying a fixed effect technique to the panel data we arrive at the following regression results:

GDP per capita = 1.25 log net fixed capital formation + country dummies
(2.80)[9]

Adjusted R^2 = 0.32; no. of observations = 313.

From the above, the regression parameter estimate associated with the country dummies is saved and used as the dependent variable in the regressions reported in Table 2.5. For reasons of space we report only a sub-set of the full results. We exclude reporting regressions including the full set of independent variables used, as detailed in Table 2.2, because a number of them proved to be statistically insignificant. Also, only the results for the combined regulatory variable are reported – estimates including the regulatory quality and regulatory effectiveness variables separately were consistent with these results.[10]

Our main interest in the regression results reported in Table 2.5 is with the role that the regulatory proxies play in explaining the variation in the country dummies. These results are consistent with those reported in Table 2.4. Even though the coefficient values for the regulatory variable are lower, the finding is that regulatory governance still significantly affects the growth performance of an economy. Also, there is no evidence of conditional convergence in this case and, while the Asia regional dummy is as before, namely statistically significant and positive, the African dummy is now significantly negative (previously it was insignificant), while the Latin America and Others (other countries) dummies are now statistically insignificant (previously they were statistically significant and positive and negative, respectively).[11] These changes in the results were investigated and seem to reflect the differences in the modelling methods used, suggesting that in this type of research the precise modelling used can affect the results. Nevertheless, the overall picture that emerges is that the quality and effectiveness of regulation has a positive effect on growth using both approaches to the modelling.

5.   CONCLUSIONS

The provision of a regulatory regime that promotes rather than reduces economic growth is an important part of good governance. The ability of the state to provide effective regulatory institutions can be expected to be a determinant of how well markets and the economy perform. The effectiveness of regulatory institutions will depend on both the *efficiency* of the regulatory policies and instruments that are used and the *quality* of the governance processes that are practised by the regulatory authorities, as discussed in the early part of this chapter.

This chapter has tested the hypothesis that the quality of regulation affects economic performance, drawing on data in Kaufmann and Kraay (2002) and World Bank data. Two proxies for regulatory quality were included separately and then combined as determinants of economic growth performance, using both cross-sectional and panel data methods. The results from both sets of modelling suggest a strong causal link between regulatory quality and economic growth and confirm that the form of regulation matters for economic performance. The results are consistent with those of Olson et al. (1998), who found that productivity growth is strongly correlated with the quality of governance, and Kaufmann and Kraay (2002), who found that the quality of governance has a positive effect on incomes.

The challenge in international business is to provide an environment conducive to mutually beneficial trade and investment. In the specific context of developing countries, the challenge is to build effective regulatory institutions that have the capacity to provide regulatory processes that stimulate inward investment and trade, while meeting the particular structural characteristics and developmental needs of the economy. As we highlighted earlier, the proxies we use for regulatory governance are correlated with a number of other institutional proxies. One could argue, therefore, that what we have established could equally hold for the link between institutional capacity in general and economic performance.

However, the literature reviewed earlier in the chapter is consistent with institutional capacity playing a strong and complementary role in regulatory governance. Also, the ability to model separately institutions in general and regulatory institutions or governance in particular remains problematic because of their complementarity. Our results are best interpreted as demonstrating the importance of regulatory quality for economic growth in the context of wider institutional capacity building. Finally, we acknowledge that the direction of causation between economic growth and regulatory quality deserves further investigation. We believe that there are good *a priori* grounds for assuming that better regulation leads to faster economic growth, but recognize that there could be some feedback from economic performance to regulatory quality. Nevertheless, despite these caveats, our results are consistent with the view that 'good' regulation is associated with higher economic growth, which in turn is conducive to the expansion of international business.

NOTES

1. One of the authors of this chapter has been involved in the design of regulatory institutions for Malawi.
2. This expresses the observed data in each cluster as a linear function of the unobserved common component of governance, plus a disturbance term to capture perception errors and sampling variation in each indicator (Kaufmann et al., 1999).
3. However, neither neoclassical nor endogenous growth theory gave regulation an explicit role. By assuming that output is at the limit provided by the available factor inputs and technology, neoclassical growth theory implicitly assumed optimal regulation.
4. Benhabib and Spiegel (1994) argue that the initial level of human capital can affect the growth path of productivity. Olson et al. (1998) also use secondary school enrolment as a proxy explanatory variable in their growth study.
5. There are two estimation procedures for panel data: fixed and random effects. In our case, the fixed effect method is the most appropriate one to use for the following reasons: (a) *a priori* we expect regulatory governance proxies to be correlated with the intercept term for each country; those with a poor or weak regulatory governance are also expected to perform relatively badly in terms of economic performance; (b) we are interested in measuring differences between countries included in our data set; the parameter estimate for country dummies (the intercept term for each country) is a proxy for these differences. Intercepts in turn are used as a dependent variable in the second-stage regression to establish the link between regulatory governance and country characteristics captured by the intercept term. The fixed effects method allows us to do this; (c) in small samples, similar to the one we are using here, there may be practical problems preventing parameter estimation when the random effect model is applied; this is not the case with the fixed effects model.
6. The series constructed are composite indexes, which are based on a number of variables generated at different points in time, mainly in the 1990s. Information for each country on these proxies, therefore, generally relates to a period rather than a specific year. Kaufmann and Kraay (2002) highlight certain issues relating to the quality of the data used, particularly when it is utilized for making comparisons across countries. However, we are not aware of better regulatory quality data, while conceding that better-quality data could reveal different results to those reported here. Nevertheless, based on the significance level of the relevant variables in our regressions, we are fairly confident that any differences in the results would relate to the magnitude of these effects rather than their sign.
7. A number of the explanatory variables were logged. In the literature the basic growth accounting model is generally exponential (e.g. Cobb–Douglas); once logged, it becomes a linear relationship which can then be estimated. For the other explanatory variables in our model, logging helped to solve problems of serial correlation and heteroscedasticity.
8. The transition economies of Central and Eastern Europe suffered from a large fall in GDP during the 1990s and this helps to explain this result.
9. The figure in parentheses is the *t*-ratio.
10. This is unsurprising given, as noted earlier, the degree of multicollinearity between the regulatory variables.
11. In this model the regional dummies identify whether there are regional similarities or differences as far as the country dummies are concerned.

REFERENCES

Asian Development Bank (2000), *Asia Development Report, 2000*, Manila: ADB.
Averch, H. and Johnson, L.L. (1962), 'Behavior of the Firm under Regulatory Constraint', *American Economic Review*, **52**, 1052–69.
Bailey, E.E. (1973), *Economic Theory of Regulatory Constraint*, Lexington, MA: D.C. Heath.

Baldwin, R. and Cave, M. (1999), *Understanding Regulation: Theory, Strategy and Practice*, Oxford: Oxford University Press.

Barro, R.J. (1991), 'Economic Growth in a Cross Section of Countries', *Quarterly Journal of Economics*, **106**, 407–33.

Barro, R.J. (1997), 'Determinants of Economic Growth: A cross-country empirical study', Development Discussion Paper No. 579, Harvard Institute for International Development.

Barro, R.J. (2000), 'Inequality and growth in a panel of countries', *Journal of Economic Growth*, **5**, 5–32.

Barro, R. and Sala-i-Martin, X. (1999), 'Convergence', *Journal of Political Economy*, **C**, 223–51.

Benhabib, J.J. and Spiegel, M.M. (1994), 'The Role of Human Capital in Economic Development: Evidence from Cross-Country Data', *Journal of Monetary Economics*, **34**, 143–73.

Birdsall, N. and Nellis, J. (2002), 'Winners and Losers: Assessing the Distributional Impact of Privatization', Working Paper No. 6, Washington, DC: Center for Global Development.

Brownbridge, M. and Kirkpatrick, C. (2000), 'Financial Regulation in Developing Countries: Survey Article', *Journal of Development Studies*, **37** (1), 1–24.

Brownbridge, M. and Kirkpatrick, C. (2002), 'Policy Symposium: Financial Regulation and Supervision in Developing Countries', *Development Policy Review*, **20** (3).

Buchanan, J.M. (1972), *Theory of Public Choice*, Ann Arbor, MI: University of Michigan Press.

Burnside, C. and Dollar, D. (1997), 'Aid Policies and Growth', Policy Research Working Paper no. 1777, Washington, DC: World Bank.

Campbell-White, O. and Bhatia, A. (1998), *Directions in Development: Privatization in Africa*, Washington, DC: World Bank.

Cave, M. and Stern, J. (1998), 'Regulatory Institutions and Regulatory Policy for Economies in Transition', in C. Robinson (ed.), *Regulating Utilities: Understanding the Issues*, London: Institute of Economic Affairs.

Chong, A. and Lopez-de-Silanes, F. (2002), 'Privatization and Labor Force Restructuring around the World', World Bank Policy Research Working Paper 2884, Washington, DC: World Bank.

Clague, C., Keefer, P., Knack, S. and Olson, M. (1995), 'Contract-intensive Money: Contract Enforcement, Property Rights and Economic Performance', Working Paper No. 151, University of Maryland: Institutional Reform and the Informal Sector (IRIS).

Cook, P. (1999), 'Privatization and Utility Regulation in Developing Countries: The Lessons So Far', *Annals of Public and Cooperative Economics*, **70** (4), 549–87.

Cook, P. and Kirkpatrick, C. (2003), 'Assessing the Impact of Privatization in Developing Countries', in D. Parker and D. Saal (eds), *International Handbook on Privatization*, Cheltenham, UK and Northampton, MA, USA: Edward Elgar.

De Castro, A.S., Goldin, I. and da Silva, L.A.P. (2002), 'Relative Returns to Policy Reform: Evidence from Controlled Cross-Country Regressions', mimeo, Washington, DC: World Bank.

Dinar, A. (2000), 'Political Economy of Water Pricing Reforms', in A. Dinar (ed.), *The Political Economy of Water Pricing Reforms*, Oxford: World Bank and Oxford University Press.

Estache, A. and Kouassi, E. (2002), 'Sector Organization, Governance and the Inefficiency of African Water Utilities', mimeo.

Gray, P. (2001), 'Private Participation in Infrastructure: A Review of the Evidence', mimeo, Washington, DC: World Bank.

Grossman, S.J. and Hart, O.D. (1986), 'The Costs and Benefits of Ownership: A Theory of Vertical and Lateral Integration', *Journal of Political Economy*, **94** (4), 691–719.

Guasch, J.L. and Hahn, R.W. (1999), 'The Costs and Benefits of Regulation: Implications for Developing Countries', *World Bank Research Observer*, **14** (1), 137–58.

Hall, R.E. and Jones, C. (1999), 'Why Do Some Countries Produce So Much More Output per Worker than Others?', *Quarterly Journal of Economics*, **114** (1), 83–116.

Hayek, F.A. (1945), 'The Use of Knowledge in Society', *American Economic Review*, **35**, 519–30.

Hood, C. (1994), *Explaining Economic Policy Reversals*, Buckingham: Open University Press.

Islam, N. (1995), 'Growth Empirics: A Panel Data Approach', *Quarterly Journal of Economics*, **110**, 1127–70.

Kauffmann, D. and Kraay, A. (2002), 'Growth Without Governance', mimeo, Washington, DC: World Bank.

Kaufmann, D., Kraay, A. and Zoido-Lobatón, P. (1999), 'Aggregating Governance Indicators', Working Paper No. 2195, Washington, DC: World Bank Policy Research Department.

Kaufmann, D., Kraay, A. and Zoido-Lobatón, P. (2002), 'Governance Matters II: Updated indicators for 2000/01', Policy Research Working Paper, Washington, DC: World Bank.

Keefer, P. and Knack, S. (1995), 'Institutions and Economic Performance: Cross-country Tests Using Alternative Institutional Measures', *Economics and Politics*, **7** (3), 207–27.

King, G. and Zeng, L. (2000), 'Improving Forecast of State Failure', mimeo, the Mid-West Science Association Conference, Chicago.

Kirkpatrick, C. and Parker, D. (2004), 'Regulatory Impact Assessment and Regulatory Governance in Developing Countries', *Public Administration and Development*, **24**, 1–12.

Knight-John, M. (2002), 'The Institutional Policy Framework for Regulation and Competition in Sri Lanka', Working Paper No. 40, Centre on Regulation and Competition, Institute for Development Policy and Management, University of Manchester.

Laffont, J.-J. (1999), *Incentives and the Political Economy of Regulation*, Oxford: Oxford University Press.

Laffont, J.-J. and Tirole, J. (1993), *A Theory of Incentives in Procurement and Regulation*, Cambridge, MA: MIT Press.

Laffont, J.-J. and Tirole, J. (2000), *Competition in Telecommunications*, Cambridge, MA: MIT Press.

Lanyi, A. (2000), 'The Institutional Basis of Economic Reforms', in S. Kähkönen and A. Lanyi (eds), *Institutions, Incentives and Economic Reforms in India*, New Delhi and London: Sage Publications.

Levy, B. and Spiller, P.T. (1994), 'The Institutional Foundations of Regulatory Commitment: A Comparative Analysis of Telecommunications Regulation', *Journal of Law, Economics and Organization*, **10** (2), 201–46.

Lucas, R.E. (1988), 'On Mechanisms of Economic Planning', *Journal of Monetary Economics*, **21** (1), 3–42.

Maimbo, S. (2002), 'The Diagnosis and Prediction of Bank Failures in Zambia, 1990–1998', *Development Policy Review*, **20** (3), 261–78.

Majone, G. (1994), 'The Emergence of the Regulatory State in Europe', *West European Politics*, **17**, 77–101.

Majone, G. (1997), 'From the Positive to the Regulatory State', *Journal of Public Policy*, **17** (2), 139–67.

Mankiw, N.D., Romer, P. and Weil, D. (1992), 'A Contribution to the Empirics of Economic Growth', *Quarterly Journal of Economics*, **107**, 407–37.

Mauro, P. (1995), 'Corruption and Growth', *Quarterly Journal of Economics*, **110**, 681–712.

Neumayer, E. (2002), 'Is Good Governance Rewarded? A Cross-National Analysis of Debt Forgiveness', *World Development*, **30** (6), 913–30.

Newbery, D. (1999), *Privatization, Restructuring and Regulation of Network Industries*, Cambridge, MA: MIT Press.

North, D.C. (1990), *Institutions, Institutional Change and Economic Performance*, Cambridge: Cambridge University Press.

Olson, M., Sarna, N. and Swamy, A.V. (1998), 'Governance and Growth: A simple hypothesis explaining cross-country differences in productivity', mimeo, Centre for Institutional Reform and Informal Sector (IRIS), University of Maryland.

Parker, D. (1999), 'Regulation of Privatised Public Utilities in the UK: Performance and Governance', *International Journal of Public Sector Management*, **12** (3), 213–35.

Parker, D. (2002), 'Economic Regulation: A Review of Issues', *Annals of Public and Cooperative Economics*, **73** (4), 493–519.

Peltzman, S. (1976), 'Toward a More General Theory of Regulation', *Journal of Law and Economics*, **14**, 109–48.

Political Risk Services (2002), International Country Risk Guide (A commercial source which regularly publishes survey data on country risks).

Reagan, M.D. (1987), *Regulation: The Politics of Policy*, Boston, MA: Little Brown.

Romer, P.M. (1986), 'Increasing Returns and Long-run Growth', *Journal of Political Economy*, **94** (5), 1002–37.

Sachs, J.D. and Warner, A.M. (1995), 'Economic Reform and the Process of Global Integration', *Brookings Paper in Economic Activities*, **0** (1): 1–95.

Sappington, D.E. and Stiglitz, J.E. (1987), 'Privatization, Information and Incentives', *Journal of Policy Analysis & Management*, **6** (4), 567–82.

Schwella, E. (2002), 'Regulation and Competition in South Africa', Working Paper no. 18, Manchester: Centre on Regulation and Competition, University of Manchester.

Shapiro, C. and Willig, R.D. (1990), 'Economic Rationales for the Scope of Privatization', in E.N. Suleiman and J. Waterbury, *The Political Economy of Public Sector Reform and Privatization*, Boulder, CO: Westview Press; also reprinted in D. Parker (ed.) (2001), *Privatisation and Corporate Performance*, Cheltenham, UK and Northampton, MA, USA: Edward Elgar.

Solow, R.M. (1956), 'A Contribution to the Theory of Economic Growth', *Quarterly Journal of Economics*, **70**, 65–94.

Stern, J. and Holder, S. (1999), 'Regulatory Governance: Criteria for Assessing the Performance of Regulatory Systems. An Application to Infrastructure Industries in the Developing Countries of Asia', *Utilities Policy*, **8**, 33–50.

Stern, N. (1991), 'Public Policy and the Economics of Development', *European Economic Review*, **35**.

Stigler, G. (1971), 'The Theory of Economic Regulation', *Bell Journal of Economics and Management*, **2**, 3–21.

Stiglitz, J. (1998), 'Private Uses of Public Interests: Incentives and Institutions', *Journal of Economic Perspectives*, **12** (2), 3–22.

World Bank (1995), *Bureaucrats in Business: The Economics and Politics of Government Ownership*, Oxford: Oxford University Press for the World Bank.

World Bank (1997), *World Development Report. The State in a Changing World*, Washington, DC: World Bank.

World Bank (2001), *Private Sector Development Strategy – Directions for the World Bank Group*, mimeo, Washington, DC: World Bank.

World Bank (2002), *World Development Report, 2002. Building Institutions for Markets*, Washington, DC: World Bank.

World Bank (2003), *Global Economic Prospects and the Developing Countries*, Washington, DC: World Bank.

Yarrow, G. (1999), 'A Theory of Privatization, or Why Bureaucrats are Still in Business', *World Development*, **27** (1), 157–68.

APPENDIX

List of countries included in the regressions:

Argentina, Australia, Austria, Bangladesh, Belgium, Benin, Bolivia, Brazil, Bulgaria, Burkina Faso, Cameroon, Canada, Chile, China, Colombia, Congo, Dem. Rep., Congo, Rep., Costa Rica, Côte d'Ivoire, Dominican Republic, Ecuador, Egypt, Arab Rep., El Salvador, Finland, France, Gabon, Gambia, Ghana, Greece, Guatemala, Guinea-Bissau, Guyana, Haiti, Honduras, Hong Kong, Hungary, Iceland, India, Indonesia, Iran, Islamic Rep., Israel, Italy, Jamaica, Japan, Jordan, Kenya, Korea, Rep., Latvia, Lesotho, Luxembourg, Malawi, Malaysia, Mali, Mauritius, Mexico, Morocco, Mozambique, Netherlands, Nicaragua, Niger, Nigeria, Norway, Pakistan, Panama, Papua New Guinea, Paraguay, Peru, Philippines, Senegal, Singapore, Spain, Sri Lanka, Sweden, Switzerland, Syrian Arab Republic, Thailand, Togo, Trinidad and Tobago, Tunisia, United States, Uruguay, Venezuela, Zambia, Zimbabwe.

3. The World Trade Organisation and domestic regulation

Peter Holmes

In 1998 Guy de Jonquières wrote an article in the *Financial Times*, 'Rules for the regulators', in which he argued that future trade negotiations would no longer be about tariffs, quotas and other measures clearly targeting trade, but would rather be about domestic regulations that had an indirect effect on trade:

> Increasingly, regulation is becoming the focus of international competition and conflict. As the borders come down in the world economy, the repercussions of inadequate or flawed regulation are becoming more immediate and more likely to cross national frontiers. This is thrusting the main global body for resolving trade disputes into new territory. As liberalisation extends deeper into countries' domestic economies, the opening of markets increasingly requires global disciplines on national regulatory policies.[1]

Some observers might disagree with the author's argument that erosion of sovereignty in this area was desirable, but there is no doubt that this comment was highly prescient.

This has proved to be particularly true in transatlantic trade diplomacy. One of the toughest trade battles at the World Trade Organisation (WTO) between the EU and the USA has been the 'Beef Hormone' dispute in which the USA and Canada challenged the EU's right to ban the sale in its markets of beef treated with growth-promoting hormones, a ban which had the effect of excluding almost all US beef from the EU market, since this method of rearing is usual in North America. The looming battle over GM (genetically modified) foods is a similar case: here the primary effect of any EU rules would be to govern the use of GM crops within the EU, but there would also be a significant effect on trade and therefore it comes within the remit of the WTO.

The intermingling of trade and regulation has a long history within the EU, though its profile has been very low until recently in the multilateral system. The traditional British jokes about 'Brussels' seeking to harmonize standards for ice cream and to force British ice cream to be labelled 'iced vegetable fat', while mythological, do have a basis in fact. When the Treaty of Rome was written the authors realized that it would not be enough to outlaw all barriers to imports that acted at borders, because border measures could be replaced by domestic measures that had an equivalent effect. In the crudest example, France could remove all customs duties on Scotch whisky but introduce a sales tax that affects whisky products but not cognac.

If the UK eliminates a 10 per cent tariff on German cars but at the same time raises value-added tax (VAT) by 10 per cent on all cars *and* introduces a production subsidy of 10 per cent, we are back where we started. Technical regulations have similar effects: even a requirement that all products be packaged and labelled in pounds and ounces in one country but in metric units in a neighbour can create a barrier to trade.

THE BASIC ECONOMICS OF NON-TARIFF BARRIERS (NTBS)

The basic economics of protection by tariffs and indeed subsidies is fairly familiar, but it is worth recalling the difference between these measures and the effects of regulatory protection. Where tariff protectionism is used, imports are taxed and the price to consumers of imported goods is raised by the amount of the tariff (as a first approximation). On imported goods this price increase goes to the state as revenue. In the case of domestic substitutes for imports, traditional theory assumes that producers match the price of imports with an equivalent rise, in which case there is a transfer of revenue from consumers to domestic producers. In the case of quotas or quantitative restrictions we can also assume that prices rise but in this case the scarcity rent goes to the exporter.

In the case of regulatory NTBs the effects are different. Here the impact of the NTB is to raise the costs of supply *for everyone* in such a way as to restrict market penetration by imports. The typical regulatory barrier takes the form of a technical regulation that requires some product or process specification that is somehow more burdensome on foreign producers than on home producers.

It is worth noting at this point that standards in themselves do not necessarily constitute trade barriers. But they can become so if there exists a compulsion to require the use of one standard rather than another. There may be regulations which make standards compulsory, or involve complex conformity assessment procedures. These are testing and certification systems that a product (or service) has to go through to prove that it complies with a regulation or standard, and one country's certificates may not be recognized by another even if products are identical. The latter often creates the most stringent barriers, as testing and certification can be very costly, and is sometimes in the hands of private domestic producers.

It has been recognized that private firms may have an incentive to lobby for national regulations that raise both their own costs and those of foreigners when a similar cost amounts to a greater burden for the foreigner. Such a situation can arise when foreign competitors operate with lower profit margins or when fixed costs can be more easily spread over the whole market by local firms (see Mattoo, 2001).

The early theoretical literature (like GATT – General Agreement on Tariffs and Trade – law, as we shall see) mainly focused on tariff barriers and taxation, but there was a literature on NTBs: these were mostly analysed in terms of subsidies and quotas. The theoretical analysis of the impact of regulatory differences (including technical barriers and service regulations) is relatively recent. The main reason for this is almost certainly that trade economists have been anxious to stress the benefits to consumers of diversity of regulations and have been aware that discussions of 'distortions' caused by domestic regulations in other countries are likely to lead to demands for harmonization which, if not met, lead in turn to pressures for traditional protectionism. As we shall note below, most trade economists seek to minimize the scope for international rules to harmonize domestic regulations.[2]

DOMESTIC POLICY AND INTERNATIONAL TRADE IN THE ECONOMICS LITERATURE

It has long been recognized in principle that many domestic policy measures can have the effect of distorting trade. A long tradition of literature in international economics has identified the conditions under which taxes and subsidies might have an effect on trade. Johnson (1965) developed the famous theoretical result that for the promotion of domestic industry an internal subsidy was more appropriate than a tariff, which is simultaneously a production subsidy and a consumption tax. To reduce consumption of the item in question (e.g. luxury goods in developing countries), a tax on all sales, not just imports, is appropriate. Conversely, this literature showed that combinations of taxes and subsidies could achieve exactly the same effect as taxes. The effect of a tariff can be mimicked by a tax on all sales of the item combined with a subsidy on domestic production. Interestingly, the theoretical literature was less preoccupied with subsidies than tariffs: the trade literature was clearly concerned about distortions but the public finance literature gave broad support to subsidies in cases where there were externalities. It was only in the 1970s and 1980s that the trade literature began to converge in its outlook with the public choice literature.[3]

We should, however, distinguish between the broad principles of taxation as they affect the relative price of all imports and domestic goods and how they might alter the relative prices of home versus foreign variants of individual commodities.

There was extensive literature in the 1960s on the trade neutrality of internal sales tax systems (i.e. origin versus destination-based tax systems). Under the destination principle, sales taxes or VAT are levied on imports but not exports (and vice versa for the origin principle). The destination principle is less likely to distort trade, given the location of production, but it could influence investment decisions.[4]

What is notable about these measures is that in most cases it is possible to design a measure that does not actually formally discriminate between home and foreign goods (apart from the example of the production subsidy which by its nature only affects domestic goods, though it might not differentiate between the nationality of firms).

It is therefore clear that any set of rules governing trade liberalization must also address domestic regulations and taxation if removal of barriers directly affecting trade is not to be simply replaced by imposition of indirect measures.

Sceptics may well ask whether the retention of alternative policy instruments might not be a good idea. This perspective, however, risks missing what many trade economists see as the key aim of trade liberalization, namely the creation of a regime of predictable rules, rather than necessarily a system of totally free trade, whether we are thinking of the EU or the WTO. Those who believe in the merits of the multilateral trade system or the single market regime do not necessarily believe that governments must abolish all interference with trade; it is increasingly argued that unpredictability of public policy has serious adverse consequences. Curiously, the point is made most often in the context of macroeconomic policy where rules (including contingent rules) are considered by many authors superior to a policy framework with total discretion.

The concept of a rule-based trade regime is founded on a similar idea. Trade liberalization is motivated by the desire to signal clearly to investors that they should not invest in sectors where the country does not have a comparative advantage. Whereas there may be arguments against the introduction of such reforms in a big bang, there is every reason to ensure that transition periods are predictable and not disrupted by offsetting subsidies or other measures.

'DEEP' VERSUS 'SHALLOW' INTEGRATION IN THE EU AND THE WTO

Historically there has been a divide between the framework rules of the multilateral trading system and those of more ambitious regional integration schemes such as the EU. This is exemplified by the perception that the GATT dealt with trade barriers while the European Common Market was intended to go further in harmonizing domestic legislation.

Since the 1960s the legal literature has extensively explored the links between trade and regulation. In a masterly account of the relationship between the EU and the GATT/WTO system, Weiler (1999) observes that both the Treaty of Rome and the GATT did address non-border regulatory measures but in different ways. Article III of the GATT 1947 provided that domestic taxes and regulations should not be applied so as to discriminate against imported goods.[5] In other words, signatories of GATT could apply whatever discriminatory barriers they wished at the border, but once inside the country, foreign goods had to be treated exactly as domestic goods. The 'national treatment' provisions of GATT enshrined non-discrimination as the cornerstone of its approach to taxes and regulations. A pure non-discrimination rule allows a country to have any tax regime or regulatory framework it wishes so long as the same rules apply to domestic and foreign goods (or services).

It soon becomes clear that such a principle is extremely tolerant of measures that are designed to effectively deny entry to foreign goods if it is confined to banning explicit *de jure* or 'facial' discrimination. In the simplest case we can mimic a tariff by a tax system that bears far more heavily on types of car that are imported than on types produced at home, or has different tax rates on spirits based on different kinds of alcohol. And for technical regulations, where there are economies of scale and scope, the requirement in a regulation that standards commonly used at home are compulsory for all goods may exclude foreign products even when the same regulations apply to them as to home products.

The classic example regarding this point in recent times has been the EU ban on the sale of hormone-treated beef. This affects all beef regardless of origin, but it can be argued to have affected imported beef more since hormone treatment of beef is not customary inside the EU (but is elsewhere).

Before moving on, it is worth examining the basic disciplines that bear on domestic regulations. Specifically, there are most favoured nation, national treatment, mutual recognition, and harmonization (see Table 3.1).

The most-favoured nation (MFN) provision lies at the core of the GATT and the WTO. Whereas a country's rules may discriminate against foreigners, all similar imported products must be treated the same. This provision prevents, for example, the use of administrative measures that exempt country A's goods from a technical requirement that is imposed on country B's goods, *for no good reason*. This provision is more significant where technical barriers to trade are concerned than for tariffs – but in particular it has much more relevance to services than goods.

The MFN principle has been at the heart of the GATT since 1947 for sound reasons of political economy. It is intended to ensure that weaker players secure all the same market access opportunities that stronger ones have. The only basic exception is for thorough-going regional integration schemes (as

Table 3.1   A summary of key terminology

	Meaning	WTO	Governance
Most favoured nation	Discriminate against foreigners, but not between them	Key principle of GATT	Minimal constraints on autonomy
National treatment	Treat foreign and home firms equally, but rules as idiosyncratic as you like	Art. III also key. Sometimes impact under-estimated TBTs; GATS subject to committments	Impact slight without binding DS. Could be big with binding DS – if implicit discrimination addressed
Mutual recognition	Equivalence assumed but subject to challenge	SPS if equivalence can be shown	Depends on freedom to choose partners and if binding DS
Harmoniza-tion/approxi-mation	Everyone has same/similar rules	TRIPs Telecoms Reference Paper	Explicit agreement in detail needed; EU QMV WTO consensus if multilateral

laid out in GATT Art. XXIV, and GATS – General Agreement on Trade in Services – Art. V), but it is clear that as the EU and the USA pursue bilateral trade arrangements the MFN principle is under threat. The relevance for domestic regulations here is that countries must not impose regulatory requirements on some countries but not others.

'National treatment' is the basic principle of non-discrimination. It says that regulations may take any form but they must be applied evenly between home and foreign goods. The sting in the tail here is that the application of the principle must be *de facto* as well as *de jure*. Harmonization of law, by contrast, represents a system for preventing technical barriers to trade. While neither the GATT nor the WTO have a means for agreeing common legislation, it is arguable that some provisions, particularly the TRIPs (trade-related aspects of intellectual property rights) agreement, get close to this.

Mutual recognition (MR) is a principle that was developed by the European Court of Justice in the 1970s in the face of the unwillingness of member states to remove the national differences in rules that created trade barriers. MR means that each EU member state agrees to accept goods made to each other's standards and to accept goods made to theirs even if the standards involved are slightly different. Inevitably this must be a selective affair: there must be a basic compatibility between the partners' approaches. Moreover, the provision is of little value unless there is also MR of testing and certification procedures. The WTO provisions have two aspects: members are enjoined to accept products made to other countries' standards when these are based on international standards. (The exact nature of this obligation will be discussed below.) But there are special rules governing bilateral mutual recognition agreements which will normally be needed to extend MR into testing and certification.

Each regime has different governance implications. Looser obligations require less complex arrangements for defining common norms, but if they are binding, leave enormous power and discretion in the hands of the dispute settlement body or court. It is a far from trivial issue to determine what are 'like products' and which must be subject to the same rules or taxes.

DOMESTIC MEASURES AND GATT

It is possible to argue that before the creation of the WTO the difference between the EC and the WTO was that the former concerned itself with the removal of non-border barriers that distorted trade flows. As a matter of practical politics this is more or less accurate but legally it is misleading. Like the Treaty of Rome, the GATT did concern itself with behind-the-border non-tariff barriers. In practice, however, this function did not assume a high priority.

The original discipline on domestic regulations in the GATT comes in the form of Article III (1947):

Article III: National Treatment on Internal Taxation and Regulation
The contracting parties recognize that internal taxes and other internal charges, and laws, regulations and requirements affecting the internal sale, offering for sale, purchase, transportation, distribution or use of products, and internal quantitative regulations requiring the mixture, processing or use of products in specified amounts or proportions, should not be applied to imported or domestic products so as to afford protection to domestic production.

This is the core non-discrimination requirement (national treatment) of GATT. It states that once an imported good has crossed the frontier it must thereafter be treated the same as 'like' domestic products.

This rule had some exceptions: it did not apply to public procurement and, quite importantly, it only applied to *new* measures until the creation of the WTO in 1994. We should note at this point that competition laws are almost certainly covered by Article III, and whilst for trade in goods there is no obligation on a member state to have a competition law, any such law must conform to Article III. Curiously, as we shall note below, the position is somewhat different with respect to services.[6]

In fact, Article III is not the only measure of relevance to domestic regulation in the original GATT. Article XI bans any measure other than 'duties, taxes or other charges' which may be used to restrict imports; it outlaws quantitative restrictions. A total ban on the sale of a type of product that has the effect of preventing the same of imported products can be seen as a zero quota.

Article XVI of the GATT 1947 forbids export subsidies – and can be used to attack any provisions of *domestic* tax law that, even in an indirect manner, treat income from export earnings more generously than domestic profits. This potentially enters quite deep into national sovereignty, as the case brought by the EU against the USA in the 'Foreign Sales Corporation' case shows.[7] Other provisions of the 1947 GATT Treaty dealt with state import and export monopolies requiring them not to discriminate against *or between* foreign goods.

Finally, on the discipline side, Article XXIII states that a contracting party may bring a complaint against another if it believes that a new measure has been introduced which has the effect of 'nullification or impairment' of market access that was provided for by the GATT agreement and the parties' schedules. This is known as the 'non-violation' because it applies when the accused party has introduced a measure that is *not* explicitly prohibited as such by the GATT and which would be perfectly legal if it did not have the effect of injuring the complainant's exports. It is, in fact, very hard to win a case under this provision.[8]

Each of these disciplines contains its own defence: obviously one can claim that differences in treatment of imports and other goods do not afford protection to domestic goods (Art. III) and perhaps, more significantly, if a foreign good is not a 'like product' compared with the domestic counterpart, then it can be treated differently.

In addition there is a general exception provision (GATT, Art. XX):

General Exceptions
   Subject to the requirement that such measures are not applied in a manner which would constitute a means of arbitrary or unjustifiable discrimination between countries where the same conditions prevail, or a disguised restriction on international trade, nothing in this Agreement shall be construed to prevent the adoption or enforcement by any contracting party of measures:
      (a) necessary to protect public morals;
      (b) necessary to protect human, animal or plant life or health;

and

> (g) relating to the conservation of exhaustible natural resources if such measures are made effective in conjunction with restrictions on domestic production or consumption.

This is the equivalent of Article 30 of the revised EC Treaty which allows general public policy exceptions. But whereas the European Court of Justice had a means of enforcing the equivalent provisions against quotas and 'measures of equivalent effect', the dispute settlement system of the pre-1994 GATT had no teeth. That is to say, if a judgment was given against a GATT contracting party (now under WTO 'member state'), it was not binding unless approved by a consensus of all states including the respondent.

THE CREATION OF THE WTO

The launch of the WTO in 1994 had two important effects. It created a series of new obligations in addition to those above, and, less well understood, it gave teeth to the original obligations for the first time.

The Technical Barriers to Trade (TBT) Agreement

There had been long discussion on the role of technical barriers to trade in the GATT, but in 1994 the conclusion of the Uruguay Round took this one step further with the creation of the WTO, a full-blown multilateral organization of which signatories of the GATT and a series of new countries became members. The technical barriers to trade (TBT) agreement consolidated a number of agreements that GATT signatories had made.

Recalling the distinction between standards, regulations and testing and certification, the TBT agreement requires members to ensure that all are implemented in such a way as to minimize distortions to trade.

Key provisions are:

Article 2.2 Members shall ensure that technical regulations are not prepared, adopted or applied with a view to or with the effect of creating unnecessary obstacles to international trade. For this purpose, technical regulations shall not be more trade-restrictive than necessary to fulfil a legitimate objective, taking account of the risks non-fulfilment would create. Such legitimate objectives are, inter alia: national security requirements; the prevention of deceptive practices; protection of human health or safety, animal or plant life or health, or the environment. In assessing such risks, relevant elements of consideration are, inter alia: available scientific and technical information, related processing technology or intended end-uses of products.

and

> *Article 2.4*   Where technical regulations are required and relevant international standards exist or their completion is imminent, Members shall use them, or the relevant parts of them, as a basis for their technical regulations except when such international standards or relevant parts would be an ineffective or inappropriate means for the fulfilment of the legitimate objectives pursued, for instance because of fundamental climatic or geographical factors or fundamental technological problems.

The most significant elements are the requirement that there should be no unnecessary obstacles to trade, and that regulations should be based on international standards unless these would be 'an ineffective or inappropriate means for the fulfilment of the legitimate objectives pursued'. It is clear that these terms are somewhat ambiguous and it will be a recurring theme of this chapter that one cannot interpret the meaning of these WTO rules without looking at the jurisprudence of the dispute settlement body.

The basic meaning of this element of the TBT agreement is that countries can pursue their own national regulatory aims but there are bounds on the means that may be used to pursue them if these restrict trade. There is a natural economists' response to this, namely that some sort of cost–benefit analysis should be employed to compare the value of the regulatory goal with the trade loss. This philosophy lies behind the use of Environmental Impact Assessment in the USA. However, it is clearly inappropriate in the WTO context. The trade-off is between gains for the importing countries and losses for exporters. The WTO dispute settlement body (DSB)[9] does not have the authority to insist on a form of redistribution of income that may be implied by such a trade-off. (We should recall that from the time of the GATT, trade rules have been expressed in mercantilist terms in which the cost of an import restriction is not viewed as the cost to consumers of inability to import; rather it is the cost of lost export revenue.)

The wording of the TBT agreement is ambiguous: it does not give countries total freedom to regulate as they wish, and implies there are circumstances in which regulations will be disregarded if they are not based on international norms. However, the TBT also implies that there is considerable freedom to regulate if a 'legitimate' aim is pursued. It was left to the DSB to sort out the meaning of the terms here in more detail than is provided in the text itself and, almost as important, to settle the burden of proof.

The Agreement on the Application of Sanitary and Phytosanitary Measures (SPS)

The SPS agreement was a new addition to the GATT structure at the time of the Uruguay Round (UR): it deals with regulations to protect human, animal or plant life or health. It has basically the same structure as the TBT agreement but it is rather more precise. The SPS agreement was motivated by the Uruguay Round decision to liberalize agriculture. It was clear that reducing tariff barriers would be of no value if spurious health and safety regulations could be invoked without scientific basis. The SPS measures were driven by a number of concerns: the USA was particularly motivated by the desire to end an EU ban on the sale of beef treated with growth hormones (wherever produced); and the EU was keen to prevent the USA from shutting out EU wine and cheese exports.

In its preamble the SPS agreement reaffirms that:

> no Member should be prevented from adopting or enforcing measures necessary to protect human, animal or plant life or health, subject to the requirement that these measures are not applied in a manner which would constitute a means of arbitrary or unjustifiable discrimination between Members where the same conditions prevail or a disguised restriction on international trade.

It summarizes the trade-off: there is no curtailment of the right to protect health, but this must not be by 'arbitrary measures' or a 'disguised restriction on international trade'.

But what is arbitrary? The agreement states that all SPS measures must be based on scientific evidence (Art. 2.2) including a scientific risk assessment (Art. 5.1). It also goes somewhat further than the TBT agreement in requiring that regulations be based on international standards.

The agreement calls for measures to minimize distortions to trade; Article 5 footnote 3 states:

> For purposes of paragraph 6 of Article 5, a measure is not more trade-restrictive than required unless there is another measure, reasonably available taking into account technical and economic feasibility, that achieves the appropriate level of sanitary or phytosanitary protection and is significantly less restrictive to trade.

Thus the SPS creates a presumption that products that conform to international food safety standards are safe. The requirement to base food safety rules on scientific evidence contained one important qualification. Article 5.7 states:

> In cases where relevant scientific evidence is insufficient, a Member may provisionally adopt sanitary or phytosanitary measures on the basis of available pertinent information . . .

This provision is closely related to the 'precautionary principle' often invoked by the EU but it does not give *carte blanche* for bans unless there is *some evidence* of a risk. The SPS agreement did not, however, oblige countries to base their regulations on international standards *in all cases*, but it defined rather precisely the conditions under which countries could impose tighter standards. This was the heart of the beef hormone dispute. The spirit of both the TBT and SPS agreements is therefore that states should be allowed to choose any legitimate regulatory objective they like, and can introduce any measures that are necessary to achieve such goals, even if trade is affected. They cannot, however, introduce regulations that affect trade but have no connection to a legitimate regulatory aim.

But what is a legitimate aim? And what is *necessary*? The rules are clear that if a state introduces a measure that is demonstrably necessary to achieve the aim of increasing food safety or which falls into one of the other 'legitimate aims' of TBT, it is hard to argue that it is illegal under the WTO, even if there is restriction to trade. But the problems arise when the aim is a TBT aim that is not on the list, when there is dispute about the validity of the aim, or in the case of SPS measures, whether there is enough scientific evidence to support it.

WTO JURISPRUDENCE ON TRADE IN GOODS

It is worth bringing together the case law that has emerged in these three areas. This law may be located in two main areas: in the first place, in the rules of the GATT itself, specifically Article III (the non-discrimination provision) and its own internal defences and the exception clause that is spelled out in Article XX. In the second place, law has arisen through the specific disciplines and gateways in the TBT and SPS agreements. It should be remembered that the WTO dispute settlement process has a number of steps. A member brings a complaint to the WTO: there are first consultations and then, if no settlement can be reached, a panel is appointed to decide. The panel judges whether the measure in question is compatible with WTO rules. If not, it will ask the respondent member to bring its policy into compliance, but no guidance is usually given about how this is to be done.

The panel's judgment then becomes a binding decision of the WTO unless:

(a) there is an appeal, or
(b) a consensus of WTO members – including the winning complainant – reject the decision.

If there is an appeal, the permanently constituted Appellate Body makes a final ruling, which is automatically binding, unless there is a consensus against it.[10] The respondent must then comply. If they do not do so, the complainant may then be authorized to take retaliatory action if a 'compliance panel' judges that the respondent has not implemented the ruling.

One issue about how much sovereignty is lost concerns whether or not it is within the rules for a respondent to agree to pay compensation instead of complying. Practice has emerged that non-compliance with compensation is becoming '*de facto* legal', but all lawyers agree that this outcome is not ideal, as if it were formally recognized, it would give powerful players the ability to buy their way out of complaints.

It is worth noting that the some of the worst fears about the intrusiveness of the WTO have not materialized in the sense that there has not been a spate of dispute settlement cases about domestic regulation, as was feared. However, some of the highest-profile cases – beef hormones and asbestos (see below) – were about the regulatory part of the rules. The most controversial aspects of this have been where exporters have challenged national measures allegedly promoting food safety but other aims and measures to enforce them have come under scrutiny. As the ultimate arbiter, the Appellate Body has tried to develop a consistent body of doctrine through its handling of Art. III/Art. XX, TBT and SPS cases.

The legal position has been summed up by Türk and Neuman and by Marceau and Trachtman (2002).[11] The Appellate Body has adopted the position that it will normally accept the declared regulatory goal of any respondent member state, but it will be prepared to examine the link between the declared aim and the actual measure adopted, in particular to explore whether the measure is really necessary or 'least trade-restrictive' for the achievement of the aim.

Thus the thread which runs through the decisions is that a state may choose its own regulatory aims, but the way its enforcement affects other countries' exports and the instruments to achieve the aims must be scrutinized.

The beef hormone case[12] under SPS was the most spectacular: in a nutshell the USA and Canada claimed the EU had introduced a ban on sale of hormone-treated beef without any scientific evidence at all that there were risks from such beef. (They argued that broccoli contained more of the hormones in question than treated beef.)

After the signing of the SPS agreement, the USA had pushed the international food safety standards authority, the *Codex Alimentarius*, for approval of a standard authorizing the use of growth hormones during the raising of cattle. This meant that the EU's ban on their use would be illegal unless it had scientific evidence to show that there was some risk which could be reduced by a regulation which did not allow US or Canadian beef to be sold in the EU. The USA set out to convince the WTO panel that there was no such evidence. It is widely acknowledged that the EU had very little, if any, evidence of possible harm from hormone-treated beef and the panel's ruling that the EU's measures were illegal came as no surprise. The Appellate Body, however, nuanced this outcome very significantly.

The Appellate Body ruled that under the SPS agreement, the EU had the right to set safety standards at higher levels than the *Codex* standard, but it ruled that the USA had shown that the EU had no scientific evidence that its ban on hormone-treated beef actually did reduce risk. The Appellate Body accepted the US case that the EU had not based its measures on a proper scientific risk assessment.

The Appellate Body overturned some elements of the initial panel decision to reaffirm the right of the EU to set the safety levels of its choice, and it ruled that the onus lay on the USA to prove that EU rules were not based on a scientific risk assessment, but accepted that the USA had done so.

The Appellate Body made it clear that the EU did not have to show conclusively that there was a danger from hormone-treated beef, merely that there was some evidence – any evidence – of a risk from even a 'minority' scientist. Critics who argued that WTO had applied a naïve 'right or wrong' view of science appear to have been mistaken. The Appellate Body stated in paragraph 194:

> We do not believe that a risk assessment has to come to a monolithic conclusion that coincides with the scientific conclusion or view implicit in the SPS measure. The risk assessment could set out both the prevailing view representing the 'mainstream' of scientific opinion, as well as the opinions of scientists taking a divergent view. Article 5.1 does not require that the risk assessment must necessarily embody only the view of a majority of the relevant scientific community. In some cases, the very existence of divergent views presented by qualified scientists who have investigated the particular issue at hand may indicate a state of scientific uncertainty.

Oddly, the EU caused considerable confusion by invoking the relevance of the 'precautionary principle'; it did not, however, give a firm definition of this and failed to invoke Article 5.7 here (see above). That is, the EU claimed there was an identifiable risk but did not reveal any evidence for this.

The beef hormone case set a number of core precedents: it established the right to set national safety levels as one wished and put the burden of proof more firmly on complainants, but it established the right of the DSB to decide whether there was a rational link between the declared objective and the trade measure.

Subsequent cases have taken this further: the Appellate Body has ruled that similar rights and burdens apply in the case of TBT and SPS measures. That is, it is up to the complainant to show that the measure in question is not based on an international standard where one exists *and* that such a departure is not needed to achieve a valid objective.

The Appellate Body has been fairly tolerant of regulatory objectives but intolerant of measures that clearly went well beyond what was needed to achieve the stated aim. One significant case was the Korean beef case,[13] where Korean law demanded that all imported beef should be sold in separate shops to ensure no possibility of a Korean consumer unwittingly buying imported meat instead of local. The Appellate Body did not question the objective but said it could be achieved equally well by other means (e.g. labelling rules) that would be less of an obstacle to importers.

This immediately gives us an insight into how the DSB might approach a dispute over GM foods. If the EU were to ban the import of GMOs, claiming them to be unsafe, it would risk losing the case unless it could show it had some scientific evidence of possible risk (even if *proof* of danger would not be required). On the other hand, if the EU argued that it wanted to impose strict labelling and segregation rules to reflect the collective wish of the EU public not to eat GM foods involuntarily, then it would be much easier to defend the case. However, the USA could still argue that ultra-strict segregation rules were more trade-restricting than necessary.

The DSB does not, however, have moral authority to make an economic trade-off between the welfare (as expressed by their subjective preferences) of EU consumers versus the profits of US cattle farmers as in a conventional cost–benefit analysis.

Another important case was the 'shrimp turtle' case.[14] Here the USA banned shrimp imports from certain Asian countries because they were not caught in US-approved nets that had a 'turtle extractor device'. The Appellate Body established the principle that the USA *did* have a right to control the sale of products produced abroad in what it considered an environmentally unfriendly way; but it said the specific measure in question discriminated against some countries whose fishermen did not harm turtles but achieved this aim without using US methods. Finally, a new US proposal was introduced that had the same effect by other means and was approved by the WTO.

The Appellate Body has tried to avoid taking a position on the merits of the objective in question: in the case of Korean beef it established the position that if the regulatory objective was legitimate, there should be no compromising the aim, but it might be asked whether other ways could be found of achieving it. But even if there were a number of alternative ways of achieving the same target, the Appellate Body would look more sympathetically on a very trade-restrictive measure in cases when the aim was a life-and-death matter. That is, if the aim is legitimate and clearly of high political salience, a measure will not be disregarded just because there is a another hypothetical measure that is as effective, but might restrict trade less.

On the other hand, if the objective is considered to be legitimate but less vital, the Appellate Body will be more sympathetic to demands that it be replaced by a less trade-restrictive *but equally effective* measure (which would not be specified, however). Thus, if the only way to achieve a legitimate aim involves banning all imports, the WTO should allow that, but if the same aim can be achieved by more or less trade-restrictive measures, the Appellate Body will consider demands that an alternative be adopted. The Appellate Body has made it clear that it will be more willing to impose the administrative nuisance of ensuring that a measure is modified to restrict trade less, while still achieving its aims in cases where the aim, while legitimate, is somehow less vital.

An interesting hypothetical case concerns the new EU regulations on the maximum tolerable levels of aflatoxin in peanut butter. World Bank economists[15] have estimated that the new tougher standards will only save two lives per billion peanut butter consumers at a cost of many hundreds of millions of dollars to very poor peanut farmers in Africa, and perhaps death through economic crisis. It argues that the price per life saved is in some sense too high. If our understanding is correct, the Appellate Body would be unlikely to challenge the EU's right to set a very tight safety limit for lives saved. Aflatoxin is a genuine health risk, and the test would not be whether the loss of many livelihoods in Africa was a legitimate trade-off against a small improvement in public health in the EU, but rather whether the same improvement in public health could be achieved in another way.

On the other hand, the Appellate Body recently (November 2003) upheld a US complaint against Japanese rules that made it impossible for apples to be sold to Japan from 48 of the 50 US states.[16] Here, the panel and the Appellate Body, while not apparently questioning Japan's right to keep its orchards free of 'fire blight', nevertheless concluded that there was in effect no risk that the 'mature symptomless apples' which were being excluded could ever be infected and, therefore, any ban on their import was not rationally related to a legitimate goal.

But what if the issue is not life and death? The WTO is open to the charge that the Appellate Body is judging the merits of the aim. It can be argued from the 'Korean beef' case that the Appellate Body is asking what priority the respondent country places on the aim in question. Here, the Koreans chose not to claim that foreign beef was unsafe, but they stressed a need to inform consumers. The Appellate Body had to decide if insisting that foreign beef was sold in separate shops was really necessary for Korea's aims. The Appellate Body report, para. 164, says:

> In sum, determination of whether a measure, which is not 'indispensable', may nevertheless be 'necessary' within the contemplation of Article XX(d), involves in every case a process of weighing and balancing a series of factors which prominently include the contribution made by the compliance measure to the enforcement of the law or regulation at issue, the importance of the common interests or values protected by that law or regulation, and the accompanying impact of the law or regulation on imports or exports.

The Appellate Body observed that Korea did not require foreign seafood or foreign pork to be sold in separate shops, nor was the objective of the law to make the probability of fraudulent sale of foreign beef zero. In the light of these considerations it ruled that Korea could devise some alternative ways of minimizing the risk of counterfeit beef being sold which was as effective but put less of the burden on foreign importers. The Appellate Body did not at any point investigate whether the Koreans had a protectionist aim here, only whether their measures had more protectionist *effects* than were needed to fulfil the aim.

The finding here was influential in the better-known asbestos case.[17] Here, Canada claimed that a French ban on the use of asbestos (all asbestos, not just imports) was illegal because it discriminated against other building materials. The panel concluded that asbestos and other building materials were 'like products' and hence France had violated Article III since there was protection for other materials that France might itself produce. However, it said that this discrimination was justifiable under Article XX because there was clear evidence that asbestos was dangerous. WTO analysts breathed a sigh of relief when the Appellate Body overturned the first part of this ruling: it declared that safe and unsafe products, though otherwise similar, were not 'like products'.

The asbestos case is one of the relatively few where the complainant has lost. The propensity of respondents to win is not really a sign that the DSB is eager to overturn every domestic measure it can; rather that in general only the most egregious cases get to the WTO. Canadian officials generally squirm when asked why their government brought the asbestos case!

In general, developing countries favour the use of tight controls on arbitrary food safety rules that prevent developed countries excluding their products for no good reason. An interesting case has occurred recently over fears that a cholera outbreak in East Africa might contaminate food exports to the EU. WHO representatives have argued in a WTO context that an import ban was inappropriate, but one can see the sensitivity that might be invoked:

> Although there is a theoretical risk of Cholera transmission associated with some food commodities moving in international trade, this has rarely proved significant and authorities should seek means of dealing with it other than by applying an embargo on importation.[18]

But will the European public be happy to see products imported that carry even a 'theoretical risk' of cholera infection?

OTHER AGREEMENTS

Trade-Related Investment Measures (TRIMs) and Subsidies

The extent to which WTO rules undermine the scope for industrial policies for development is hotly debated. There is not space here to cover the whole issue, but it is useful to make a few points relating to the link between internal and external rules.

The WTO provisions considered here are the 'TRIMs' agreement on 'trade-related investment measures' and the agreement on subsidies and countervailing measures (SCM agreement), which governs which subsidies are allowed and what retaliation is allowed against them.

One rather surprising point is that the text of the TRIMs agreement is extremely narrow in scope (Bora, 2002). The text refers to investment incentives of all kinds that affect firms' ability to export – it is not about foreign investment *per se*.

Article 2 implies that the only purpose of TRIMs is to clarify, give effect to and allow temporary derogations from the existing Articles III and XI of the GATT. The TRIMs agreement actually addresses rules about trade in goods but not rules about foreign investment. In fact, the text does not define a 'TRIM' but it gives examples: it states that it would be inconsistent with the existing Article XI of the GATT to give advantage to any firms which, for example, make access to foreign exchange for imports conditional on export performance; and that it would be inconsistent with Article III to privilege in any way enterprises that limit their imports. These rules apply for domestic and foreign firms alike. The relatively narrow scope of the TRIMs agreement is, of course, behind the EU's drive to conclude a 'trade and investment' agreement under the WTO (and the ill-fated Multilateral Agreement on Investment (MAI) talks).

The narrow scope of TRIMs does not mean that its provisions have no impact on freedom to make policy. Combined with the SCM agreement, which limits export subsidies, it presents a real issue from a development policy perspective. In principle, the SCM agreement does not limit all subsidies for development. It allows 'non-specific subsidies' and strict limits on 'specific subsidies'. The latter are divided into 'prohibited' and 'actionable'. Subsidies directly conditional on export performance or for import substitution are prohibited.

The World Bank argues that the SCM agreement still leaves developing countries free to use the most effective instruments of industrial policy and the promotion of export competitiveness. This judgment is sensitive to the belief that selective subsidy schemes tend to be ineffective and, from an economic perspective, a case can be made against the TRIMs rules.

Trade in Services: The General Agreement on Trade in Services (GATS)

Whilst it is as controversial, the GATS agreement is based on rather different principles from the GATT, so we need to look at it differently. Its preamble states

Recognizing the right of Members to regulate, and to introduce new regulations, on the supply of services within their territories in order to meet national policy objectives and, given asymmetries existing with respect to the degree of development of services regulations in different countries, the particular need of developing countries to exercise this right.

It cannot therefore be claimed that GATS takes away the right of developing countries to regulate.

What makes GATS special is that:

- virtually all the measures affected are domestic regulations: there are generally no tariffs on traded services;
- the trade liberalization and national treatment obligations only apply to sectors that countries have chosen to schedule.

It is, however, not strictly correct to say that the GATS system only creates obligations for 'scheduled' sectors. It is worth noting that GATS creates an MFN obligation for scheduled and unscheduled sectors alike: that is, however restrictive your rules on entry of foreign service suppliers, you must not discriminate *between* foreign countries.

More controversial have been the provisions for market access and national treatment. The contrast with trade in goods is striking: whilst in goods trade essentially all tariffs must be bound for WTO members, market access and national treatment commitments in services only cover those sectors and 'modes of supply' that are explicitly scheduled by members of the WTO.

The GATS agreement is a 'positive list' agreement and an opt-in arrangement. It identifies 4 'modes of supply':

- Mode 1, 'from the territory of one Member into the territory of any other Member';
- Mode 2, 'in the territory of one Member to the service consumer of any other Member';
- Mode 3, 'by a service supplier of one Member, through commercial presence in the territory of any other Member';
- Mode 4, 'by a service supplier of one Member, through presence of natural persons of a Member in the territory of any other Member'.

Mode 1 would apply if, for example, a buyer used the services of a company based elsewhere using the Internet while Mode 2 would embrace tourism. Mode 3 is the classic example of establishment, i.e. FDI abroad. Mode 4 is least discussed, but it is where developing countries have been pressing for liberalization by the 'North'; in effect it involves short-term movement of people to undertake specific service tasks, for example an Indian engineer travelling to the USA to set up a piece of software.

The WTO has statistical categories for each service sector and member states declare which of the sectors and sub-sectors and modes they commit themselves to opening. If a sector is opened Article XVI (2) of the GATS lists a series of measures that cannot be applied in that sector *unless* there is a specific exemption taken:

> In sectors where market-access commitments are undertaken, the measures which a Member shall not maintain or adopt either on the basis of a regional subdivision or on the basis of its entire territory, unless otherwise specified in its Schedule, are defined as:
>
> (a) limitations on the number of service suppliers whether in the form of numerical quotas, monopolies, exclusive service suppliers or the requirements of an economic needs test;
>
> (b) limitations on the total value of service transactions or assets in the form of numerical quotas or the requirement of an economic needs test;
>
> (c) limitations on the total number of service operations or on the total quantity of service output expressed in terms of designated numerical units in the form of quotas or the requirement of an economic needs test;
>
> (d) limitations on the total number of persons that may be employed in a particular service sector or that a service supplier may employ and who are necessary for, and directly related to, the supply of a specific service in the form of numerical quotas or the requirement of an economic needs test;
>
> (e) measures which restrict or require specific types of legal entity or joint venture through which a service supplier may supply a service; and
>
> (f) limitations on the participation of foreign capital in terms of maximum percentage limit on foreign shareholding or the total value of individual or aggregate foreign investment.

Article XVII further requires that any domestic regulations that apply (whether because not barred by Art. XVI or because an exception has been scheduled) must be applied in a non-discriminatory way – again unless a specific exemption is scheduled. It states that

> in the sectors covered by its schedule, and subject to any conditions and qualifications set out in the schedule, each member shall give treatment to foreign services and service suppliers treatment, in measures affecting supply of services, no less favourable than it gives to its own services and suppliers.[19]

A typical GATS schedule starts by listing those sectors that are to be open to foreign suppliers; then it lists all the exceptions. First these will be 'horizontal exceptions' where the EU states, for example: 'In all EC Member States services considered as public utilities at a national or local level may be subject to public monopolies or to exclusive rights granted to private operators.'

In addition to general provisions there are special sectoral sub-agreements, for example in telecommunications. In this case a 'Reference Paper' on basic telecommunications sets out a standard set of commitments that countries can sign up to. This text is somewhat more precise than the general GATS agreement.

From an economic perspective one of the key issues to be resolved – and there has been little jurisprudence on this – is what might be regarded as discriminatory rules. If, for example, insurance regulations in a country required that all firms kept funds deposited in local liquid assets, then this might deprive foreign firms, which keep their assets elsewhere, of part of their natural comparative advantage.

One major case has been brought to the dispute settlement system, concerning telecommunications policy in Mexico.[20] In this case, which was not appealed (so only the panel decision is available), the USA claimed that Mexico was not fulfilling the obligations it had taken on in signing up to the Reference Paper. The Reference Paper[21] obliges signatories to prevent anti-competitive behaviour by dominant firms, in particular that which deters entry. Signatories must allow foreign telecommunications operators access to the networks of major domestic service suppliers on 'reasonable' and 'cost-based' terms and ban 'anti-competitive' practices by major suppliers, normally former monopolists. In this case, the Mexican government allowed the former state monopoly Telmex to set the interconnection rates to be charged by all Mexican networks (including some foreign-owned) for calls coming in from the USA. The Mexicans argued that this was a way to prevent anti-competitive predatory pricing by foreign networks, but the USA argued that it was an illegal state-run cartel.

The decision rejected Mexico's position, making it clear that the dispute settlement system may well decide for itself what is and is not an effective competition law under GATS.[22]

The panel decision makes quite a lot of economic sense but it is one of many factors making developing countries increasingly reluctant to sign on to further WTO disciplines in diplomatically ambiguous texts whose meaning might then become more constraining as legal precedents develop. The ruling surprised some analysts,[23] who felt that the Reference Paper was intended primarily to deal with unfair cross-subsidies.

The Trade-Related Aspects of Intellectual Property Rights (TRIPs) Agreement

This agreement has been extremely widely debated. The present discussion will limit its comments to just a few of the less commonly discussed elements. Broadly speaking, the TRIPs agreement requires all WTO members (with some initial transition period for developing countries) to adopt IPR laws very similar to those of the EU and the USA. It defines minimum periods for patents and specifies what must be patentable and what exceptions may be allowed. Careful reading of the TRIPs text shows that there is more 'wiggle room' than appears at first sight.

TRIPs allows countries to use their own definitions of non-obviousness and patent breadth. For example, in patent literature it is now widely understood that there is not a simple trade-off between innovation and diffusion, with the former being helped by tough IPRs and the latter discouraged. Rather, increasing innovation is seen as incremental, where strong rights for the first inventor will make it harder for the next generation of innovations to appear. Developing countries are likely to need rules that favour downstream rather than upstream innovators.[24]

TRIPs does not require a country to recognize patents of others that they consider invalid: for example the USA may issue a patent to an American firm for a form of Basmati rice, but it cannot demand that India recognize this within India. In particular, the provisions for compulsory licensing (e.g. for pharmaceuticals) provide for compulsory licensing to be relatively freely usable in cases where an anti-competitive abuse can be shown to have taken place (Article 31k). This paragraph states that in such cases compulsory licences can be issued for export as well as home production.[25] And one of the most striking provisions of TRIPs is Article 6:

> Exhaustion
> For the purposes of dispute settlement under this Agreement, subject to the provisions of Articles 3 and 4 nothing in this Agreement shall be used to address the issue of the exhaustion of intellectual property rights.

'Exhaustion' refers to the ability of an IPR holder to control the rights of the person who has bought a product affected by IPR and to do what they see fit with it, for example to sell it on to another country. Thus the TRIPs agreement excludes the possibility of disputes about parallel imports. It seems very likely that the USA would have lost any case it might have brought against South Africa over Aids drugs, which concerned re-import of drugs legally marketed elsewhere at lower prices. The TRIPs agreement cannot easily be used to bring cases against countries for authorizing parallel imports of products lawfully sold elsewhere, though it could be used to attack exports of generic drugs that might have been sold without the patent holder's permission. The post-Doha negotiations have sought to clarify when public health emergencies can justify compulsory licensing for either home or export use.

The basic economics of TRIPs is well understood – or rather there is general agreement that there is *no* general agreement about the optimal extent of IPR rules and there is no efficiency case for demanding a degree of harmonization in this area that goes well beyond that of food safety or technical standards, where the negative impact on trade of non-harmonized rules is obvious. It is well known that global rules on IPRs are likely to generate rents for countries that possess stocks of existing patents: there is very much less evidence of any effect to promote innovation where it is not flourishing.

CONCLUSIONS

The key conclusion from our review is that in technical standards, SPS measures and services, there are comprehensive and specific rules governing the way domestic regulations must be implemented to minimize the effect on trade. There are looser rules under the old GATT non-discrimination provisions. All of these rules were the product of diplomatic negotiation and have an element of ambiguity. Their exact implications will emerge as they are tested in the disputes settlement body. For developing countries, it is far from clear that they will lose more in terms of regulatory autonomy than they will gain. This is because the WTO gives them the ability to pin down developed countries and constrain arbitrary protectionism.

The Appellate Body has so far been extraordinarily adept at reconciling regulatory autonomy and trade needs. There have been few challenges to regulations in developing countries so far. If anything, the complaint that developing countries have is that the Appellate Body has been too sympathetic to the wishes of developed countries to regulate more extensively their (the developing countries') home markets. This, on occasion, has made it harder for developing countries to export. The shrimp turtle dispute is a case in point:[26] the USA was given the right to address the environmental consequences of production methods in developing countries. Defenders of this decision say that the USA needed to address a critical global 'externality'. However, many developing countries argued that it was not for the USA to take on such extra-territorial environmental regulatory concerns.

The problem therefore is not that the WTO rules have been enforced so as to prevent domestic regulation: scope for such regulation still very much exists. Nevertheless, the very ambiguity of the rules and the power of the Appellate Body will remain a major issue. This problem cannot be made to go away: so long as domestic rules can affect market access it is essential to have in place a framework for handling disputes stemming from them at a multilateral level. The position of developing countries has become increasingly hostile to the EU's proposals for further international negotiations on 'norms'. But if the EU's membership prefers not to negotiate, the Appellate Body will intervene whenever disputes arise. The general provisions of the GATT and the GATS already cover many aspects of domestic regulation, and the meaning of these rules will be left to the dispute settlement system if it is not otherwise dealt with.

NOTES

1. *Financial Times*, 2 March 1998.
2. See, for example, Bhagwati and Hudec (1996).
3. See Brock and Magee (1978) as applied to tariffs.
4. See Johnson et al. (1968).
5. All GATT/WTO texts are available at www.wto.org and where cited have been downloaded from there.
6. The present chapter does not deal in detail with WTO rules affecting trade and competition. See Holmes (2002).
7. United States – Tax Treatment for 'Foreign Sales Corporations'.
8. The USA brought a case against Japan known as 'Kodak–Fuji' and lost heavily. Japan – Measures Affecting Consumer Photographic Film and Paper.
9. This is the general term to cover the panels, the Appellate Body and the General Council.
10. No decision has been rejected by such a consensus.
11. See also Young and Holmes (2004).
12. EC Measures Concerning Meat and Meat Products (Hormones).
13. Korea – Measures Affecting Imports of Fresh, Chilled and Frozen Beef.
14. United States – Import Prohibition of Certain Shrimp and Shrimp Products.
15. Otsuki et al. (2001).
16. Japan – Measures Affecting the Importation of Apples.
17. European Communities – Measures Affecting Asbestos and Asbestos-Containing Products.
18. The WTO agreements and public health P. 60 www.who.int/emc-documents/cholera/docs/whocddser9216rev1.pdf
19. WTO Secretariat October 1999, Trade in Services Division 'An Introduction to the GATS'.
20. Mexico – Measures Affecting Telecommunications Services.
21. Telecommunications services: reference paper, 24 April 1996 at http://www.wto.org/english/tratop_e/serv_e/telecom_e/tel23_e.htm
22. The imprecision of the GATS rules and the contrast between GATT and GATS on competition law provides a case for saying that WTO rules already create obligations on competition law and that negotiations are needed to define the scope of these obligations. But this is beyond the present chapter. See Holmes 2002.
23. See Marsden (2004).
24. See Dumont and Holmes (2002).
25. Technically, where an anti-competitive practice is occurring a state is exempted from Article 31f, which states 'any such use shall be authorized predominantly for the supply of the domestic market of the Member authorizing such use'.
26. United States – Import Prohibition of Certain Shrimp and Shrimp Products.

REFERENCES

Bhagwati, J. and Hudec, R. (1996), *Fair Trade and Harmonization*, Vols 1 and 2, Cambridge, MA: MIT Press.
Bora, Birjit (2002), 'Trade Related Investent Measures', in Bernard M. Hoekman, Philip English and Aaditya Mattoo (eds), *Development, Trade, and the WTO: A Handbook*, Washington, DC: World Bank.
Brock, William and Magee, Stephen P. (1978), 'The Economics of Special-Interest

Politics: The Case of the Tariff', *American Economic Review*, **68** (May), 246–50.

Dumont, Beatrice and Holmes, Peter (2002), 'The Breadth of Intellectual Property Rights and their Interface with Competition Law and Policy: Divergent Paths to the Same Goal', *Economics of Innovation and New Technology*, **11** (2), 149–62.

Holmes, Peter (2002), 'Trade, Competition and the WTO', in Bernard M. Hoekman, Philip English and Aaditya Mattoo (eds), *Development, Trade, and the WTO: A Handbook*, Washington, DC: World Bank.

Johnson, Harry G., Wonnacott, Paul and Shibata, Hirofumi (1968), *Harmonization of National Economic Policies Under Free Trade*, Toronto: University of Toronto Press.

Johnson, H.G. (1965), 'Optimal Intervention in the Presence of Domestic Distortions', in R.E. Caves, P.B. Kenen and H.G. Johnson (eds), *Trade, Growth and the Balance of Payments: Essays in Honor of Gottfried Haberler*, Amsterdam: North-Holland, pp. 3–34.

Marceau, Gabrielle and Trachtman, Joel (2002), 'The Technical Barriers to Trade Agreement, the Sanitary and Phytosanitary Measures Agreement, and the General Agreement on Tariffs and Trade – A Map of the WTO Law of Domestic Regulation of Goods', *Journal of World Trade*, **36** (5), 811–81.

Marsden, Philip (2004), 'Trade and Competition: WTO Decides First Competition Case with Disappointing Results', *Competition Law Insight*, May, 3–9.

Mattoo, A. (2001), 'Discriminatory Consequences of Non-discriminatory Standards', *Journal of Economic Integration*, **16** (1), 78–105.

Otsuki, Tsunehiro, Wilson, John S. and Sewadeh, Mirvat (2001), 'What Price Precaution? European Harmonisation of Aflatoxin Regulations and African Groundnut Exports', *European Review of Agricultural Economics*, **28** (3), 263–84.

Weiler, J.H.H. (1999), 'The Constitution of the Common Market Place: The Free Movement of Goods', in P.P. Craig and G. de Bùrca (eds), *The Evolution of EU Law*, New York: Oxford University Press.

Young, Alasdair and Holmes, Peter (2004), 'Protection or Protectionism? EU Food Safety Rules and the WTO', at www.polisci.berkeley.edu/faculty/bio/permanent/ansell,c/foodsafety/HY.pdf.

WTO

EC Measures Concerning Meat and Meat Products (Hormones) – AB-1997-4 – Report of the Appellate Body.

Japan – Measures Affecting Consumer Photographic Film and Paper – Report of the Panel 31/03/1998.

Korea – Measures Affecting Imports of Fresh, Chilled and Frozen Beef – AB-2000-8 – Report of the Appellate Body.

European Communities – Measures Affecting Asbestos and Asbestos-Containing Products – AB-2000-11 – Report of the Appellate Body.

United States – Import Prohibition of Certain Shrimp and Shrimp Products – AB-1998-4 – Report of the Appellate Body.

United States – Tax Treatment for 'Foreign Sales Corporations' – AB-1999-9 – Report of the Appellate Body.

Japan – Measures Affecting the Importation of Apples – AB-2003-4 – Report of the Appellate Body.

Mexico – Measures Affecting Telecommunications Services – Report of the Panel, April 2004.

WTO/WHO *The WTO Agreements and Public health* www.who.int/emc-documents/ cholera/docs/whocddser9216rev1.pdf.

4. Learning to love patents: capacity building, intellectual property and the (re)production of governance norms in the 'developing world'*

Christopher May

TRIPs: Article 67, Technical Co-operation
In order to facilitate the implementation of this agreement, developed country members shall provide, on request and on mutually agreed terms and conditions, technical and financial co-operation in favour of developing and least-developed country members. Such co-operation shall include assistance in the preparation of domestic legislation on the protection and enforcement of intellectual property rights as well as on the prevention of their abuse, and shall include support regarding the establishment or reinforcement of domestic offices and agencies relevant to these matters, including the training of personnel. (GATT, 1994, Article 1C: 29)

Since 1995, intellectual property rights (IPRs) have been subject to the trade-related aspects of intellectual property rights agreement (TRIPs), which is overseen by the World Trade Organisation (WTO). While this agreement does not determine national legislation, for members of the WTO to be TRIPs-compliant their domestic intellectual property law must support the protections and rights that are laid out in TRIPs' 73 articles. The agreement covers not only general provisions and basic principles, but also represents an undertaking to uphold certain standards of protection for IPRs and to provide legal mechanisms for their enforcement. Perhaps most importantly, the robust dispute settlement mechanism (DSM), which is a central aspect of the WTO, now encompasses international disputes about IPRs. Before 1995, while there were long-standing multilateral treaties in place regarding the international recognition and protection of IPRs, overseen by the World Intellectual Property Organisation (WIPO), these were widely regarded as essentially toothless in the face of 'piracy' and the frequent disregard for the protection of non-nationals' intellectual property outside the most developed countries (and even sometimes between them).

In addition to the advantages to be gained by having a tougher multilateral enforcement mechanism, the US government (alongside allies in the European Union) wanted to move the international regulation of IPRs into the new WTO (at the expense of regulatory competence located with the WIPO) because negotiators felt they were more likely to gain agreements to their advantage by linking these issues to the international trade regime (Braithwaite and Drahos, 2000: 61–4). Therefore, it is perhaps unsurprising that the TRIPs agreement represents a particular view of the role of IPRs in economic relations, a view that has emerged primarily from the US private sector.[1] Furthermore, the inclusion of the TRIPs, the General Agreement on Trade in Services (GATS) and a number of other agreements (ranging from investment to antidumping) in the Uruguay Round final settlement was the culmination of a general strategy on behalf of the USA and the EU to force developing countries to adopt multilateral agreements in sectors which they had hitherto resisted (Steinberg, 2002). By withdrawing from their previous commitments under GATT 1947 and therefore terminating their obligations under that agreement, the USA and EU forced developing countries to accede to a much wider agreement under the WTO if they wished to regain the trade arrangements with which they had started the Uruguay Round.

Although there are still some members of the WTO who are in a transitional period, the TRIPs agreement establishes for the first time a potentially global settlement on the recognition and protection of IPRs. For the developed countries TRIPs compliance has involved some legislative reorientation and occasionally new laws (or judicial reinterpretations of existing laws). For the developing countries, often with little or no tradition of IPRs, compliance is considerably more difficult and expensive to achieve. Or as K. Kalan, puts it, 'trying to insert a patent system deriving primarily from the tenets of Western thought into a country shaped primarily by non-Western thought may invoke the classic square-peg-in-a-round-hole situation' (Kalan, 2000: 1447). In recognition of these difficulties, most developing-country members of the WTO are currently covered by the transitional arrangement (recently extended to 2016 in regard to pharmaceutical patents). They have been allowed an interim period in which they are expected to develop the legal and governance structures that full accession to the TRIPs agreement requires.

During this transitional period developing countries have been in receipt of extensive technical support (under Article 67 of the agreement) to enable them to build the legal capacity to establish TRIPs compliance. On one side there is a need to fully understand the agreement because it is not only complex, but in many ways is a subtle and quite flexible set of negotiated undertakings. Hence legal capacity building can have clear benefits for developing countries that may be able to use newly conversant legislators and specialists to take advantage of these opportunities to make the agreement do what they need it to. However, on the other hand, such capacity building and legal training may also lead to the effective 'epistemic lock-in' of specific views of how IPRs should be treated.[2] Thus the danger of these programmes is that they implicitly socialize developing-country legal practitioners into a specific way of dealing with IPRs, a tendency that is already of course widely manifest in the TRIPs agreement.

My central concern in this chapter is to examine the tensions that stem from contrasting views of the social utility of 'owning' knowledge: on one side the US/European acceptance of the legitimacy and usefulness of IPRs; on the other a widespread suspicion by NGOs (non-governmental organizations) of the benefits of commodifying knowledge, as well as some doubt in developing countries about what IPRs seem intended to do. It is far from clear to many that IPRs represent a reflection of customary practice in developing countries, and without this link legal innovation becomes relatively more difficult to sustain. This is not a new problem. As Graeme Dinwoodie has noted:

> It is not a new lesson that real approximation [harmonization] of laws, one that will endure, does not come from the transplanting of disembodied concepts . . . It is economic and social contexts that *sustain* these laws [of intellectual property], and if similar social setting does not exist, merely harmonising text may be of little value. (Dinwoodie, 2000: 311–12, emphasis added)

First I briefly lay out the basics of IPRs (which anyone familiar with patents, copyrights and other forms of IPRs can easily skip) and some important aspects of the TRIPs agreement, before moving to set out the scope of support that is currently made available to developing countries to support their accession to full TRIPs compliance. I then explore some of the political and social tensions that the imposition of a putative global legal culture on diverse local developing countries' legal formations engenders. I conclude by suggesting that the debates about IPRs need to be rescued from the realm of technical assistance and efficiency maximization, and returned to the realm of political economy where they belong, linking this to Stephen Gill's arguments regarding the emergence of the 'new constitutionalism'.

WHAT IS INTELLECTUAL PROPERTY?

When knowledge and/or information becomes subject to ownership, intellectual property rights express ownership's legal benefits: the ability to charge rent for use; to receive compensation for loss; and demand payment for transfer. Intellectual property rights are subdivided into a number of groups, of which two generate most discussion: industrial intellectual property (patents) and literary or artistic intellectual property (copyrights). Conventionally the difference between patents and copyrights is presented as between a patent's protection of the idea itself, and copyright's protection of its expression. Laws of intellectual property attempt to support the rights of individuals over their creative endeavours, while at the same time recognizing that the extensive social benefits from the diffusion of innovation, in terms of economic and social advance, should be relatively unlimited by cost. This important balance between private reward and public interest is at the heart of all intellectual property legislation and is expressed through time limits on IPRs. Unlike property rights in material things, IPRs are formally temporary: once their term has expired they return to the public realm, where no price can be exacted.

For patents the knowledge which is to be registered and thus made property should be applicable in industry. To gain the rights attached to a grant of patent an idea must be:

- *new*, not already in the public domain or the subject of a previous patent;
- *non-obvious*: it should not be common sense to any accomplished practitioner in the field who, having been asked to solve a particular practical problem, would see this solution immediately; it should not be self-evident using available skills or technologies; and
- *useful*, or *applicable in industry*: it must have a stated function, and could immediately be produced to fulfil this function.

Following the harmonization of national legislation across all members of the WTO through the TRIPs agreement, once these three conditions have been fulfilled, an idea can be patented within each member's territorial jurisdiction. The patent application (detailing the idea and all its relevant details or specification) is lodged at the national patent office (or with the European Patent Office). For an agreed fee national patent offices allow others access to the patent document, but perhaps more importantly the office supports legal action against unauthorized usage when infringement is reported. Essentially, patents are an institutionalized bargain between the state and the inventor: the state agrees to ensure that the inventor is paid for their idea when others use it (for the term of the patent) while the inventor allows the state to lodge the idea in its public records, to ensure public dissemination of innovation.

Unlike patent, copyright is concerned with the form of knowledge and information that would normally be termed 'literary and artistic works', and needs no formal initial registration. Among those forms of expression that are usually regarded as subject to copyright are: literary works (fiction and non-fiction); musical works (of all sorts); artistic works (of two- *and* three-dimensional form and, importantly, irrespective of content – from 'pure art' and advertising to amateur drawings and doodles); maps; technical drawings; photography; audiovisual works (including cinematic works, video and forms of multi-media); and audio recordings. However, the underlying ideas, the plot, the conjunction of colours, the musical key or chords do not receive protection, only each specific creative expression attracts copyright.

Copyright is intended to ensure that creative expression should not be reproduced without the express permission of its author or producer. These rights can be legally transferred to another person or company who then exercises them in their own interest. In Anglo-Saxon countries (reflecting the common-law tradition) these rights are limited to an economic right, where the creator (or copyright owner) is legally entitled to demand a share of earnings from the utilization or reproduction of the copyrighted work. In continental Europe (and in jurisdictions drawing from the Roman law tradition), there is an additional moral right not to have work tampered with or misrepresented. In all cases, failure to agree terms prior to the act of reproduction or duplication may result in any income being awarded to the original copyright holder by the court if an infringement is deemed to have taken place. Unlike patents, however, copyright resides in the work from the moment of creation; all that is required is that the creator prove that any supposed infringement is a reproduction of the original work.

Trademarks are an important third form of IPRs. These distinguish the products of one company from another and can be made up of one or more distinctive words, letters, numbers, drawings or pictures, emblems or other graphic representations. Generally trademarks need to be registered to ensure that the mark is not already in use. A particular trademark is unlikely to succeed in being registered if it is too similar to, or liable to cause confusion with, a trademark already registered by another company or if it is already in common use. Of all IPRs, trademarks have perhaps the longest history, tracing their origins back to makers' marks on early pottery and before that to tribal animal branding. There are other sorts of intellectual property from process patents (which cover processes as opposed to actual machines) to geographical indicators (such as 'champagne' and 'Parma ham'), but these share the key characteristics noted above; they construct a form of information or knowledge as ownable property.

The most important aspect of IPRs is their formal construction of scarcity where none necessarily exists. Knowledge and information, unlike material things, are not necessarily rivalrous; coincident usage does not detract from utility. In this sense, most of the time knowledge (before it is made property) does not exhibit the characteristics of material things before they are made (legal) property.[3] Property in a legal sense can only be what the law says it is; it does not exist waiting to be recognized as such, but rather is the codification of particular social relations, those between owner and non-owner, reproduced as rights. However, in its very materiality, that which is potentially tangible property (as it is sometimes called) exists prior to its recognition in a way the IPRs do not. Material property is 'naturally' scarce and therefore is rival in potential use, whereas knowledge in most cases is non-rival before becoming intellectual property. In cases where knowledge may produce advantage for the holder (information asymmetries), by enabling a better price to be extracted, or by allowing a market advantage to be gained, information and knowledge *is* rivalrous. If there were perfect information (universal access), then the knowledge holder's benefits would evaporate.[4] However, in general, knowledge and information are non-rival, and it is difficult to extract a price for the use of non-rival goods. Therefore a legal form of scarcity is introduced to ensure a price can be obtained for use.

As this scarcity is far from natural or of self-evident benefit to all, significant time and effort is spent telling stories about intellectual property that are meant to justify its existence as a set of legal rights (May, 2000: 22–9). These narratives revolve around three claims for the usefulness of making knowledge and information property which are frequently deployed in arguments about IPRs. The first argument is that effort deserves reward. This draws on a long line of political theory which asserts that where man has improved nature he deserves to have property in the fruits of the effort that has been put in. This started as John Locke's argument about property rights in previously common land being awarded to the diligent cultivator, and has now become a more general argument that effort requires reward. In intellectual property this justification is expressed as both a reward and an incentive. Only by allowing innovators and creators ownership rights over their creations can we reward their efforts (and by doing so also encourage further effort). Thus the construction of scarcity serves the social need to encourage and reward effort and innovation. Second, IPRs also reflect the rights of individuals to own the products of their own efforts, in that these efforts reflect the expression of an individual's self-identity. Thus individuals should be allowed to own intellectual property in the products of their mental activity, because it is *their* mental work that has produced that which might subsequently be made property. This argument is not as often utilized (although it is frequently alluded to in arguments about piracy), as it raises questions about the legitimacy of transferring ownership of IPRs to others.

The third narrative of intellectual property reflects the capitalist character of modern society. Here, the argument is concerned with the benefits of introducing markets into any particular area of social existence. Markets, we are told, promote efficiency of use, and therefore if we want to ensure that ideas and knowledge are used efficiently, for the maximum benefit of society, we need to introduce markets into the distribution of knowledge and ideas. This will ensure that those who value knowledge and information most highly will pay most for it (rewarding the innovators) and will be also forced by a competitive market to enhance their efficiency in using these knowledge resources. Here, the imposition of scarcity promotes efficient use, because knowledge can be costly to produce, and the drive to enhance efficiency itself produces further surplus to spend on more knowledge. These three stories appear in various combinations and in various ways, but wherever IPRs are contested, disputed or merely discussed, these stories are (re)told and have become part of the 'common sense' of treating knowledge as property.

THE GLOBAL GOVERNANCE OF IPRS: FROM WIPO TO TRIPS

From the emergence of IPRs in a prototypical form in Venice in the fifteenth century (May, 2002b), for the best part of four centuries the governance of intellectual property was essentially a *national* issue. However, in the last years of the nineteenth century, two sets of conferences focused on the inter-national coordination of protection for IPRs, reflecting the success of political campaigning in support of the internationalization of intellectual property protection (Machlup and Penrose, 1950). These conferences resulted in the Paris Convention (covering patents), which was completed by an Interpretative Protocol in Madrid in 1891, and the Berne Convention for the Protection of Literary and Artistic Works (1886).

While these conventions grew and developed over the subsequent century, as early as 1893 the common issues across both had led to the establishment of a combined secretariat, functioning under various names until the estab-lishment of WIPO at the end of the 1960s. An agency of the United Nations since 1974, WIPO also administers other international treaties covering intel-lectual property (including trademarks, geographic indicators and industrial designs) and is responsible for promoting technology transfer by supporting the recognition of IPRs in developing countries.

These conventions aimed to ensure that the rights of owners could be easily exercised in foreign jurisdictions, utilizing common processes and levels of protection. However, not only did the conventions themselves (and thus WIPO's secretariat) have no explicit rules on enforcement; there was no settled and robust mechanism for the settlement of disputes between members regarding the protection offered non-nationals (Matthews, 2002: 11). Members enjoyed enormous discretion over how they legislated to protect IPRs and many potential signatories of the various conventions who were IPR importers did not perceive accession as in their immediate national interest.

These differing perceptions of national interests undermined attempts in the 1970s and 1980s to establish a more workable dispute settlement procedure. While the conventions allowed some voluntary harmonization of protection across the various forms of IPRs, growing concerns among important industrial sectors in the richer, developed countries (especially the content industries) regarding piracy were largely frustrated, at a time when IPRs were moving steadily to the centre of the commercial concerns of a number of important globalizing industrial sectors. Nevertheless, 'co-operation with developing countries' remained at the heart of WIPO's self-nominated role. Extensive legal support through training, model legislation and advice was intended to aid the creation, or modernization, of IPR-related laws, to establish a knowledgeable judiciary as well as knowledgeable legal professionals, and to generally support developing countries in establishing a robust legal structure for the protection of IPRs (WIPO, 1993: 55–7) (all of which continues under TRIPs).

The main political pressure from the developed countries to include intellectual property in the Uruguay Round originated in the response by the content industries to a series of technological innovations, centred on information and communications technologies (ICTs) which enhanced both the possibilities of an international (commodity) trade in information- and knowledge-related goods, but also enlarged the possibilities of 'theft' and 'piracy' (May, 2000: 81–5). Trade negotiators from the developed countries were heavily (and successfully) lobbied on this issue while they themselves also argued that the complex of 24 multilateral treaties administered by WIPO produced too much rule diversity. But this did little to stimulate developing countries' interest in including IPRs in multilateral trade negotiations. To 'encourage' a change of heart the US trade representative threatened bilateral trade sanctions (under the Special 301 section of the Omnibus Trade and Tariff Act, 1988), utilized against the Indian pharmaceutical industry among others (Matthews, 2002: 31).

The statutory authority on which this is based (and which is helpfully reproduced in each annual *Special 301 Report*) also notes that the section was 'amended in the Uruguay Round Agreements Act to clarify that a country can be found to deny adequate and effective intellectual property protection *even if it is in compliance* with its obligations under the TRIPs agreement' (USTR, 2003: 9, emphasis added). As Duncan Matthews notes, if a country does not respond to this surveillance and reporting process, then 'trade sanctions may then be imposed under Special 301 in the form of increased tariff duties or import restrictions' (Matthews, 2002: 26). In other words, even now the USTR sees the TRIPs agreement as insufficient as regards the 'needs' of its industry clients, and has the ability to restrict access to the world's largest market as a device for 'encouraging' policy changes to induce compliance with the required standards of protection.

During the Uruguay Round of multilateral trade negotiations this stick was combined with the carrot of a promise to open up agricultural markets and an offer to abolish the Multi-Fibre Arrangement which constrained developing countries' textile exports (May, 2000: 88). The developing countries generally lacked the expertise and resources to fully resist this firm bilateral pressure. As John Braithwaite and Peter Drahos point out, 'Negotiating fatigue among weaker states is one explanation . . . why 100 states signed the TRIPs agreement' (Braithwaite and Drahos, 2000: 197). The combination of political pressure and weakened resistance due to the complexity of the negotiations relative to the limited resources developing countries could dedicate to them ensured that when the developing countries joined the new WTO they had to accede (with some transitional arrangements to be sure) to the TRIPs agreement as well.[5]

Since the conclusion of the Uruguay Round of multilateral trade negotiations, and the formation of the WTO, the legal regime for intellectual property has been effectively globalized. Although the TRIPs agreement does not dictate national laws, it does require members of the WTO to ensure that their laws in this area produce certain mandated patterns of governance. The preamble to the TRIPs agreement which itself was subject to some considerable negotiation was finally agreed on the basis that the signatories desired

> to reduce distortions and impediments to international trade, and taking into account the need to promote effective and adequate protection of intellectual property rights, and to ensure that measures and procedures to enforce intellectual property rights do not themselves become barriers to legitimate trade. (GATT, 1994, Article 1C: 2)

The recognition that 'intellectual property rights are private rights' was partly balanced by an explicit allowance of the need for the 'public policy objectives of national systems for the protection of intellectual property, including developmental and technological objectives'. The previous problems of international enforcement of IPRs are reflected in the desire to promote 'adequate' protection through the application of a global set of standards.

The keystone of the TRIPs agreement is the adoption in the realm of intellectual property of the principles that are central to the WTO (like the GATT before it): national treatment; most-favoured-nation treatment (MFN); and reciprocity. While reciprocity as a principle does little in itself to change the intellectual property regime, the introduction of MFN does change the international governance of IPRs somewhat. Under the auspices of WIPO there were many smaller-scale treaties and conventions on various aspects of intellectual property; under TRIPs, and because of MFN, all such specialized agreements immediately apply to all the members of the WTO. Where there had been resistance to incorporate particular sectoral conventions in the past, by inclusion into the WTO their scope becomes as wide as the main IPR conventions. Furthermore, national treatment ensures favouritism accorded domestic inventors or prospective owners of IPRs relative to non-nationals is rendered illegal. This is an important shift as many national IPR systems have favoured domestic 'owners' either through legislative or procedural means.

Indeed, in the past, many industries in then developing countries (such as the US publishers in the nineteenth century) 'pirated' non-national intellectual property because protection was awarded to nationals who were known not to be the original innovators.

At the dawn of the new millennium, however, the central intention of the TRIPs agreement is to provide a legal framework for a single intellectual property regime throughout the international system. The TRIPs agreement presents WTO members with a single framework for dealing with the diverse aspects of intellectual property, replacing WIPO's more fragmented set of treaties and sectoral agreements. That said, it is not a model piece of legislation that can be incorporated directly into national law. Rather, it sets the minimum standards that should be reflected in the national legislation of all WTO members. It does not preclude members setting more rigid or stronger protection for IPRs except where such extensions above and beyond the minimum standards represent an infringement of the agreement's articles in some way. National legislatures are required therefore to ensure that IPRs are protected, but the method for this protection is only important as regards its consequences, not its form; the agreement is concerned with ends, not means. But national legislative enaction of the TRIPs agreement's principles are subject to the WTO's dispute settlement mechanism under the agreement. Therefore, unlike the WIPO's stewardship of previous conventions, the WTO offers a considerably more robust mechanism for states to appeal to where the national laws of a particular country are seen to impede the rights of other nationals.

While the character of intellectual property – what is actually to be protected – is modified to some extent by the agreement (especially for computer programs), the main area of discontinuity with prior practice is in the national protection of IPRs. By bringing intellectual property under the purview of the WTO, the TRIPs agreement stipulates that 'procedures shall be applied in such a manner as to avoid the creation of barriers to legitimate trade' (GATT, 1994, Article 1C: 19). The protection of intellectual property rights (or more often their non-protection) should not be used to disrupt trade flows. For instance, if only nationals are protected this would act as a barrier to non-nationals, who would receive no protection for the IPR element of goods or services they wished to export to that jurisdiction. Non-discrimination must be explicitly part of a clear and fair registration procedure for IPRs, where they require registration, to be recognized (the exceptions being copyright and trade secrets – 'undisclosed information'). The agreement provides a set of conditions which national legislation for registration must fulfil, broadly based on the requirements of openness and prompt enacting of procedures.

The members of the WTO are required to enact suitable procedures to ensure the 'effective action against any act of infringement of intellectual property . . . including expeditious remedies to prevent infringements and remedies which constitute a deterrent to further infringement' (GATT, 1994, Article 1C: 19). These procedures must be fair and equitable and available under civil law. In the section of the agreement covering Civil and Administrative Procedures and Remedies there are a number of requirements which national legislation should include, ranging from the need for courts to have powers to obtain evidence of infringements to the need to produce fair settlements in regard to damages. The agreement also mandates clear limits to the parallel importation of licensed goods from other jurisdictions. However, this is expanded in TRIPs to cover not only trademarked goods but also 'pirated copyright goods . . . [and] goods which involve other infringements of intellectual property rights' (GATT, 1994, Article 1C: 23). Currently, the most obvious effect of this aspect of TRIPs is to render the importation of pirated generic pharmaceuticals illegal for any WTO member, even if they have enacted the health emergency provisions of the agreement, as reasserted within the Doha ministerial declaration.[6]

Overall, this extension of the protection of intellectual property in the international realm as well as the harmonization of law across WTO members represented a major triumph for the 'US pharmaceutical, entertainments and informatics industries that were largely responsible for getting TRIPs on the agenda' of the Uruguay Round (Hoekman and Kostecki, 1995: 156). The TRIPs agreement is significant in the extension it represents for the rights of the owners of intellectual property. Indeed, Kurt Burch contends that this expansion of ownership rights also 'extends an essentially liberal conception of social life as relations organized and understood by reference to exclusive property rights . . . [promoting] the vocabulary of rights and property and the liberal conceptual framework they help define' (Burch, 1995: 215). Furthermore, Samuel Oddi argues that the use of a natural *rights* discourse (utilizing the narratives of justification I briefly laid out above) tries to establish that

> these rights are so important that individual [WTO] member welfare should not stand in the way of their being protected as an entitlement of the creators. This invokes a counter-instrumentalist policy that members, regardless of their state of industrialization, should sacrifice their national interests in favour of the posited higher order of international trade (Oddi, 1996: 440)

While the TRIPs agreement includes instrumentalist justifications alongside the more rights-oriented language, Oddi (and others, including myself) argue that it is the rights side of any balance between individual rights and public developmental benefits that are systematically privileged throughout the agreement's text.

Therefore, while the agreement itself is a complex and wide-ranging set of requirements on signatories,[7] at its core is a particular set of norms regarding the treatment of knowledge as property. These norms underpin the entire agreement and are based on the notion that the private ownership of knowledge as property is a major spur to continued economic development and social welfare. They further emphasize the development of knowledge as an individualized endeavour, and the legitimate reward of such individualized effort.

Most obviously, this includes a robust norm of commodification of knowledge and information. While the agreement is potentially quite flexible, as evidenced by the negotiations over the Doha ministerial declaration, the forces which support a particular reading of the agreement are difficult to overcome. The Doha declaration itself, despite extensive negotiations, *only* reasserted the broad thrust of the original text's invocation of health emergencies as legitimate reasons for the suspension of IPR laws for pharmaceuticals. However, these norms of property ownership (especially as regards knowledge and information) are hardly universal and therefore represent a major problem for the legitimization of the *global* governance of IPRs.

In this sense, a one-size-fits-all strategy may not self-evidently serve many developing countries' immediate best interests, even though this is the model which well-funded capacity-building and 'awareness-raising' programmes aim to reproduce. The World Bank, WTO, WIPO and a number of other multilateral, national and private agencies are expending significant effort in this area to 'help' developing countries establish TRIPs compliance. Furthermore, and paradoxically, as Peter Drahos has pointed out, in an attempt to ensure their clients are not caught up in costly IPR-related trade disputes with developed-country members of the WTO, the staff of WIPO have often encouraged developing countries to adopt legislation that goes beyond the formal requirements of the TRIPs agreement (Drahos, 2002: 777). Indeed, in the wake of bilateral trade agreements with the USA (reflecting the commitment under 'Special 301' to go beyond *mere* TRIPs compliance), a number of developing countries have found themselves needing 'TRIPs-plus' legislation, which again reinforces this dynamic within the assistance programme at WIPO. Thus, in trying to help developing countries avoid trade disputes, the assistance programme has undermined the possibilities of diplomatic (and democratic) critical engagement with the agreement itself.

In addition to the practical problems that these capacity-building programmes encounter (not least, the fit with developing countries' previous political and legislative traditions), TRIPs has also engendered a political response especially in those developing countries where significant groups remain to be convinced of the appropriateness of the TRIPs model (of which the farmers' rights movement in India is perhaps the best-known example). Recent debates have ranged across a number of sectors, sometimes focusing on perceptions of bio-piracy (Shiva, 2001: 49–68), elsewhere concerned with pharmaceutical products (May, 2002a), or the piracy of software, and the 'theft' of traditional knowledge (Gervais, 2002). These debates, and their effects on the legitimacy of IPRs in developing countries, impact directly on the legitimacy of the norms which are being 'imported' through the legal assistance supporting TRIPs compliance. Indeed, the advice and support from many NGOs active on IPR-related issues (such as Oxfam and the Quaker Office at the UN) emphasize the problems these debates have thrown up, in direct contrast to the positive emphasis of much multilateral aid which seeks to reproduce the normative settlement set out in TRIPs. However, as Braithwaite and Drahos point out, whatever critiques may be mobilized against these norms of propertization, the global regime governing IPRs sets 'strong limits on a state's capacity to define territorial property rights in ways that enhance national welfare' (Braithwaite and Drahos, 2000: 75). It is these welfare effects in developing countries that are the central problem in the global governance of IPRs.

Essentially, this is the key issue underlying this chapter: how is this liberal conception of right (re)produced across the WTO's membership, and most especially the developing countries? This particular legal culture, with its set of norms regarding the treatment of knowledge as property, underlies the entire TRIPs agreement. However, this legal culture is by no mean uncontested and, therefore, the continuing concern to aid capacity building in developing countries was reasserted in the Doha declaration.

THE EXTENT OF ASSISTANCE PROGRAMMES FOR CAPACITY BUILDING

A number of agencies have been particularly active in helping developing countries construct the capacity to fulfil their TRIPs-related obligations. The World Intellectual Property Organisation (WIPO) in Geneva runs the 'Co-operation for Development Programme' providing support and training for countries developing the legal structures that TRIPs' undertakings require. The European Patent Office (EPO) has also undertaken various programmes although here the focus is more on the states which are seeking to join the European Union. Other organizations ranging from multilateral agencies like the WTO and the United Nations Conference on Trade and Development (UNCTAD) to some non-governmental organizations provide various forms of support to developing countries struggling to develop legal systems that will enable them to establish TRIPs compliance. Most developing countries are likely to be dependent on such assistance if they are to hope to establish the mechanisms and legal infrastructure required to fulfil their TRIPs obligations. Such political–legal transformations can require considerable resources and investment.

The WIPO 'Co-operation for Development Programme' has two distinct elements, an assistance programme and the maintenance of a documentation collection. The Collection of Laws section of the WIPO has centralized the archiving of the legislative texts which are received by the International Bureau of WIPO. These are available electronically to all members, to aid the drafting of their own legislation, and the section also publishes periodicals, distributed to members, drawing attention to aspects of the collection. The assistance programme is conducted by express agreement with the WTO and explicitly aimed at transitional developing countries to enable them to draft TRIPs-compliant legislation. As WIPO notes, this assistance may take a number of forms:

> Depending on the content of the request [from a member developing country] and on the situation of the country concerned, it may take the form of the submission of a WIPO draft law on any aspect of industrial property or on copyright and related rights, or of WIPO comments or studies on draft laws prepared by the government or on existing laws as regards their compatibility with relevant international treaties ... or any legal advice on any specific aspect of intellectual property law. *To the extent possible* the advice given takes into account the specific needs of the country concerned, in harmony with its legal, economic and political system. (WIPO Assistance, no date, emphasis added)

While members' concerns may be heeded, this can only take place within the constraints of the requirements of the agreement itself. This support is available to all members of WIPO, and draft laws and other legal instruments frequently circulate between a government legislative team and WIPO a number of times before a final draft is settled on. These negotiations may also include visits to the country concerned by WIPO officials or invitations for key legislators and/or civil servants to Geneva for consultations. After the law has been enacted, WIPO offers national workshops on the adopted legislation, judicial symposia and training for enforcement officers.

Following a decision by the WIPO general assembly in September 2001, a unit for developing countries was established to coordinate WIPO's technical assistance activities, to ensure the non-duplication of work both within WIPO itself and also between WIPO and other agencies. To give an idea of the scale of WIPO's own capacity-building and technical support operations, between January 1998 and June 2001 WIPO provided the following technical assistance for developing countries:

- 2,087 intellectual property officials from the developing countries received training in awareness building and human resources development (1,451 from Africa, 383 from Asia-Pacific, 225 from Arabic-speaking developing countries and 28 from Haiti);

- 34 developing countries have received assistance in building-up or upgrading their intellectual property offices with adequate institutional infrastructure and resources, qualified staff, modern management techniques and access to information technology support systems;
- WIPO has sponsored study visits through the WIPO Worldwide Academy for officials from the developing countries, and organized study tours for officials from many developing countries to offices in industrialized countries to study various aspects of modernization;
- 32 developing countries have been beneficiaries of WIPO assistance on legislation in the areas of intellectual property, copyright and neighbouring rights and geographical indications;
- in close co-operation with other international organizations, WIPO has organized national, regional and interregional meetings for the developing countries on the implementation of the TRIPs Agreement. (WIPO Assistance, no date)

The extent of this work reflects the agency's opinion that a 'clear and balanced view of the Agreement enables the developing countries to assess the conformity of their existing national legislation vis-à-vis the provisions of the TRIPs Agreement'. While this dwarfs most other provision, this is not to say no other agencies are providing important sources of support in this area.

Although much of its IPR-related training is delivered through WIPO, the WTO also continues to provide IPR-related support to its members. For instance, the WTO has an ongoing project in Indonesia with a budget of US$14.7 million, while an earlier project to establish an agency to implement industrial property (patent) laws in Mexico cost US$32.1 million between 1992 and 1996. In 2002, the WTO and WIPO jointly organized two regional workshops, one for sub-Saharan Africa and Haiti, and the other for the Asia-Pacific region, to introduce key officials to TRIPs compliance. This joint initiative is planned to develop specific action plans for developing-country members of the WTO, focusing on preparing legislation, institution building, modernizing intellectual property systems and enforcement issues (WTO, 2001).

The European Patent Office (EPO) also has a number of programmes, from the EC–ASEAN Patents and Trademark Programme, to their Projects for Africa and the Middle East. Its programmes centre on training, advice and assistance, as well as the provision of patent (and other IPR-related) documentation. Although the EPO limits most of its work to 'awareness raising' and its programmes are more focused on direct trading partners, it has also done considerable work in the former communist states of Eastern Europe. In 1997 it established its own academy, and in 1999 for instance 422 trainees from 80 states attended the 23 courses it ran.

Alongside these activities the EPO has a strong outreach programme arranging seminars for patent attorneys, judges and administrators in Eastern European countries and across Asia. Most significantly, given China's accession to the WTO and therefore TRIPs (alongside their long-noted problem of 'piracy'), the EPO has also been working with the State Intellectual Property Office to improve its in-house training and the two offices are now linked by a direct data transfer connection to aid Chinese officials access to European legal documentation (EPO, 2000: ch. 5). One of the key elements of the EPO's activities has been the provision of European national legislation and collections of patent applications as learning materials. These collections are intended to help legislators draw up laws that reflect the procedures and protections that are found in European law. As with the WIPO activities outlined above, training involves the composition of model laws and the importation of specific elements of extant European law.

Unlike WIPO and the EPO, the World Bank is perhaps a little more cautious in its support for the universalization of the TRIPs standards of IPR protection. In the 2002 *Global Economic Prospects* report, the chapter on IPRs concludes:

> While promising some eventual benefits, the new [TRIPs] regime is asymmetric in its likely effects across countries. Low-income economies may expect to incur net costs for some time, suggesting that patience and assistance are needed, along with programmes to limit potentially negative effects in areas such as new medicines. (World Bank, 2002: 148)

Nevertheless, the World Bank has included IPRs in its own wider legal training programme, and continues to aid countries develop the legal capacity to establish their TRIPs-compliant legislation and practices. In the 1990s World Bank-sponsored programmes included:

- Brazil – primarily supporting the implementation of the 1996 industrial property law, covering the training of IPR administration staff, some reform of administrative structures and the development of new local agencies to specialize in domestic IPR assistance (US$4 million);
- Indonesia – programme to aid the development of the necessary legal infrastructure to support the 1997 IPR laws (potentially bringing Indonesia into TRIPs compliance) covering administrative improvements, staff training, and further legal reforms (centred on regulations regarding the topography of integrated circuits, trademarks and trade secrets) (US$14.7 million);
- Mexico – from 1992 to 1996 a programme to speed up patent awards and increase domestic enforcement activities, including administrative improvements and a new IPR agency, staff training, the computerization

of the patent application process, and training in enforcement procedures for courts' staff (US$32 million). (Finger and Schuler, 1999:
51–2)

More recently, World Bank programmes have included IPRs in more general
good governance and general legal capacity-building projects. Other recent
more general projects have included a new *Legal Yearbook* to be distributed to
governments (including legal materials, case studies and articles), legal education for the general public (in Russia and elsewhere), and a wide range of
'best-practice' programmes. The Bank's legal programmes have flourished
under the rubric of good governance, and given the key issue of legal compliance with multilateral commitments it is no surprise that considerable emphasis continues to be given to TRIPs-related activities.

In the realm of bilateral aid, USAID now spends around a quarter of its
annual budget on legal and regulatory training including a major programme
focusing on trade policy/regulatory activities.[8] This general work helps developing countries with little experience of 'Western' legal practices to develop
some of the skills that can be subsequently deployed for IPR legislation, and
underpins much of the focused work undertaken by the specialist agencies.
Furthermore, USAID has launched a number of initiatives in developing countries to build capacity related to the accession to the WTO. Between 1999 and
2001 the USA, through USAID, provided US$7.1 million to aid developing
countries related to TRIPs compliance. This has mostly taken the form of technical assistance from the US Patent and Trademark Office (USPTO) to help
countries bring their domestic legislation into compliance with TRIPs, ranging
from assessments of draft laws to recommendations regarding existing laws
and the manner in which they can be brought into compliance.

The USPTO also runs a visiting scholars programme which includes
'hands-on' training in the administration of intellectual property law, and has
assisted a number of countries with seminars and training programmes for
officials and legislators (including Kenya, Ghana, Mozambique, India, Brazil,
Poland, Mexico, Russia, Georgia, Lithuania, Macedonia, Malaysia, Sri Lanka,
Thailand, Uzbekistan, Oman, the Dominican Republic, Lebanon and Cyprus)
(USAID, 2002: ch. 2). Thus USAID is supporting the development of a
specific legal culture in developing countries at the general level of legal infrastructural building and at the particular level of specific legislative policies
linked to IPRs. However, as Jacques de Lisle warns, this should not necessarily be taken to mean that all assistance uncritically promotes US models of
law, even if, as he also notes, the role of legal education at US and US-
affiliated law schools *does* promotes a specific view of the manner in which
law should function (de Lisle, 1999). Therefore, due to the use of legal educa-
tors from outside government to facilitate much of this bilateral aid, the 'hard'

message of TRIPs compliance may be somewhat diluted 'twixt cup and lip'.

The United Nations Conference on Trade and Development (UNCTAD) was severely marginalized by the shift of global IPR regulation from WIPO to the WTO, reflecting the critical line it had taken previously to the IPR-related demands of the developed countries (which were finally codified in TRIPs). The agency continues to carry out feasibility studies for developing countries' capacity enhancement, ranging in projected costs from nearly US$2 million to train staff to administer IPR laws effectively in Egypt, to nearly US$6 million to modernize India's patent office (Finger and Schuler, 1999: 53–5). However, John Braithwaite and Peter Drahos note that UNCTAD, 'the one UN organ with high levels of analytical expertise on trade and intellectual property, has largely become irrelevant in affecting intellectual property standard-making' (Braithwaite and Drahos, 2000: 68). Nevertheless, the agency continues to provide analysis and advice to developing countries, and is currently running a programme in conjunction with the International Centre for Trade and Sustainable Development on capacity building which aims to provide documents and advice aimed at policymakers and trade negotiators from developing countries.[9] Additionally, where intellectual property law touches environmental law there is also the possibility that a new joint programme with the UN Environment Programme, a Capacity Building Task Force on Trade, Environment and Development, may look at some IPR-related law, although the first projects have not done so.

It is not just multilateral and state-aid agencies that are active in the provision of assistance and legal training. In the private/NGO sector, the Rockefeller Foundation recently introduced a programme to help developing countries develop TRIPs-compliant legislation and infrastructure to protect IPRs. In a recent list of 'foreign-supported' training events focusing on WTO compliance issues in China, organizations delivering training/educational support ranged from the US Department of Commerce and offices of the US Embassy in Beijing, as well as EU, British, Australian and Japanese aid, to programmes delivered by the US–China Business Council, The Ford Foundation and the Asian Foundation. While not all these focused centrally on IPRs, the US–China Legal Co-operation Fund has been supporting the training of Chinese judicial officers in IPR-related issues and the EU–China IPR Co-operation Programme has been working for the last three years explicitly on 'realigning' China's IPR regime with 'international norms' (Goldstein and Anderson, 2002). Of course, the bilateral assistance from the US government was tied to a Chinese agreement to upgrade its IPR protection in the face of 'Special 301' bilateral sanction under US trade law (de Lisle, 1999: 223). China may be a special case, where many private and multilateral organizations have identified a 'need' for their support, but throughout the developing countries, similar, if perhaps less extensive, training and support is being mobilized.

Finally, many NGOs, like Oxfam and Action Aid, are offering policy advice to developing countries, which, unlike the 'official' aid on offer, is intended to help policymakers and legislators resist some of the political pressure stemming from the developed states and the multilateral agencies for full and comprehensive TRIPs compliance. Although these voices have at times been drowned out by the vast and continuing resources dedicated to (re)producing the particular reading of the TRIPs agreement favoured by the developed countries, they were also instrumental in supporting the renewed negotiated resistance that culminated in the Doha declaration's passages on IPRs.

SOME PROBLEMS WITH 'ENCOURAGING' TRIPS COMPLIANCE

Capacity-building programmes aim to help countries that have no tradition or expertise in the field of IPRs, or whose legislative experience regarding IPRs is at variance with the TRIPs model, develop the mechanisms and human resources that will be required for the establishment or reorientation of national IPR-related legal regimes in line with TRIPs. Additionally, as I have already noted, in an attempt to ensure that their clients are not caught up in costly IPR-related trade disputes with developed-country members of the WTO (most obviously the USA), the staff of WIPO have often encouraged developing countries to adopt legislation that goes beyond the formal requirements of the TRIPs agreement.

Given that the USTR has access to what Drahos and Braithwaite (2002: 101) have described as 'a global surveillance network, consisting of American companies, the American Chamber of Commerce, trade associations and American embassies, a network that gathers and reports on the minutiae of [countries'] social and legal practices when it comes to US intellectual property', it is perhaps understandable that policymakers in developing countries feel under pressure as regards IPRs. It has been noted by the USTR that in the couple of months prior to their annual report on IPRs, many countries endeavour to pass legislation or conduct high-profile investigations into 'piracy' to positively affect their listing in the report: the designation *Priority Foreign Country* (currently only the Ukraine is so designated) can result in withdrawal from the US General System of Preferences (GSP); *Priority Watch List* countries can be subjected to considerable bilateral pressure (threats of withdrawal of GSP 'privileges' and enaction of WTO–DSM cases against them); *Watch List* countries are essentially 'on notice' and are regarded as trying to achieve in good faith, if having not actually achieved, the policy and enforcement outcomes desired by the USTR.

Overall there are three broad areas where developing countries need to act (and are receiving support to act) if they are to bring their legal systems into TRIPs compliance: legislative reform (either new laws of the redrafting/ reorganization of existing laws); administrative development (from computerization and streamlining to cope with the expansion of applications and work, to the development of previously absent mechanisms); and effective enforcement (including the development of effective judicial systems as well as training for law enforcement agencies). While the development of administrative practices and enforcement mechanisms is important for the protection of IPRs (and indeed are the focus of considerable attention from the USTR through the 'Special 301' process), the foundation of any capacity building must be the legislation itself. Unless this is brought into compliance, the best administrative and enforcement practices will do little to ensure that developing countries are able to fulfil the undertakings on IPRs which form an important element of their WTO membership.

Although the TRIPs agreement does not actually mandate the forms of law that any member may adopt, as J. Michael Finger and Philip Schuler have concluded, at the WTO the tendency has and continues to be

> to give the benefit of the doubt to established standards. Finding grounds for moving away from established standards may be particularly difficult in the area of intellectual property rights. They are, after all, an existential matter of legal definition, not a scientific matter of empirical estimation . . . [Thus] the benefit of the doubt will rest with systems presently in place in the industrialized countries. (Finger and Schuler, 1999: 20)

This supports the suggestion that the type and scope of capacity building encouraged in the programmes previously outlined would not tend to support novel and different solutions to the problems of IPR protection. Rather, as the statement from WIPO noted above, advice may 'to the extent possible . . . take into account the specific needs of the country concerned' but only where this does not conflict with the TRIPs agreement's invocation of required legal effect, and the 'best practice' acknowledged by the various agencies involved in capacity-building programmes.

As noted in the previous section, both the WTO and the World Bank have funded programmes in Indonesia to support the development of TRIPs-compliant IPR laws. A brief examination of this case reveals the problems which capacity building for IPRs may suggest more generally. One of the first problems encountered by any legislative reform in Indonesia is the traditional customary law known as *adat*, which K. Kalan suggests is 'not so much a clear legal code as it is a malleable, yet deep seated way of making sense of the world' (Kalan, 2000: 1467).[10] Furthermore, *adat* is not a unified system of law, but rather has quite significant regional variations. Despite considerable internal differences, there are also four major differences between *adat* and Western law: (1) no distinction between real rights and personal rights; (2) no distinction between moveable and immoveable property; (3) no distinction between public and private law; and (4) no distinction between civil and criminal delicts. (Kalan, 2000: 1467, fn. 151)

At the heart of *adat* is the stability of the community, and hence the awarding of property (in material things or goods) has to be judged by virtue of its impact on community. Kalan argues that patents would be construed under *adat* 'as an advantage to the owner at the expense of the community, and thus as disruptive to the vital societal equilibrium' (Kalan, 2000: 1468). Neither does *adat* have a clear philosophy of enforcement, not least of all as the community rather than individuals are the focus of law. All of this makes the coordination of traditional law and TRIPs-compliant legislation difficult, to say the least.

Above the 'bedrock' of *adat* are layers of Islamic legal conceptions, the formal Dutch Civil Code of 1847, and the 1945 Constitution. For instance, the patent system itself rests on a three Presidential decrees from 1989 and 1991, which themselves rest on this complex and multi-layered legal underpinning. In 1997 the government acceded to the agreements that compromise the legislative content of the TRIPs agreement (the Paris and Berne Conventions, and others).[11] Previously, between 1912 and the declaration of independence in 1945 Indonesia had an externally imposed and administered (colonial) patent law, but after independence this was rejected as a colonial imposition.

Additionally, in order to thwart the control of the domestic publishing industry by Dutch publishers (from the ex-colonial power), in 1960 Indonesia withdrew from the Berne Convention (Heath, 1997: 307; Drahos and Braithwaite, 2002: 78). The failure to pass even a promised patent law led to a hiatus until 1989 by when over 13 000 patent applications were submitted in response to the continually promised but never enacted law. The move in the 1990s to a more robust set of laws regarding IPRs was prompted by external pressures, both from investors and from multilateral agencies which the Indonesian government was keen to join (the WTO being the most important). This reflected the shift in Indonesia from import-substitution to export-led development, a development at least partly triggered by the decline in income from oil and gas (Antons, 1997: 321). And Kalan suggests that '*Adat* and Islam would not, by themselves, generate intellectual property laws; the patent laws are Indonesia's response to the pressures of the global economy' (Kalan, 2000: 1472). That said, the successful implementation of TRIPs-compliant laws has been very difficult, and remains incomplete (especially as regards the USTR's continuing demands).

Indonesians may still have difficulty conceptualizing property other than material objects, while the country's overall agrarian character means that the role of IPRs is outside the majority population's experience or interest. There has been limited success in producing effective IPR protection, not least of all due to the

> relative infertility of Indonesia's cultural soil to nurture the seeds or to support the trellis for maintaining such a harvest of invention. The mentality of Indonesia, shaped by years of *adat*, Islam, agrarian existence, and colonial rule, place a premium on the idea of community ownership and shared assets – a contrary view to the individualistic, monopolistic tenets of patent law . . . as evidenced by the country's retiring and leisurely approach to legislation and its weak record of enforcement. (Kalan, 2000: 1476)

And therefore, despite the legislative capacity, there is still some need to expand the administrative and enforcement capabilities if Indonesia is to comply fully with its TRIPs commitments. In the case of patent law, there is also a perception that unlike copyright (where there is a relatively vocal and growing supportive industrial constituency of content producers), the legislative changes resulting from the accession to TRIPs are too strongly influenced by foreign interests. Christoph Antons identifies 'a substantial lobby of local industry that feels threatened by stronger patent protection that would make its products much more expensive' (Antons, 1997: 346). Furthermore, as intellectual property is traditionally viewed as a criminal matter in Indonesia, partly because of the lack of civil enforcement mechanisms, investigation and enforcement have fallen to the police. However, Simon Butt suggests that the police do not treat IPR-related crime seriously, leaving enforcement often to confiscation but not prosecution, if alleged infringements are investigated at all (Butt, 2002: 435). Thus, even if Indonesia does pass TRIPs-compliant laws, it is not clear that this will deal with the problems which the USTR and other agencies have identified, primarily regarding 'piracy'.

Given the historical context briefly alluded to above, it is perhaps little surprise that in Butt's view,

> With the probable exception of senior intellectual property officials, the Indonesian Government and bureaucracy reject intellectual property law outright, or more commonly, are indifferent to it or more preoccupied with more pressing issues. This has meant that generally speaking, the government has done the minimum required to give the appearance of compliance . . . while simultaneously avoiding the more fundamental reforms that must be made to the bureaucracy and legal system if an effective intellectual property regime is to be established. (Butt, 2002: 436)

Thus, given the social and cultural divide between the putative law and societal practice, it is less than surprising that Indonesia remains on the US watch list as regards IPR infringement. Indeed, for the last three years Indonesia has been cited as a *Priority Watch List* country in the USTR's annual report, having also spent most of the 1990s in this position. In the most recent report, the USTR notes that 'overall protection of intellectual property remains weak . . . [while] long delays remain in prosecuting intellectual property cases and the Indonesian Government has not promulgated sentencing guidelines with deterrent penalties' (USTR, 2003: 14). This contrasts with Malaysia, which while sharing a similar (but not identical) cultural background, has made more strenuous efforts to move towards the US-mandated model of IPR protection. As a result, Malaysia has been downgraded from the *Priority Watch List* to merely a *Watch List* country.[12]

In contrast to Indonesia, Malaysia possesses a legal system rooted in British law (though with some elements of Islamic law held over). As Meredith Woo-Cummings notes, the judiciary and the judicial process still operate 'under the profound influence of the English common law and equity, judicial precedents, principles, ideas and concepts' (Woo-Cummings, 2003: 217). This makes the adoption of TRIPs-compliant legislation less problematic than it is in Indonesia. Furthermore, despite this heritage of common law and several decades of working within the 'rule of law', Dr Mahathir's control of the state apparatus has also allowed any resistance to legislative change to be brushed aside (ibid.: 219). Thus the normative foundations are closer to those which support IPRs, while resistance to TRIPs-compliant laws can be largely ignored by legislators.

Furthermore, with state-led developmental projects like the Malaysian Multimedia Super Corridor, the government has identified strong IPR laws as a key element in the development of national competitiveness (Wong, 1999), extending to a number of measures that directly reflect the USTR's demands in the area of copyright 'piracy', most importantly 'optical media production' (USTR, 2003: 3). This contrasts with the mid-1980s, when only US pressure in the form of 'Special 301' measures prompted Malaysia to rework its copyright laws (including coverage for software) and become signatories to the Berne Convention in 1990. However, the USTR's 2003 report keeps Malaysia on the *Watch List* because 'prosecution is a weak link in the enforcement chain and the judicial process remains slow' (USTR, 2003: 26). That said, over the last four years the comments in the annual *Special 301* report have become less antagonistic while at the same time those regarding Indonesia have become more caustic.

Quite apart from any historical or legal differences between Indonesia and Malaysia, there is also a question of their relative economic development. In July 2001, while Indonesia was designated a *low-income* country, Malaysia was identified as an *upper middle-income* country by the World Bank (2002: 250, table 1). Though such a distinction is crude, it does suggest in broad terms that Malaysia might be regarded as more economically developed than Indonesia. When this is compared to the experience of the newly industrialized countries of East Asia, then a further reason for the difference in IPR legislation comes into focus. Surveying a number of studies, Nagesh Kumar concludes that

> the east Asian countries, viz., Japan, Korea and Taiwan, have absorbed substantial
> amount[s] of technological learning under weak IPR protection regime[s] during the
> early phases [of economic development]. These patent regimes facilitated the
> absorption of innovation and knowledge generated abroad by their indigenous
> firms. They have also encouraged minor adaptations and incremental innovations
> on the foreign inventions by domestic enterprises. (Kumar, 2003: 216)

As these local industries started to innovate themselves, a stronger regime of
protection was established, *but only then*. Malaysia seems likely to be nearer
this sort of threshold than Indonesia, which has led Darko Djaic to argue:

> enforcement problems continue because protection intellectual property is simply
> not in Indonesia's interest. As Indonesia imports more intellectual property than it
> exports, [the] authorities realize that the new TRIPs-based intellectual property
> regime, based on Western standards, protects foreign intellectual property. (Djaic,
> 2000: 466)

While under pressure from the USTR, Indonesia has slowly updated and
expanded its IPR-related legislation, a process that can thus hardly be said to
be voluntarily undertaken. Therefore, it seems likely that the political economy of Indonesia itself will need to change (or develop) before the demands
of the USTR and the US government are likely to be met.

The Indonesian and Malaysian cases alert us to a major issue in building
capacity for IPRs in developing countries. Where prior legal culture and the
TRIPs-compliant laws come into conflict it is by no means certain that the new
laws will be regarded as legitimate. Furthermore, despite the enactment of a
legal framework that is broadly TRIPs-compliant, supported by capacity-
building projects, enforcement practices may remain underdeveloped. Indeed,
without clear cultural support legislation will be seen merely as the imposition
of foreign laws. However, where economic development stimulates the emergence of an industrial constituency which is likely to support stronger protection, then capacity building may find more fertile ground. Hence considerable
political effort is being expended to start to (re)produce the globalized norms
and justifications which are at the heart of the TRIPs agreement.

Law cannot work if it is only followed when there is continual explicit
enforcement. This is even more the case where the very law itself disturbs the
common character of that which it regulates (in this case through the construction of scarcity in knowledge and/or information). Thus, while the possession
of material goods and the provision of personal services may be protected (or
access and use withheld by force), this is not the case for knowledge and infor-
mation-made property. In the absence of socially accepted IPRs (and therefore
the difficulty of establishing scarcity as it relates to use), it is difficult to
govern access to knowledge and information unless it is kept altogether secret.
Few, if any, knowledge-related businesses can expect to thrive without reveal-

ing the knowledge/informational base of their products or services. Thus the construction of knowledge scarcity, if not seen as legitimate, makes it almost impossible to operate knowledge- or information-related commerce through a set of market relations.

Certainly, the TRIPs agreement is far from uncontested in many other developing countries which are experiencing similar mismatches between custom or tradition and the TRIPs-related laws that their membership of the WTO requires. The provision of training and technical assistance to build capacity is itself part of the reproduction of the dominant (TRIPs-constituted) view of IPRs and is therefore a site of considerable political struggle. By trying to shift elite perceptions away from these previous models of (non-)ownership of knowledge resources, capacity building is explicitly trying to engender a normative shift in members' societies.

While there is no fixed developing-country position on IPRs across sectors or countries, the current (TRIPs-engendered) social bargain between private rewards and public benefits at the heart of the legal construction of IPRs may not be as appropriate to developing countries as it is to developed and wealthy countries. On one side, many developing-countries elites and governments are keen to join the international trading community and see the need to adopt the increasingly universalized rules of the system as part of this process (not least in the realm of electronically delivered services, where India and some Caribbean countries are developing significant sectoral capacity). But, conversely, there are vocal constituencies in many countries which have prompted a political response less supportive of an unqualified adoption of TRIPs-related standards. Policymakers and legislators are also starting to question the claims made on behalf of the TRIPs-related settlement by developed countries' trade negotiators.

The manner in which the majority of patents are used in Africa does little to support the rhetoric of their supporters as regards the developmental advantage of IPRs. Rather than facilitating the importation of new technologies for production (or service fulfilment), patents have historically been used to maintain import monopolies (Kongolo, 2000: 275). They have not been 'worked' and therefore do the precise opposite of what is intended: the patent holder is protected from any copying or competition regarding their technology, while also gaining new markets through imports. Local production either by the patent holder or by imitators is foreclosed, ensuring no real developmental benefits can be gained (apart from the direct consumption of the product). Of course, this should be no real surprise: the driving force behind TRIPs-related diplomacy was an agenda of *trade*, not development; and considerable efforts were mobilized in the negotiations behind TRIPs to ensure that the notion of 'working' patents was diminished as a justification for compulsory licence.

In the slightly different context of economic policy reform, Deborah

Bräutigam has suggested that 'economic reformers need to be able to communicate with and (often) compensate losers' (Bräutigam, 2000: 262). She
stresses that some form of 'safety-net' or compensation package needs to be
put in place to ensure that the 'losers' from any particular set of reforms do not
become a critical block of resistance. She also argues that 'political sustainability may dictate less orthodox reform sequences' (ibid.). That is, the immediate adoption of all structures 'required' by liberalization may itself be
counterproductive in the medium term. Indeed, both these issues are at the
forefront of problems with the establishment of TRIPs compliance through
legislative reform and capacity building. Although capacity building at the
national level may be one element of constituting a global legal structure for
the protection of IPRs, there is also a need to (re-)recognize the central balance
between private rewards and public benefits that have been central to the legal
history of IPRs in national legislation.

The history of the international recognition of IPRs is considerably shorter
than any of its (various) national histories. In the late nineteenth century the
Paris and Berne Conventions attempted to construct an international regime
for the protection of IPRs, but it was only with the TRIPs agreement over one
hundred years later, linking IPRs to the dispute settlement mechanism at the
WTO, that the international regime gained any teeth. Thus, only for the last
seven years has there been a truly global legal regime for IPRs, although many
developing countries are still navigating transitional periods.

The final achievement of this potential 'one-size-fits-all' settlement has
revealed the central problem for the globalization of IPRs. Its effects already
suggest that without a well-developed global society able to mediate between
private rewards and social goods/public benefits, the notion of a global regime
for IPRs is difficult (if not impossible) to justify. Before the end of the nineteenth century (and for many countries, into the twentieth), non-national intellectual property was seldom recognized. Indeed, from Venice onwards the
legal recognition of IPRs was dependent on national registration or national
production. Famously, the US publishing industry thrived in the nineteenth
century, publishing 'unauthorized' work of European authors, but perhaps less
often noted, US industrialization proceeded apace with technologies that were
patented abroad, but freely available (essentially through 'piracy') to entrepreneurs in America, especially in the petrochemical sector.

The character of national laws (only recognizing national invention or
creation) supported a similar appropriation of foreign knowledge and information when the USA, and, before that, Britain, were 'developing countries',
as it did more recently in East Asia. Since the fifteenth century restrictions on
who was recognized as an owner of IPRs represented a strategic development
policy to encourage the importation of innovation by domestic companies (and
before them artisans). Thus it is ironic that having reached the heights of

economic development, the governments of the most developed countries now argue in multilateral negotiations that the very protection they ignored in their years of speedy expansion will actually aid and support the economic development of other countries. Their claims regarding the benefits of IPR protection fail to recall that the social bargain they wish to reproduce was constructed through national political mediation of interest, and not the imposition of a 'one-size-fits-all' model across the global system.

CONCLUSION

We are currently in a transitory period, where the global governance regime for IPRs has been established, but the political community on which the justification of intellectual property depends (alongside the socio-legal recognition of the private/public balance at the heart of the construction of IPRs) is far from globalized. This closely reflects the depiction of the contemporary (global) polity suggested by Richard Higgott and Morten Ougaard: while there is a 'thick interconnectedness' between 'political structures, agents and process, with transnational properties', these are as yet only linked by a 'thin community that transcends the territorial state' (Higgott and Ougaard, 2002: 12). The TRIPs agreement and the political economy of its negotiation, alongside the international (industry-based) lobbying groups involved in establishing and expanding the (specific) agenda of IPR governance discussed above, all fit with the notion of 'thick interconnectedness'. Not only via the Internet (which itself is very unevenly globalized), but also through the use of new (patented) technologies and the increasingly globalized reach of brands, as well as the capacity-building programmes detailed herein, the *globalized* interconnectivity of the political economy of knowledge commodification has become more pronounced by the day. However, there remains only a 'thin community' as regards the socio-political justification of IPRs on which the TRIPs agreement's normative aspects are founded.

While mechanisms exist at the national level to ameliorate problems that the balance of private rewards and public benefits might produce, few mechanisms exist at the global level. There is little way for developing countries to meaningfully factor in the national social costs of strong IPR laws. Whereas in national political debates, those groups shouldering the immediate social costs may have a number of political avenues through which countermeasures may be mobilized, with the exception of breaking international agreements, there is much less scope for such mediation at the global level. Indeed, where there is little tradition or history of legal structures of some similarity to those promoted through TRIPs, there are few if any avenues for developing an alternative vision of how knowledge and informational resources might, or should, be governed.

As Rochelle Cooper Dreyfuss and Andrea Lowenfeld point out, developing countries have handicapped themselves by acceding to the TRIPs agreement: 'Instead of following the strategy (which many developed countries once pursued) of absorbing the world's knowledge base and coming up to technological speed before protecting foreign intellectual property, a country that enters into the TRIPs Agreement at this stage . . . may well raise the costs of acquiring the knowledge it needs' (Dreyfuss and Lowenfeld, 1997: 303). These costs are quite high: the World Bank has estimated annual 'net patent rents' on full implementation of the TRIPs agreement (in 2000 dollars). These figures suggested that the USA will receive payments of around US$19 billion, while the republic of Korea (being at the forefront of TRIPs compliance, and a model of economic development for many) will experience a net outflow of over US$15 billion. While some developed countries gain rents (the UK nearly US$3 billion; Germany US$6.8 billion), some will experience net outflows (New Zealand just over US$2 billion and Canada US$0.6 billion). More interesting still are the estimates of annual outflows from developing countries. For Brazil these are set to be US$0.5 billion, for China US$5.1 billion and for India US$0.9 billion) (World Bank, 2002: 133, table 5.1). These net transfers do not include those countries with less developed local industrial sectors, which may see IPR-related payments by multinational corporations added to the transfer of funds.

The world is not sufficiently globalized (whatever commentators celebrating the 'borderless world' claim) for any political and legal settlement to closely follow previous national political bargains. The justifications that have previously been used to underpin IPRs do not have sufficient purchase on the current global situation without a mechanism for recognizing the social costs side of any 'bargain' which promotes private rewards. As Graeme Dinwoodie stresses,

> the incorporation of intellectual property agreements within trade mechanisms might (if trade concerns become paramount) deprive intellectual property policy-making of the rich palette of *human values* that historically has influenced its formulation. Considering only the ability to exploit comparative advantage in the ownership of intellectual property rights would appear to make international intellectual property policy less multi-dimensional. (Dinwoodie, 2002: 1004, emphasis added)

In a nutshell, it is this lack of multidimensionality that is the key problem: given the vast inequalities evident in the world, the impact of these inequalities is not recognized when the social costs that are required for the continued support for private rewards remain largely hidden in policy discussions.

The current settlement for IPRs may work well for the developed countries, but for developing countries the central bargain at the centre of IPRs makes little sense. The private rights of IPR 'owners' in the richer states are being purchased at too great a social cost in the developing world. Before TRIPs this was essentially recognized in the *de facto* acceptance of widespread 'piracy' outside the developed countries. This was by no means a perfect solution, and a return to the essentially ungoverned character of the pre-TRIPs world of intellectual property is improbable. However, the current settlement does not command significant support outside the developed world. Hence the potential tensions that surround attempts at capacity building are hardly likely to be transitory. The best efforts at norm (re)production will come up against the very real problems that TRIPs compliance produces in many developing countries. Indeed, Jerome Reichman suggests that behind the ratcheting up of IPR enforcement standards is a protectionist rationale, to protect high-tech companies from the sorts of competition that commodity manufacturing and agriculture have had to deal with in the past (Reichman, 1997). The challenge is to square the problems of 'protection' with the real need to offer some protection of the rights of innovators and creators.

This, then, returns us to the global political realm. Intellectual property is of course not the only policy area where the USA has mobilized considerable political economic pressure (not least through bilateral trade instruments). As Daniel Drezner has noted, 'Scratch the surface, and it is surprising how much transnational law is created through military, economic and diplomatic coercion' (Drezner, 2001: 334), although perhaps less surprising to those viewing US practices from outside America's borders. Furthermore, again as Drezner suggests, 'the more the United States succeeds in creating top–down legal standards, the more such attempts will be made in the future' (ibid.: 333). Thus the capacity-building efforts and political pressure towards accelerated and globalized TRIPs compliance utilized by various agencies of the US government are probably emblematic of the manner in which the 'rule of law' will be extended multilaterally. There is much more at stake politically for the US government than merely the governance of IPRs.

Stephen Gill has termed this wider political dynamic the 'new constitutionalism', an attempt 'to make transnational liberalism, and if possible liberal democratic capitalism, the sole model for future development' (Gill, 2003: 132). While the global governance of IPRs is only one, albeit important, part of this 'project', its general contours are clearly discernible. The TRIPs-mandated settlement on governance of intellectual property stresses and privileges the rights (and needs) of knowledge 'owners' while denuding the 'democratic' public realm of substantial knowledge and information resources. As Gill suggests, under this new constitutionalism 'public policy is increasingly premised on the goal of increasing security of property (owners) and minimising the uncertainty of investors' (ibid.: 196). In the governance of IPRs these goals have been enacted in developing countries by the extensive capacity-building programmes (in the legislative realm and in enforcement practices) that I have discussed above.

Additionally, Gill identifies the bilateral pressure (through market access and investment agreements) that the US government is able to bring to bear to further drive this political trajectory (Gill, 2003: 134), which as I have noted above also has played a major role in the move to TRIPs compliance in developing countries. In policy terms, the 'new constitutionalism' stresses the 'need to strengthen surveillance mechanisms, and institutional capabilities to reinforce . . . market discipline at the multilateral level, and to help to sustain the legal and political conditions for transnational capital' (ibid.: 177). This 'new constitutionalism' has prompted the utilization of extensive political and economic resources to 'support' TRIPs compliance through aid for institution building, 'support' in legislative development and the provision of training to those policymakers and public servants who will need to 'govern' IPRs in each national jurisdiction.

Finally, although I would not argue for setting aside law, it does not follow that there is necessarily one legal model which suits all countries at all levels of development. If the global political economy of IPRs tells us one thing it is that the world is far too insufficiently globalized for the imposition of a global legal settlement that does not allow for the divergent national social developmental interests to be recognized (and acted upon). In the governance of IPRs this requires not only greater historical sensitivity to the manner in which IPRs have been governed in the past; it also requires an explicit recognition of the social bargain that lies at the centre of the justification of intellectual property. Again, this requires some historical sensitivity, perhaps starting from the recognition that patents and copyrights originated in the award of limited monopolies not the recognition of unlimited 'rights' (Sell and May, 2001). Critiques are now starting to emerge and, despite the efforts at norm construction outlined above, they may yet have a major impact on the future of the global governance of IPRs. Whether this impact will redirect the trajectory of the 'new constitutionalism' in the globalizing realm of IPR protection and enforcement remains to be seen.

NOTES

*   An earlier version of this chapter was presented at the International Studies Association conference, Portland, 2003. I thank all those who commented on it there, but especially the discussant, Richard Stubbs, who suggested a number of improvements to the argument from which the current version has benefited greatly.
1.   The private sector played a major role in the negotiations which led to the TRIPs agreement, drafting the majority of the document which became the broadly successful position advocated by the office of the US Trade Representative during the Uruguay Round (see May, 2000: 82–4; Drahos and Braithwaite, 2002; Matthews, 2002; and Sell, 1998).

2. I owe this apt phrase to Dwijan Rangnekar of University College, London.
3. Take the example of a hammer (as material property); if I own a hammer and we would both like to use it, our utility is compromised by sharing use. I cannot use the hammer while you are, you cannot while I am; our intended use is rival. Thus, for you to also use my hammer, either you have to accept a compromised utility (relying on my goodwill to allow you to use it when I am not) or you must also buy a hammer. The hammer is scarce. However, the idea of building something with hammer and nails is not scarce. If I instruct you in the art of simple construction, once that knowledge has been imparted, your use of that information has no effect on my own ability to use the knowledge at the same time; there is no compromise to my utility. We may be fighting over whose turn it is to use the hammer, but we do not have to argue over whose turn it is to use the idea of hammering a nail into a joint; our use of the idea of cabinet construction is non-rival. Ideas, knowledge and information are generally non-rivalous.
4. For instance, many problems for buyers in the second-hand car market could be ameliorated if all car dealers where required to reveal *all* they knew about the cars they were selling. This would probably reduce the price they could obtain for much of their stock, but would enhance the general satisfaction (and even safety) of second-hand car buyers.
5. Extended discussions of the negotiations that led to TRIPs can be found in Matthews (2002: ch. 2) and Stewart (1993: 2245–333).
6. For a discussion of IPRs, AIDS and the pharmaceutical industry see May (2002a).
7. Space precludes a detailed account of TRIPs numerous sections; Keith Maskus (2000: ch. 2) offers a good concise summary of the agreement, as does Matthews (2002: ch. three) but also see my discussion in May (2000: ch. 3).
8. Space precludes a detailed account of the activities, but for a comprehensive account see de Lisle (1999).
9. The project webpage is <http://www.ictsd.org/iprsonline/unctadictsd/description>
10. See also Butt (2002: 434–5) and Djaic (2000: 463–4).
11. For a brief history of Indonesia's patent law see Antons (1997: 322–4).
12. Designation of Indonesia and Malaysia in last four years' USTR's *Special 301 Report*.

	2000	2001	2002	2003
Indonesia	WL	PWL	PWL	PWL
Malaysia	PWL	PWL	WL	WL

Note: PWL: priority watch list (high risk of sanctions); WL: watch list (lower risk of sanction).

Source: Compiled from USTR (2000; 2001; 2002; 2003).

REFERENCES

Antons, C. (1997), 'The Indonesia Patent Act of 1989', *International Review of Industrial and Copyright Law*, **28** (3), 320–47.

Braithwaite, J. and Drahos, P. (2000), *Global Business Regulation*, Cambridge: Cambridge University Press.

Bräutigam, D. (2000), 'Foreign Aid and the Politics of Participation in Economic Policy Reform', *Public Administration and Development*, **20** (3), 253–64.

Burch, K. (1995), 'Intellectual Property Rights and the Culture of Global Liberalism', *Science Communication*, **17** (2), 214–32.

Butt, S. (2002), 'Intellectual Property in Indonesia: A Problematic Legal Transplant', *European Intellectual Property Review*, **24** (9), 429–37.

Dinwoodie, G. (2000), 'The Integration of International and Domestic Intellectual Property Lawmaking', *Columbia VLA Journal of Law and the Arts*, **23** (3/4), 307–14.

Dinwoodie, G. (2002), 'The Architecture of the International Intellectual Property System', *Chicago Kent Law Review*, **77** (3), 993–1014.

Djaic, D. (2000), 'Why does the Enforcement of Indonesia's Intellectual Property Laws continue to be a Problem?', *European Intellectual Property Review*, **22** (10), 454–69.

Drahos, P. (2002), 'Developing Countries and International Intellectual Property Standard Setting', *Journal of World Intellectual Property*, **5** (5), 765–89.

Drahos, P. and Braithwaite, J. (2002), *Information Feudalism. Who Owns the Knowledge Economy?*, London: Earthscan Publications.

Dreyfuss, R.C. and Lowenfeld, A.F. (1997), 'Two Achievements of the Uruguay Round: Putting TRIPs and Dispute Settlement Together', *Virginia Journal of International Law*, **37**, 275–333.

Drezner, D.W. (2001), 'On the Balance Between International Law and Democratic Sovereignty', *Chicago Journal of International Law*, **2** (2), 321–36.

European Patent Office [EPO] (2000), *EPO Annual Report*, Munich: EPO [available online at <http://www.european-patent-office.org/an_rep/2000/html> (20 February 2002)].

Finger, P. and Schuler, P. (1999), 'Implementation of Uruguay Round Commitments: The Development Challenge', paper for the WTO/World Bank Conference on 'Developing Countries in a Millennium Round', WTO Secretariat, Geneva, 20–21 September].

General Agreement on Tariffs and Trade [GATT] (1994), *Final Act Embodying the Results of the Uruguay Round of Multilateral Trade Negotiations*, Geneva: GATT Publication Services.

Gervais, D.J. (2002), 'The Internationalisation of Intellectual Property: New Challenges from the Very Old and the Very New', *Fordham Intellectual Property Media and Entertainment Journal*, **12** (4), 929–90.

Gill, S. (2003), *Power and Resistance in the New World Order*, Basingstoke: Palgrave Macmillan.

Goldstein, B.L. and Anderson, S.J. (2002), 'Foreign Contributions to China's WTO Capacity Building', *China Business Review*, **1** (January–February), at <http://www.chinabusinessreview.com/0201/goldstein> (29 January 2003).

Heath, C. (1997), 'Intellectual Property Rights in Asia – An Overview', *International Review of Industrial and Copyright Law*, **28** (3), 303–9.

Higgott, R. and Ougaard, M. (2002), 'Introduction: Beyond System and Society – Towards a Global Polity', in M. Ougaard and R. Higgott (eds), *Towards a Global Polity*, London: Routledge.

Hoekman, B.M. and Kostecki, M.M. (1995), *The Political Economy of the World Trading System. From GATT to WTO*, Oxford: Oxford University Press.

Kalan, K. (2000), 'Property Rights, Individual Rights and the Viability of Patent Law Systems', *University of Colorado Law Review*, **71** (5), 1439–78.

Kongolo, T. (2000), 'The African Intellectual Property Organisations', *Journal of World Intellectual Property*, **3** (2), 265–88.

Kumar, N. (2003), 'Intellectual Property Rights, Technology and Economic Development', *Economic and Political Weekly*, **38** (3), 209–25, at <http://www.epw.org.in/showArticles.php?root = 2003&leat = 01&filename = 5391&filetype = pdf> (23 January 2003).

de Lisle, J. (1999), 'Lex Americana?: United States Legal Assistance, American Legal Models and Legal Change in the Post-Communist World and Beyond', *University of Pennsylvania Journal of International Economic Law*, **20** (2), 179–308.

Machlup, F. and Penrose, E.T. (1950), 'The Patent Controversy in the Nineteenth Century', *Journal of Economic History*, **10**, 1 (May), 1–29.

Maskus, K. (2000), *Intellectual Property Rights in the Global Economy*, Washington, DC: Institute for International Economics.

Matthews, D. (2002), *Globalising Intellectual Property Rights: The TRIPs Agreement*, London: Routledge.

May, C. (2000), *A Global Political Economy of Intellectual Property Rights: The new enclosures?* London: Routledge.

May, C. (2002a), 'Unacceptable Costs: The Consequences of Making Knowledge Property in a Global Society', *Global Society*, **16** (2), 123–44.

May, C. (2002b), 'The Venetian Moment: New Technologies, Legal Innovation and the Institutional Origins of Intellectual Property', *Prometheus*, **20** (2), 159–79.

Oddi, A.S. (1996), 'TRIPs – Natural Rights and a "Polite Form of Economic Imperialism" ', *Vanderbilt Journal of Transnational Law*, **29**, 415–70.

Reichman, J.H. (1997), 'From Free Riders to Fair Followers: Global Competition under the TRIPs Agreement', *New York University Journal of International Law and Politics*, **29**, 11–93.

Sell, S. (1998), *Power and Ideas. North–South Politics of Intellectual Property and Anti-Trust*, Albany, NY: State University of New York Press.

Sell, S. and May, C. (2001), 'Moments in Law: Contestation and Settlement in the History of Intellectual Property', *Review of International Political Economy*, **8** (3), 467–500.

Shiva, V. (2001), *Protect or Plunder? Understanding Intellectual Property Rights*, London: Zed Books.

Steinberg, R.H. (2002), 'In the Shadow of Law or Power? Consensus-Based Bargaining in the GATT/WTO', *International Organisation*, **56** (2), 339–74.

Stewart, T.P. (1993), *The GATT Uruguay Round. A Negotiating History (1986–1992)*, Deventer: Kluwer Law and Taxation Publishers.

United States Agency for International Development (USAID) (2002), *Trade Capacity Survey Report*, at <http://www.usaid.gov/economic_growth/tradereport> (13 September 2002).

[Office of the] United States Trade Representative (USTR) (2000), *2000 Special 301 Report*, Washington, DC: USTR, at <http://www.ustr.gov/sectors/intellectual.shtml> (8 May 2003).

[Office of the] United States Trade Representative (USTR) (2001), *2001 Special 301 Report*, Washington, DC: USTR, at <http://www.ustr.gov/sectors/intellectual.shtml> (8 May 2003).

[Office of the] United States Trade Representative (USTR) (2003), *2002 Special 301 Report*, Washington, DC: USTR, at <http://www.ustr.gov/sectors/intellectual.shtml> (8 May 2003).

[Office of the] United States Trade Representative (USTR) (2003), *2003 Special 301 Report*, Washington, DC: USTR, at <http://www.ustr.gov/sectors/intellectual.shtml> (8 May 2003).

Wong, C. (1999), 'Malaysia's MSC and Intellectual Property Protection', *Jaring Internet Magazine*, **2** (8), 17–18.

Woo-Cummings, M. (2003), 'Diverse Paths Towards 'the Right Institutions': Law, the State, and Economic Reform in East Asia', in L. Weiss (ed.), *States in the Global Economy: Bringing domestic institutions back in*, Cambridge: Cambridge University Press.

World Bank (2002), *Global Economic Prospects and the Developing Countries*, Washington, DC: International Bank for Reconstruction and Development.

World Intellectual Property Organisation (WIPO) (1993), *WIPO: General Information*, Geneva: WIPO.

World Intellectual Property Organisation (WIPO) (no date), 'Assistance in the Field of Intellectual Property Legislation', at <http://www.wipo.int/cfdiplaw/en/assistance_ip.htm> (12 September 2002).

World Trade Organisation (WTO) (2001), 'WIPO and WTO Launch New Initiative to Help World's Poorest Countries' (Press/231) 14 June, at <http://www.wto.org/english/news_e/pres01_e/pr231_e> (4 December 2002).

PART II

The Latin American Experience

5. From the developmental to the regulatory state: the transformation of the government's impact on the Brazilian economy*

Edmund Amann and Werner Baer

Brazil's recent large-scale privatization programme presents the image of an economy in transition from state domination to one in which market forces prevail. The aim of this chapter is to show that such a characterization of the changes in the institutional structure of the Brazilian economy is somewhat overblown and that the state has retained a surprisingly strong grip on the development of the industrial and public utilities sectors. The state's lingering influence is held to stem from an interlinked combination of financial fragility among enterprises, dependence on public sector financing and changes in regulatory stance.

To substantiate our argument we begin by briefly charting the evolution of state participation in the economy in the period stretching from the 1930s to the late 1970s. Particular stress is placed on the influence of the state in shaping the industrialization process. In addition, we shall review the transformation of state-owned enterprises from being a mainly positive influence on the Brazilian economy to becoming increasingly dysfunctional. This will be followed by a brief overview of the extent of the privatization process of the 1990s, and the resulting change of the role of the state in the country's economy, that is, from being a direct participant to being mainly a regulatory agent. In a concluding section, we shall speculate on both the positive and negative economic aspects of the state being mainly a regulator.

THE PARTICIPANT STATE: 1930–1980

Beginning in the 1930s and accelerating in the post-World War II period, the

* Reprinted from *Quarterly Review of Economics and Finance*, vol. 45 (2005), Edmund Amann and Werner Baer, 'From the developmental to the regulatory state: the transformation of the government's impact on the Brazilian economy', pp. 421–31, copyright 2005, with permission from Elsevier.

state enterprise sector became dominant in public utilities, heavy industry, the exploitation of natural resources and the financial sector. It was complementary to the private domestic and multinational sectors, that is, each ownership sector specialized in specific sectors in the economy where it had the greatest comparative advantage. By the 1970s a large proportion of the steel industry (approximately 70 per cent of capacity) was in the hands of state enterprises. Similarly, state enterprises were heavily involved in the exploitation of natural resources, as was the case with Petrobrás (petroleum and various derivative industries) and Vale do Rio Doce (mineral extraction).[1] In addition to these areas, public sector ownership was widespread in the field of public utilities, railroad transportation, ports and the banking and financial sector (which includes the gigantic development bank – BNDES, and commercial banks owned either by the federal or state governments).

The importance of the state can also be gauged from the following facts: (a) a 1974 survey of the 5113 largest incorporated firms showed that over 39 per cent of assets belonged to state-owned enterprises (SOEs), while these same firms were responsible for 16 per cent of the value of sales; (b) a 1985 survey of the 8094 largest firms revealed that the share of net assets of state enterprises amounted to 48 per cent, while the share of these enterprises in total sales was 28.1 per cent.[2] The state also had an extremely powerful position in the financial sector.

The loans of the BNDES, together with other federal and state development banks, and official savings banks amounted to about 50 per cent of gross capital formation in the 1980s. The state also had a considerable influence in the commercial banking sector. For instance in 1985 the Banco do Brasil (the federally owned commercial bank) held 24 per cent of all funds on deposit in Brazil's 50 largest commercial banks, including some commercial banks owned by the state governments. Finally, at the beginning of the 1980s, the national development bank, the national housing bank (now extinct), the Bank of the Northeast and various development banks of individual states provided more than 70 per cent of the loans devoted to investment purposes. What was the impact of this substantial presence of the state in the Brazilian economy and was it necessarily harmful to the interests of the private sector?

It has been argued that for a long period of time this large-scale presence of the state in the economy was beneficial to both the domestic and foreign-owned private sectors.[3] State firms provided relatively cheap inputs to the private sector (steel, electric power etc.). The state was also the major source of finance for both public and private investment activities. In fact, there was a remarkable growth of savings in the 1960s and 1970s which was due to the government sector. The latter created and administered many forced saving funds through various social security levies. For instance, in 1974, 64 per cent of Brazil's savings were due to publicly administered social security funds; by

1980 this had risen to over 70 per cent. All these factors went some way to contributing to the accelerated growth which Brazil enjoyed between 1950 and 1980. However beneficial the impacts regarding growth, the hefty presence of the state failed to address the worsening pattern of income distribution.[4]

THE DECADENCE OF STATE ENTERPRISES

By the late 1970s a number of weaknesses inherent in the extensive presence of state enterprises had become apparent. The main features of the decadence of state enterprises were the following: (a) the use of state enterprises as macroeconomic policy instruments, for instance forcing state enterprises to restrain their prices and the tariffs they charged for their products in order to repress inflationary pressures. This did not halt inflation but caused large deficits in the affected enterprises, undermining their efficient operations and forcing the state to subsidize the losses incurred, which in turn, worsened the government deficit; (b) the political pressure to over-employ in SOEs and a tendency to hire individuals with personal connections to executive positions; (c) the increasing number of cases of corruption resulting from the quasi-monopoly position of state firms in certain sectors; (d) the use of public enterprises to borrow more on the international market than they needed so as to provide for accelerated capital inflows. This placed many SOEs in a precarious financial position.[5]

In the 1980s the combination of the debt crisis, the fiscal crisis and bouts of hyperinflation forced Brazil to adopt a set of neoliberal policies, one of whose main features was privatization. The pressure to adopt privatization policies came not only from within, but also externally from Brazil's major external creditors, most especially the IMF and the World Bank.[6]

THE PRIVATIZATION EXPERIENCE

Starting timidly in the late 1980s but accelerating markedly after 1994, Brazil engaged in one of the world's largest privatization programmes. At first privatization was concentrated in the steel and petrochemicals sectors, later embracing such state firms as the airplane manufacturer Embraer. From 1994 on the privatization programme expanded rapidly, as it now included public utilities, such as telecommunications, electricity distribution, railroads, ports and some of the major highways. At first foreign participation was limited. After a number of constitutional amendments which allowed foreign firms to participate in public utilities, the involvement of foreign capital in the privatization process increased dramatically. By 2002, receipts for privatization amounted to US$105.3 billion. Of this, foreign participation totalled US$42.1 billion and on a sectoral basis privatization of public utilities amounted to 63 per cent.[7]

It is important to note that a substantial source of domestic participation in the privatization auctions was constituted by the public sector using the resources of forced savings schemes. In this regard, the role of public sector pension schemes should be highlighted. For instance, in the case of the steel industry – among the earliest privatizations – the Banco do Brasil pension fund, Previ, was a key player. By 1997 it had acquired a substantial (23.9 per cent) stake in Acesita (a special steels company) which, in turn, owned important stakes in two other steel enterprises, Indústrias Villares and Aços Villares (De Paula, 1998). Within the same industry, a consortium of other public sector pension funds had managed to acquire a substantial stake in Belgo Mineira, a key enterprise in the speciality steels market. Of course, the role of the public sector pension funds in the privatization process extended to well beyond the steel sector. In the case of Previ,[8] it can be shown that by the end of 2002, the fund had acquired major stakes across a range of key privatized companies.[9]

THE ROLE OF THE STATE AS A REGULATOR

One notable feature of Brazil's privatization has been the fact that public utility privatization has been carried out through the granting of concessions rather than a permanent transfer of assets. The winner of the concession contract would be running a facility for a limited period of time (usually 20–25 years), at the end of which the assets would revert to the state unless a new concession were granted either to the old firm or a newcomer after an appropriate auction. During the concession period, the concession contract would be in force. It would include provisions for rate or tariff readjustments, investment obligations for both maintenance and upgrading the relevant facilities etc. For instance, in the telecommunications sector, strict targets have been set for increasing provision of fixed and cellular lines, while service quality is also monitored and enforced.[10]

The administration of the concession contract would be in the hands of special regulatory institutions (e.g. ANATEL; ANEEL) and in some cases government ministries. As one commentator noted, the introduction of these agencies established 'an array of sectoral regulatory–normative federal agencies that . . . have changed not only the procedures but indeed the culture of Brazilian public sector management primarily in the area of infrastructure. Previously line ministries or public enterprises under their jurisdiction have carried out not only policy-making functions but also economic alterations . . .'[11]

An additional aspect of privatization through concessions was that the

BNDES development bank helped to finance both domestic and foreign bidders in the auction process.

THE REGULATORY STATE AND ITS ECONOMIC INFLUENCE

Since public utilities privatization through the concessions model had the heaviest weight in the privatization process, regulation has become one of the most important channels through which the state can influence economic activity.[12] Of the state's various regulatory responsibilities, one of the most significant concerns the setting of tariffs. In formulating policy in this regard the state has had to balance the influence of competing constituencies. In the period of rapid privatization, the state in an effort to attract bidders to its concession auctions prioritized the interests of investors, raising tariffs sharply in order to raise the rate of return and thus attract the maximum number of bidders.[13]

As a result of the regulator's lenient policies towards the new concessionaires, profitability of public utilities increased dramatically. For instance, in the case of electricity generation, from being negative, average profitability rose to 1.8 per cent as a percentage of turnover in 1996 to 4.3 per cent in 1999.[14] For the electricity distribution sector, too, the initial years post privatization proved a favourable period: between 1995 and 1999 average profitability increased from 4.3 per cent to 5.9 per cent, having been negative for much of the first half of the decade.

An important consequence of privatization was that the concessionaires were required to substantially upgrade the facilities they administered under the concession contract. This was often made easier by the government through generous loans made to the concessionaires via the BNDES. In the case of the electricity sector, between 1995 and 2000 no less than 43.8 per cent of total investments carried out by the newly privatized utility enterprises was financed using funds from the BNDES. Such funding resulted in a surge in fixed capital formation: between 1994 and 1999 installed capacity in the generating sector leapt from 54.1 GW to 64.0 GW.[15] The railroad transportation system has also been realizing a quantum leap in investment following its privatization through the launch of concessions. Once again the BNDES is proving a key player in financing rises in fixed capital formation: between 2000 and 2004 the Bank has committed itself to funding 47 per cent of the projected rise in network capacity.[16]

In the case of the 9945 km of privatized federal and state highways, the BNDES has also proven an active participant in the financing of infrastructural improvements. Since the launch of the concessions, the Bank has provided funding amounting to 31 per cent of total investments in highway upgrading.

POLITICAL CHANGE AND ITS REGULATORY IMPLICATIONS

By 2002 the harmonious relationship between the government and the concessionaires had begun to unwind. There have been a number of reasons for this. For instance, the high interest rate policies adopted in order to defend the exchange rate contributed to low economic growth and to an increase in the burden of debt incurred by the concessionaires. This was reinforced by the devaluation of the real in January 1999 and the continued depreciation of the currency up to the final quarter of 2002. The resulting rise in the cost of the debt of many concessionaires made them demand generous increases in their tariffs.

However, as early as 1998 the attitude of the government was already becoming less favourable to the concessionaires and more sympathetic to the needs of the low-income population and to other hard-pressed users of public utilities. For example, in the case of highway concessions, the protests of associations of truck drivers in various states forced the government to reduce tolls.[17] These reductions in turn were contested by a number of concessionaires, who went to court claiming that by reducing tolls the government had violated the concession contracts.[18] This demonstrates an early example of the pressures from different groups to which regulators were subject. In the case of the telecommunications sector, the election of the Lula administration in October 2002 appears to herald similar downward pressure on tariffs. By 2003 telecommunications enterprises were seeking to maintain in place arrangements by which tariffs are adjusted in line with general price inflation. However, according to the Minister for Communications, Miro Teixeira, this regulatory approach is unlikely to survive for long with the 'elimination of rate indexation and the promotion of increased competition'.[19] Such downward pressures on tariffs have the potential to result in a change of the ownership landscape. Indeed, there have been recent signs that some concessionaires are seriously thinking of abandoning their concession contracts.

Another key regulatory issue faced by the concessionaires in the wake of privatization has had less to do with the level of tariffs *per se* than with uncertainty over their future path and the transparency which attaches to their setting and enforcement. In this regard, the performance of some of the regulatory agencies has been more investor-friendly than that of others. In the case of the electrical energy sector, for example, the regulator, ANEEL, has come under consistent criticism for the opacity, complexity and inconsistency of its management of tariff setting. For Landau (2002, p. 5) ANEEL comes in for criticism 'for its failure to adopt clear, unequivocal and rational rules on tarification. This factor has contributed significantly to insufficient private investment in power generation (because investors did not know the relative prices of inputs and outputs of generation plant, leading to shortages).'

ACHIEVEMENTS AND FAILURES OF REGULATION

Of course, it should be recognized that the post-privatization period in Brazil has been associated with regulatory achievements as well as failures. The case of telecommunications offers a sharp contrast with that of electrical energy. The telecommunications regulator, ANATEL, has succeeded in presiding over a surge in both capacity and in competition, whether in the fields of fixed-line or mobile services.[20]

Some of the recent difficulties encountered by the regulatory state are slowly being discussed in the academic literature. For instance, a recent article by Brazilian policy makers[21] in the regulatory field argues that in electricity generation and distribution, the future need for massive investment will have to come from the private sector. In order to encourage the latter they emphasize the need by the regulatory authorities to provide stimulative tariff regimes and also to provide some guarantees that these regimes will remain favourable for long periods of time.

While these observations may be valid within a permanently privatized public utilities setting, they imply that the socio-political preferences of society will not change and that, therefore, it is possible for the regulatory agencies to be permanently inclined towards favouring the private investor. It has, however, been shown in this chapter that in a democracy such as Brazil there may be substantial swings in the mood and preferences of society. If, for any reason, this mood swings in the direction of more populist policies, that is, placing equity above the need to entice private capital, the possibility of more lasting guarantees facing investors will be ruled out.

With the election of President Lula da Silva in October 2002 the regulatory agencies established under President Cardoso have come under acute pressure. According to a recent article in the *Washington Times*, President da Silva is seeking to curb the regulators' powers after having accused these agencies of overseeing excessively investor-friendly pricing regimes. In particular, President da Silva is quoted as stating that '[the regulators] are procuring the political power of Brazil. They've created a wall between themselves and the government.' The article further states that the new president and his team have been studying the country's regulators, targeting them for changes which are said to benefit certain sectors more than the population in general. Among the issues of contention between the government and the regulators is the linkage of price rises for intermediate inputs such as steel and ethanol to movements in the US dollar.

The article further states that the new government has put the brakes on recent attempts to increase energy rates by more than 40 per cent over the next four years. Finally, a senator, Aloizio Mercadante, a confidant of the president, and the government's then leader in the Senate, said that 'there are serious problems with the agencies, from the area of tariffs to that of regulation. The government has lost the ability to regulate important sectors such as utilities.' Another politician close to the president, Congressman Roberto Jefferson, is quoted by the article as saying 'we are certain that the regulators [are acting] above the law ... They're treated like a parallel power. I think the performance of these agencies is really an abuse.'[22]

Changes in the political atmosphere alluded to above could also manifest themselves in the government's policy regarding the appointment of key personnel to the regulatory agencies.[23] Landau (2002, pp. 8–9) has observed that up to the end of the Cardoso administration the government gave preference in its nominations to

> expertise over partisan allegiance or the exchange of political favours, but the vagaries of politics in the future may intrude on this very sensitive process. The outstanding example of an agency governed by personalities of acknowledged stature is ANATEL, whose resolutions tend to be politically neutral whereas ANEEL, where nominations are made on the basis of political rather than technical criteria, has often produced resolutions that result in controversy, to say the least, and that are disputed (often in court) by both concession-holders and consumer groups.

Another perceptive observation relating to the inevitably political nature of the regulatory mission emerges from a recent international report.[24] The report draws attention to the fact that

> it is one thing for countries to make a policy decision to create an independent regulatory agency, and quite another to empower the agency to act independently and effectively ... Inevitably (regulatory agencies) are the products of political, social and legal conditions that exist at fixed points in time, in each country ... regulatory approaches and policies change, and agencies change with them. (International Telecommunications Union, 2001, p. 1)

Some might even doubt that investor-friendly regulatory policies will attract a substantial amount of private investment. As we have indicated, a large proportion of the financing of public utilities in Brazil was supplied by the BNDES using public money. Were the financially parlous state of the utilities sector to result in its progressive re-nationalization, then, in the absence of investor-friendly regulatory policies, much-needed increases in investment could only be implemented either through direct subsidies of consumers or through direct public sector capital investment. In other words, it is ironic that whether the administration of public utilities remains within the private sector or reverts to direct government control, in either case the resources of the state will always be required to sustain investment programmes. Of course, one might take the view that, whatever the role of the state in providing capital, these resources might be used more efficiently by privately administered entities.

THE REGULATORY STATE: THE DAWN OF A NEW STYLE OF INTERVENTION?

At the beginning of the twenty-first century it would seem that the major influence of the Brazilian state on the productive sector is through its regulatory agencies and through the development bank. Through regulation it influences the country's electric power supply, its telecommunications system, its rail and road transportation network, its oil exploration and production sector (both through the still publicly owned Petrobras and the regulation of the activities of foreign oil prospectors). In addition, the state development bank is still the major source of investment funds. Through these instruments – both as a regulator and as financier – the state continues to exercise a major influence over the development of these sectors. More specifically, given the existence of thin capital markets – which necessitate borrowing at subsidized interest rates – and regulated prices, two of the most important dimensions of the economic environment faced by 'privatized' enterprises are set by the state.

Above and beyond any regulatory or financing role, it should be remembered that the state has not entirely relinquished its position as the channel through which savings are accumulated (forced savings through pension funds) and then directed at favoured sectors. We have shown that among the most favoured sectors have been the privatized utilities and such industries as steel.

With a subdued domestic market, and the financially parlous state of many multinational utilities groups (especially in telecommunications), many enterprises in the Brazilian utilities sector have been experiencing liquidity problems which the state is increasingly less willing to address through favourable tariff adjustments. This may lead many of the concessionaires to abandon their contracts, in essence leading to a 're-nationalization' of the utility.

An interesting example of the difficult situation of the utilities sector is provided by the case of Eletropaulo, the São Paulo electricity distributor whose concession was obtained by the US group AES in 1998. AES has run into difficulties with its Brazilian subsidiary as tariffs and consequently revenues have failed to rise in line with the enterprise's debt payment obligations to its creditors, most especially the BNDES. Owing the BNDES US$1.13 billion, of which US$600 million is past due, AES has found itself – temporarily at least – unable to continue with its repayments, triggering heated negotiations between itself and the Bank. The regulatory and financial conflict between AES and organs of the Brazilian state has now become something of a test case regarding public policy response to the deteriorating condition of the utilities sector. Mindful of the implications for other foreign investors, the US State Department has become involved, with the US Ambassador to Brazil attempting to intercede.[25]

AES/Eletropaulo is not the only example of a foreign-owned utility in financial difficulties. In the case of the French-owned EDF, its Rio de Janeiro electricity distributor, LIGHT, owes more than US$125 million to a consortium of domestic and foreign banks.[26] In addition, the Minas Gerais-based distributor SEB/CEMIG (also partially owned by AES) is overdue on some US$87 million debt payment to the BNDES.

While in many regards the liberalization of the Brazilian telecommunications sector has proved more successful than in the case of electricity, the sector may nevertheless face serious problems. In particular, some enterprises will struggle to extract themselves from the trap of heavy indebtedness and lack of liquidity. These problems initially surfaced following the depreciation of the real in early 1999. Since then, a number of service providers have been struggling to meet their debt obligations, faced with a mismatch between foreign-currency-denominated debts and local-currency-denominated revenue streams. To make matters worse, revenues have been constrained by a combination of price regulation and the failure of market demand to expand to the extent originally anticipated. In the most recent casualty of these unfavourable conditions, the São Paulo cellular service operator BCP was taken over by its creditors in April 2003, forcing the exit of a major US shareholder, Bell South.

In order to prevent future recurrences of such cases, the authorities need to ensure that tariff alterations appropriately reflect the evolving cost base of telecommunications enterprises. On this score, the outlook for the sector is not especially favourable. In June 2003, hot on the heels of criticism from President da Silva himself, a series of legal injunctions overturned ANATEL-agreed tariff increases nationwide.[27] More troublingly still for ANATEL, a draft presidential decree released in May 2003 mandated the handing back of much responsibility for the oversight of the telecommunications sector from the regulatory agency to the Ministry for Communications. In particular, the decree requires that ANATEL be stripped of its decision-making functions in terms of tariff setting and the establishment of service obligation rules. So long as uncertainty continues to surround the regulation of the telecommunications sector, it is difficult to envisage a renewed wave of investment of the type experienced in the 1990s.

Instances such as this clearly raise an important issue for the government: can it any longer attract the bidding of new concessionaires, and in order to do this, would it be obliged to offer more generous tariff conditions? If any privatized enterprises should return to the hands of the public sector, would the state be in a position to run a deficit-generating public utility? If the latter, the implication may be a decline in the rate of return accruing to the investments of the 'forced savers' administered by the BNDES. In the past such a reduction may have been feasible against the backdrop of a relatively young population. Nowadays, however, with an ageing population relying increasingly on savings through the social security system, there would be less scope for such financing arrangements.

CONCLUSION

In this chapter we have shown that Brazil's economy in the aftermath of privatization has not become as fully exposed to market forces as one might have expected. All of the important public utilities sectors are subject to substantial regulation, and a large proportion of all productive sectors remain heavily dependent on the state for investment financing. We would not wish to claim that the post-privatization period has witnessed no meaningful alteration in the scope of state intervention in the productive sector. In particular it should be emphasized that privatized enterprises now have much greater control over their internal functioning, their cost base and, most important of all, the size and composition of their labour force, which is no longer subject to political interference.[28]

However, we have shown that a more populist stance in regulating public utilities and the precariousness of the debtors of the development bank (due to interest and exchange rate movements) may augur a period of progressive re-nationalization and, at the same time, could jeopardize the security of the forced savings of the public. It is thus clear that the evolution of the Brazilian productive sector will continue to be strongly conditioned by the actions of the state.

NOTES

1. For details see Baer (2001), Ch. 12 and Amann et al. (2002); also Baer (1969).
2. Baer (2001).
3. See Evans (1979); Amann (2000); Baer (2001).
4. Wells (1976); Werneck (1986).

5. Baer (2001), pp. 283–4.
6. Castelar Pinheiro (1999).
7. BNDES (2003).
8. Previ had by the end of the 1990s acquired a 13.8 per cent stake in CSN, Brazil's largest and oldest steel company (Amann et al., 2002).
9. For instance, among Previ's R$13.4 billion in total equity holdings in December 2002 the following privatized companies featured prominently: Acesita R$39 million; Brasil Telecom R$143 million; Eletropaulo R$22 million; Embraer R$852 million; CVRD R$307 million (Source: Previ Annual Report 2002).
10. BNDES (2000a), p. 9.
11. Landau (2002), p. 2.
12. For a comprehensive review of the rise of the regulatory state in alternative national contexts see Glaeser and Shleifer (2003).
13. In the city of Rio de Janeiro, for example, while the consumer price index rose by 189.7 per cent between August 1994 and February 2000, the price index for public services rose by 264.7 per cent.
14. BNDES (2000b).
15. Ibid.
16. BNDES (2000c).
17. In 1998 truck driver protests resulted in a 50 per cent reduction in tolls; in 1999 tolls were reduced between 20 and 28 per cent and in July 1999 there was a brief national truckers' strike demanding a toll reduction.
18. BNDES, Seminário de Privatização, November 2000.
19. Fleischer (2003).
20. International Telecommunications Union (2001). Another comprehensive review of the accomplishments in the telecommunications area can be found in a chapter by Siqueira in Lamounier and Figueiredo (2002), pp. 215–40. The same volume also contains a chapter on the accomplishments in the transport sector written by De Toledo, pp. 241–92.
21. Linhares Pires et al. (2002).
22. Brooks (2003).
23. This is also emphasized in a general survey of Latin America's electricity sector: see Fischer and Serra (2000), pp. 188–9; Spiller and Cardilli (1997) and Spiller and Viana-Martorell (1996).
24. International Telecommunications Union (2001).
25. *Estado de São Paulo* (2003); *Jornal do Brasil* (2003).
26. VALOR, 2 Julho de 2003, p. B 1.
27. A 41.7 per cent readjustment of rates which had been authorized by ANATEL was suspended by the Court of Justice of Rio de Janeiro: *Jornal do Brasil*, 30 June 2003, p. A7.
28. In the case of the railroad sector, for example, employment since privatization has declined substantially. Employment in that part of the railroad network formerly controlled by the RFFSA has fallen from 28 639 in 1996 to 12 807 in 2000 (Ministério de Transportes, 2000).

REFERENCES

Amann, E. (2000), *Economic Liberalisation and Industrial Performance in Brazil*, Oxford and New York: Oxford University Press.
Amann, E., De Paula, G. and Ferraz, J. (2002), 'Ownership Structures in the Post-privatized Brazilian Steel Industry: Complexity, Instability and the Lingering Role of the State', mimeo, University of Manchester.
Baer, W. (1969), *The Development of the Brazilian Steel Industry*, Nashville, TN: Vanderbilt University Press.
Baer, W. (2001), *The Brazilian Economy, Growth and Development*, 5th edn, Westport, CT: Praeger.

BNDES (2000a), *Telecommunicações: Cenário Pós-Privatização no Brasil*, Rio de Janeiro: BNDES.
BNDES (2000b), *O Setor Elétrico Pós-Privatização no Brasil*, Rio de Janeiro: BNDES.
BNDES (2000c), *As Concessões Ferroviárias*, Rio de Janeiro: BNDES.
BNDES (2003), *Privatizações no Brasil*, Rio de Janeiro: BNDES.
Brooks, Bradley (2003), 'Brazil May Curb Regulators' Powers', *Washington Times*, 20 February.
Castelar Pinheiro, A.C. (1999), 'Privatização no Brasil: Por quê? Até onde? Até quando?', in F. Giambiagi and M. Mesquita Moreira (eds), *A Economia Brasileira nos Anos 90*, Rio de Janeiro: BNDES.
De Paula, G.M. (1998), 'Privatização e Estrutura de Mercado na Indústria Siderúrgica Mundial', unpublished doctoral dissertation, Instituto de Economia, Universidade Federal do Rio de Janeiro, Rio de Janeiro.
Estado de São Paulo (2003), 12 and 13 March.
Evans, P. (1979), *Dependent Development: The Alliance of Multinational, State and Local Capital in Brazil*, Princeton, NJ: Princeton University Press.
Fischer, R. and Serra, P. (2000), 'Regulating the Electricity Sector in Latin America', *Economia*, 1 (1), 155–98
Fleischer, D. (2003), *Brazil Focus*, 24 February.
Glaeser, E.L. and Shleifer, A. (2003), 'The Rise of the Regulatory State', *Journal of Economic Literature*, **XLI** (2), 401–25.
International Telecommunications Union (2001), *Effective Regulation – Case Study: Brazil*, Geneva: International Telecommunications Union.
Jornal do Brasil (2003), 12 March.
Lamounier, B. and Figueiredo, R. (eds) (2002), *A Era FHC: Um Balanço*, São Paulo: Cultura Editores Associados.
Landau, G.D. (2002), 'The Regulatory–normative Framework in Brazil', *Policy Papers on the Americas*, **XIII** (April), Study 2, Washington, DC: Center for Strategic and International Studies.
Linhares Pires, J.C., Giambiagi, F. and Sales, A.F. (2002), 'As perspectivas do setor eletrico após o racionamento', *Revista do BNDES*, **18** (Dezembro), 163–203.
Ministério de Transportes (2000), *Relatórios Trimestrais de Acompanhamento de Concessões*, Brasília: Ministério de Transportes.
Spiller, P. and Viana-Martorell, L. (1996), 'How Should it be Done? Electricity Regulation in Argentina, Brazil, Uruguay and Chile', in R.G. Gilbert and E.P. Kahn (eds), *International Comparisons of Electricity Regulation*, Cambridge: Cambridge University Press, 82–125.
Spiller, P. and Cardilli, C.G. (1997), 'The Frontier of Telecommunications De-regulation: Small Countries Leading the Pack', *Journal of Economic Perspectives*, **11** (4), 127–38
Wells, J. (1976), 'Underconsumption, Market Size and Expenditure Patterns in Brazil', *Bulletin of the Society for Latin American Studies*, No. 24, March.
Werneck, R.F. (1986), 'Poupança estatal, divida externa e crise financeira do setor público', *Pesquisa e Planejamento Econômico*, **16** (3).

6. Brazilian regulatory agencies: early appraisal and looming challenges

Andrea Goldstein and
José Claudio Linhares Pires

What are we doing in practice? Creating regulatory agencies, a new State. And when I say regulation, I mean a radicalization of democracy. Improved control deepens democracy.

Fernando Henrique Cardoso (1997)

Brazil is undergoing an institutional transition in which the provision of public services, long the domain of state monopolies, is increasingly in the hands of the private sector. A core element in this process has been the creation of a new form of public sector institution – the regulatory agency – with supposed operational and financial autonomy. Regulatory agencies operate in an environment characterized by technical complexity and are required to handle arbitrage conflicts and potential clashes of interests with other government bodies. At the same time, regulatory agencies face the constant need to avoid regulatory capture, an ever-present risk given their repeated interaction with a restricted number of private firms. Despite the short timespan of Brazil's regulatory agencies,[1] they have produced a considerable volume of regulatory decisions and their media profile is relatively high. While some articles have provided *ex ante* assessments of the normative framework in which regulators operate, this chapter is among the first studies to analyse their activity in detail.[2]

The objectives of this chapter are twofold:

- to evaluate the performance of Brazil's three largest regulatory agencies – those for electricity (ANEEL – Agência Nacional de Energia Elétrica – National Electrical Energy Agency), natural gas and oil (ANP – Agência Nacional de Petróleo – National Petroleum Agency), and telecommunications (ANATEL – Agência Nacional de Telecommunicações – National Telecommunications Agency);
- to analyse the main challenges so as to formulate policy proposals aimed at improving regulator performance, and also to draw lessons for other industries that are still in the process of establishing regulatory arrangements.

The organization of the chapter is as follows. First, on the basis of a selective review of the economic literature on regulation we define a few analytical criteria. In particular, following Berg (2000) and Levy and Spiller (1994), we distinguish between regulatory incentives – i.e. behaviours that should be regulated and mechanisms for developing and enforcing rules – and regulatory governance – i.e. how new regulatory agencies are insulated from ongoing political pressures, while utilizing processes that promote participation, transparency and predictability. Next, we sketch out the main characteristics of the Brazilian regulatory experience and study the process leading to the appointment (and sometime the renewal in office) of the agencies' directors,[3] their relationship with other government bodies and state-level regulatory bodies and, more generally, the political economy of Brazilian regulation. Finally, we proceed to analyse the agencies' most important decisions – resolutions (*resoluções*), decrees (*portarias*) and administrative acts (*atos administrativos*). Following Artana et al. (1998), we assess:

- whether the interventions have been based on the terms set in the original contracts or on their subsequent modification;
- whether decisions have been motivated by an expected event and/or contractual imperfections;[4]
- whether the decisions have been challenged by the enterprises (or other interested parties), how such disputes have been solved, and who has been involved in this process.

In the conclusions we place Brazil in a comparative perspective and identify the main challenges for policymakers.

A GENERAL FRAMEWORK TO ASSESS UTILITIES' REGULATION

Utilities differ from other (formerly) state-owned firms because they have natural monopoly components. Thus the welfare benefits of transferring ownership to a private investor may not be large if the utility continues to act as a monopolist. As Galal et al. (1994, p. 579) note: 'it is an essential truth that trading a public monopolist for its unregulated private equivalent is not guaranteed to enhance either the enterprise's efficiency or the government's chances of being kept in office by satisfied consumers'. This is why it is argued that privatization must be accompanied by regulatory reform and that – because of the nature of the services supplied by the utilities (assets' specificity and non-tradability) – this process hinges on the (prior or simultaneous) development of safeguarding institutions (Spiller, 1993). These must improve *regulatory governance*, signalling policymakers' commitment not to engage in opportunistic behaviour and reassuring potential and actual investors against the risk of administrative expropriation of their assets. This in turn reduces the regulatory risk and interest rate premia on financial markets. Specific norms on issues such as market structure, tariffs and interconnection rules constitute the *regulatory incentives.*

Those with a significant interest in a decision incur costs when negotiating the amelioration of a market failure, so regulation is best viewed as a contracting problem. Political and social institutions not only affect the ability to restrain administrative action, but also have an independent impact on the type of regulation that can be implemented, and hence on the appropriate balance between commitment and flexibility. In particular, to complement regulatory procedures in a welfare-enhancing way, three mechanisms restraining arbitrary administrative action must be in place. According to Levy and Spiller (1994) these are: (a) substantive restraints on the discretion of the regulator; (b) formal or informal constraints on changing the regulatory system; and (c) institutions that enforce the above formal – substantive or procedural – constraints.

These principles are relatively general. All around the world, issues in the reform of regulatory governance include the designation of regulatory authorities, the definition of their powers, the provision of guarantees against unmotivated removal, the scale of financial autonomy, the choice of the tariff-setting formula, the existence of fora to arbitrate disputes, and the role of the existing antitrust authority in monitoring access to networks. In developing countries, agencies may be more permeable to the temptation of kick-backs, as the state is weak and civil servants' salaries are often low in absolute terms and always lower than in regulated firms. The recipe is therefore rather simple: introduce meritocratic recruitment and pay competitive salaries. A final issue concerns the degree of discretion. While clear mandates which specify limits, either through licences or through legislation, may reduce the risk of expropriation, rules such as price caps and incentive schemes demand some flexibility in order to adapt to ever-changing technology and demand circumstances.

There is then an important trade-off between constraining discretion and retaining the flexibility to pursue efficiency and other goals. Thus, unless the country's institutions allow for the separation of arbitrariness from useful regulatory discretion, systems that grant too much administrative discretion may underperform in terms of investment and welfare.[5] Smith (1997b) argues that the allocation of responsibilities between agencies and ministries should be decided on the basis of four factors: (a) whether political or technical criteria should take precedence; (b) whether significant conflicts of interest may occur through the sharing of responsibilities; (c) whether there are learning-by-doing effects and economies of scope that may favour concentration of responsibilities; and (d) whether political authorities have confidence in the agency.

The discussion so far has hinted at the importance of a 'transaction costs political economy' which would give an active and central role to institutional design (Estache and Martimort, 2000). The normative and positive agenda, however, should not be limited to the 'depoliticization' of the economy by strengthening the rules on bureaucratic conduct and setting up independent agencies (Chang, 2002). In the public domain individuals have motivations other then pure self-seeking, though as Smith (1997a) puts it, 'persons appointed to these positions must have personal qualities to resist improper pressures and inducements. And they must exercise their authority with skill to win the respect of key stakeholders, enhance the legitimacy of their role and decisions, and build a constituency for their independence.' Equally important, the rights and obligations that underlie markets are political constructs and result from political struggle.

A GENERAL OVERVIEW OF THE BRAZILIAN REGULATORY EXPERIENCE[6]

The pre-privatization regulatory regime, by giving state-owned enterprises (SOEs) planning and policy execution responsibilities, clearly blurred the relationship between the regulator and the regulated, allowing a high degree of discretion in the exercise of monopoly power. Moreover, regulatory competencies were split among several ministries, local authorities, public companies and national committees, except for administered price setting, which has been the responsibility of a single government committee, the CIP (Conselho Interministerial de Preços – Interministerial Price Council). The practice of hiring bureaucrats from the SOEs also did little to foster the development of independent and autonomous capacities within regulatory bodies. Pricing decisions were often subordinated to macroeconomic or social policy objectives, such as inflation control or equity considerations. None of these objectives was achieved, but long-run inefficiencies nevertheless did result. Moreover, while Brazil has had a competition law since 1962, CADE's (Conselho Administrativa de Defesa Economica – Administrative Council for Economic Defence, Brazil's main antitrust agency) action remained subdued for many years. The modern era of competition policy in Brazil only began in 1994, when a new competition law was enacted, granting independence to CADE.[7]

Between 1994, when the sell-off process started in earnest with the disposal of state assets in the steel industry, and 1998, when the sale of Telebrás made Brazil by far the world's largest privatizer, almost 170 SOEs were transferred to the private sector and total revenues amounted to close to US$83 billion. As far as the three industries under examination are concerned, regulatory incentives are clearly different. In telecommunications, a master plan released in late 1995 pointed to the benefits of competition and privatization in hitting the target of almost doubling the number of phone lines. It was only in July 1997, however, that Congress finally approved the General Telecommunication Law (LGT – Lei Geral de Telecommunicações). The law, which affects telephony, does not cover cable TV or radio broadcasting.[8]

The period following the implementation of the LGT saw rapid change. First, the telecommunications system was completely reorganized by grouping the 27 operators in three separate holdings (one of which serves São Paulo state); by carving up mobile telephony into nine regional A-band operators competing with B-band private concession-holders; and by establishing the long-distance carrier Embratel as a separate holding. Second, the master plan's goals – increasing fixed lines by 89 per cent (by 2001) and wireless lines by 148 per cent (by 2003) – were incorporated in the new Universalization Plan, that the new operators are expected to follow. Third, the mechanism for differentiated sharing of long-distance revenue between Embratel and the operators of individual states was replaced by a tariff-based interconnection for long-distance calls.[9] Fourth, an RPI-X formula was established. For the tariffs of fixed-line companies, the X-factor was set equal to zero for the 1998–2002 period, but equal to 10 for interconnection charges, in order to allow new competitors (the concessionaires of so-called mirror, or *espelho*, licences) to challenge the incumbent. The state-owned incumbent, Telebrás, was sold very successfully in July 1998. Two *espelho* local concessions were then granted on 14 January 1999 to compete with the former Telebrás holdings until 2002, when entry into the Brazilian telecoms market would become unrestricted.[10] July 1999 saw the launching of the multi-carrier system that allows consumers to choose their long-distance carrier.

The 1993 electricity reform created a single transmission system to unify the national grid and provide open access to all suppliers.[11] In September 1997 a report commissioned by the government from an international consultancy recommended some standard measures for electricity privatization, such as a gradual unbundling of the assets of Eletrobrás, the state-owned incumbent utility. The report also called for the creation of a wholesale power market and the operation of the transmission network by an independent operator (possibly to remain state-owned) (MME, 1997). Except for the Angra nuclear reactors and for Brazil's stake in Itaipú, the federal government sought to privatize all generation and distribution companies – an objective that it has largely fulfilled. Following the introduction of rules on unbundling and on access to the transmission network, industrial users with consumption in excess of 10 MWh (3 MWh since mid-2000) can purchase power in the recently established wholesale market (Mercado Atacadista de Energia Elétrica, MAE). In this market, short-term electricity transactions not covered by bilateral contracts take place. New investment in hydroelectric and thermal generation is governed at the federal level by the concession regime, while entry regulation in gas distribution, also through concession, is a state responsibility. For technological reasons, however, market competition in electricity finds its limit in the need to assure centralized coordination (planning and dispatch order). So, even in this more competitive setting, the MAE remains subject to the decisions of the National System Operator (Operador Nacional do Sistema Elétrico, ONS), a private non-profit body in charge of coordinating and controlling the operation of electricity generation and transmission facilities.

Finally, in the case of oil, where prices and quantities already responded to (international) market signals, the government strategy in the 1990s has been cautiously to open up new exploration opportunities to private participants, usually in partnership with Petrobrás, whose state-owned status remains unquestioned.[12] The situation is more complex in the case of gas. The Transportadora Brasileira Gasoduto Brasil–Bolívia (TBG), the Petrobrás subsidiary that operates the Brazil–Bolivia gas pipeline, maintains 20 years' contracts with separate clauses to determine dollar prices for gas and to index readjustments to the variation of oil prices on the world market. Increases in the price of gas are passed through by distributors, who define an overhead before charging the final consumers.

As far as regulatory governance is concerned, three new independent bodies have been created (Tables 6.1–6.4).[13] A positive feature is the fact that the regulatory regime is embodied in law, thus making it more difficult to change without a debate in Congress. The law-making process itself, however, substantially watered down the government's initial propositions, regarding for instance the regulators' ability to access information, provide firms with efficiency-enhancing incentives, and institute safeguarding mechanisms to protect against expropriation. Moreover, as will be made explicit below, the decision to create two separate agencies for the energy sector has brought serious inefficiencies, especially in so far as it has contradicted the goal of increasing the use of gas. Finally, only ANEEL, the electricity regulator, has signed a management contract detailing its operational targets.[14]

THE GENERAL CONTEXT: IDEAS, POLITICS AND INSTITUTIONS

Discussing the conditions for establishing a 'regulatory compact' requires a normative analysis, specifically concerning the optimal nature of norms and regulations in imperfectly competitive markets. An institutional analysis is

Table 6.1 Brazilian regulatory agencies: summary data

	ANATEL	ANEEL	ANP
Industry-wide regulation	Law 9472 (16 Jul. '97)	Law 8987 (13 Feb. '95)	Art. 177 of the Constitution
Founding legal act	Decree 2338 (7 Oct. '97)	Law 9427 (26 Dec. '96)	Law 9478 (6 Aug. '97)
Management contract	No	2 Mar. '98	No
Inauguration	5 Nov. '97	2 Dec. '97	16 Jan. '98
Headquarters	Brasília	Brasília	Rio de Janeiro
Regional offices	In each state	No	Brasília, São Paulo, Salvador
Number of directors	Director-General + 4	Director-General + 4	Director-General + 4
Background of Director-General	Renato Navarro Guerreiro: former Executive Secretary, Ministry of Telecommunications, and President of the Board of Directors, Telebrás.	José Mário Miranda Abdo: former Director-General, Departamento Nacional de Águas e Energia Elétrica.	David Zylbersztajn: Ph.D., Institut d'Economie et de Politique de l'Energie (Grenoble), former Energy Secretary, state of São Paulo
Number of employees	No more than 1496	No more than 325	No more than 657
Of whom graduates			
Of whom temporary consultants			
Of whom former civil servants			
Annual budget (R$ million) in 1999	278	106	439 (2000)
Source of funding	Telecom fiscalization tax (Fistel) + Budget Law	Electricity fiscalization tax + Budget Law	Concession fees + windfall gain tax + Budget Law

Source: Authors' elaboration.

Table 6.2 *Regulatory incentives*

	ANATEL	ANEEL	ANP
Sector characteristics	Markets	Markets	State-owned enterprise and markets
Type	Fully competitive	Partially competitive	Vertically integrated state monopoly
Extent of monopoly		In transmission and distribution	Prospecting concessions, wholesale distribution
Extent of competition	Favour new entrants through regulatory asymmetry	In generation and commercialization	
Granting of licences and concessions	No	Yes	Yes
Tariff setting (formula, frequency)	Price cap over a basket of services (until 2001); possibility for the agency to free companies from this requirement	Price cap in distribution, revenue cap in transmission. Annual adjustment + revision every 4 years	Ministries of Finance and Mining/Energy (until 31 Dec. 2001?). Gas tariffs are determined by state governments
Contractual objectives			
Quality standards	Yes	Yes	Yes
Investment targets	Yes	No	Yes
Meeting demand needs	Yes (universalization)	Yes	No

Table 6.2 (continued)

	ANATEL	ANEEL	ANP
Contractual requirements			
Access to essential facility	Free negotiation	Yes	Partially
Universalization	Yes	No	No
Review of anti-competitive conduct	Control, prevent, and sanction anti-competitive behaviours, without infringing CADE's legal responsibilities	Avoid the exercise of monopoly power through restrictions on market participation. No agent can (a) control more than 20% of nationwide capacity or distribution (25–35% at the regional level) and (b) have cross-ownership in generation and distribution in excess of 30%. Distribution companies can self-generate 30% of their own consumption	Informs CADE and SDE about anti-competitive behaviour

Source: Authors' elaboration.

Table 6.3 Formal safeguards of Brazilian regulatory agencies

	ANATEL	ANEEL	ANP
Legal mandate (freedom from ministerial control)	Yes	Yes	Yes
Criteria for appointment	No specific requirements, but rules to prevent conflict of interest	No specific requirements, but rules to prevent conflict of interest	No specific requirements, but rules to prevent conflict of interest
Appointment process	By the President of Brazil, following approval of his proposal by Senate	By the President of Brazil, following approval of his proposal by Senate	By the President of Brazil, following approval of his proposal by Senate
Staggering terms	No, except for the first Board	Yes	Yes
Length of mandate	5 years	4 years	4 years, renewable
Terms of removal	Upheld sentence or administrative sanction	Unmotivated in the first four months only; motivated at any time (upheld sentence, administrative sanction, unmotivated failure to comply with management contract)	Unmotivated

Table 6.3 (*continued*)

	ANATEL	ANEEL	ANP
Quarantine	A former director cannot make a complaint to the Agency on behalf of any actor for the 12 months following the end of the mandate	A former director cannot work for any company in the electricity sector for the 12 months following the end of the mandate. During this period s/he remains an employee of the Agency	A former director cannot work for any company in the oil sector for the 12 months following the end of the mandate. During this period s/he remains an employee of the Agency
Exemptions from civil service salary rules	Yes	Yes	Yes

Source: Authors' elaboration.

124

Table 6.4 *Accountability of Brazilian regulatory agencies*

	ANATEL	ANEEL	ANP
Transparency Open decision-making	Public hearings and sessions	Public hearings and sessions	Public hearings and sessions
Publication of proceedings	Yes	Yes (minutes)	Yes
Justification of decisions	No	No	No
Consultative/advisory boards	12-member Conselho Consultivo	No	No
Ouvidor	Yes	Yes	Yes
Appeal procedures	Agency, ordinary justice	Agency, ordinary justice	Agency, ordinary justice
Grounds of appeal (error of fact or of law, incl. failure to follow a required process)	Decisions are subject to three levels of internal administrative appeals	Decisions are subject to three levels of internal administrative appeals	Decisions are subject to three levels of internal administrative appeals
Scrutiny of the budget	No	No	No
Management contract	No	Yes	No
Scrutiny of conduct	Internal auditing, Congress (with General Accounting Office – Tribunal de Contas da União), ordinary citizens can appeal to justice	Internal auditing, Congress (with General Accounting Office – Tribunal de Contas da União), ordinary citizens can appeal to justice	Internal auditing, Congress (with General Accounting Office – Tribunal de Contas da União), ordinary citizens can appeal to justice

Source: Authors' elaboration.

also required, tackling the question of the conditions required such that future public regulation can be made more effective than the direct state intervention of the past. The perspective employed in this chapter is informed by the idea that political institutions interact with regulatory processes and economic conditions in exacerbating or ameliorating the potential for administrative expropriation or manipulation, and hence determining the utilities' economic performance. Core elements of the institutional endowment include informal norms and values, legislative and executive bodies, and judicial power (Abdala, 2000).

The impact of values on economic policies has been studied extensively in the case of trade policy, especially in the USA (Goldstein, J., 1993), though much less so in other policy domains. There is no doubt, however, that the leeway that regulatory agencies have in implementing their mandate is constrained not only by their institutional embeddedness but also by the degree of acceptance that the populace – and the elites in particular – have for their autonomy. The conventional wisdom, often found in the financial press, is that in Brazil the ideology of state-led development – even at the cost of macroeconomic imbalances – remains deeply rooted and that market reforms find their limit there. The picture is more nuanced and points to the prevalence of contingent priorities over generic, ideological goals. McDonough's (1981) seminal contribution demonstrated the existence of complex cleavages in the elites, especially regarding the trade-offs between capital accumulation and social equity. Studying a more recent period, Kingstone (1999) has also high-lighted how two powerful sectors of the elite, industrialists and business associations, have by and large supported trade opening. However, such support has been dependent on perceptions of the ability of government leaders to deliver on their promises.

That pragmatism has informed the attitude of societal interests that had long enjoyed the benefits of protection by the state from market pressures is clear when looking at the political economy of Brazilian privatization. Indicators as diverse as opinion polls, electoral success of market reformers, and frequency of strike actions, directly or indirectly related to the sell-off programme, all show that in Brazil ownership transfer has not elicited strong passions (Goldstein, A., 1999). This is not to say, however, that privatization is being supported wholeheartedly. By August 1999, the difference between supporters and opponents of privatization was statistically insignificant in tele-coms and road transport, and negative in electricity.[15]

By turning internal bureaucratic conflicts into formal legal processes, regulatory agencies can facilitate the transition from populist democracy to rule-based state regulation.[16] Legislative and executive bodies can constrain the action of regulatory authorities, usually limiting their independence and/or making it more costly for them to gain credibility *vis-à-vis* investors and other

stakeholders. While it is intuitive that a credible government willing to coop-
erate with a Congress with a common political platform makes the regulators'
life less complex, there is no clear-cut formula to determine the optimal political regime. Spiller (1999) identifies three key issues – the centralization of
decision-making, the extent of discretionary powers and the degree of procedural specificity – and argues that, depending on the country, various combinations may maximize institutional credibility. Indeed, almost a decade after
the virtues of insulated bureaucracies were influentially extolled as a building
block for economic transformation (Williamson, 1994), this thesis has been
questioned as too mechanical.

In Brazil, the executive has exercised almost unchallenged leadership in
designing and implementing the programme of privatization. As in many other
countries, the 1990s have seen a rising resort to temporary decrees to advance
the policy goals of the government; interestingly, this has not reflected the need
to by-pass Congress, which, quite on the contrary, has rarely been strong enough
to amend government proposals (Almeida, 1999).[17] For this reason, in Brazil
challenges to regulatory politics may stem less from excessive politicization and
more from the lack of effective mechanisms allowing coherent bargaining over
policy design. In other words, so far as regulatory decisions are concerned, the
executive may be under too little pressure to hear signals from other parties and
to search for compromise. Hence, ill-advised decisions may result.

There is, however, an element in the public administration that has consistently opposed reforms. The Brazilian judicial system has traditionally func-
tioned rather badly, with a poor track record in upholding private property or
contracts and a statistically significant negative impact on growth (Pinheiro,
2000).[18] As shown in Table 6.5 (which does not portray the particularly heated

Table 6.5   Judicial interventions in the privatization process, 1991–97

Sector	Number of privatizations	Number of cases
Steel	8	92
Chemical	14	105
Fertilizers	4	35
Electricity	6	35
Railroads	1	19
Mining	1	148
Banking	1	4
Other	3	22
Total	38	460

Source: Data taken from Almeida (1999).

case of Banespa in 2000), the judiciary has repeatedly and consistently sided with plaintiffs seeking an injunction against the sale of state assets. Not surprisingly, judges are also opposed to relinquishing their powers to independent authorities. More than half of magistrates consider that courts should not refrain from overhauling the decisions of the agencies, not only on procedural but also on substantive grounds (Pinheiro, 2001, Table 22).

REGULATION IN BRAZIL: AN EARLY APPRAISAL

The previous sections have shown the large steps taken in the second half of the 1990s in reducing the role of the state in the Brazilian economy, the scrupulous adoption of the lessons from international experience concerning the design of the regulatory agencies, and the institutional and political conditions that have surrounded the whole process. Here, on the basis of Table 6.6, which provides a synoptical view of the ten most important decisions taken by the agencies, we analyse the regulators' behaviour.

ANATEL

Our analysis of this agency is based on decisions concerning ownership changes, fulfilment of interconnection conditions and redefinition of the regulatory environment in the mobile phone market. It is important to emphasize that in this sector the dynamics of technological progress and wide differences in corporate strategies make our task relatively difficult, since it is not easy to separate regulatory failures from strategic errors made by managers. In its decision-making, ANATEL has been helped by the fact that clear sectoral rules had been set before its creation. None the less, it has also faced obstacles that could undermine its credibility: (a) the operators' initial difficulty in meeting quality objectives, given the simultaneous fast expansion of services supply;[19] (b) the adoption of new technical norms to introduce competition in long-distance intraregional telephony one year after the introduction of the new industry framework; (c) the threat of losing control over the Universalization Fund to the Ministry of the Communications;[20] (d) the fact that, in a context of fast technological convergence, ANATEL does not exercise regulatory governance over radio and TV services, whose concession is the responsibility of Congress; and (e) lack of competition in local fixed-line phone services because the 'mirror firms', that were created after Telebrás's privatization, have little power in the local market.

The LGT prohibits a single operator from owning shares in a controlling consortium in more than one region. ANATEL has taken three decisions in this area and has even signed an agreement with the National Securities

Table 6.6   The main decisions taken by Brazilian regulatory agencies

Event	Type of contractual revision	Subjective evaluation of the decision	Adequacy of contractual design	Context in which the decision was taken	Visibility of the decision	Participation
ANATEL						
1. Share sale	Intervention in the CRT's board (20 June 2000 until 27 June 2001)	Right: application of sector's law avoided market concentration	Adequate: applied LGT	Conflict of interest, judiciary appeals	Average	Industry, state and federal governments
2. Redefinition of mobile phone regulation	ANATEL resolution No. 253 (21 December 2000)	Right: supported convergence	Adequate: applied the General Concession Plan	Conflict of interest between incumbent and challengers	High	Public hearings with industry participants
3. Interconnection rights	ANATEL arbitrations (several between 1998 and 2001)	Right but insufficient: strong information asymmetry	Insufficient: the lack of reference tariffs made free negotiation difficult	Conflict of interest between incumbent and challengers, judiciary appeals	Average	ANATEL's Câmara de Arbitragem
ANEEL						
4. Escelsa's tariff revision	ANEEL resolution No. 246 (3 August 2001)	Right: included productivity gains in pricing formula and started timid readjustment	Insufficient: the revision was not foreseen in the concession contract, thus risk of opportunism and hold-up	Erosion of consumers' trust in the agency, black-outs in various parts of Brazil	High	Public hearings with industry participants and consumers

129

Table 6.6 (continued)

Event	Type of contractual revision	Subjective evaluation of the decision	Adequacy of contractual design	Context in which the decision was taken	Visibility of the decision	Participation
5. Pass-through of increases in distributors' non-controllable costs	Non-application of clause in the concession agreement (several between 1998 and 2001)	Wrong: created a hold-up problem that increased regulatory risk	Insufficient: the concession agreement does not clarify terms for pass-through	Erosion of investors' trust in the agency, inflationary pressures, intervention of Finance Ministry	High	Public hearings with industry participants and consumers, judiciary appeals
6. Intervention of the MAE	ANEEL resolutions Nos 160, 161 and 162 (20 April 2001)	Right but overdue: overcome a deficiency in the model	Insufficient: MAE is a private concern	Energy crisis and erosion of investors' trust in the agency	High	Threat of judiciary appeals
ANP						
7. Exploration and production licence tenders	Public tenders (June 1999, 2000 and 2001)	Right: boosted competition	Adequate, application of Oil Law	Conflict of interest between Petrobrás and challengers	High	Industry participants

8. Free access to the Bolivia–Brazil gas pipeline	Decision of the Director-General based on decree No. 8 (18 January 2001, 14 February 2001 and 16 April 2001)	Right but insufficient: unsustainable boost to competition	Insufficient: lacking a Gas Law, ruling is not sufficient to break entry barriers	Conflict of interest between Petrobrás and challengers	Average	Only interested parties (Enron, Gaspetro)
9. Withdrawal of licences of fuel distributors	ANP resolution of 26 December 2000	Correct	Adequate	Conflict of interest between incumbents and challengers, protect consumers	Average	None
ANEEL/ANP 10. Emergency measures to overcome the energy crisis	Resolutions of the Comitê de Gestão da Crise de Oferta de Eletricidade (21 resolutions between 16 May and 26 June 2001)	Necessary but far from perfect: trade-off between policy coordination and agencies' independence	Industry laws did not make it possible to ensure supply expansion and coordination	Various conflicts of interest	High	Government bodies, industry participants

Source: Authors' elaboration.

Commission (Comissão de Valores Mobiliários, CVM) to improve its understanding of corporate finance issues. The first intervention concerned the acquisition of Telesp by Telefónica,[21] the Spanish group which had already bought CRT, a company independent from the Telebrás group that provides local fixed telephony services in the state of Rio Grande do Sul. A series of conflicts had erupted between the shareholders of CRT and Brasil Telecom – which operates in the same region as Telesp, already held 8 per cent of the latter's ordinary shares, and was also interested in gaining control. As these were delaying the sale of shares in the CRT consortium, ANATEL first considered the possibility of suspending the licence and eventually took over the company in June 1999 to verify the possible existence of legal, regulatory, or contractual wrongdoings by CRT or its controlling shareholders. After a tense legal battle – which also involved the state government – and under pressure from the agency's president and the Minister of Telecommunications, Brasil Telecom finally agreed to pay US$800 million to gain control.[22] This unusual situation has shown the costs associated with failing to appoint an arbitrator to settle the dispute.

In other interventions, ANATEL was concerned about the effects in Brazil of the planned global merger between Sprint and MCI – both of which already had stakes in the two long-distance operators. ANATEL suspended the voting rights of Macal Investimentos on the board of directors of Telemar, in September 1999, as it suspected the former of transferring its shares to Grupo Garantia before the expiration of the five-year grace period set by the LGT.[23]

The second important event concerns the terms of interconnection. The international experience of the last decade clearly shows that the market power of the incumbent firm makes it very difficult to introduce competition in the market for infrastructure. In the case of telecoms, in particular, the incumbent has strong monopoly power over the local loop, so that its position will hardly be challenged unless the regulator proactively seeks to promote access by setting the rate of interconnection on the basis of marginal cost. This is a key issue in Brazil, where the local monopolist in one given region can also provide long-distance data transmission and Internet services in others, so that the terms of interconnection can give rise to a set of strategic games played in different markets.

The LGT allows free negotiation between the parties and foresees an intervention by the agency only at the parties' request. However, information asymmetries between the parties have increased transaction costs and opportunistic behaviour in negotiating interconnection agreements. ANATEL, moreover, lacks the experience to operate in this environment. When Embratel appealed against a set of decisions by the Arbitration Chamber of ANATEL that had favoured mobile phone operators in various regions, ANATEL denied it a suspension of the rulings. At the same time, Embratel asked the agency to arbitrate in its dispute with local concessionaires over the use of the 'last mile' to supply high-speed Internet access. As local fixed-telephony operators enter the Internet service providers' (ISP) market, more disputes will emerge. Embratel charges a capacity rent – and not a tariff, as it does in basic phone services – for the use of its backbone, which already accounts for almost two-thirds of total traffic. Only learning-by-doing by both regulators and the private sector will change this situation.

ANATEL's activity in the area of competition is made easier by the fact that it is the only agency empowered to prepare a case and refer it to CADE. In the other instances, the responsibility to prepare cases falls under the duties of the SDE in the Ministry of Justice.[24] This power gives it more flexibility and efficiency to oppose mergers that amount to an abuse of market power and produce anti-competitive behaviours. The action of ANATEL in regulating competition and arbitraging conflicts, however, finds its limit in the Brazilian institutional context. For example, in July 2000 ANATEL ruled that the revenue for fixed-to-mobile calls made between June 1998 and July 1999 belonged to the long-distance operator and forced Telefonica to pay some US$20 million to Embratel.[25] Telefonica successfully appealed the decision in court.

The third and final event refers to the auctions for licences to provide personal mobile communications service (Serviços Móveis Pessoais, SMP).[26] The Lei Mínima carved the country into respectively nine and ten areas for the A and B mobile telephony bands; for local fixed services the Plano Geral de Outorgas, as foreseen in the LGT, created a duopoly in three multi-state regions; and finally, long-distance calls are supplied at the national level. In setting up the SMP model, ANATEL has tried to induce convergence between fixed and mobile operators and the creation of conglomerates of sufficient size to exploit economies of scale. The licences for C, D and E bands are to operate in areas which cover regions that are different from those of fixed telephony, while cellular phone companies licensed on bands A and B have been encouraged to migrate to the SMP standard.

Although the strategic interest of gaining access to the C, D and E band markets should be clear, the auctions have not yet been completed. Brazil has not escaped the negative fall-out of the worsening financial standing of the main global players, whose level of indebtedness has risen dramatically since 2000 as they overpaid for licences in Europe and the USA. The SMP model, moreover, is a so-called 2.5G technology, and investors have been cautious before committing large sums to an option that may be outdated in a short time. Despite these problems, there are indications that ANATEL has been at least partly successful in meeting its twin goals of convergence and consolidation – for example Telemar and Telecom Italia bought mobile licences in the same areas where they were already operating fixed services (see Table 6.7).

Table 6.7 Regional distribution of telecoms operators

Area	Mobile services				Fixed services	
	A Band	B Band	D Band	E Band	Concessionary	'Mirror'
REGION I						
Amazonas, Amapá, Pará, Maranhão and Roraima	Telesystem, Opportunity Pension Fund	Inepar	Telemar	Telecom Italia	Gutierrez, Inepar, Macal and others	Telecom Americas[1]
Alagoas, Ceará, Paraíba, Pernambuco, Piauí and Rio Grande do Norte	Telecom Italia[2]	Bell South				
Bahia and Sergipe	Telefonica	Telecom Italia				
Rio de Janeiro and Espírito Santo	Telefonica	Telecom Americas[1]				
Minas Gerais	Telesystem, Opportunity, Pension Fund	Telecom Italia				

REGION II					
Acre, Distrito Federal, Goiás, Mato Grosso, Mato Grosso do Sul, Rondônia and Tocantins	Splice	Telesystem, Telecom Americas[1]	Telecom Italia	No bidders as of 05/06/2001	Telecom Italia, Oportunity Pension Fund	GVT
Paraná e Santa Catarina	Telecom Italia	Inepar				
Rio Grande do Sul	Telefonica	Telesystem, Telecom Americas[1]				
REGION III						
São Paulo (Capital)	Portugal Telecom	Bell South	Telecom Italia	No bidders as of 05/06/2001	Telefonica	Telecom Americas[1]
São Paulo (Interior)		Telia				
REGION IV (Long distance fixed services)					MCI	France Telecom, National Grid

Notes:
[1] Joint venture between Bell Canada, SBC and Telmex.
[2] Telecom Italia had to renounce D and E bands' rights in order to respect the provision forbidding regional overlapping with A and B bands' frequencies.

Source: Based on BNDES data.

The number of players is likely to fall rapidly once the large fixed-line operators fulfil their expansion goals.

ANEEL

Four main reasons explain the much greater difficulties experienced by the electricity regulator in its operation:

(a) As ANEEL was established when the restructuring process had already started, its legitimacy in dispute settlement and arbitration is contested. The capacity to enforce obligations on the private sector was weak from the very beginning as the first two contracts with privatized distributors had been signed.
(b) As the process of privatization is still far from complete and some state-owned companies have strong market power in generation and transmission, the government's direct role as an investor (in generation and transmission) and indirect role as regulator gives rise to a conflict of interest. Furnas (an SOE), for example, was fined by ANEEL in September 2000 for not paying its debt to the MAE, but it has not complied so far.
(c) As most of ANEEL's top management is formed by former DNAEE (Departamento Nacional de Energia Elétrica – National Department of Electrical Energy) officials, the signal given to private investors is that the crux of the regulatory game still concerns technical, legal and operational issues, and not the creation of the economic incentives necessary to create a really competitive market.
(d) There is an insufficient degree of institutional coordination between ANEEL and ANP and the water agency, despite the fact that some important issues for the functioning of the electricity sector – such as the use of water rights or the structure of the gas industry – fall under the responsibility of other such bodies.

Reflecting all such factors, ANEEL has often lacked the flexibility to define key rules to encourage entry, to stimulate investment, and to increase electricity capacity. To give just one example, the delays accumulated in defining transmission charges or the pass-through mechanism for the purchase price of imported gas have slowed the start of the auctioning of licences for, respectively, new transmission lines and new-generation projects. In what follows we focus on three case studies, namely the revision of Escelsa's tariffs, the decision not to allow pass-through of distributors' non-controllable cost, and the decision to assume the management of the MAE.

Escelsa was the first electricity distribution company to be privatized by the federal government, well before the creation of ANEEL. Its concession contract was revised just three years after ownership transfer, reflecting the fact that in 1995 the regulatory environment was still very uncertain.[27] When it started to revise the contract, ANEEL was being criticized on account of the continuous blackouts around the country, in particular in Rio de Janeiro and Ceará. Because of these events, public opinion started questioning the logic of privatization and the tariff conditions set by the government. In particular, there was concern that the formula for final consumers did not include a productivity factor.

Conscious of the serious risk of a backlash, in the case of Escelsa ANEEL established a process of public consultation and deliberation. In real terms, the tariff was reduced by 3.4 per cent on average, while the rate structure for different users was also modified. In relation to the yearly tariff readjustments for 1999–2001, ANEEL decided to make these conditional on the fulfilment of additional targets for quality and universalization.[28] This action allowed users to share the benefits from the improvement in efficiency that privatization had brought about. Although the original contract did not take into account the increase in productivity – so that in theory ANEEL's intervention amounted to a hold-up – Escelsa's management welcomed it. A possible explanation is that the contract ended up being the same as those of the other distributors, although in such other cases the initial X in the RPI-X formula was equal to zero.

If, in this case, private investors did not complain about the intervention by ANEEL, the same cannot be said of its denial to the distributors' request to pass through increases in their non-controllable costs.[29] On several occasions ANEEL came out against the request by the concessionaires for extraordinary tariff revisions, for instance in January 2000 when Escelsa sought authorization for a 4.3 per cent increase to reflect the higher input costs. While acknowledging that non-controllable costs had indeed risen, ANEEL ruled that, even without the tariff revision, Escelsa's economic and financial position was not being placed in peril. The regulator's position mirrors that of the Ministry of Finance concerning the risk that price readjustments pose for inflation and the need to modify the reference index used in concession agreements.[30] In practice, by adopting an approach not foreseen in the contracts, ANEEL may have increased the regulatory risk, not least because a number of non-controllable costs did indeed increase dramatically. One cost index rose by more than 125 per cent in the first five months of 2001, although its weight in the distributors' cost structure is small.[31]

Of course the risk that regulatory agencies may lose credibility as a result of ill-advised choices is heightened in the case of Brazil. Because of its recent inflationary past, private investors, and foreigners in particular, are sensitive to any signal that government may tamper with tariff policy as a tool to fight inflation. To make things worse, before the debate on this issue formally started, ANEEL's director-general argued that, to avoid a pass-through of the 1999 revisions on inflation, the index used to quantify controllable costs could be altered, as could some clauses in the concession agreements.[32]

We now turn to the third event, the decision taken by ANEEL on 20 April 2001 to take over control of the MAE in order to 'increase the flexibility of negotiations in the electricity market, preserve competition, support investments to expand supply, and defend the public interest'.[33] Since its establishment, the operation of MAE has been marred by the conflicting interests of the state as regulator and producer and the vague definition of the enforcement regime for penalties.

Regarding the first factor, as the federal government owns the main generators, in practice it has failed to signal to other industry participants that it was expecting such companies to respond to the same pressures. As observed above, a clear indication in this sense has been the fact that when ANEEL fined Furnas US$240 million for its failure to respect an agreement with MAE to supply power generated at the Angra II nuclear plant, the company refused to comply. The second factor relates to flaws in MAE's governance structure, based on shared management by agents that intervene in the pool market at different stages. In this regard Brazil seems to share many problems with California. According to Besant-Jones and Tenenbaum (2001, pp. 12–18):

> the market and system operator must be genuinely independent in ownership and decision-making from market participants (generators, distributors, retail and wholesale suppliers and final customers). The governance system in California resembled a mini-legislature and . . . suggests four lessons. First, the board cannot be too large or it will be ineffective as a decision-making body. Second, the voting rules must ensure that one or two classes cannot control the board's decisions. Third, the regulator must be able to step in and make a decision if the board is dead-locked. Fourth, consumer representatives or advocates should be viewed as market participants.

The intervention has brought about three key changes:

(a) the MAE's Executive Committee (Coex), a collegiate body, has been suppressed and substituted by the Conselho do Mercado Atacadista de Energia (COMAE), managed professionally;[34]
(b) guarantees and penalties have been set for trading energy on the MAE, with an upper limit set at 10 per cent of a firm's total turnover; and
(c) the ASMAE, which was previously an independent and self-regulated institution, is now regulated and supervised by ANEEL.

ANEEL's decision is correct, although probably overdue considering that in two years no transactions have been concluded on the MAE.

ANP

The biggest difficulty encountered by ANP in establishing its credibility as the 'referee' in the market for oil and gas is the degree of market power exercised by Petrobrás in all upstream and downstream segments. A further limit stems from the fact that ANP is not responsible for the regulation of prices and tariffs. These, over the current transition period, remain under the control of the Ministry of Finance. A modification in the tax structure – in the sense of either creating a single tax on fuels or adding an extra rate, earmarked to the states, to the VAT on imports – is a prerequisite to phase out the so-called Fund of Compensation (Parcela de Preços Específica – Specific Pricing Package or PPE), the special formula that permits cross-subsidization between different refined products and covers Petrobrás against variation in the difference between the price of oil in Brazil and on the international market. Pursuant to the Oil Law's target of liberalizing fuel imports by August 2001,[35] ANP sent to Congress a package of constitutional revisions authorizing the imposition of duties on refined products, which were exempted by the 1988 Constitution. Until the PPE is removed, it is not possible to open the market to imports, since Petrobrás would be obliged to compete with companies that are not subject to the cross-subsidization requirement and could therefore underprice Petrobrás. But this process requires a constitutional amendment, which in turn has to be approved by a two-thirds majority in both congressional houses.

Yet, despite this great limit on its operational autonomy, so far ANP has successfully accomplished its mission of implementing the competitive model in the oil and gas industry. Our evaluation is based on the analysis of three key events: the tender for the exploration and production licences, the debate on the free access to the Bolivia–Brazil gas pipeline, and the closing down of fuel forecourts.

In July 1998 ANP issued the list of the oil exploration and production blocks left to Petrobrás and those to be tendered. Out of a total of 6 436 000 km^2 of blocks in 26 basins, only 7.1 per cent were retained by Petrobrás. One year later, the ANP started tendering for exploration, development and production licences. Three rounds were held between June 1999 and 2001 for a total of 103 blocks, bringing dozens of companies, including all the international majors, to drill for oil and gas both on and off shore.[36] While in the first round there was one only bidder for 15 blocks out of 27, one year later there was competition for 21 out of 23 blocks. Another difference between the two rounds – and a partial explanation for the more heated contests of 2000 than 1999 – is that the government initially imposed a high minimum price for licences. As a result no Brazilian company, except Petrobrás, took part in the first round, while some participated in the second and third, as did second-tier and smaller international companies.

This event should be viewed positively since ANP was responsible for surveying, delimiting and auctioning the blocks. In other words, despite the existence of transaction costs and strong information asymmetries – Petrobrás traditionally monopolized technical knowledge in the oil business in Brazil – ANP created a set of attractive assets. ANP is also playing an active role in monitoring the fulfilment of contractual obligations, as in the recent warning addressed to Coastal (an oil exploration enterprise) for not informing the agency of the discovery of gas in Bacia do Paraná.

The second event refers to the application of the free access principle – established by Article 58 of the Oil Law and regulated by ANP decree no. 169/98[37] – in the case of the Gasbol gas pipeline run by TBG. The agency initially set the transmission volumes at 1 million m³/day (between April and August 2001) for Enersil (controlled by Enron) and between 800 000 and 1 million m³/day (September 2001 to December 2003) for British Gas (BG).[38] ANP intervened following a request by these two companies, which alleged they were finding it difficult to close contracts with TBG. Enron asked for more gas delivery points along the TBG's pipeline as part of a contractual agreement signed with Petrobrás in September 2000. British Gas then asked for the same conditions. On 16 April 2001, ANP awarded BG transport rights from Bolivia to the state of São Paulo, in the form of firm contractual arrangements, to the tune of 700 000 m³/day for April–August 2001 and 2.1 million m³/day between September 2001 and December 2002. BG had requested that these conditions apply until December 2003, but ANP argued that, from that date, supply would be made in the form of interruptible contractual arrangements, i.e. that any interruption has to be notified to ANP for approval.

Because the pipeline is clearly a natural monopoly, ensuring free access is one key issue, possibly the most important, in promoting competition in the gas market. For this very reason, the ANP decision was right: as explained in its ruling, the agency found that TGB was preventing the sharing of the essential facility it controls.[39] TBG modified the original planning of the pipeline's maximum capacity in such a way that it could only respect the contracts signed with Petrobrás. Concerning the tariff applied on the BG–TBG firm contractual arrangement, ANP upheld the same criterion adopted in solving the conflict over interruptible contractual arrangements with Enron, that is, introducing a distance factor into the definition of the values between the source and the delivery location.

Our evaluation is that this measure will prove insufficient to guarantee full competition in the Brazilian gas market.[40] The only action that may avoid conflicts of interest and abuse of market power is the unbundling of Petrobrás, separating the transport facility from both upstream and downstream activities.[41] Contrary to ANATEL, ANP does not enjoy the power of preparing antitrust cases and CADE has not studied the sector so far. A further problem is that ANP's jurisprudence does not cover the distribution and marketing of gas, since for these activities the Constitution established a principle of subsidiarity, granting responsibilities to the states. The biggest challenge is to design an adequate model for the natural gas sector. In Brazil gas exploration is associated with oil, and Petrobrás has always treated the former as a complementary product of its main activity. The events of 1997 have not modified this situation and Petrobrás continues as a monopoly in gas exploration and transportation while distribution is in the hands of regional monopolies.

Finally, we examine the possibility that the decision to increase to 750 000 litres the minimum storage capacity directly owned by wholesale fuel distribution companies may have reduced competition by raising a barrier to entry and exit. ANP has defended its decree on the grounds that the excessive number of market participants – 409 in 1997, of which most were acting as intermediaries – made it impossible to exploit economies of scale and induced enterprises to increase financial margins by adulterating fuel and dodging taxes. As a result of the decree and of more efficient monitoring, the number of agents has fallen to 202, of which 194 have market shares of 0.1 per cent each.[42] In this sense, the possibly negative effects on competition have been more than offset by the reduced risk that consumers are jeopardized by opportunistic behaviour and predatory competition.

THE ENERGY CRISIS MANAGEMENT COMMITTEE (COMITÊ DE GESTÃO DA CRISE DE ENERGIA)

In 2001 the fortunes of the Brazil's energy sector – and more generally the credibility of the country's market liberalization programme – became overshadowed by power shortages that forced production cuts in industry and slowed economic growth. Although a discussion of the origins of the crisis goes well beyond the goals of this chapter,[43] the crisis has shown the limits of the institutional model adopted to regulate the energy sector, based on separate agencies for electricity and oil and gas. For the purposes of the present discussion, it is interesting to analyse the first joint decision taken by ANP and ANEEL, which, in June 2001, led to the adoption of the emergency programme to reduce energy consumption.[44]

The 1997 Law envisaged the creation of the National Energy Policy Council (Conselho Nacional de Política Energética, CNPE) to advise the Presidency of Brazil in the formulation of the national energy policy. The Law, however, did not foresee any role for either ANEEL or ANP, and at any rate the CNPE only became operational in June 2000.[45] Although increasing competition in power generation largely hinges on the greater use of gas, the lack of clear coordinating mechanisms has made it much more difficult to attain this goal. Decisions on at least two key issues – how to adjust the price for imported gas (by ANP) and how to define the maximum value of the pass-through (by ANEEL) – have been postponed. Added to the inefficiencies caused by Petrobrás's market power, this indefinition has created bottlenecks in supply that have paralysed new investment in gas-powered stations.

In May 2001, as the energy crisis worsened, the Comitê de Gestão da Crise de Energia (CGE), chaired by Pedro Parente, President Cardoso's Chief of Staff, was established.[46] As shown by the high number of resolutions approved (15 in the month to 15 June), the CGE has proven rather efficient in taking emergency measures to reduce consumption and increase supply – and has attracted positive comments from the business press.[47] By including a large number of ministries, departments and government agencies, however, the CGE has effectively taken over most of ANEEL's statutory responsibilities, such as setting the spot price on the MAE, marketing excess capacity produced by independent generators, and fixing objectives to curb consumption. The initial intention of extending the CGE's emergency powers by making it impossible to take legal action against its decisions, which was later over-turned by President Cardoso, is also rather questionable. Indeed, it would have been deeply in contrast to the desire, expressed in the quotation at the beginning of this chapter, to make regulatory efficiency a building block for a virtuous circle of democratic governance.

Although the CGE is also responsible for decisions in the gas industry, ANP has been able to gain increasing power and credibility, at least indirectly at the expense of ANEEL. The agency's director-general proposed the emergency plan that, with some changes, was finally preferred to a competing plan sponsored by ANEEL. In June 2001, ANP met another success when the CGE altered its initial decree – sponsored by the Ministries of Finance and Energy – setting the price conditions for supplying the new plants included in the Priority Thermoelectric Program (Programa Prioritário de Termeletricidade, PPT).[48] The intervention by ANP was motivated by the desire to remove certain elements in the original decree – such as the power for Petrobrás to set in dollars the tariff for transporting gas from Bolivia – that risked jeopardizing the entry of new market participants.[49] Then, on 13 June 2001, ANP refused to grant Petrobrás the right to expand by 10 million m³/day the gas volume shipped on the pipeline. In agreement with the CGE, it decided to put this right up for auction and to limit Petrobrás to 4 million m³/day. We think that this decision was right. The credibility of the agency increased in so far as it had demonstrated its unwillingness to sacrifice the long-term objective of creating a competitive market on the altar of any short-term solution needed to overcome the crisis.

CONCLUSIONS

In this chapter we have analysed the performance of Brazil's regulatory agencies from an institutional perspective. While undertaking a comparative assessment was not among the goals of this chapter, it is fair to conclude that Brazil has not performed worse than its peers. Simple indicators such as price, quantity and quality of services, as well as financial results and productive efficiency, all show across-the-board improvements.[50] In Table 6.8 we draw together the regulatory experiences of Brazil and three other countries: the United Kingdom for being a privatization pioneer, Argentina because it is a neighbour whose record Brazilian policymakers have closely studied, and Italy for being another country where utilities have been transformed in the second half of the 1990s. Three implications emerge from the international experience. First, agencies' success in gaining autonomy from the government, the regulated firms and consumers strengthens the regulatory environment. The second finding is that this process takes time and that learning-by-doing effects are sizeable. Third, as suggested by Levy and Spiller (1994), commitment can be developed even in what are *prima facie* problematic environments and that without such commitment long-term investment will not take place.

Of course this does not mean that all is well in Brazil. There are four main problems:

(a) insufficient coordination between different agencies;
(b) unclear definition of their respective competencies;
(c) lack of regulatory sovereignty; and
(d) inadequacies in design of the new antitrust agency.

Turning to the first of these problems, there are clear deficiencies in governance which hinder effective coordination between different regulatory bodies. Political infighting and lack of coordination between energy authorities have inhibited private sector investment and have been associated with periodic energy crises, with serious consequences for short-term economic prospects and perhaps even for the medium-term sustainability of reforms. While setting up the CGE has allowed the rapid implementation of emergency measures, this still represents an imperfect form of intervention. Over the long term, enhancing policy coherence and credibility requires the return of decision-making powers to the regulatory agencies, the consolidation of rule-making bodies and the achievement of superior coordination capabilities. In this sense it may be appropriate to transfer regulatory competencies over electricity and gas to a single agency – following the British example.[51] Indeed, as observed by one of the authors in another paper, even in the case of railways

Table 6.8 Regulatory agencies in selected countries: a comparative summary

	Argentina	Brazil	Italy	United Kingdom
Institutional endowment and regulatory design	While politicians have largely relinquished control on macroeconomic policy by adopting the currency board, they have kept discretionary powers in utilities' regulation	Neutral effect, although the judiciary may impact negatively on the performance of the agencies	Strong resistance by Parliament and the judiciary to the institution of independent authorities, governments in favour but weak	Supportive, although the choice of individual, rather than collegiate, regulators has been criticized
Regulatory governance	High degree of specificity of the contractual arrangement has made regulation individualized and politicized	Agencies have generally abided by the spirit of the respective industry laws; uneven development of due process procedures; the debate on how to improve accountability is still in its infancy;	The media regulator has dual responsibilities for telecoms and television and its cumbersome structure results in politicization of decisions; its procedures are rather murky, while	Excessive discretion has not encouraged consistency between regulators and adherence to common principles in addressing core issues; the Monopolies and Mergers Commission has reinforced the regulators' discretion

		lack of coordination between electricity and oil/gas regulators	those of the gas and electricity agency are very transparent	rather than constrained it
Regulatory incentives	The very generous conditions granted in some cases (telecoms and water in particular) are making it difficult to open up markets; the risk of reneging on signed contracts outweighs the possible benefits; the energy wholesale market is highly competitive	Competition has been introduced to the largest possible degree in telecoms, while the costs of the delayed sell-off of generators are proving sizeable	In electricity and gas the very limited dilution of state ownership in the integrated incumbents is delaying the introduction of competition; some asymmetrical competition in telecoms, although the privatized incumbent still has more than 90 per cent of the market	Achieving the current large degree of competition has required continuous adaptations (e.g. duopoly review in telecoms, British gas demerger); the RPI-X approach has resulted in excessive costs of capital and has tended to benefit investors over consumers

Sources: Abdala (2000) and Spiller (1999) for Argentina; this chapter for Brazil; Abate and Clô (2000), Pontarollo and Oglietti (2000) and Ranci (2000) for Italy; Domah and Pollitt (2001) and Helm (2000) for the United Kingdom.

the consolidation of the existing regulatory bodies into a new independent agency, whose mandate may extend to other transport industries, is an imperative given the powerful positions enjoyed by concessionaires (Estache et al., 2001).

Second, the need to better define each agency's competencies, while more evident in the energy sector, is also clear when observing the debate raging around the definition of the rules governing digital TV operations. As technologies and corporate strategies converge, Brazil requires a single point of contact to negotiate with industrial and financial investors and to set the rules over both media and telecommunications. Such a body may indeed be ANATEL, and clear benefits in terms of transparency and accountability may be derived from removing the right of granting licences from politicians – especially in Brazil where many members of Congress hold media concessions. There is, however, also a risk in completely isolating decision-making procedures. Society at large should have a voice and, while there is no reason to think that a regulatory agency is not the appropriate forum, its functioning should be adapted accordingly.

Third comes the issue of the legal status of the agencies' decisions, which in Brazil can be overturned by any judge (Araújo and Pires, 2000). A constitutional amendment is required so that the decisions of the regulatory bodies can be made equal to the ruling of a first-instance court. It is imperative to restrict the ability that parties currently enjoy to call on the judiciary to step into the fray and delay business decisions.

A fourth point has to do with the current debate over a single agency responsible for consumer protection and competition (Instituto Nova Cidadania, 2001; Oliveira, 2000; Pittman, 2001). The draft proposal to establish the National Consumer Defence and Competition Agency (Agência de Defesa do Consumidor e da Concorrência – ANC) contains positive developments in regulatory incentives – in particular the idea that mergers and acquisitions should be examined before, and not after, they are concluded. In light of the experiences analysed in this chapter, however, there are clear governance risks. Appointing a director-general, instead of a committee, may reduce transparency, *a fortiori*, if the mandate coincides with that of the President of Brazil, while the defence of competition and the protection of consumers are separate issues that should probably be left apart.

NOTES

1. ANATEL was established in 1997, ANEEL in 1996 and ANP in 1997.
2. FGV (2001) is similar to our chapter, although the focus is on specific contractual arrangements rather than the performance of the regulatory agencies. Mueller and Pereira (2000) is also similar in the use of an institutional approach, although their analysis is clearly *ex ante*.

In view of the theory's capacity to derive a number of interesting predictions about which interests will be represented, the extent to which the intensities of their stakes will be translated into effective political participation, and the relative allocation of rents by the regulatory process, it is not surprising that the empirical work (regardless of the specific approach) lags behind.

3. In the three agencies, directors have been changed at least once.

4. Since contracts are incomplete by definition, they may be renegotiated because numerous contingencies were unforeseen.

5. A mirror-image problem may occur when the agencies take the 'opportunity to engage in "shirking" – consciously failing to pursue the policy objectives that elected political leaders would desire' (Noll, 1989, p. 1277).

6. This section builds on, and expands, previous work by the authors, especially Goldstein, A. (1999), Pires (1999) and Pires and Piccinini (1999).

7. The 1994 law broadly resembles the competition laws of other countries, proscribing anti-competitive conduct, including single-firm conduct by monopolists or dominant firms and anti-competitive agreements and anti-competitive mergers. The Brazilian system is unique, however, in that, beyond CADE, two other government bodies, SDE in the Ministry of Justice and SEAE in the Ministry of Finance, are designated in the competition law as having principal advisory and investigative roles in competition enforcement. Cases are begun in SDE, which, with the assistance and advice of SEAE, conducts preliminary investigations and administrative proceedings before submitting the file and its recommendations to CADE, which renders the final judgment. CADE does have power to request further information from entities whose transactions or actions are being reviewed. According to a multi-country survey of regulatory bodies (Global Competition Review, 2000), this agency is warmly endorsed, although its independence – or at least its willingness to antagonize the government – has been questioned.

8. The 1996 lei minima governs cellular B-band 15-year concessions. To avoid cherry-picking, Brazil was divided into two groups comprising ten regions; no competing group could bid for more than two regions and only one bid could be placed in each group. Concessionaires are forbidden from adopting overly competitive practices, such as providing subsidies or free handsets.

9. ANATEL has established a rate per minute, plus an additional temporary surcharge (PAT) per minute, that will be abolished in 2002.

10. In August 2000 ANATEL awarded the first *espelhinho* concessions, to offer fixed telecom services in 413 municipalities not served by the *espelhos*.

11. Sintrel has never worked in practice because state concessionaires opposed it and transmission tariffs were not defined.

12. While the government must hold, by law, a controlling majority in the company, in August 2000 some 250 000 Brazilians bought Petrobrás's share in the first sale of a state-owned company specifically targeted at retail investors. The government raised US$4 billion and reduced its stake from 81.7 per cent to 55 per cent of the voting capital.

13. State-level multi-utility agencies have also been set up in Bahia, Ceará, Pará, Rio de Janeiro, Rio Grande do Norte, Rio Grande do Sul and São Paulo. The National Water Agency (ANA) was instituted in 2000 (Law 9984).

14. The Bill establishing ANEEL generated a great deal of controversy and Congress significantly watered down the initial text presented by the executive (Abranches, 1999).

15. 'Pós-privatização', special supplement, *Folha de S. Paulo*, 20 August 1999. It is noteworthy that in May 2001, 10 per cent only of respondents considered privatization as the main cause of the electricity crisis – against 42 per cent blaming government responsibility and 27 per cent lack of rain, although 69 per cent of Brazilians are against the electricity power privatization programme according to Datafolha Research (3 July 2001).

16. Majone (1997) distinguishes between two views of democracy, the 'majority' or 'populist' model and the 'state regulator' one. In the former, the majority controls the entire government apparatus, while in the latter execution tasks and control responsibilities are delegated to non-government public bodies.

17. At 95 per cent, the approval rate of law proposals presented by the current government to

Parliament since 1998 beats by far the records set since 1985 (according to data by Argelina Figueiredo and Fernando Limongi quoted in 'Orçamento é livre na luta contra as trevas', *Valor Econômico*, 18–20 May 2001).
18.	Similar considerations apply to administrative tribunals. At least formally, an important advance has been the approval of constitutional revision no. 19/1998, which introduces the efficiency principle in article 37 of the Constitution.
19.	'Telefonia sob pressão', *Folha de S. Paulo*, 2 June 2001.
20.	The Fund (Fundo de Universalização dos Serviços de Telecomunicações, FUST) was created in August 2000 (Law 9998). It is financed through a 1 per cent levy on the gross profits of each telecoms operator, plus other sources. It will be used to supply telephone lines and high-speed Internet connections to public schools, libraries and hospitals (draft version of Decree 3624/2000).
21.	The consortium that took over both companies was formed by Telefónica, Iberdrola, BBVA and RBS.
22.	The final ruling is still pending and the shareholders of Brasil Telecom and Telefónica may still be fined for their failure to reach an agreement concerning the ownership of CRT.
23.	ANATEL decided to return management rights over Telemar to Macal as it emerged that control had not changed hands. Garantia and Macal had simply agreed to coordinate their votes, although the latter may still be fined for withholding this information from ANATEL.
24.	The National Agency for Health Monitoring (Agência Nacional de Vigilância Sanitária, ANVS), however, is empowered to both investigate and take decisions.
25.	Until the concession contracts were signed in June 1998, the receipts for all fixed-to-mobile calls accrued to the local operator; with the introduction of the multi-carrier system the process was inverted and it is now the trunk operator that receives the receipts.
26.	Brazil has opted for the European GSM technology to operate in the 1.8 GHz SMP band because this standard makes it easier to introduce more competition in the short run and migrate to the 1.9 GHz band when the International Mobile Telecommunications-2000 (IMT-2000) third-generation mobile systems become operational worldwide.
27.	Contrary to later concession contracts, that of Escelsa did not specify any tariff regime, simply setting the average rate and the structure for different services.
28.	According to ANEEL's director-general, 'after the first revision, a price cap lower than the inflation index should be used to stimulate the concessionaire to seek higher efficiency' (*Estado de São Paulo*, 5 May 1999).
29.	Contracts divide tariffs into two different components. One, revised every year, reflects costs that are under the firm's direct control (personnel and administration); the other, whose revision is decided following a request by the concessionaire, includes non-controllable items such as energy purchases, special regimes (Reserva Global de Reversão – RGR, Conta de Consumo de Combustíveis – CCC) and transmission and distribution access charges.
30.	The price index chosen for energy – IGP-M – is more sensible to changes in wholesale prices, rather than exchange rate variations because the Wholesale Price Index (IPA) represents 60 per cent of IGPM.
31.	The CCC had been created in 1975 to subsidize the use of fossil fuel for thermal plants.
32.	Abdo declared that, in order to meet both goals of showing commitment to investors and keeping inflation under control, ANEEL and the Ministry of Finance were studying how to define an appropriate index. According to the press, this initiative was resisted by the Minister of Communications. See 'ANEEL e Ministro divergem sobre contratos com concessionárias', *Estado de São Paulo*, 2 December 1999.
33.	For more details see http://www.aneel.gov.br/scripts/not/Noticias.idc.
34.	COMAE consists of six professional members, independent from market participants and subject to a quarantine obligation upon expiration of their mandate. Consumers, producers and ANEEL appoint two members each. ONS and ASMAE (Administradora de Serviços do MAE) each have one non-voting director.
35.	However, by the end of 2000 only imports of LPG, aviation kerosene and fuel oil have been authorized, while imports of naphtha diesel oil and gasoline remain controlled by Petrobrás. After a first postponement to January 2001, the final opening of the fuel retail market was again postponed until January 2002.

36. At June 2001, exploration and production rights for 50 blocks, representing 3.2 per cent of the total area managed by ANP, have been tendered.
37. This decree was revoked on 16 April 2001 and ANP has started public hearings on the subject.
38. The two decisions were taken in December 2000 and January 2001.
39. According to ANP, 'TBG has consistently sought to impede third-party access to the transport infrastructure, by either creating entry barriers to new gas suppliers or putting off negotiations and decisions' (see http://www.anp.gov.br/gasnatural.htm).
40. As shown below, ANP took other initiatives, but they had to be submitted to the Comitê de Gestão da Crise de Energia.
41. ANP argued that limiting vertical cross-ownership is imperative for implementing the free access principle and making it possible to introduce competition.
42. At the end of 2000, ANP had withdrawn the licence from eight fuel distributors, while a further 75 had not yet complied with the new requirements.
43. These have included consumption growth rates much above supply expansion, lower rainfalls in the summer period (January–April), uncertainty regarding progress in the privatization process, and the willingness of private participants to invest in new-generation capacity while the regulatory framework was not clarified (Pires et al., 2001). As the risk of blackouts dramatically increased in Brazil's industrial belt (South-East) and in other regions (Centre-West and North-East), the government decided to implement a rationing programme.
44. Over a minimum of six months, small commercial and industrial users will have to reduce their consumption by 20 per cent. Large consumers are required to reduce consumption by 15–25 per cent (10 per cent in rural areas), depending largely on the employment and value added they generate and power they consume. All face substantially higher electricity rates and selective power cuts if they do not meet the targets.
45. The CNPE consists of seven ministers, a representative for the States and the Federal District of Brasília, a specialist in energy policy, and a university professor. Its objectives are to protect consumers and the environment, promote energy conservation, new investment and competition, optimize the energy mix between different fuels, and fix guidance for specific programmes such as those on gas, coal, nuclear power, alcohol and other biomass.
46. While ANEEL's director-general blamed the low level of rainfall, the government instituted the Comissão de Gerenciamento da Racionalização da Oferta e do Consumo de Energia Elétrica (CGRE) on 18 April 2001. This was replaced by the CGE on 15 May 2001, at the same time as a special commission, chaired by the director-general of the National Water Agency (Agência Nacional de Águas, ANA), was set up to assign responsibilities for the crisis.
47. 'A inércia versus a eficiência da Câmara de Gestão', *Valor Econômico*, 12 June 2001.
48. The PPT offers incentives to those power plant developers able to start generating before the end of the first semester of 2003. The government, through Petrobrás, will set price ceilings for 15-year fuel-supply contracts, so as to reassure investors concerned about gas-price fluctuations.
49. Until the recent decision on exchange rate risk, only Petrobrás had started projects in gas-powered generation.
50. See data on http://www.bndes.gov.br/pndnew/palestra/priv2002.exe. An important qualification, however, is that competition in local fixed-phone services is still minimal, because the 'mirror firms' have found it difficult to challenge the incumbents.
51. ANP already has very considerable regulatory powers, so that the alternative option of merging it outright with ANEEL to create a 'super' energy agency has sizeable risks. Even if there were economies of scale, diseconomies of specialization are likely to be greater. On the other hand the experience during the crisis shows that there are large gains from coordination that can be internalized by putting electricity and gas under a common roof.

REFERENCES

Abate, Antonio and Alberto Clô (2000), 'La regolazione elettrica in Italia, alcune prime valutazioni', *L'Industria*, **21** (4), 645–68.

Abdala, Manuel (2000), 'Institutional Roots of Post-Privatization Regulatory Outcomes', *Telecom Development*, **24** (8/9), 645–68.

Abranches, Sérgio (1999). 'Privatização, mudança estrutural e regulação: uma avaliação do programa de privatização no Brasil', in Velloso, J. (ed.), *A crise Mundial e a Nova agenda de crescimento. Fórum Nacional*. Rio de Janeiro: José Olimpyo Editora.

Almeida, Maria Hermínia Tavares de (1999), 'Negociando a Reforma: A Privatização de Empresas Públicas no Brasil', *Dados*, **42** (3), 254–81.

Araújo, C. Helena and José Claudio L. Pires (2000), 'Regulação e Arbitragem nos Setores de Serviços Públicos no Brasil: Problemas e Possibilidades', *Revista de Administração Pública*, September/October, 134–55.

Artana, Daniel, Fernando Navajas and Santiago Urbiztondo (1998), 'Regulation and Contractual Adaptation in Public Utilities: The Case of Argentina', Inter-American Development Bank, IFM–115.

Berg, Sanford (2000), 'Developments in Best-Practice Regulation: Principles, Processes, and Performance', *Electricity Journal*, July, No. 13, pp. 11–18.

Besant-Jones, John E. and Bernard W. Tenenbaum (2001), 'The California Experience with Power Sector Reform: Lessons for Developing Countries', The World Bank, Energy and Mining Sector Board, April.

Cardoso, Fernando Henrique (1997), 'As Razões do Presidente', interview with Roberto Pompeu de Toledo, Veja, 10 September.

Chang, Ha-Joon (2002), 'Breaking the Mould: An Institutionalist Political Economy Alternative to the Neo-Liberal Theory of the Market and the State', *Cambridge Journal of Economics*, **26** (5), 539–59.

Dnes, Anthony and Jonathan Seaton (1999), 'The Regulation of Electricity: Results from an Event Study', *Applied Economics*, **31** (5), 609–18.

Dornah, Preetum and Michael Pollitt (2001), 'The Restructuring and Privatisation of the Electricity Distribution and Supply Businesses in England', *Fiscal Studies*, **22** (1), 107–46.

Estache, Antonio and David Martimort (2000), 'Transaction Costs, Politics, Regulatory Institutions, and Regulatory Outcomes', in Luigi Manzetti (ed.), *Regulatory Policy in Latin America: Post-Privatization Realities*, Boulder, CO: Lynne Rienner.

Estache, Antonio, Andrea Goldstein and Russell Pittmann (2001), 'Privatization and Regulatory Reform in Brazil: The Case of Freight Railways', *Journal of International Competition and Trade*, **1** (2), 203–35.

FGV (2001), 'Private Participation in Infrastructure Projects and Determinants of Observed Contractual Arrangements: The Case of Brazil', Inter-American Development Bank, Working Papers, No. 413.

Galal, Ahmed, Leroy Jones, Pankay Tandon and Ingo Vogelsang (1994), *Welfare Consequences of Selling Public Enterprises*, Oxford and New York: Oxford University Press.

Global Competition Review (2000), *Rating The Regulators*, available on-line at http://www.global-competition.com/rating/rtng_fs.htm.

Goldstein, Andrea (1999), 'The Brazilian Privatization in International Perspective: The Rocky Path from State Capitalism to Regulatory Capitalism', *Industrial and Corporate Change*, **8** (4), 673–710.

Goldstein, Judith (1993), *Ideas, Interests, and American Trade Policy*, Ithaca, NY: Cornell University Press.

Helm, Dieter (2000), *Making Britain More Competitive: A Critique of Competition and Regulatory Policy*, Royal Bank of Scotland/Scottish Economic Society lecture, 6 November.

Instituto Nova Cidadania (2001), 'Comentários sobre o Antiprojeto de Criação da Agência de Defesa da Concorrência', mimeo.

Kingstone, Peter (1999), *Crafting Coalitions for Reform*, University Park, PA: Penn State Press.

Levy, Brian and Pablo Spiller (1994), 'The Institutional Foundations of Regulatory Commitment: a Comparative Analysis of Telecommunications Regulation', *Journal of Law, Economics and Organization*, **10** (2), 201–46.

Majone, Giandomenico (1997), 'From the Positive to the Regulatory State: Causes and Consequences of Changes in the Mode of Governance', *Journal of Public Policy*, **17** (2), 139–67.

McDonough, Peter (1981), *Power and Ideology in Brazil*, Princeton, NJ: Princeton University Press.

MME (1997), *Restrucuração do Setor Elétrico Brasileiro*, Ministério de Minas e Energia.

Mueller, Bernardo and Carlos Pereira (2000), 'Credibility and the Design of Regulatory Agencies in Brazil', presented at the Annual Conference of the International Society for New Institutional Economics, Tübingen, 22–24 September.

Noll, Roger (1989), 'Economic Perspectives on the Politics of Regulation', in R. Schmalensee and R. Willing (eds), *Handbook of Industrial Organization*, Vol. II, Amsterdam: Elsevier.

Oliveira, Gesner (2000), 'Novidades no controle de fusões', *Folha de S. Paulo*, 4 November.

Pinheiro, Armando C. (2000), 'O judiciário e a economia: evidéncia empírica para o caso brasileiro', in Armando C. Pinheiro (ed.), *Judiciário e Economia no Brasil*, São Paulo: Sumaré.

Pinheiro, Armando C. (2001), 'O judiciário e a economia na visão dos magistrados', presented at the seminar 'Reforma do Judiciário', Idesp, 27 April.

Pires, José Claudio L. (1999), 'Capacity, Efficiency and Contemporary Regulatory Approaches in the Brazilian Energy Sector: The Experiences of Aneel and Anp', *Ensaios BNDES*, No. 11.

Pires, José Claudio L., Fábio Giambiagi and Joana Gostkorzewicz (2001), 'O Cenário Macroeconômico e as Condições de Oferta de Energia Elétrica no Brasil', BNDES, *Texto para Discussão* no. 85.

Pires, José Claudio L. and Maurício S. Piccinini (1999), 'A Regulação dos Setores de Infra-Estrutura no Brasil', in Fabio Giambiagi and Maurício Mesquita Moreira (eds), *A Economia Brasileira nos Anos 90*, BNDES.

Pittman, Russell (2001), 'Proposed Changes in Brazil's Antitrust Law', *Boletín Latinoamericano de Competencia*, No. 12, 203–35.

Pontarollo, Enzo and Andrea Oglietti (2000), 'La performance dell'Autorità per le Garanzie nelle Comunicazioni: un primo esame', *L'Industria*, **21** (4), 643–60.

Ranci, Pippo (2000), 'Un contributo per valutare l'Autorità per l'energia elettrica e il gas', *L'Industria*, **21** (4), 749–64.

Smith, Warrick (1997a), 'Utility Regulators: The Independence Debate', The World Bank, Public Policy for the Private Sector, *Viewpoint*, No. 127.

Smith, Warrick (1997b), 'Utility Regulators: Roles and Responsibilities', The World Bank, Public Policy for the Private Sector, *Viewpoint*, No. 128.

Smith, Warrick (1997c), 'Utility Regulators: Decisionmaking Structures, Resources, and Start-up Strategy', The World Bank, Public Policy for the Private Sector, *Viewpoint*, No. 129.

Spiller, Pablo (1993), 'Institutions and Regulatory Commitment in Utilities' Privatization', *Industrial and Corporate Change*, **2** (3).

Spiller, Pablo (1999), 'La regulación de los servicios públicos en la Argentina: una propuesta de reforma institucional', Fundación Gobierno y Sociedad, *Cuaderno*, No. 3.

Williamson, John (ed.) (1994), *The Political Economy of Policy Reform*, Washington, DC: Institute for International Economics.

7. Corporate governance, regulation and the lingering role of the state in the post-privatized Brazilian steel industry

Edmund Amann, João Carlos Ferraz and Germano Mendes de Paula[1]

Beginning in 1988, Brazil embarked on one of the world's largest privatization programmes. Over the course of the next few years a great many enterprises were transferred to the private sector, across a cluster of industries ranging from steel, to petrochemicals to public utilities. Privatization has involved substantial transfer of assets from the public to the private sector and has also been argued to have radically altered patterns of efficiency. The majority of analyses so far conducted regarding privatization in Brazil and elsewhere have been characterized by a focus on two types of issues: the economic success of privatization in terms of its contribution to public finances, and in relation to its impacts on productive efficiency once private owners take the helm of companies.

While these relationships are unquestionably important, they are not the only ones worthy of attention by academics and policymakers. In the course of this chapter we wish to shed light on issues that have been up to now somewhat overlooked. Specifically, using the Brazilian steel industry as our case study we will pay attention to two questions: (a) does privatization deliver enhanced corporate governance standards? and (b) does privatization necessarily entail the final exit of the state as an investor?

In examining these questions it is found that in large part due to regulatory shortcomings, enhanced corporate governance did not result from privatization. Thus, despite improved financial performance, the privatized Brazilian steel companies proved unable to attract increasing participation from minority shareholders. For this reason, privatized steel enterprises have continued to rely on the state as a key source of external finance.

This chapter consists of four sections, including this introduction. The next section (Section I) is dedicated to a review of the historical development of the Brazilian steel industry. Section II concerns itself with the investigation of the privatization programme and considers the post-privatization performance of the steel sector, analysing ownership structure and corporate governance issues after privatization. The third and final section summarizes the main findings.

I. A BRIEF HISTORICAL REVIEW OF THE BRAZILIAN STEEL INDUSTRY

The Brazilian steel industry started its operation in 1925, when Companhia Siderúrgica Belgo-Mineira commissioned the Sabará works, in the State of Minas Gerais. It is important to stress that this company was established in 1921, as an association between the Luxembourg-based group Arbed and local investors. In 1935, Belgo-Mineira initiated the construction of the João Monlevade works, also in Minas Gerais, and until now still the company's largest mill (Baer, 1970, p. 88). From 1924 to 1946, Brazilian steel production rose from 4.5 to 342 thousand tons, of which Belgo-Mineira was responsible for 70 per cent of the total (De Paula, 1998, pp. 226–7).

A second landmark event for the Brazilian steel industry was the establishment of Companhia Siderúrgica Nacional (CSN), in the State of Rio de Janeiro, which was the pioneer in flat steel production in Brazil. The Volta Redonda works, Brazil's first coke-integrated mill, came on stream in 1946.[2] Two years later, the complex was finally completed, and the company was producing a wide range of products, such as hot and cold rolled coils, galvanizing sheet and tinplate. As is stressed by many authors, such as Mangabeira (1993, p. 65), the constitution of CSN, during the Vargas term, was aimed at fostering the industrial development of the country. Moreover, the development of CSN was part of a strong nationalist policy, trying to reduce dependence on foreign economic influence. The state-owned steel enterprise played three roles simultaneously: (a) to make up for the lack of domestic private capital; (b) to substitute imports, allowing the local supply of a basic input for industrialization; and (c) to present a showcase to the world demonstrating new-found economic sovereignty.

Closer relationships between domestic private capital, foreign investors and the state were further developed in the 1950s. One company (Acesita) was established in 1951 by a foreign investor, but due to the lack of capital, was eventually acquired in 1952 by the government-owned bank Banco do Brasil (Gomes, 1983, p. 355). Furthermore, Mannesmann of Germany began the operation of a subsidiary in Brazil to supply tubes to Petrobrás, the state-owned oil and gas monopoly. Next, in the late 1950s, two new companies were established, Usiminas and Cosipa. The first corresponded to a joint venture between the Brazilian state and Japanese companies, led by the then Yawata Steel (now Nippon Steel). It should be highlighted that this was the first foreign investment ever made by the Japanese steel industry.[3] Cosipa, for its part, was controlled by the state itself and other SOEs.

During the 1960s, the steel industry was chosen as a high-priority sector by the government. The then Banco Nacional de Desenvolvimento Econômico (BNDE), which had been established in the previous decade, lent the majority of its funds to the steel industry. In the period 1960–65 around 69 per cent of total lending carried out by the BNDE was directed at the steel industry. In the first half of the 1960s, Usiminas and Cosipa were started up. In 1968, the First National Steel Plan was issued, consisting of four main pillars: (a) an interministerial committee to establish sectoral policies; (b) a holding company to embrace SOEs; (c) another committee to foster private steel companies; (d) the National Steel Fund, which was never founded. The main consequence of these actions was the launch of the state-owned holding company, Siderbrás, in 1974.

The 1970s can be considered the golden age of the SOE model in Brazilian steel. The intermediate goods industry as a whole was among the sectors most favoured by a huge investment programme headed by the state. The so-called Second National Development Plan (PND II) prioritized steel, petrochemicals, fertilizers and pulp and paper, which at the time were generating large trade deficits. The priority areas of PND II were: (a) the production of capital goods and intermediate goods; (b) the transportation and communication infrastructure; (c) the development of alternative energy sources, with the intent of diminishing reliance on foreign supplies (Batista, 1987, p. 69). In the 1974–80 period, US$13.5 billion were invested in Brazilian steel, of which Siderbrás was responsible for 77 per cent (De Paula, 1998, p. 230). Among the SOEs, the 1970s saw not only the expansion of CSN, Usiminas and Cosipa, but also the establishment of new large SOE mills, CST and Açominas. In the case of CST, this development consisted of a joint venture of the Brazilian state with Japanese (Kawasaki Steel) and Italian (Finsider, at the time a SOE itself) investors.

In the mid-1970s the Brazilian steel market structure could be summarized as follows. First, large SOE mills (CSN, Usiminas and Cosipa) dominated the flat steel business. Second, foreign investors had a multiplicity of involvement in the sector. This varied from leading long steel (Belgo-Mineira) and tube (Mannesmann) market segments, associated with SOE-controlled companies (i.e. Usiminas and CST) and also partnerships with domestic private companies. In addition, small mills came to be controlled by the government due to their financial fragility (Cofavi and Cosim, for instance) or in order to diversify the type of energy consumed (Usiba and Piratini).

Repeatedly viewed as a 'lost decade', the 1980s was, while not a golden age for Brazilian steel, then at least the beginning of an 'export age'. During this decade, three important steel mills were commissioned: CST, Açominas and Mendes Jr. Although the last, a joint venture with a heavy construction company, was the smallest, for our purposes it can be considered the most significant in terms of illustrating the evolving relationship between the state and the private sector. First of all, the government pressured Mendes Jr to enlarge the original size of the mill by factor of 10, due to a jump in forecast demand. However, as a consequence of the plant's new dimensions, Siderbrás was obliged to hold a 49 per cent equity stake, because the light long steel business was 'reserved' for the private sector (both domestic and foreign). Meanwhile, the production of crude steel jumped from 15.3 (in 1980) to 25 million tons (in 1989).

II. PRIVATIZATION, PERFORMANCE AND OWNERSHIP STRUCTURE

The Process of Privatization

The privatization of the Brazilian steel industry can be divided into two phases: (a) the sale of small-sized companies, in the period 1988–92; (b) the transfer to the private sector of Big Six companies (1991–93). The Big Six comprised Usiminas, CST, Acesita, CSN, Cosipa and Açominas.

Regarding the first phase, six small firms were sold. They had become SOEs for two reasons: (a) financial necessity (Cosim, Cimetal, Cofavi and Cosinor); (b) the need to diversify energy sources (Usiba and Piratini). The main consequence of this first step of steel privatization was to strengthen the market control of the Brazilian company, Gerdau, which bought Cimetal, Cosinor, Usiba and Piratini.[4] Moreover, two companies originally acquired by Dufer, Cosim and Cofavi, changed their ownership afterwards. Belgo-Mineira is currently the owner of what was known as Cofavi.

In the case of Gerdau, it should be stressed that during the 1990s, the company engaged in an intense strategy of international as well as internal ownership restructuring. Indeed, Gerdau was committed to a large asset restructuring. The parent company has consolidated its various companies by merging 28 of them and reducing the number of publicly traded companies from six to only two: Metalúrgica Gerdau (holding) and Gerdau S.A. (operating). The final phase of this restructuring was completed in June 1997.

The Big Six Brazilian steel SOEs were privatized during the 1991–93 period. Steel and petrochemicals were among the first sectors to be transferred to private investors by means of public auctions. Indeed, the administration of President Collor de Melo viewed privatization as a symbol of its commitment to radical economic reform. Three features should stressed: (a) in an international comparison among 22 countries that privatized 37 steel companies in the period between 1984 and 1997, De Paula (1998) notes that Brazil was the only country that chose auctions as the technique of privatization for steel companies; (b) a 40 per cent ceiling on purchases of voting stock was imposed on foreign investors; (c) there were serious concerns that the government had paid too little attention to the future ownership structure of the steel industry after privatization. In relation to this last feature, it is worth recalling a contemporary World Bank report:

> There seems to be an apparent absence of timely industry-wide strategic thinking prior to privatization. More time should be spent substantially ahead of the sale studying strategic aspects of the industry, how an industry might ideally be organized, what legal, policy and regulatory changes are needed for the industry to reach international competitiveness, attract buyers and maintain competitive pressure, and how the mode of privatization might be modified to accomplish this strategy. (World Bank, 1992, p. vi)

The privatization of the Big Six steel companies started with the sale of Usiminas, in late 1991. The privatization was divided initially into three blocks, consisting of an auction of common shares (representing the majority control), an auction of non-voting shares and a public offering of heavily discounted shares directed exclusively at employees. The largest acquirers were domestic banks (mainly, Bozano Simonsen), the pension funds associated with SOEs, the mining company Companhia Vale do Rio Doce (CVRD) and steel distributors – see Table 7.1. A first impression is that the government promoted a dispersion of ownership. However, this interpretation is misleading. First, CVRD was at the time an SOE itself. The decision to buy stemmed from the fact that CVRD had accumulated non-paid debentures of Siderbrás (received in exchange for unpaid iron ore bills) and was able to use these 'junk bonds' to gain participation in connected businesses within the steel industry. Nevertheless, it cannot be denied that the government allowed an SOE to participate as a bidder in a privatization auction. Second, we should note that the largest pension funds in Brazil are related to SOEs too. In fact, Previ, which is the largest pension fund in the country (belonging to Banco do Brasil employees – a group of public sector workers), acquired a strategic stake in Usiminas.[5] Therefore, this evidence shows that privatization did not lead to wholesale transfer of assets from the public to the *bona fide* private sector.

Much the same pattern was observed in the remaining privatizations. CST and Acesita were sold in 1992. In the first case, the main buyers were a combination of domestic banks (Bozano Simonsen and Unibanco) and the pension fund Previ. The original international stakeholders Kawasaki Steel and Finsider had the right to acquire 14 per cent of the voting capital, reaching the 40 per cent ceiling maximum set. The employees were also beneficiaries of a public offering of shares with substantial discounts. Acesita, differently from

Table 7.1 Privatization of the big steel companies in Brazil, 1991–94

Companies	Capacity (Mt/y)	Date of sale	Privatization technique	Value of sale (US$M)	Proportion of total holding sold (%)	Main acquirers (% of voting capital)	Combined pension funds' participation (% of voting capital)	Combined foreign investors' participation (% of voting capital)
Usiminas	4.2	Oct. '91	Auction	1461	70	Bozano Simonsen (7.6%), other banks (20.6%), CVRD (15%), Previ (15%), other pension funds (11.1%), steel distributors (4.4%)	26.1	4.5
		Sept. '94	Public offering of shares	480	16			
CST	3.0	Jul. '92	Auction	354	90	Bozano Simonsen (25.4%), Unibanco (20%), CVRD (15%)	1.7	0.7
Acesita	0.85	Oct. '92	Auction	465	74	Previ (15%), other pension funds (21.1%), banks (18.6%)	36.1	1.8
CSN	4.6	Apr. '93	Auction	1495	91	CVRD (9.4%), Vicunha (9.2%), Bamerindus (9.1%), Bradesco (7.7%), other banks (18.3%), pension funds (2.7%)	8.5	2.7

Cosipa	3.9	Aug. '93	Auction	360	60	Usiminas (49.7%), Bozano (12.4%), steel distributors (12.4%)	0.2	2.6
		1994	Public offering of shares	226	24			
Açominas	2.4	Sept. '93	Auction	599	100	Mendes Jr (31.7%), Villares (6.2%), state-owned banks of Minas Gerais (7.4%), CVRD (5%)	0.6	0.0
Total				5444				

Source: De Paula (1995, 1998).

the other big companies, belonged to Banco do Brasil. On the first day of the auction, the sale was unsuccessful. There were rumours that the government, in an attempt to prevent this failure from halting the privatization process, pressured the public sector pension funds to buy Acesita. Previ once more played a prominent role, leading other pension funds to participate in the privatization of Acesita. Paradoxically, the largest shareholder changed from Banco do Brasil itself to Previ, the pension fund of Banco do Brasil employees.

Following the impeachment of President Collor de Mello, the new incumbent, Itamar Franco, continued the privatization programme. CSN, which was considered a symbol of nationalism in Brazil, was sold in 1993. In the auction, the main acquirers were the mining company CVRD, the textile group Vicunha and the domestic bank Bamerindus. Cosipa, for its part, was purchased by Usiminas, Bozano Simonsen and a group of steel distributors. Finally, Açominas was bought by a consortium headed by Siderúrgica Mendes Jr, Villares (a private-owned special steel producer), CVRD and banks controlled by the State of Minas Gerais.

Regarding the involvement of foreign investors, it should be noted that the exclusive mode of participation was portfolio investment. During the auctions, foreign participation was almost insignificant. Indeed, even in the case of Usiminas and CSN, in which it was greater, foreign capital purchased only 4.5 per cent and 2.5 per cent of voting capital, respectively. In fact, this situation was only reversed in the second phase of the privatization of Usiminas, when investors from abroad acquired US$361 million in equity. According to our estimates, foreign investors invested US$565 million in the Brazilian Big Six privatization programme, which was equivalent to only 10.4 per cent of the total privatization revenue. However, even this sum may be an overestimate. The Brazilian government accepted its own 'junk bonds' in return for shares without the market discount that was prevalent at that moment. The only exception was the case of external debts, to which were applied a 25 per cent discount.[6]

Pinho (2001, p. 7) estimates that the total privatization revenue of Brazilian steel firms reached almost US$5.0 billion. This figure differs from ours, probably because we explicitly considered the second phase of privatization of Usiminas and Cosipa, in which the mechanism of public offering of shares was utilized. Pinho (2001) shows that the participation of domestic capital was equivalent to 90.4 per cent of the privatization proceeds. Within this group, it should be highlighted that SOEs (to a large extent, CVRD) accounted for 12.2 per cent. Moreover, the pension funds, which were almost exclusively related to SOEs themselves, were responsible for another 15.0 per cent. This offers striking evidence that during the privatization itself, the visible hand of the state continued to play a significant role as a provider of equity capital.

Despite the prominent role of the public sector, domestic private sector banks purchased the largest share of the Big Six steel firms. According to Pinho (2001, p. 16), their investments amounted to US$1.7 billion, or 33.6 per cent of the total privatization revenues. This would strongly affect the owner-ship structure trajectory of the sector, as we shall see shortly. On the other hand, the participation of the Brazilian private sector domestic groups was quite disappointing. They invested only US$1.1 billion (or 21.8 per cent). This is somewhat troubling, especially considering the fact that privatization usually represents a once-and-for-all opportunity for enterprises (foreign or domestic) to enter new branches of industry.

Among the Big Six steel company privatizations, beyond the auction sale, the government opted for a public offering of shares specially focused on attracting minority shareholders. However, this approach was adopted in just three cases: Usiminas, CSN and Cosipa. In the first case, its important to stress that Usiminas was chosen to be the first privatized steel company, due to its image of efficiency and good management. The government offered 10 per cent of Usiminas shares in the public offering, but only 6 per cent were sold. The lack of demand from minority shareholders also occurred in the experi-ence of CSN. The government had reserved 13.9 per cent for the public, though only 9.9 per cent were subscribed. Solely in the case of Cosipa was the public offering (equivalent to 10.3 per cent of its shares) totally subscribed. Thus the privatization of the Brazilian steel industry was unable initially to attract minority shareholders.

The Performance of Privatized Steel Companies

Perhaps the most significant expected benefit of privatization is that it will give rise to an improvement in efficiency in the enterprises to which it is applied. Megginson et al. (1994) established a widely followed approach to the study of the impacts of privatization on corporate performance. Their methodology, centring on the Wilcoxon Signed Rank Test and the Sign Test, was applied in the Brazilian case by Pinheiro (1996). Pinheiro analysed the performance of 50 Brazilian companies that were privatized during the 1980s and 1990s. He found that, for those enterprises sold in the 1991–94 period, performance improved in accordance with expectations in all variables. This period witnessed the sale of the Big Six steel companies. In the case of those enterprises privatized in the 1980s, performance improved in all indices bar profit per employee, return on sales, leverage and investment per unit of assets. The third column of Table 7.2 shows Pinheiro's combined results for all companies privatized in the period 1981–94.

Moonen (1999), also employing the Megginson et al. methodology, estab-lished a positive relationship between privatization and various indicators of

Table 7.2 *Expected and actual performance of Brazilian steel companies post privatization*

Variable	Proxy	Expected change	Actual change for all companies	Actual change for steel companies
1. Profitability	Return on sales = net income/sales	↑	↑	↑
	Return on assets = net income/total assets	↑	n.a.	↑
	Return on equity = net income/equity	↑	↑	↑
2. Operating efficiency	Sales efficiency = real sales/total number of employees	↑	↑	↑
	Net income efficiency = net income/total number of employees	↑	↑	↑
3. Capital expenditure	Capital expenditure to sales = capital expenditure/sales	↑	↑	↑
	Capital expenditure to assets = capital expenditure/total assets	↑	↑	↑
4. Output	Real sales = nominal sales/consumer price index	↑	↑	↑
5. Employment	Total employment = total number of employees	↓	↓	↓

6. Leverage   Debt to assets = total debt/total assets → → ← ← →

     Long-term debt to equity = long-term debt/equity   n.a.

7. Dividends   Dividends to sales = cash dividends/sales   n.a.

     Dividend payout = cash dividends/net income   n.a.

8. Exports   Exports to sales = exports/sales   n.a.

Source: Pinheiro (1996); Moonen (1999).

163

efficiency for the Brazilian steel industry. The fourth column of Table 7.2 illustrates the actual changes observed among the Big Six Brazilian steel companies. The comparison concerning performance was made in the 5–9-year period encompassing privatization. As can be seen, in the vast majority of cases, the theoretical expectation of enhanced performance was borne out in reality, the only exception being that of exports (which actually decreased).

Another important performance characteristic is constituted by capital investment. In the period between 1974 and 1983 average annual investment in the Brazilian steel sector reached US$2 billion. However, in the years 1984–93, average annual investment dropped to US$476 million, even considering that new greenfield plants, whose construction began in the 1970s, were inaugurated in the mid-1980s: Mendes Jr (in 1984) and Açominas (1986). Privatization has been associated with a second boom of investment. In the 1994–2002 period Brazilian steel companies invested US$1.36 billion per year.

Regarding labour productivity, Andrade et al. (2001, p. 10) demonstrate that privatization has given rise to substantial improvements. Between 1990 and 1994 labour productivity (measured in terms of tons per employee per year) rose from 155 to 264. By 2000 Andrade et al. estimated that labour productivity had reached 493 tons per employee per year. Whereas the authors referred to above have focused on issues of financial and productive efficiency, we of course wish to draw attention to a far less researched area: the impacts of privatization on patterns of ownership and corporate governance.

Ownership Structure in the Post-privatization Period

As we noted in the introduction, one of the principal objectives of this chapter is to establish the relationship between privatization and patterns of corporate governance. Bearing this in mind, we want to stress two features regarding corporate governance: complexity (defined as where the assets of a given corporation are controlled by a relatively small number of investors from different origins, grouped together in different formats, either directly or through a holding company) and instability (defined as where there are recurrent changes in the composition of the largest shareholders).

We will illustrate this argument by analysing the ownership structure of the Brazilian steel industry in the post-privatization period. Regarding complexity, Figure 7.1 shows very confused ownership relations among companies and investors. For instance, there was a cross-ownership relation between CSN and CVRD, which in its turn was privatized in 1997.[7] The mining company CVRD held 9.9 per cent of CSN. The latter controlled 25.2 per cent of the holding company Valepar, which had a 52.2 per cent stake in CSN itself.

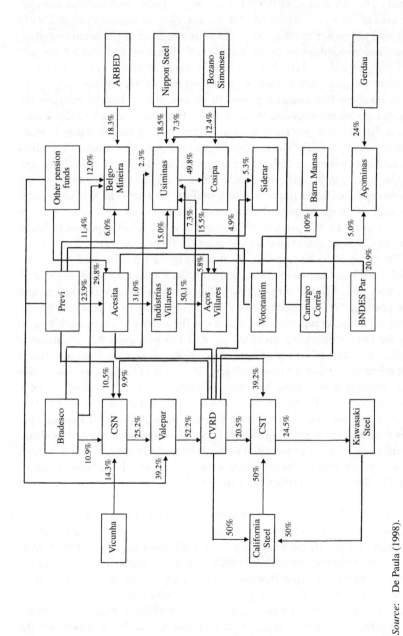

Source: De Paula (1998).

Figure 7.1 The ownership structure of the Brazilian steel industry in 1997

It should be remembered that CVRD, at the time it was a SOE, bought a minority stake in privatized steel companies other than CSN. In the late 1990s, it had a 20.5 per cent stake in CST, a 5.0 per cent stake in Açominas and 15.5 per cent of Usiminas, which had for its part 49.8 per cent of Cosipa. CVRD was also the owner of 50 per cent of California Steel, a US-based company, which had an additional 4 per cent stake in CST. Acesita had also 5.8 per cent of voting capital of Aços Villares and 31 per cent of the voting capital of Indústrias Villares, which controlled 50.1 per cent of Aços Villares.

To complete this surrealist picture of the complexity that characterizes the post-privatization ownership structure of the Brazilian steel industry, it should be emphasized that two types of shareholders had significant stakes in more than one steel company. The leading domestic bank Bradesco controlled a 10.9 per cent equity stake in CSN, 11.4 per cent of Belgo-Mineira and 2.3 per cent of Usiminas. On its own, the pension fund Previ held 10.5 per cent of the voting capital of CSN, 15 per cent of Usiminas, 23.9 per cent of Acesita and 6 per cent of Belgo-Mineira. Furthermore, Previ, jointly with other pension funds, controlled 39.2 per cent of Valepar. These funds had important stakes in Acesita (29.3 per cent) and Belgo-Mineira (12.0 per cent) too.

Therefore, it can be seen that privatization of the Brazilian steel companies heightened the complexity, or in other words, a relatively small number of investors from different origins, controlling newly privatized corporations and grouped together in a multitude of different configurations, either directly or through holding companies. The opacity of these patterns of ownership is, to say the least, striking. To stress the point, it can be argued that privatization implied a pattern of corporate governance that was very far from any model that might be conducive to transparency, the forging of common investor goals or a sustainable ownership structure. In other words, this kind of complex ownership reduces the attractiveness of investing for minority shareholders for two main reasons: (a) since the large investors have stakes in different companies (and even in competing firms), they may forge alliances among themselves in order to seek their ultimate goals instead of the best interest of each company individually; (b) the largest shareholders can sell their stakes, appropriating the majority control premium, which is far from accessible to the minority.

The key point to note is that the privatization programme, though a success judged in terms of rapidly divesting the public sector of assets, did not pay sufficient attention to the regulatory framework governing the control of those assets following their sale. This meant that minority shareholders did not have the legal means to assert themselves effectively or represent themselves at board level. To all intents and purposes they were shut out of key strategic decision-making, which was vested in a very restricted set of hands. At the same time, no regulatory reform was instituted that might have increased the more general public accountability of the boards of the privatized enterprises, a critical omission given the environmental and social sensitivity of the steel industry. As time went on following privatization, the failure to institute regulatory reform of corporate governance procedures went hand in hand with increasing complexity of the Brazilian steel industry's ownership structure. As will be seen, this had important implications for the sector's ability to tap private, as opposed to public, sector sources of capital.

The second main characteristic of the ownership structure is instability. We believe that this is a result of two main factors. On one hand, Brazil was the only country that used auctions as a privatization technique to sell steel companies. Therefore, in contrast to other countries that utilized tenders, it proved easier for the shareholders to exit the company. Using tenders, investors establish a consortium and changes of ownership happen within these groupings, while new outside investors do not emerge.[8] When public offerings of shares were employed, by contrast, the dispersed ownership structure meant that acquisitions and selling of shares did not necessarily imply alterations in the main strategic orientation of the firms. On the other hand, this instability is a clear consequence of the fact that the main motivation underpinning the original acquisitions was financial, specifically to realize value from state 'junk bonds' (in the case of CVRD), to realize profits after turning the companies around or experiencing a steel price recovery (banks) or even to invest in a long-term, low-income, low-risk business (pension funds).

Regarding ownership structure instability (meaning frequent consecutive changes in partnership composition after privatization), De Paula (2002) finds that, excluding privatizations, between 1993 and 2002, there were 23 ownership transactions and three instances of asset leasing implemented in the Brazilian steel industry. In an attempt to summarize the diversity of these ownership changes, Table 7.3 divides the transactions into eight categories.

First and most importantly, some banks decided to exit the steel sector and realize their gains. Thus, Banco Bamerindus exited CSN in 1995, Bozano Simonsen did the same in relation to Usiminas and CST in 1996 and Unibanco sold its shares in CST in the same year. Indeed, Pinho (2001, p. 42), after raising some concerns about the accuracy of the figures, estimated that Bozano Simonsen bank gained some 52 per cent of profits in reselling its stake in Usiminas. Nevertheless, this extraordinary gain was superseded by the sale of Bamerindus's participation in CSN (a 181 per cent profit) and Bozano Simonsen and Unibanco's stake in CST (388 per cent).

To be fair, not all transactions could trace their roots to the privatization process. This is the case of the long steel business, in which SOEs had not played a significant role. In Table 7.3 we identify three ownership changes related to companies that had always been in the private sector, and three cases of asset leasing. Although these operations were quite important in terms of

The Latin American experience

Table 7.3   Ownership changes in the Brazilian post-privatized steel industry,
by category, 1993–2002

Type of ownership change	Number of transactions
Changes in the internal composition of main shareholders	7
Financial institution sale of equity stakes	5
New international entrants	3
Acquisition of traditional private sector companies[1]	3
Leasing of assets	3
Acquisition of majority control of a former SOE	2
New domestic group entrants	1
Other cases (including CVRD–CSN separation)	2
Total	26

Note: [1] Companies that were always in the private sector.

Source: Adapted from De Paula (2002).

their absolute number, they were not significant in relation to the overall financial value of transactions.

It should be emphasized that, in the post-privatization age, changes in ownership have significantly modified the market structure of the Brazilian steel industry. In this connection, the case of Açominas is instructive, especially for understanding the continuing role played by the state. For the privatization auction, two consortia were formed: one headed by Usiminas, Gerdau and Belgo-Mineira; another led by Siderúrgica Mendes Jr with the support of state-owned banks from the State of Minas Gerais. The auction was won by the second consortium. However, Mendes Jr arguably abused its position as the largest shareholder (a classic problem of corporate governance) and main client, since it did not pay for the semi-finished products that it received from Açominas. As a consequence, a set of ownership transactions was carried out. These culminated in the sale of the stakes of Mendes Jr, CVRD, Banco Econômico and the state-owned banks of Minas Gerais to Gerdau. The last thereby assumed almost 80 per cent of the voting capital of Açominas. Thus Gerdau, even though it did not participate in the privatization of the Big Six steel companies, eventually became the majority shareholder of Açominas.

The lack of importance of foreign investors during the privatization of Big Six companies has been reversed since 1997. Since then, three foreign newcomers have entered the industry. The Singapore-based company NatSteel bought a stake in Açominas in 1997. Afterwards, as a consequence of the withdrawal of Mendes Jr, CVRD and the state-owned bank of Minas Gerais, the Asian firm came to be the second-largest shareholder of Açominas. However, immediately after Gerdau attained a majority position, NatSteel agreed, in early 2002, to sell its stake to Gerdau. The other newcomers are Usinor (which was merged with the European steel companies Arbed and Aceralia, and renamed Arcelor) and Sidenor. The then French company Usinor made a strategic investment in Acesita, in 1998, and became an important indirect shareholder in CST. The Spanish company Sidenor assumed majority control of Aços Villares, a speciality long steel company, in 2000.

Regarding the second key question posed in the introduction, that of the changing role of the state, the phenomenon of public institutions acting in conjunction with foreign investors should be stressed.[9] For example, State of Minas Gerais banks were equity partners alongside NatSteel in Açominas; in the case of Usinor–Acesita, the second-largest shareholder continues to be Previ; in Aços Villares, although never an SOE, the second-largest shareholder is a subsidiary of the public bank BNDES. While foreign steel companies have a large influence on the management and operation of the Brazilian steel firms, it may be seen that the state – in its various forms – continues to play a significant role, benefiting foreign investors in two ways. First, due to the fact that the state, in its new guise as investor rather than operator, does not have the technical knowledge to operate the steel works, it can be considered a politically influential silent partner. Second, the state's participation has assisted international investors by effectively diminishing the amount of money that they have been required to inject into steel companies in order to ensure adequate operation.

The case of Usiminas is interesting in terms of a privatized corporation expanding its sectoral presence and promoting association with local capital. First, the company set in motion a very complex ownership restructuring of its Cosipa subsidiary in early 1999. This involved the division of Cosipa into two companies, with one of them merging with Usiminas. This represents a case of reverse acquisition, because, although the acquirer was Cosipa, for fiscal considerations, the new company held on to the name of Usiminas. Moreover, in late 2001, Usiminas converted the debentures of Cosipa, diluting the share of minority shareholders and enlarging its stake from 32 per cent to 93 per cent of total capital. Naturally, this dilution has received a great deal of criticism from minority shareholders.

Second, Votorantim, Brazil's largest diversified group, bought a 7.3 per cent stake in Usiminas in 1998. The case of Votorantim well illustrates the cautious posture adopted by local private capital. Votorantim has operated a long steel mill – Barra Mansa – since 1937 and is an economic group focusing on activities where large barriers to entry, homogeneous product and natural-resource-oriented businesses prevail. Consequently, the group has come to specialize in the production of such industrial commodities as aluminium, nickel, zinc, cement, pulp and paper. Thus one might expect that Votorantim would be a prime candidate in any equity purchases of steel companies. However, it only acquired a minority stake in Usiminas six years after the company's privatization and after having lost the bidding contest for CVRD.[10]

In contrast with Votorantim, whose main strategy can be defined as conservative, Vicunha, another leading Brazilian company, aggressively used the opportunities that privatization opened up to enter new businesses. Indeed, Goldstein and Schneider (2000, pp. 21–2) stress that Vicunha has turned into a conglomerate through privatization. It entered the steel industry by purchasing a 14 per cent stake in CSN in 1993. Four years later, Vicunha's CEO, Benjamin Steinbruch, was the architect of the consortium that won the auction for CVRD. Moreover, via a joint venture with Telecom Italia, Vicunha won a mobile-phone licence for the State of Bahia.

According to Goldstein and Schneider (2000), Vicunha's acquisitions and investments demonstrate a strategy to gain control of assets that would otherwise take generations to assemble. Moreover, this strategy poses an additional problem regarding corporate governance in general and cross-ownership in particular. Vicunha gained control over CVRD through its stake in CSN, which can be viewed as quasi-pyramidal corporate control.[11] On the other hand, in order to do this, Vicunha took a few risks. It was prepared to borrow to gain control of CVRD – most of CSN's 39 per cent stake was covered by a US$1.1 billion loan – and to accept shared control in all its ventures. According to Goldstein and Schneider (2000, pp. 22–3):

> [Steinbruch's] empire, however, soon faced the conglomerate dangers of management overstretch and lack of focus. Moreover, CVRD's complex shareholder structure and a jumble of non-core business interests dragged the share price down by nearly half since privatization. Steinbruch was therefore obliged to reshuffle his impressive industrial portfolio. In 1999 CSN sold its Ribeirão Grande cement firm to Votorantim . . . Most importantly, the cross-ownership between CSN and CVRD is being severed (descruzamento).

The elimination of cross-ownership between CSN and CVRD resulted from two transactions. First, Bradespar (an investment company that was spun off from Bradesco, the largest Brazilian private bank, in March 2000) and Previ (the country's largest pension fund) sold all their shares in CSN to Vicunha, for a consideration of US$1.18 billion. Due to the fact that Bradespar and Previ held, respectively, 17.9 per cent and 13.8 per cent of CSN shares, Vicunha enhanced its stake in CSN from 14 per cent to 46 per cent (Figure 7.2). Simultaneously, CVRD sold to Valia (CVRD's employee pension fund) 10.3 per cent of CSN's total capital, for US$250 million, in order to eliminate

Valia's actuarial deficit. To help finance ownership restructuring, CSN also distributed huge dividends in 2000 – around US$920 million – larger than the company's net income in that year (US$840 million). This measure was connected with the financial resources that Vicunha had to raise to finance the increase of its stake in CSN. However, it also demanded further credit from the development bank BNDES and even from Bradespar and Previ. In total, Vicunha issued US$1 billion in debentures. Thus the state, via BNDES, had to expand its exposure to Vicunha in order to disentangle the cross-ownership structure arising from the privatization process.

Second, CVRD's ownership restructuring was carried out as follows. Bradespar and Previ purchased the shares belonging to CSN in Valepar for US$1.32 billion. Valepar is a holding company established during the CVRD privatization process. It holds 42 per cent of the voting capital and 27 per cent of the total capital of CVRD. As CSN used to control 32 per cent of Valepar shares, it indirectly had 8.65 per cent of the total capital of CVRD. With this second transaction, Litel, a specific-purpose company controlled by Previ (in which other pension funds, such as Petros, Funcef and Funcesp, also take part), augmented its stake in Valepar to 42 per cent from 25 per cent. Bradespar, directly and indirectly, via Eletron (a joint venture with the Brazilian investment bank Opportunity), raised its share in Valepar to 35 per

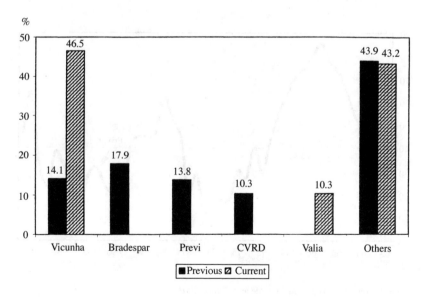

Source: Based on data from CSN.

Figure 7.2   CSN's ownership structure, 2000–2001

cent from 21 per cent. The other shareholders of Valepar in mid-2002 were: Sweet River (a holding belonging to international investors, which sold its stake to Litel and Bradespar in March 2003) and Investvale (an investment fund owned by CVRD's employees).

One additional feature should be highlighted. In the 1960s, the BNDES focused its lending on the sector to such an extent that it became known as the 'Steel Bank'. The same happened, though without similar intensity, during the course of the following decade. However, since the mid-1980s, due to efforts to reduce the size of the state in the Brazilian economy, the BNDES has been barred from lending money to SOEs (by Resolution 2005 of the National Monetary Council), including public sector steel companies. This prohibition was, of course, lifted once these companies were privatized. Indeed, as Figure 7.3 shows, the dependence of the Brazilian steel companies on financing provided by the public sector bank BNDES increased from 9.7 per cent (in 1989) to 23.2 per cent (in 1991, the year that marked the beginning of the Big Six privatizations) to over 45 per cent in the period 2000–2001.

Before concluding this section, it is worth considering the relationship between economic performance and the pattern of corporate governance. This relationship can be viewed through two prisms, one quite optimistic and one less so. According to the first, the Brazilian steel industry can be viewed as a

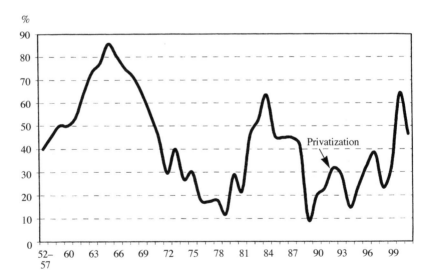

Source: Based on data from Andrade and Cunha (2003).

Figure 7.3   BNDES loans to the steel industry as a proportion of total sector investment, 1957–2001

case where the economic performance improvements were so substantial that, even retaining and reinforcing an unsatisfactory pattern of corporate governance, the financial results were extremely favourable. However, viewing the situation through another prism, it could be argued that even given the good financial results, the capability of the Brazilian steel industry to internationalize could have been better fostered had a superior corporate governance standard been mandated by the authorities and then adopted by the sector.

The sense that corporate governance deficiencies stemming from regulatory flaws act as a brake on the sector's development has yet further dimensions. Although the Brazilian steel companies have enhanced their financial performance, they have been unable to escape from two tough realities. First, the number of shareholders has not increased. For example, in the case of Usiminas, the number of such investors has been stagnant during the last five years. Thus the presence of good results alone is not necessarily sufficient to attract minority investors. Second, given the dearth of minority shareholders, Brazilian equity markets are neither as deep nor as liquid as their counterparts in Europe or North America. In contemplating accelerated investment, therefore, steel companies cannot count on equity finance to any great extent. This is an especially serious limitation given the very high interest rates that prevail in the private sector domestic financial market. Consequently, enterprises have needed to depend on the state-owned bank, the BNDES.

CONCLUSIONS

This chapter tackled two specific questions, using the Brazilian steel industry as a case study. In the first place, the chapter attempted to assess whether privatization had delivered enhanced corporate governance standards. In the second, it attempted to determine whether privatization necessarily entailed the final exit of the state as an investor.

Regarding the first question, it was shown that privatization did not prove the catalyst for improved corporate governance standards, whether imposed in regulatory form by the state or adopted voluntarily by enterprises. For the Brazilian steel industry, this led to a very complex and unstable ownership structure.[12] This characteristic, taken together with a lack of formal rights, did not assist in attracting minority shareholders to the sector. Partly for this reason, the pattern of corporate funding in the Brazilian steel industry tended to centre itself still more firmly on the accumulation of state bank debt rather than the raising of equity capital. Thus, to answer the second question, the state has remained a vital source of finance for the steel sector despite privatization.

Looking to the future, the ability of Brazilian enterprises to invest, grow and penetrate new markets will clearly in part depend upon cost-effective access to equity finance. Such access will in turn depend on the development of improved corporate governance standards that more generously favour the interests of minority shareholders. Although this chapter presented a somewhat bleak picture, change is now very much in the air. In early 2003 a new legal framework, the Lei das S.A. (the Law of Limited Companies) came into force, the effect of which is to boost minority shareholder rights. Although the Law disappointed some observers with its perceived timidity, it nevertheless marks a break with the past and possibly heralds an era in which more dispersed, transparent and accountable patterns of corporate ownership will become the order of the day. Were this hope to be realized (and it is still too soon to tell for certain), then the repercussions for the Brazilian industrial sector can only be positive.

NOTES

1. The authors would like to express their thanks for the financial support provided by the Conselho Nacional de Desenvolvimento Científico e Tecnológico (CNPq) and the Fundação de Amparo à Pesquisa do Rio de Janeiro (FAPERJ). The views expressed here are the responsibilities of the authors and do not necessarily represent the views of the United Nations Economic Commission for Latin America and the Caribbean (ECLAC).
2. Coke integrated mills are plants which convert iron ore into semi-finished or finished steel products. Traditionally, this required coke ovens, blast furnaces, steel-making furnaces and rolling mills.
3. The initial investment made by the Japanese consisted of a 40 per cent stake. Later on this stake was reduced to 14 per cent and eventually even to 4.65 per cent. However, just before the privatization of the company, in order to solve a legal problem, they had the right to pay US$28.5 million in order to improve their share to 12.88 per cent. Currently, Japanese investors possess a 18.39 per cent stake in the voting capital of Usiminas and 9.45 per cent of the total capital.
4. Gerdau's growth was based mainly via the utilization of mini-mill plants. This kind of plant uses scrap instead of iron ore. This technology is more compact, starting at the steel shop.
5. Rabelo and Coutinho (2001, p. 48) state that, by the end of 1999, Brazilian pension funds had some US$60 billion in assets. Of this total, 30 per cent was invested in shares. These institutions owned approximately 15 per cent of the total value of companies listed in the São Paulo Stock Exchange (Bovespa). At that time, Previ's assets totalled US$17.8 billion. Vieira (2001, p. 103) draws attention to the fact that Previ is not only the largest Brazilian pension fund, but has also traditionally had the largest exposure to the capital markets. Vieira estimates that, in the period 1990–99, Previ allocated almost 41 per cent of its total asset portfolio to equity markets. At the same time, Petros (which belongs to Petrobrás employees) and Sistel (belonging to former Telebrás employees) invested 29 per cent and 26 per cent, respectively, of their assets in shares.
6. According to Brumer (1994, p. 294), the average of the market discount at the time of privatization of steel companies was: Usiminas (50 per cent), CST (50 per cent), Acesita (55 per cent), CSN (45 per cent), Cosipa (35 per cent) and Açominas (60 per cent). Taking into the consideration these six privatizations, the average discount reached 49 per cent.
7. CVRD was privatized in May 1997. Two consortia took part in the auction, one led by CSN and the other by Votorantim. The first one emerged the winner, being formed by CSN itself, pension funds (Previ, Petros, Fundação CESP and Funcef) and financial institutions

(Opportunity and National Banks). This consortium bought 42 per cent of voting capital of CVRD for a consideration of US$3.3 billion (Mello, 2000, p. 94). As a consequence, a cross-ownership relation between CSN and CVRD was generated.

8. The case of the Argentinean telecommunications privatization offers an interesting contrast with that of Brazilian steel. Regarding the technique of privatization, it was decided to divide the incumbent state monopoly in two prior to sale (Herrera, 1992). In both cases, a consortium was formed by an international telecom company, a diversified domestic group and an international financial institution. Afterwards, the major trend regarding corporate ownership was the increase of the stake belonging to the international telecommunication company. This situation is very different from that of Brazilian steel, in which the complexity and instability of corporate control was much more intense.

9. In the past, the Brazilian state assisted multinational corporations and local domestic groups in developing greenfield sites. This business–government relationship became well known internationally with the publication of Peter Evans's 1979 book *Dependent Development: The Alliance of Multinational, State, and Local Capital in Brazil*. In the particular case of the steel business, coke-integrated mills were solely constructed by SOEs. Nowadays, this relationship is connected with brownfield investment and the division of tasks is not so clearly defined.

10. According to Ruiz (1997, p. 181), during the 1980–87 period, Votorantim's corporate strategy was based on the reduction of indebtedness and investing only its own capital in mutually related activities. Only at the end of 1980s did the group expand its investments. The selected sectors, pulp and paper and citrus juices, had already become internationally competitive. This could be considered a rather conservative strategy. For Goldstein and Schneider (2000, pp. 25–6), Votorantim's big asset is a strong balance sheet. In spite of operating in capital-intensive industries, total debt is less than cash holdings. In the 1990s, being already the country's largest private electricity generator, Votorantim became an important investor in the privatized energy business, through a joint venture with the heavy construction group Camargo Corrêa and the domestic bank, Bradesco.

11. The existence of pure or quasi-pyramidal structure, naturally, does not stem solely from privatization. In the experience of the Brazilian steel industry, Gerdau has a prominent role. The Gerdau Johannpeter family controls the company, via holdings, with just 8.3 per cent of total capital (Rabelo and Coutinho, 2001, p. 16).

12. Siffert Fo (1998, p. 11) shows that the participation of the shared stockholding control in the cumulative revenues of the 100 largest non-financial companies in Brazil increased from 3.5 per cent (in 1990) to 12.4 per cent (in 1997). The author stresses that this new trend is largely associated with the privatization process. Therefore, the growing complexity of ownership structures following privatizations is clearly not confined to the steel industry.

REFERENCES

Andrade, M.L.A. et al. (2001), *Impactos da Privatização no Setor Siderúrgico*, Rio de Janeiro: BNDES.

Andrade, M.L.A. and Cunha, L.M.S. (2003), *O Setor Siderúrgico*, Rio de Janeiro: BNDES.

Baer, W. (1970), *Siderurgia e Desenvolvimento Brasileiro*, Rio de Janeiro: Zahar.

Batista, J.C. (1987), 'A estratégia de ajustamento externo do Segundo Plano de Desenvolvimento', *Revista de Economia Política*, **17** (2), pp. 66–80.

Brumer, W.N. (1994), Presentation. *Steel Survival Strategies IX*, New York: American Metal Market–World Steel Dynamics, pp. 281–97.

De Paula, G.M. (1995), 'A privatização da indústria siderúrgica Brasileira. Grupos econômicos industriais no Brasil' and 'A política econômica: estrutura, estratégia e desafios', Working Papers. Campinas: Instituto de Economia, Unicamp.

De Paula, G.M. (1998), 'Privatização e Estrutura de Mercado na Indústria Siderúrgica Mundial', unpublished doctoral dissertation, Instituto de Economia, Universidade Federal do Rio de Janeiro, Rio de Janeiro.

De Paula, G.M. (2002), *Cadeia Produtiva da Siderurgia. Estudo de Competitividade por Cadeias Integradas: Um Esforço Coordenado de Criação de Estratégias Compartilhadas*, Campinas: Instituto de Economia, Unicamp.

Evans, P. (1979), *Dependent Development: The Alliance of Multinational, State, and Local Capital in Brazil*, Princeton, NJ: Princeton University Press.

Goldstein, A. and Schneider, B.R. (2000), 'Big Business in Brazil: States and Markets in the Corporate Reorganization of the 1990s', Paper presented at Institute for Latin American Studies, University of London, 7–8 December.

Gomes, F.M. (1983), *História da Siderurgia Brasileira*, Belo Horizonte: Itatiaia; São Paulo: Editora da Universidade de São Paulo.

Herrera, A. (1992), 'La privatización de La Telefonía Argentina', *Revista de la CEPAL*, No. 47.

Mangabeira, W. (1993), *Os Dilemas do Novo Sindicalismo: Democracia e Política em Volta Redonda*, Rio de Janeiro: Relume-Dumará.

Megginson, W., Nash, R. and Randenborgh, M. (1994), 'The Financial and Operating Performance of Newly Privatized Firms: An International Empirical Analysis', *Journal of Finance*, **49** (2), pp. 403–52.

Mello, E.M.R. (2000), 'Mineração e Enclave: estudo de caso da Companhia Vale do Rio Doce em Itabira', unpublished masters dissertation, Instituto de Economia, Universidade Federal de Uberlândia, Uberlândia.

Moonen, J. (1999), 'Does Privatization Work? The Case of the Brazilian Steel Industry', unpublished masters dissertation, Maastricht University, Maastricht.

Pinheiro, A.C. (1996), 'Impactos Microeconômicos da Privatização no Brasil', *Pesquisa e Planejamento Econômico*, **26** (3), pp. 357–98.

Pinho, M.S. (2001), 'Reestruturação Produtiva e Inserção Internacional da Siderurgia Brasileira', unpublished doctoral dissertation, Instituto de Economia, Unicamp, Campinas.

Rabelo, F.M. and Coutinho, L.G. (2001), *Corporate Governance in Brazil*, Paris: OECD Development Centre.

Ruiz, R.M. (1997), 'The Restructuring of Brazilian Industrial Groups between 1980 and 1993', *CEPAL Review*, No. 61, 167–86.

Siffert Fo, N. (1998), *Corporate Governance: International Standards and Empirical Evidence in Brazil during the 1990s*, Rio de Janeiro: BNDES.

Vieira, E.R. (2001), 'Análise da Forma de Atuação dos Fundos de Pensão Brasileiros: Condicionantes Institucionais', unpublished masters dissertation, Instituto de Economia, Universidade Federal de Uberlândia, Uberlândia.

Young, P. (1993), 'A transferência da experiência de privatização Británica para outros Países', in A.A. Zini Jr (ed.), *O Mercado e o Estado no Desenvolvimento Econômico nos anos 90*, Brasília: IPEA, pp. 99–111.

PART III

The African Experience

8. Privatization and regulation in South Africa: an evaluation

Afeikhena Jerome

After decades of poor performance and inefficient operation by state-owned enterprises, governments all over the world have, since the 1980s, embraced privatization as a means of fostering economic growth, attaining macroeconomic stability and reducing public sector borrowing requirements. More than 100 countries have privatized well over 100 000 medium and large enterprises in one form or another in the last two decades (Megginson and Netter, 2001).

Although privatization has been relatively less successful in Africa than in other regions,[1] Africa was not left out in the race to sell off state enterprises. Currently, only nine countries in Africa have yet to initiate a privatization programme. Even war-torn countries such as Liberia, Rwanda and Sierra Leone have begun to privatize some enterprises. Rwanda, still recovering from the genocide of 1994, has a very active privatization programme. Namibia is perhaps one of the very few with no plans to privatize, largely because its state enterprises are generally well run (Harsch, 2000; Ariyo and Jerome, 2003).

Despite the mounting evidence that associates privatization with improved performance, higher profitability, output and productivity growth, fiscal benefits, quality improvements and better access for the poor (Boubakri and Cosset, 1998 and 1999; Megginson et al., 1994; Dewenter and Malatesta, 2001; Chong and López-de-Silanes, 2003), there is increasing disenchantment with privatization. The initial trend has lost momentum and there is growing resentment and questioning of the benefits of privatization by both populist and intellectual voices. This has occurred in the face of some high-profile failures in infrastructure privatization and concern that privatization does not produce macroeconomic and distributional gains equivalent to its microeconomic benefit. As a result, the pendulum is currently swinging back toward increased governmental provision and supervision (Kikeri and Nellis, 2004).

Privatization has generally been oversold as a panacea for all economic ills, often misunderstood and all too often imperfectly implemented. This applies in South Africa, where the programme has from the outset been

179

highly controversial and contentious. There is also increasing recognition of the importance of a regulatory framework to counter pervasive market failures as a result of natural monopolies, information failure, externalities and other social concerns. Governments across sub-Saharan Africa, often at the prodding of multilateral institutions, have established, or are establishing, regulatory agencies for utilities, inspired mostly by the industrial countries' model rather than their peculiar national context. In spite of its growing importance, infrastructure regulation has remained under-researched in Africa. Arguably, with the exception of South Africa where the literature is gradually evolving, not much is known about the post-privatization transition to utility regulation in Africa, especially within the context of region-specific peculiarities.

Given the increasing interest in privatization and regulation, this chapter evaluates South Africa's privatization experience in the light of a decade of democracy. It attempts to make a distinct contribution to the literature inasmuch as many evaluations so far of South Africa's privatization programme are few and disjointed, with a good number assuming an ideological disposition. Existing empirical studies are confined mainly to evaluating water privatization (Bayat and Moolla, 2003). Apart from complementing the growing volume of research on privatization in South Africa (Schwella, 2002; Jerome and Rangata, 2003; BusinessMap, 2004), this chapter sets out to be the first comprehensive evaluation of the programme a decade after the demise of apartheid. This is particularly relevant in view of growing uncertainty about South Africa's privatization plans in the wake of recent changes in ministerial portfolio after the April 2004 elections.

Arguably, privatization in South Africa had been slow, with few visible results and a general feeling among observers and donors that governments' commitment to the process was generally half-hearted. Consequently, most of the intended objectives have remained unrealized. Despite the growing unease about privatization, it should neither be abandoned nor reversed. Rather, there should be a strengthening of efforts to privatize correctly: by better tailoring privatization to local conditions; deepening efforts to promote competition and regulatory frameworks; enforcing transparency in sales processes; and introducing mechanisms to ensure that the poor have access to affordable essential services. It is necessary to 'lock in' the gains and prevent backsliding.

The remainder of the chapter is structured as follows. Section I gives a brief overview of the critical success factors for privatization and regulation; Section II examines the privatization programme in South Africa itself. An evaluation of this programme is conducted in Section III, and analysis of the regulatory framework takes place in Section IV. Finally, a conclusion is reached in Section V.

I. CRITICAL SUCCESS FACTORS FOR PRIVATIZATION AND REGULATION

Despite the extensive adoption of privatization, it has from the outset been highly controversial and politically charged. This relates to the agency and credibility problems that are unleashed by the exercise as well as its implications for income distribution. At the heart of much of the criticism is the perception that privatization has been unfair, hurting the poor, the disenfranchised and in some cases beleaguered workers (Birdsall and Nellis, 2002). In spite of the fact that there is no universally applicable approach to privatization, and given that the attempt to apply a 'one-size-fits-all' approach has proven ineffective and counterproductive, the literature has identified the necessary features of a legitimate and acceptable national policy. This constitutes a universal benchmark for evaluating the design, implementation process and outcome of national (privatization) policies and programmes. These include broad-based participation, political commitment, competition and transparency, among others.

Privatization requires strong political commitment. It is intensely political since most transactions produce winners as well as losers and the gains are usually diffused and only realized in the longer term. At the same time, the costs are short term and borne by vulnerable but vocal groups, such as labour. Privatization thus requires careful handling by the political and administrative leadership to explain alternatives, build coalitions for change, and deal with the disaffected. Top-level political commitment is a necessary but not sufficient condition for successful privatization efforts. Public perceptions of success are important for the privatization process. The building of widespread public understanding among a larger group of stakeholders is essential. In this regard, the availability of information is key. Many countries have found public information campaigns to be helpful. Such campaigns are particularly effective when combined with mechanisms to ensure broad-based participation and to mitigate political and social costs (e.g. procedures for transparency, labour programmes, and share ownership schemes in firms being sold).

The difficulties of SOE reform and the substantial empirical evidence on privatization strongly support the importance of ownership. Contract theory notes, however, that ownership structure matters only if complete contracts cannot be written (Grossman and Hart, 1986). Indeed, a handful of empirical studies ascribe performance improvements after sale to competition rather than a change in ownership. Sachs et al. (2000), for example, examine the empirical evidence across 24 transition economies and conclude that ownership alone is not enough to generate economic performance improvements. It is when ownership change is combined with institutional reforms aimed at the removal of barriers to entry and exit, improving prudential regulation and corporate governance, hardening budget constraints, and developing capital markets that one sees substantial and enduring progress. Galal et al. (1994) also demonstrates that while ownership matters, competitive markets reinforce the benefits of private ownership. Maximum impact is produced when market competitiveness, hardened budget constraints and improved regulatory frameworks coincide with privatization. The higher the level of institutional reforms, the more positive the economic performance impact from a change of ownership. At the same time, institutional reforms do not guarantee performance improvements unless there is a minimum level of ownership change. Thus, while ownership matters, policies and institutions matter just as much.

Rapid and extensive divestment without a proper framework can lead to disastrous results, as the experience of Eastern Europe has demonstrated (Nellis, 1999, pp. 16–19). For each transaction, proper planning, execution, monitoring and assessment are necessary. Transparency is an integral part of the privatization. It includes timely access to relevant information, respect for rules of the game and procedures, as well as control. Lack of transparency often leads to allegations of corruption and provides ammunition to political and other opponents of privatization. It often creates backlash from investors and the public at large, and threatens to halt the process. In Russia, the mass privatization programme permitted insiders to engage in extensive 'self-dealing', while the subsequent privatization 'auctions' were a massive give-away of the most important assets at bargain prices to a handful of well-connected oligarchs, who, in the absence of adequate legal and institutional arrangements, continued to act that way (Black et al., 2000). As a result, the public came to oppose privatization, associating it with corruption and wealth transfers to a chosen few.

Regulation is now recognized as an important instrument in the development toolkit, which when properly conducted can support market-led pro-poor growth and development (Parker and Kirkpatrick, 2002). After a decade of infrastructure privatization and liberalization in Africa and some high-profile failures, there is increasing recognition of the importance of a regulatory framework. Governments across sub-Saharan Africa, often at the prodding of multilateral institutions, have established or are establishing regulatory agencies for utilities, inspired mostly by the industrial countries' model rather than their peculiar national context. The main rationale for regulation is to counter pervasive 'market failures' where competition is either not feasible or does not produce results compatible with the public interest. In infrastructure industries, this may take the form of natural monopolies, where private monopolists may seek to levy prices significantly above marginal costs, or public monopolies, which may allow costs to rise above efficient levels or offer services of inferior quality; information failures such that consumers are able to assess the quality of the service they are paying for;

externalities with implications for controlling environmental standards, public health and safety; and social concerns since many infrastructure services are considered essential to life.

When infrastructure reforms were introduced in developing and transition economies, many of them had little or no precedence to guide the design of regulatory mechanisms. Under pressure from multilateral institutions, investment bankers and financial advisers, many of these countries hastily adopted regulatory templates from developed countries. These models were rarely adapted to the political and institutional features prevalent in these economies, including lack of checks and balances, limited technical expertise, weak auditing, accounting and tax systems, and widespread corruption and regulatory capture (Laffont, 1996). As a result, such efforts have had limited successes or failed woefully. Many government entities, especially sector ministers, have resisted giving up their regulatory functions and limiting their roles to policy oversight,[2] assessing industry development and adjusting policies accordingly (World Bank, 2004).

Lessons from the past decade indicate the importance of planning for credible and efficient regulation, including its economic content and institutional architecture prior to reform (Willig, 1999). There is growing consensus around the key design features for a modern regulatory agency. The main features of effective regulation of privatized utilities are coherence, independence, accountability, predictability, transparency and capacity (Noll, 2000 and Stern and Holder, 1999). No matter the sophistication of the regulatory design, utility regulators usually face a number of challenges, which have been outlined by Smith (2000). These include:

- Developing and applying the expertise required to address challenging issues in highly complex and increasing dynamic industries. While understanding the technical features of the regulatory industry is clearly essential, the regulator will need to draw expertise in economics, finance, law and engineering to understand the art and science of regulatory decisions.
- Resisting undue pressure or influences from political authorities (political capture), who are often interested in short-term gains.
- Resisting undue pressure from regulated firms (regulatory capture) to ensure that the balance between consumer and producers interest is struck in their favour.
- Obtaining information from regulated firms. Well-informed decisions also require inputs from a diffuse range of consumers, who individually have limited incentives to provide full or accurate information.
- Exercising their responsibilities in a way that builds public support for their role and decisions, and thus helps to sustain reform.

Furthermore, newly created agencies in developing countries typically face more severe constraints, particularly when they are established as part of broader reforms including privatization. In the face of weak personnel, or non-existent data on the regulated firm, they may be required to introduce unpopular tariff increases at a time when privatization remains contentious and consumers have unrealistic expectations about the timing of service improvement.

II. THE PRIVATIZATION AND RESTRUCTURING PROGRAMME IN SOUTH AFRICA

The post-apartheid government inherited well over 300 state-owned enterprises. A startling 50 per cent of South African fixed capital assets were in state hands when the Mandela government took office in 1994, while the private sector was dominated by a handful of closely held conglomerates operating in a loosely regulated and inherently anti-competitive setting. These enterprises were established primarily to strengthen import-substitution industries, which had started to grow during World War I, by providing infrastructure improvements and basic materials. Eventually, they were used as platform for 'white' employment and social benefits as well as creating a support base among the white working class and Afrikaner business owners. These enterprises were incurring losses, and the low efficiency of some of them was a source of continued criticism of the government.

In 1985, privatization was accepted as part of the economic policy in South Africa for many of the same reasons that have made it a new economic creed almost worldwide. State corporations had been the major recipients of large foreign loans that were called in and cut off in 1985, leaving them with serious capital shortages. It was envisaged that sales of the corporations' assets could both ease the debt burden and provide the government with new revenue for much-needed social programmes.

In 1987 the government's position was formulated and spelled out in a White Paper (White Paper on Privatization and Restructuring, 1987). However, except for the contracting out of certain government services, for example building and maintenance of roads and toll roads and the introduction of compensatory tariffs, the privatization drive lost some momentum by the beginning of the 1990s and was eventually put on hold during the period of constitutional negotiations. The initial attempt suffered from two major drawbacks. Many multinational enterprises were reluctant to buy South African enterprises because of international sanctions. More fundamentally, it met with stiff opposition from anti-apartheid organizations and trade unions led by COSATU (Congress of South African Trade Unions). The African National

Congress (ANC), which was expected to come to power in the near future, perceived it as a ploy to deny them control over the family jewels even after they achieve majority rule.

The results were that of the five state institutions that were originally earmarked for privatization, only Iscor (a steel company) was eventually sold in 1989 for 3 billion rand,[3] while corporatization policies, in which government retained ownership, were successfully adopted for others (Schwella, 2002).[4]

For many years prior to the democratic elections in 1994, there had been a heated debate in the ANC and other political organizations about the future of the economy, and privatization was a key issue in this debate (ILRIG, 1999). The position of the ANC has been anti-privatization, deriving from the freedom charter. The first economic blueprint of the new democratic government outlined in the Reconstruction and Development Programme (RDP) was published just before the 1994 elections. It opted for a development state in a mixed economy and an expansive role for the state. On privatization, the RPD was ambivalent and stated:

> There must be significant role for public sector investment to complement private sector and community participation in stimulating reconstruction and development. The primary question in this regard is not the legal form that government involvement in activity might take at a given point, but whether such actions strengthen the ability of the economy to respond to the inequalities in the country, relieve the material hardship of the majority of the people, and stimulate economic growth and competitiveness.

In the various debates on economic policy by labour, business and government, there was an agreement that the state needed to be restructured. The disagreement borders more on the nature of the restructuring. While labour opted for a developmental state with increased service provision to redress the backlogs of apartheid, business preferred a leaner and more efficient state. COSATU held demonstrations in response to privatization proposals by the newly elected government.

The conflict between government, business and labour on privatization appeared resolved in the National Framework Agreement (NFA) signed through the National Development and Labour Council (NEDLAC) in 1995 by COSATU, the Federation of Unions of South Africa (FEDUSA), the National Council of Trade Unions (NACTU) and the government of National Unity. The NFA was the first occasion on which the government and organized labour successfully negotiated around the policy of privatization. It marked a change in the policy stance of COSATU. Before NFA, COSATU had rejected privatization but in the NFA it accepted that privatization could take place in certain instances.

On NFA and workers, the Framework Agreement stated, *inter alia*:

> The ultimate aim of restructuring is to improve the quality of life for all South Africans. Therefore, the underlying approach is that restructuring should not occur at the expense of workers in state enterprises. Every effort must be made to retain employment. Where restructuring potentially has negative effects on workers, a social plan must be negotiated with the relevant unions at the enterprise level which takes account of the workers' interest.

The NFA outlined the goals of restructuring of certain state assets and the steps that were to be followed in the process. It set up a number of joint structures of government and labour to discuss plans for restructuring.

In June 1996, the government released its macroeconomic strategy tagged 'Growth, Employment and Redistribution' (GEAR), which envisions a broad-based privatization programme (although the term privatization was not used in the document). It outlined the process of restructuring of state-owned assets, the need for appropriate regulatory policies and the creation of public–private partnerships (PPPs) in recognition of the limited capacity of fiscal resources. According to the document:

> The nature of restructuring, as outlined in the framework agreement, may involve the total sale of the asset, a partial sale to strategic equity partners or the sale of the asset with government retaining a strategic interest. Work is in progress to address the outstanding issues on the restructuring of the remaining state enterprises. The restructuring will take place in a phased manner so as to ensure maximum value and adequate regulatory frameworks. Specific policy issues and further elaboration will be dealt with by the responsible Ministers.

Once GEAR became the economic policy of the government, restructuring was conducted in a number of state enterprises. Thambo Mbeki, then Deputy President, announced plans for a wide-sweeping privatization programme in late 1995 and this provoked strong protests from labour unions over the threat of job losses and labour's exclusion from the policy decision.

The programme eventually got under way in 1996 though the sales of enterprises actually began in 1997. The government, under pressure from the unions, proceeded very cautiously with what is now referred to as the 'restructuring of state assets'. A policy distinction between 'strategic' and smaller 'non-strategic' enterprises was initially made by the new government: the partial sell-off of minority stakes in strategic institutions (e.g. the telecommunications sector) was only initiated in 1997, while some of the other smaller 'non-strategic' enterprises (e.g. public resorts) were to be sold out of hand once the necessary corporatization and turnaround strategies had been implemented.

Six radio stations owned by the South African Broadcasting Corporation were sold. A 30 per cent stake in Telkom was sold to a consortium of US-based

SBS Communications (18 per cent) and Telkom Malaysia Benald (12 per cent) for a consideration of R750 million. The interests are held via an investment holding company, Thintana Communications LLC. Sun Air was sold for R97 million to Black Empowerment: the new stakeholders were Rethabile Group (35 per cent), coordinated network instruments (19 per cent) and the National Empowerment Fund (15 per cent) and staff (5 per cent). By August 1999, the company ceased operation. This was followed by the sales of 20 per cent stake in South African Airways (SAA) in 1999 to Swissair for R1.4 billion but repurchased subsequently by Transnet in 2002 due to problems in Swissair. A 20 per cent stake in the Airports Company of South Africa (ACSA) which controls all major airports in South Africa was sold to Italy's Aeroporti Di Roma and a further initial public offering (IPO) of shares is planned. Strategic management partners were appointed for the Aventura Leisure Group, the Alexkor Diamond Mine and the South African Post Office, although the management contract with the New Zealand Post Office was terminated in 2001. About R2.5 billion was also raised from partial sales of Transnet's holdings in cellular telephone operator MTN. Denel, the defence firm, was partially privatized and foreign strategic partners BAE systems and Turbomecca have been introduced. Some of the nation's forests and Mossgas were also sold.

The privatization programme, however, suffered from lack of policy credibility. Both the business community in South Africa and organized labour criticized the privatization process and the attitude of the government. Criticism from the business community (*Business Times*, 25 April 1999) centres on the perceived slowness of the government in implementing GEAR and especially the delay in privatizing state assets. Business South Africa argues that the government is sending the wrong signals to the investor community and delaying much-needed investment (Pape, 1998). Labour's criticism, especially that of COSATU and its affiliates, is based on its analysis that GEAR contradicts and abandons the RDP, and that privatization of state assets endangers the delivery of basic social needs and leads to loss of employment. Labour also believes that the economy can be kick-started by heavy investment that would lead to consumption and growth (Pape, 1998; Mostert, 2002).

At a meeting on 29 November 1999, the Interministerial Cabinet Committee on the Restructuring of State Assets (IMCC) directed that a more comprehensive policy framework be prepared to guide the restructuring process into the twenty-first century. This policy framework would ensure a consistent approach to restructuring across government and address perceived market uncertainties about government's restructuring priorities.

In August 2000, in what amounted to a renewed commitment to the privatization programme, the Department of Public Enterprises published the Policy Framework for an accelerated agenda for the restructuring of state-owned enterprises. The document endorsed NFA's objectives and aims at increasing SOE efficiency through improved governance and competition, while seeking to attract foreign investment, technology and expertise through full or partial privatization. It anticipates that at least R40 billion, representing about 5 per cent of GDP, would be generated over the period 2002–2004. It targeted the four key enterprises: Telkom (telecommunications), Transnet (transport), Eskom (electricity) and Denel (defence), collectively described in the government's policy framework as 'key enterprises'. They account for the 86 per cent of the sector's aggregate turnover, 94 per cent of total income, 77 per cent of all employment in the top SOEs and 91 per cent of total assets (Mostert, 2002). Completion of the restructuring programme was scheduled for the end of 2004.

New guidelines were also put forward with regard to five key areas, namely the economic and social effects of restructuring; the development of appropriate regulatory and competitive frameworks; promoting empowerment; corporate governance; and improving the restructuring process.

In April 2001, a further 3 per cent of Telkom, South Africa's only fixed-line telecom operator, was sold to Ucingo, a BEE grouping. A public listing of the second tranche of 20 per cent of Telkom shares was due in 2000/2001 but this was delayed due to adverse market conditions. Major privatizations in the year 2002 include the sales of Aventura resorts in January for R29 million, 51 per cent of Denel's Altimotiv division in July 2002 for R50 million, a 20 per cent stake in cellphone group M-Cell in August and a 51 per cent stake in Apron Services in October for R117 million.

On 14 April 2003, the Minister of Public Enterprises, while presenting the DPE Budget Vote to the National Assembly, highlighted the major developments in the restructuring of SOEs. According to the Minister, government conducted 11 transactions in 2002 to bring the total number of transactions since 1997 to 27. These included outright disposals, equity sales, participation of BEE groups, dividend payments, proceeds from the rationalization of interests across SOEs, and the Telkom IPO. Total privatization proceeds have been estimated at R35.5 billion, with the National Revenue Fund absorbing just under R22.5 billion (Radebe, 2003). No major privatizations took place in 2003, with the exception of the final disposal of Aventura Resorts and the listing of Telkom, the state telecommunications company.

Amidst turbulent equity markets, a further sale of a 28 per cent stake in Telkom took place in 2003, reducing the government's shareholding to 39 per cent. The sale involved a primary listing on the Johannesburg Stock Exchange and a secondary listing on the New York Stock Exchange on 4 March. Proceeds have been, however, lower than expected, around 0.4 per cent of GDP, compared to a target of 1 per cent, owing to the weak state of the global telecommunications market. Telkom IPO was implemented in the context of the government black economic empowerment objectives, through equity ownership, procurement and skill transfer. In particular, a two-tiered offering was structured to target historically disadvantaged people. To date, this has been the largest global IPO and the largest telecommunications IPO in Europe, the Middle East and Africa since the listing of Burberry in July 2002. However, Telkom continues to retain a stranglehold on the sector. Competition, which was legally supposed to begin on 7 May 2002, with Telkom losing its statutory monopoly on basic services, is being delayed. The SNO and the underserviced area licences had not been launched as at February 2004, while cheap bandwidth remains elusive.

Since the April 2004 elections, there has been growing uncertainty about South Africa's privatization plans. On 14 June, Alec Erwin,[5] the new Minister of Public Enterprises, told Parliament that he had no plans to sell off any of the large state-owned companies that have long been destined for privatization.

III.   EVALUATION OF THE PROGRAMME

The South African approach to restructuring and privatization is unique as it does not really fit any of the models applied elsewhere in the world. The general thrust puts more emphasis on the restructuring of the state sector than on privatization. The government is generally not in favour of full privatization. Rather, it has pursued partial privatization by selling equity to 'strategic equity partners' and black empowerment groups while retaining a majority interest (as in the case of Telkom, the Airports Company and South African Airways). In some ways, South Africa has followed the French example, where the state remains a majority stakeholder after partial privatizations. However, where the French prefer domestic private investors, the South African approach has been to involve foreign investors, but then only as minority partners (Schwella, 2002). This approach to restructuring and privatization has been shaped by the political need to maintain the Tripartite Alliance of the African National Congress, the South African Communist Party and COSATU.

The main objectives of the government's privatization initiatives are to facilitate economic growth, to promote the development of historically disadvantaged communities and black economic empowerment, to extend private ownership of government-controlled assets to employees and to previously disadvantaged persons, to reduce the national borrowing requirement and to promote skills transfer and fair competition. On the macroeconomic front, the programme aims to attract foreign investment, reduce public borrowing requirements and assist in the development of an economic context that promotes industrial competitiveness and fuels economic growth.

Judged against these objectives, the programme has not achieved much. Very large state-owned enterprises (SOEs) remain prominent in the transport, telecommunications, broadcasting, energy and armaments sectors. In the main, the programme has largely focused on divestiture of 'non-core business' such as broadcasting stations, resorts, and related services in the transport sector as well as selling minority stakes in utilities to so-called strategic equity partners and black economic empowerment groups.

Since inception, the programme has been characterized by a series of 'fits and starts' instead of a consistent approach where government benefit from a learning curve (Jackson, 2004). The tepid approach, especially in relation to the four major enterprises, has not yielded the desired results. Owing to the slow pace of the exercise, the government has not generated as much revenue as envisaged. By March 2004, total proceeds amounted to R35.6 billion, with the National Revenue Fund absorbing just under R22.5 billion. Total sales proceeds since inception are equivalent to just 2.59 per cent of Year 2003 GDP at market prices.

The programme has also delivered very little in the area of black economic empowerment (BEE). This is illustrated by the case of Telkom, which had a 3 per cent shareholding by a BEE consortium Ucingo from its earlier privatization. The consortium was forced to cede the stake to financiers as it was unable to finance it at listing price levels.

IV. REGULATION IN SOUTH AFRICA

Regulation in South Africa is conducted by a diverse and wide range of independent regulators. These are supplemented by many others that function in provincial and municipal spheres of government. Given limitations of space, but, more importantly, given the importance of the affected sectors in output terms, we evaluate only the utility regulators in electricity and telecommunications.

The Independent Communications Authority of South Africa (ICASA)[6]

The Independent Communications Authority of South Africa (ICASA) regulates the telecommunications and the broadcasting sectors. It was established in July 2000 by Act No. 13 of 2000 as a result of the merger of two previous regulators, the South African Telecommunications Regulatory Authority (SATRA) and the Independent Broadcasting Authority (IBA), to facilitate effective and seamless regulation of telecommunications and broadcasting and to accommodate the convergence of technologies.

ICASA regulates the telecommunications and broadcasting industries in the public interest. Its statutory functions are to make regulations and policies that govern broadcasting and telecommunications; issue licences to providers of telecommunication services and broadcasters; monitor the environment and enforce compliance with rules, regulations and policies; hear and decide on disputes and complaints brought by industry or members of the public against licensees; plan, control and manage the frequency spectrum; and protect consumers from unfair business practices, poor-quality services and harmful or inferior products.

It is the policy of the Government of South Africa that all people should have access to basic telecommunications services at affordable prices. The role of ICASA as a regulator is central to achieving this goal, and the ownership and control of telecommunication and broadcasting services by people from historically disadvantaged groups. The Authority promotes the attainment of universal service and access by putting requirements in operator's licences to roll out services in underserviced areas and ensuring that licensees contribute to the Universal Service Fund.[7]

In practice, the telecommunications sector in South Africa is not regulated in the same way as broadcasting. ICASA is guided by ministerial policy directions, with a severely constrained form of independence, as demonstrated in Box 8.1.

BOX 8.1   INEFFICIENCIES IN TELKOM

Telkom has enormous monopoly power over the fixed line network. While South Africa was hailed as one of the early starters of reform on the continent in the mid-1990s, the strategy of privatization of the incumbent monopoly coupled with a period of exclusivity and restrictions on liberalization has not delivered on national objectives.

The price cap method was adopted by a Ministerial determination on 7 May 1997 and was set for three years following section four of the Telecommunications Act. There was no direct experience and Telkom productivity data to guide the determination of the productivity improvement factor X. The cap was negotiated with very limited information and understanding.

In 2001, the new regulator published a new draft price cap regulation, received public comments and forwarded the decision to the Minister for approval. Telkom lobbied the Minister and approval of ICASA's new price regulation was delayed. Before the regulation was implemented, Telkom filed for new price

increases in 2002 based on the old regime, including a 23.9 per
cent increase in local call charges. ICASA rejected Telkom's filing
and the matter ended in the courts. Finally, a negotiated settlement was reached whereby Telkom's price increase was
approved subject to the introduction of a new lifeline service to try
to keep customers in the network. This and other amendments
were belatedly approved by the Minister on 24 October 2002.

South Africa is one of the few countries where progress in fixed
line network development has been declining. The cost of a local
three-minute call at peak time has increased at 26 per cent per
annum between 1997 and 2002. By the end of the five-year
exclusivity period, two million subscribers have been disconnected due to the high price of services. South Africa has slipped
in international benchmark comparisons from the best in Africa to
fifth.

Source: Adapted from Melody (2002).

The National Electricity Regulator (NER)

The South African electricity industry is dominated by a state-owned and
vertically integrated utility, Eskom, which ranks among the five largest in the
world. It supplies reliable electricity at among the lowest prices in the world.
The national electricity utility is commercially run, with no recourse to the
national treasury. It raises all its finance through debt, off its balance sheet,
mostly through issuing bonds, which are well supported by local and international capital markets. The industry has accomplished an unprecedented
national electrification programme, connecting about 2.5 million additional
households over the past six years, thereby increasing the proportion of the
population with access to electricity from about one-third of the population to
about two-thirds.

The NER is the regulatory authority over the electricity supply industry
(ESI) in South Africa. It is a statutory body established by the Electricity Act,
No. 41 of 1987, as amended by the Electricity Amendment Acts of 1994 and
1995. The NER was established on 1 April 1995 as the successor to the
Electricity Control Board. The Minister of Minerals and Energy appoints
board members, but once appointed, the NER acts independently and reports
to Parliament. The Board of the NER consists of a chairperson, a CEO and
seven other members, all of whom are knowledgeable and experienced in
broader electricity supply industry issues. Members do not act as representa-

tives of stakeholder interests but serve in their individual capacities. The Board is supported by a small, full-time support staff, which includes functional experts in technical, financial, economics, customer and support services areas.

The NER is funded from a levy imposed on generators of electricity, which is passed on to all customers. However, there is jurisdictional conflict between the competition commission and NER.

Section 21 (1) of the Competition Act provides that the Competition Commission

(h) Negotiate agreements with any regulatory authority to co-ordinate and harmonise the exercise of jurisdiction over competition matters within the relevant industry or sector, and to ensure the consistent application of this Act.
(i) Participate in the proceedings of any regulatory authority;
(j) Advise, and receive advice from any regulatory authority;
(k) Over time, review legislation and public regulations, and report to the Minister concerning any provision that permits uncompetitive behaviour.

On the other hand, the Electricity Act of 1987 (amended in 1994) gives the NER statutory responsibility to regulate market access to electricity suppliers (through licensing) and to approve all electricity prices. A formal agreement between the Competition Commission and the NER does not yet exist. A common understanding would need to be developed between the two regulatory bodies and government on the scope and pace of restructuring to achieve competition in the electricity industry and the respective roles in overseeing competition.

The NER will in the future have to face up to serious pricing challenges as current generating capacity is reaching its limits. The combination of excess capacity, ready availability of cheap, low-grade coal and innovative coal-fired techniques enabled Eskom to become one of the lowest-cost electricity producers in the world.[8] Eskom has been able to feed rising demand for electricity over the past ten years during which the customer base increased from 500 000 to 3.5 million, while the real price of electricity has declined by an estimated 15 per cent.

CONCLUSIONS

Ten years after the fall of apartheid and the installation of a democratic government, South Africa has made remarkable progress in all major spheres. Its noteworthy achievements in surmounting economic challenges have been widely acknowledged, especially in the restoration of macroeconomic stability. While significant progress has been made in addressing development challenges, the legacy of the past is still disturbingly apparent. The country still faces the daunting task of reducing unemployment, stimulating economic growth and tackling poverty, which has become pervasive. Dealing with these backlogs, while simultaneously placing the economy on a more sustainable growth path, probably remain the two key conundrums facing policymakers and economic analysts in contemporary South Africa.

South Africa has the most sophisticated free market economy on the African continent. With only 3 per cent of the surface area, it accounts for approximately 28 per cent of the continent's gross domestic product and 40 per cent of industrial output. It has developed institutions comparable to those in any part of the world with regard to regulatory law and commercial practice. Property rights are generally well-defined. The country's well developed legal culture combines elements of several traditions. Much of the law about property, sales and contract can be traced to the Dutch–Roman law that the early European settlers brought with them in the seventeenth century. Company financial and intellectual property derives from English sources, a connection with the nineteenth-century development of large-scale undertakings related to mining (OECD, 2003). The financial, communications and transport infrastructure is well developed and modern. The stock exchange is among the world's ten largest. South African entrepreneurs and business professionals are generally highly educated, skilled and competitive. These are all essential features for privatization. Yet privatization has been less successful relative to other regions in Africa.

Arguably, privatization in South Africa had been slow, with few visible results and a general feeling among observers and donors that governments' commitment to the process was generally half-hearted. Consequently, most of the intended objectives have remained unrealized.

The missing link appears to be the institutional framework. Privatization or restructuring got under way with no clearly defined 'frames' or 'waves'. Various government departments were involved, depending on the industry concerned. The lack of clarity about the different roles both within government and between government and state-owned enterprises and other stakeholders created significant bottlenecks. Despite the growing unease about privatization, it should neither be abandoned nor reversed. Rather, there should be a strengthening of efforts to privatize correctly: by better tailoring privatization to local conditions, deepening efforts to promote competition and regulatory frameworks, enforcing transparency in sales processes, and introducing mechanisms to ensure that the poor have access to affordable essential services.

It is necessary to 'lock in' the gains and prevent backsliding. The piecemeal privatization efforts thus far now need to be replaced by a comprehensive policy structure replete with legislative reform to create a robust and transparent investment framework. The critical factors in the success of any privatization programme are embracing privatization in its totality and not on a transactional basis. The commitment to privatization in particular and to private sector development in general should be based on pragmatic considerations and the demonstrated benefits associated with such a commitment. A more rapid and wider privatization programme, especially in infrastructure, will stimulate competition, allay investors' confidence and encourage private investment and capital inflows.

NOTES

1. Sales revenue in Africa accounted for 3 per cent of total developing country proceeds during 1990–99. Estimated revenues over the decade for 37 sub-Saharan states totalled $9 billion, less than the amount raised by sales in New Zealand alone (Nellis, 2003) and about a third of the value of two Brazilian telecommunications auctions in the mid-1990s.
2. The oft-cited example is Morocco Telecommunications, where the very successful erstwhile Director of ARNT, M. Terrab, had to resign over disagreement with the Secretary of State for Information Technology, Nasr Hejji.
3. There had been an attempt to sell ISCOR in 1929, just a few years after its creation, but there were no buyers.
4. The South African Transport Services, for example, was transformed into a public company, Transnet, and the Department of Post and Telecommunications into two public companies, Telkom and the South African Post Office.
5. According to Mr Erwin, he would prefer to make state-owned firms work better first, rather than preside over 'some sell-off type of privatisation'. See *The Economist*, 24 June 2004; 'South African Privatisation on hold?'
6. ICASA derives its mandate from four statutes. These are the ICASA Act of 2000, the Independent Broadcasting Act of 1993, the Broadcasting Act of 1999 and the Telecommunications Authority Act No. 103 of 1996. See http://www.icasa.org.za/.
7. ICASA does not, however, administer the Universal Service Fund, but merely receives monies on behalf of the Universal Service Agency (USA).
8. An international survey conducted by NUS ranked Eskom's power rates as the lowest among 14 countries. These countries included Italy, the USA, the United Kingdom, France, Canada and Australia. The second cheapest country, Sweden, was 58.5 per cent more expensive.

REFERENCES

Ariyo, A. and A. Jerome (2003), 'Privatisation in Africa: Lessons from the Ghanaian and Nigerian Experience', *African Development Yearbook*, Institute for World Economics and International Management (IWIM), University of Bremen, Germany.

Bayat, Ameina and Zunaid Moolla (2003), 'Private Participation in the Privatisation of Water Services: The Case of Nelspruit', TIPS/DPRU Forum 2003: The Challenge of Growth and Poverty: The South African Economy Since Democracy, 8 September 2003–10 September 2003, Indaba Hotel, Johannesburg.

Birdsall, N. and J. Nellis (2002), 'Winners and Losers: Assessing the Distributional Impact of Privatization', Centre for Global Development, Working Paper 6, May.

Black, B., R. Kraakman and A. Tarrasova (2000), 'Russian Privatization and Corporate Governance: What Went Wrong?', *Stanford Law Review*, **52** (6), 1731–808.

Boubakri, N. and J. Cosset (1998), 'The Financial and Operating Performance of Newly Privatised Firms: Evidence from Developing Countries', *Journal of Finance*, **53**, 1081–110.

Boubakri, N. and J. Cosset (1999), 'Does Privatization Meet the Expectations? Evidence from African Countries', Working Paper, Montreal: Ecole des HEC.

BusinessMap (2004), *Restructuring 2004: A Change of Pace*, A BusinessMap Foundation Report, Johannesburg: BusinessMap.

Chong, A. and F. López-de-Silanes (2003), 'The Truth about Privatization in Latin America', Working Paper No. R-486, Inter American Development Bank, October.

Dewenter, K. and P. Malatesta (2001), 'State-Owned and Privately Owned Firms: An Empirical Analysis of Profitability, Leverage, and Labour Intensity', *The American Economic Review*, **91** (1), 320–34.

Galal, A., L. Jones, P. Tandon and I. Vogelsang (1994), 'Welfare Consequences of Selling Public Enterprises', Washington, DC: World Bank.

Grossman, S.J. and O.D. Hart (1986), 'The Costs and Benefits of Ownership: The Theory of Vertical and Lateral Integration' *Journal of Political Economy*, **94**, 691–719.

Harsch, E. (2000), 'Privatization Shifts Gear in Africa', *Africa Recovery*, April.

ILRIG (1999), *An Alternative View of Privatisation*, Globalisation Series No. 4, Cape Town: International Labour and Information Group.

Jackson, J. (2004), 'Lessons from Restructuring: Structuring Sales Transaction and Getting it Right', *Restructuring 2004: A Change of Pace*, A BusinessMap Foundation Report, Johannesburg: BusinessMap.

Jerome, Afeikhena and Moses Rangata (2003), 'The Tortuous Road to Privatisation and Restructuring of State Assets in South Africa: Lessons from African Privatisation Experience', TIPS/DPRU Forum 2003: The Challenge of Growth and Poverty: The South African Economy Since Democracy, 8 September 2003–10 September 2003, Indaba Hotel, Johannesburg.

Kikeri, Sunita and John Nellis (2004), 'An Assessment of Privatization', *The World Bank Research Observer*, **19** (1), 87–118.

Laffont, J.J. (1996), 'Regulation, Privatization, and Incentives in Developing Countries', in M.G. Quibira and J.M. Dowling (eds), *Current Issues in Economic Development – An Asian Perspective*, Oxford and New York: published for the Asian Development Bank by Oxford University Press, Chapter 6.

Megginson, W.L. and J.M. Netter (2001), 'From State to Market: A Survey of Empirical Studies on Privatization', *Journal of Economic Literature*, **39**, 321–89.

Megginson, W., R. Nash and M. Randenborgh (1994), 'The Financial and Operating Performance of Newly Privatized Firms: An International Empirical Analysis', *Journal of Finance*, **49**, 403–52.

Melody, W. (2002), 'Assessing Telkom's 2003 Price Increase Proposal', LINK Centre Policy Research Paper No. 2, November.

Mostert, C. (2002), 'Reflections on South Africa's Restructuring of State-Owned Enterprises', Occasional Paper No. 5, Johannesburg: Friedrick Ebert Stifting, March.

Nellis, J. (1999), 'Time to Rethink Privatization in Transition Economies?', IFC Discussion Paper No. 38, Washington, DC: International Finance Corporation: http://www.ifc.org/economics/pubs/dp38/dp38.pdf.

Nellis, J. (2003), 'Privatization in Africa: What Has Happened? What is to be Done?', Center for Global Development Working Paper 25, February.

Noll, R. (2000), 'Telecommunications Reform in Developing Countries', in A.O. Krueger (ed.), *Economic Policy Reform: The Second Stage*, Chicago: University of Chicago Press.

OECD (2003), *Competition Law and Policy in South Africa. An OECD Peer Review*, Paris: Organisation for Economic Cooperation and Development, May.

Pape, C.W. (ed.) (1998), *An Alternative View of Globalisation*, Cape Town: ILRIG.

Parker, David and Colin Kirkpatrick (2002), 'Researching Economic Regulation in Developing Countries: Developing a Methodology for Critical Analysis', CRC Working Paper No. 34, Manchester: Centre on Regulation and Competition, University of Manchester.

Radebe, J. (2003), Budget Vote Presented by Jeff Radebe, Minister of Public Enterprises, Cape Town, South Africa.

Sachs, Jeffrey, Clifford Zinnes and Yair Eilat (2000) 'The Gains from Privatization in Transition Economies: Is "Change of Ownership" Enough?', Consulting Assistance on Economic Reform II Discussion Papers 63, Harvard University, Center for International Development, Cambridge, MA.

Schwella, E. (2002), 'Regulation and Competition in South Africa', Working Paper No. 18, Manchester: Centre on Regulation and Competition, University of Manchester.

Smith, Warrick (2000), 'Regulating Utilities: Thinking about Location Questions', Discussion Draft, World Bank Summer Workshop on Market Institutions, July, Washington, DC.

Stern, J. and S. Holder (1999), 'Regulatory Governance: Criteria for Assessing the Performance of Regulatory Systems. An application to infrastructure industries in the developing countries of Asia', *Utilities Policy*, **8**, 33–50.

Willig, R. (1999), 'Economic Principles to Guide Post-Privatization Governance', in F. Besanes, E.M. Uribe and R. Willig (eds), *Can Privatization Deliver? Infrastructure for Latin America*, Washington, DC and Baltimore, MD: Inter-American Development Bank and The Johns Hopkins University Press.

World Bank (2004) *Reforming Infrastructure: Privatization, Regulation, and Competition*, Washington, DC: World Bank.

9. A comparative analysis of the performance of public and private water utilities in Africa

Colin Kirkpatrick, David Parker and Yin-Fang Zhang

Donor agencies advocate the privatization of public utilities in lower-income economies to promote more efficient operation, increase investment and service coverage, and to reduce the financial burden on government budgets (World Bank, 1995). In response, a range of services, including water supply, has been opened up to private capital. By the end of 2001 there had been over US$755 billion of investment flows, involving nearly 2500 infrastructure projects in developing countries (Harris, 2003). This chapter looks at the economic impact of water services privatization in Africa using statistical, DEA (data envelopment analysis) and stochastic cost frontier measures. Recent studies have suggested that the impact of privatization has been more complex than expected in telecommunications and electricity generation (e.g. Wallsten, 2001; Zhang et al., 2003a, 2003b). Perhaps the same applies to water services.

The provision of high-quality water services remains a priority for most developing economies. According to the World Bank (2003, p. 1), more than 1 billion people in the developing world lack access to clean water and nearly 1.2 billion lack adequate sanitation. An estimated 12.2 million people die every year from diseases directly related to drinking contaminated water. Improved investment in water services and their more efficient management are a development priority (OECD, 2000). The Millennium Development Goal is to halve the number of people using unsafe water by 2015 (Hulls, 2003, p. 32). The pressing question for public policy is the extent to which privatization is critical to achieving that objective.

In this chapter, we first review the existing econometric evidence on the impact of water privatization. We then provide results using a data set for African water utilities and statistical, DEA and stochastic cost frontier measures. The statistical and DEA results suggest that utilities with private capital do seem, in the main, to perform better than pure state-owned water suppliers. However, the stochastic cost frontier analysis finds no statistically significant difference in public–private performance. The chapter goes on to consider the difficulties that face privatization in water services, in terms of the technology of water provision and the nature of the product, transaction costs and regulatory weaknesses. We then separately model the effects of regulation in a repeated stochastic cost frontier analysis, but find no statistically significant effect. This result possibly reflects inadequacies in the available data on water regulation in Africa.

THE EXISTING EVIDENCE

Private water suppliers exist in all developing countries in the form of water vendors at the street level, but there was little privatization of piped water services in developing countries before 1990 (Snell, 1998; Collignon and Vézina, 2000). Where privatized services existed, for example in Côte d'Ivoire, these were usually French-speaking ex-colonies that had inherited a reliance on private firms for water services, as exists in France. Between 1984 and 1990 only eight contracts for water and sewerage projects were awarded to the private sector worldwide and the cumulative new capital expenditure in private water services totalled less than US$1 billion.

However, during the 1990s there was increased water privatization activity, stimulated by donor agency pressures, and in 1997 the total figure for private investment had risen to US$25 billion. By the end of 2000, at least 93 countries had privatized some of their piped water services, including Argentina, Chile, China, Colombia, the Philippines, South Africa and the transition economies of Central Europe, as well as Australia and the UK (Brubaker, 2001). Taking the period from 1990 to 2002, there were 106 such projects in Latin America and the Caribbean, and 73 in East Asia and the Pacific region. By contrast there were only seven projects in the Middle East and North Africa and 14 in sub-Saharan Africa. In terms of the amounts invested, Latin America and the Caribbean and East Asia and the Pacific accounted together for over 95 per cent of the total investment (calculated on the basis of data from the World Bank PPI Database). Table 9.1 provides a summary of the largest investments in water services during the period 1990 to 2002. Clearly, a small number of countries accounted for most of the privatization of water services, and within these countries figures were dominated by a few large contracts. Indeed, one project, Aguas Argentinas, accounted for US$4.9 billion or 20 per cent of the investment in the whole of Latin America, while five Philippines contracts accounted for 38.4 per cent of the total private investment in water services in East Asia.

Table 9.1   *Largest investments in water services in developing countries,*
              1990–2002

	US$ billion	No. of projects
Argentina	7.23	10
Philippines	5.87	5
Chile	3.95	13
Brazil	3.17	33
Malaysia	2.75	6
China	1.93	44
Romania	1.04	3
Turkey	0.94	2
Indonesia	0.92	8

Source: Calculated using data from the World Bank PPI Project Database,
http://rru.worldbank.org/PPI.

Evidence suggests that the privatization of monopolies produces ambiguous results in terms of improving economic performance (Megginson and Netter, 2001) and it is to be expected that the institutional requirements to ensure that privatized monopolies perform well, notably an effective system of state regulation and supporting governance structures, will be particularly missing in many developing countries (Parker and Kirkpatrick, 2004). Privatizing water services is normally associated with contracts that take the following forms: service contracts (contracts to provide specialist services such as billing); management contracts and leases for existing facilities (private companies operating existing facilities but without new private sector investment); concessions (requiring the private sector to invest in facilities); divestitures (sale by the state of some or all of the equity in SOEs); and greenfield investments (including build–operate–transfer [BOT] type schemes) (Johnstone and Wood, 2001, pp. 10–11). In practice, contracts under which private firms provide the services but government remains the ultimate owner of the water system and may remain responsible for some investment are commonplace (OECD, 2003). Of 233 water and sewerage contracts with the private sector arranged between 1990 and 2002 on the World Bank's PPI Database, 40 per cent involved concession contracts and these accounted for 64 per cent of the total amount invested (see Table 9.2).

Where greenfield projects have occurred, for instance in China, they have often involved the building and operation of new water treatment plants; while BOT schemes for water supplies have been largely restricted to Latin America and the Caribbean. Divestitures or the sale of state-owned water businesses to the private sector have been rare, accounting for only 15.6 per cent of all water

Table 9.2   Types of private water and sewerage projects in developing countries, 1990–2002

Type	Total investment (US$ bn)*	%	No. of projects	%
Concessions	22.31	64.0	93	40
Greenfield	7.00	20.0	75	32
Operations and management	0.18	0.5	46	20
Divestiture	5.48	15.6	19	8

Note: *This is the total invested in projects with private participation and not necessarily the private sector's commitment alone.

Source: Calculated using data from the World Bank PPI Project Database, http://rru.worldbank.org/PPI.

projects and 8 per cent of the total funds invested. Also, although privatization of water services has occurred, it is important not to exaggerate its importance. At present little more than 5 per cent of the world's population is provided with drinking water through private operators (OECD, 2003) and since the Asian economic crisis of 1997/98 there has been a marked slowdown in infrastructure privatization in lower-income economies, including in the water sector (Harris, 2003). The forms water privatization takes raise issues about the transfer of risk from the public to the private sector. We return to this subject later in the chapter in a discussion of transaction costs in water service contracting.

The existing case study evidence on the results of water privatization presents a mixed picture, with some improvements in the reliability and quality of services and population served, but instances of much higher water charges and bouts of public opposition leading to cancelled schemes. This evidence is reviewed in Kirkpatrick and Parker (2004). Turning to the few published papers that have attempted a statistical or econometric analysis of the effects of water privatization in lower-income economies, these too present mixed results. The earliest such study was undertaken by Estache and Rossi (1999). They compared private and public water companies in the Asian and Pacific region, using 1995 survey data from the Asia Development Bank, and found that private operators were consistently more efficient than state-owned ones. The data included 50 utilities and a stochastic cost frontier method was adopted. In stark contrast, however, a follow-up study by the same authors came to exactly the opposite conclusion (Estache and Rossi, 2002). Using again stochastic cost frontier modelling and this time applying error components and technical efficiency effects models, but seemingly with data from the same 1995 survey by the Asian Development Bank, they concluded that efficiency was not significantly different in the private and state water sectors. Fifty water enterprises were included in their study from 29 Asian and Pacific region countries, with 22 having some form of private sector participation.

A further study, this time by Estache and Kouassi (2002), used a sample of 21 African water utilities for the period 1995/97. They estimated a production function from an unbalanced panel data set and used Tobit modelling to relate resulting inefficiency scores to governance and ownership variables. The study concluded that private ownership *is* associated with a lower inefficiency score. However, only three firms in their sample had any private capital, and levels of corruption and governance were far more important in explaining efficiency differences between firms than the ownership variable.

Finally, a study of water supply in Africa in the mid- to late 1990s by Clarke and Wallsten (2002) reported greater service coverage under private owner-ship. On average, they found that supplies for lower-income households (prox-ied by educational attainment) were smaller where there was a state sector operator. Clarke and Wallsten (2002) therefore concluded that private partici-pation in water schemes leads to more supplies to poorer households than where there is a reliance on state-owned suppliers. Their study suggests that privatization can improve service provision. However, there may be offsetting service difficulties and especially higher charges when supplies are privatized. In other words, drawing strong conclusions on the desirability of water priva-tization based on one measure, such as service coverage, may mislead. In the analysis below we use a range of performance measures in an attempt to address this problem.

ASSESSING PERFORMANCE IN PRIVATIZED AFRICAN WATER UTILITIES

To advance understanding of the results of privatization in water services, we accessed data from the Water Utility Partnership's SPBNET Africa website (http://www.wupafrica.org/spbnet/angl/index.html). This database includes up to 110 water utilities in Africa and was developed with financial and technical support from the Department of International Development (DFID) in London. The data collected, usually by questionnaire survey, relate mainly to the year 2000.[1] In our data set nine utilities situated in eight countries reported private sector involvement. However, not all of these firms could be included in each stage of the analysis because of incomplete data entries. Also, ideally we would use information on the forms private sector involvement takes to judge the degree of privatization, but unfortunately the data source only permitted ownership to be modelled as a binary variable. This is a limitation of our study, but a limitation shared with the earlier econometric studies, referred to above. Suppliers are categorized as either state owned or privately owned, with the latter capturing most forms of private sector involvement except for leasing and similar, which the database treats as continued public ownership. As explained above, such arrangements simply involve the use of private contractors to provide specialist services or to operate the system but with no new private investment.

Conclusions on the impact of water privatization may be sensitive to the precise performance measure used. Therefore, to assess the impact of private capital on performance in water services, a range of performance measures was calculated. First, a number of statistical measures were computed from the data set, including:

- labour productivity, labour costs to total costs, number of staff to number of water connections and staff per million cubic metres of water distributed – all of these measures will reflect *efficiency in the use of labour*;
- the proportion of operating costs spent on fuel and chemicals – to reflect *economies in non-labour operating costs*;
- the percentage of capital utilized – to reflect *capital stock efficiency*;
- average tariffs – to reflect the *costs of services to consumers*;
- the percentage of the population served, unaccounted for water (water losses), and hours of availability of piped water per day – to reflect the *quality of service to consumers*.

Average figures were computed for both state-owned and privately owned water suppliers and the results are provided in Table 9.3, with standard deviations shown in parentheses. This stage of the analysis involved between 61 and 84 utilities, depending upon the performance measure.

The figures in Table 9.3 confirm that, on average, private sector water utilities have higher labour productivity (both a lower number of staff per connection and per million cubic metres of water distributed) and a lower proportional spend on labour in operating costs than state-owned firms. On average, the private sector is also more economic in its use of other inputs, namely fuel and chemicals, and achieves a slightly higher capital utilization, of 67 per cent as against 60 per cent. Turning to tariffs, charges are on average 82 per cent higher in the private sector and more customers have their water consumption metered where services are privatized. Metering water can be a means of extracting higher revenues from consumers by linking payments to the volumes of water used. The private sector also achieves a lower percentage of water losses, averaging 29 per cent as against 34.8 per

Table 9.3   Performance ratios in African water utilities, 1999–2001

Labour productivity
Labour costs in total costs:
| | |
Average for state-owned firms — 29% (17)
Average for privately owned firms — 21% (27)

Staff per thousand water connections
Average for state-owned firms — 20.1 (19.9)
Average for privately owned firms — 13.1 (14.4)

Staff per million m^3 of water distributed
Average for state-owned firms — 123 (519.7)
Average for privately owned firms — 78 (151.8)

Operating costs
Proportion spent on fuel:
Average for state-owned firms — 20% (16)
Average for privately owned firms — 11% (12)

Proportion spent on chemicals
Average for state-owned firms — 17% (16)
Average for privately owned firms — 4% (5)

Capital
Capital utilization:
Average for state-owned firms — 60% (21.6)
Average for privately owned firms — 67% (21.8)

Consumer charges (US$ per m^3)
Average tariff:
Average for state-owned firms — 168 (473)
Average for privately owned firms — 305 (440)

Quality of service
Percentage of population served:
Average for state-owned firms — 63% (29.8)
Average for privately owned firms — 64% (30.2)

Unaccounted-for water
Average for state-owned firms — 34.8% (13.5)
Average for privately owned firms — 29.0% (13.1)

Availability of piped water (hours per day)
Average for state-owned firms — 17 (6.7)
Average for privately owned firms — 16 (9.3)

Percentage of customers metered
Average for state-owned firms — 60 (41.5)
Average for privately owned firms — 79 (38.4)

cent for state-owned water firms (probably assisted by more metering). But, interestingly, other measures of customer service suggest fewer differences between the private and state sectors. On average, state-owned firms supply piped water for 17 hours per day, while the private sector records a slightly lower figure of 16 hours. The state and private sectors serve about the same percentage of population in their areas, 63 per cent and 64 per cent respectively. These results, however, may simply reflect that it is where services are poor that governments have been most inclined to turn to the private sector for a solution.

What is clear is that there are major differences in the scale of water operations in the state and private sectors. Calculations using the SPBNET database suggest that in Africa privately owned water utilities are on average over twice as large as state-owned ones in terms of the total volume of water distributed (92 million as against 36.4 million m^3 per day) and have more connections to their systems (averaging 159 600 in the case of the private utilities as against 94 500 in the case of the state-owned firms). This suggests that the private utilities' superior performance, in particular in terms of labour use, may be at least partially explained by the different scale of production.

Nevertheless, the performance ratios in Table 9.3 reveal interesting differences across the private and state-owned water firms in Africa, but with the standard deviation figures (in parentheses) confirming a high degree of variance in performance within both the state and private sector categories. This suggests that conclusions based on average performance need to be interpreted with care. To provide a fuller appraisal of relative performance, two further sets of performance measures were calculated drawing on the same database for Africa:

- data envelopment analysis (DEA) efficiency scores; and
- a stochastic cost frontier analysis.

Whereas a cost function analysis is to be favoured because it distinguishes inefficiency from random error, non-parametric DEA does not require a prior specification of the appropriate functional form. Given that our data come from a wide number of countries, where it might be expected that functional forms could differ, DEA has obvious attractions. However, DEA scores can be easily biased by outliers and errors in the data. Therefore, arguably DEA results are best assessed alongside those from the cost function analysis. By computing *both* DEA efficiency scores and stochastic cost function results, using the SPBNET database, each measure provides a cross-check on the other. When both sets of results are considered alongside the statistical ratios above, the result is a triangulation of the analysis of the data. The outcome should be a more robust set of conclusions on the impact of water privatization than can be obtained from one performance measure alone (Bauer et al., 1998). The Appendix to the chapter provides a brief explanation of both the DEA and stochastic cost frontier models for those unfamiliar with the methods.

THE DEA AND THE COST FUNCTION ANALYSIS

A DEA was undertaken in which water distributed represented the volume of output produced, and hours of piped water available per day was used as the proxy for the quality of water services (as a cross-check, unaccounted-for water was also used as the quality of service proxy and the results were very similar). An input-oriented, variable-returns-to-scale model was used and the number of utilities entered into the analysis was 71, of which eight were privately owned. A constant-returns-to-scale model produced a similar set of results but with lower overall scores,[2] but the utilities vary in size and we would expect variable returns to apply in the water sector. The inputs used were initially the number of staff and number of connections, the latter acting as a proxy for the capital input in the absence of other data on fixed assets. A subsequent Tobit regression of the resulting DEA scores on other possible variables that might affect water outputs, including GDP per capita, water resource availability[3] and a 'freedom index', showed that water resources and the degree of freedom in a country were correlated with the efficiency scores. GDP per capita was found to have a statistically insignificant effect (at the 10 per cent level). The DEA was therefore repeated but including water resources and the freedom index as additional inputs. The freedom index used, developed by the Fraser Institute (http://www.freetheworld), takes account of policies within countries affecting the size of government (public spending, tax levels and state ownership), legal structure and security of property rights, access to sound money, freedom to trade, and regulation of credit, labour and business.

Good governance in the form of sound finance and regulatory systems and protection of property rights has been found to be an important explanation of economic performance differences (North, 1990; Jalilian et al., 2002; Kauffman et al., 2002), including in water services (Estache and Kouassi, 2002). The freedom variable was therefore included to capture wider governance or regulatory effects on performance in water utilities, which might otherwise have been attributed to ownership.[4] Ideally, another factor that should be taken into consideration in deriving efficiency scores is the geography of the area served because this can be expected to affect the amount of water distributed and the quality of service. However, we have no data on topography or other geographical factors that might affect performance, other than the data on renewable water resources. In the Tobit regression, the water resources variable was found to be negatively correlated with the efficiency scores. While this was initially surprising, it can be explained in terms of countries with large renewable water resources taking less care to distribute available water efficiently through their water systems and by people having better access to informal water services, such as direct extraction from rivers, where water resources are more abundant.

Table 9.4 summarizes the DEA results according to the number of utilities that achieved a score of 100 per cent efficiency, 90 per cent to 99 per cent efficiency and 80 per cent to 89 per cent efficiency under private and state ownership.[5] Although state-owned firms helped to form the efficiency frontier, demonstrating that state ownership does not necessarily lead to low relative efficiency, the number on the frontier amounted to 18 out of the 63 firms or 29 per cent of the total of state-owned firms in the data set. By contrast, three privately owned firms populated the frontier accounting for 38 per cent of the private sector firms included in the analysis. All private sector firms achieved scores of above 80 per cent relative efficiency, while 8 per cent of state-owned firms (5 firms out of 63) recorded scores of less than 80 per cent.[6] The lowest score, 72 per cent, was recorded by a state-owned water utility in Malawi. The DEA results suggest, therefore, that private ownership leads to higher efficiency scores, but also that many state-owned water firms in Africa seem to perform relatively efficiently.

A stochastic cost frontier was also estimated on the basis of the SBPNET database. The reason for choosing a cost frontier instead of a production frontier lies in the fact that most water utility firms are required to meet demand and are not free to choose the level of output. With output set exogenously, the firm is expected to minimize the costs of producing a given level of output. Compared to the deterministic cost function, the stochastic frontier decomposes the error term into stochastic noise and cost inefficiency. When the inefficiency term enters into the cost function (additively after logs are taken), the level of the cost efficiency of individual firms can be estimated.[7]

Various distributions have been suggested for the inefficiency term. But the

Table 9.4   A summary of the DEA

	Utilities with 100% relative efficiency		Utilities with efficiency of 90% to 99%		Utilities with efficiency of 80% to 89%	
	No.	%	No.	%	No.	%
State-owned	18	29	18	29	22	35
Privately owned	3	38	2	25	3	38

half-normal distribution (Aigner et al., 1977) is the most commonly used in empirical studies. To avoid imposing such an arbitrary assumption, Stevenson (1980) proposed that the more flexible truncated-normal distribution be used. The truncated-normal distribution is a generalization of the half-normal distribution, obtained by the truncation at zero of the normal distribution, with mean, μ, and variance, σ_{μ}^2. Pre-assigning μ to be zero reduces the truncated distribution to the traditional half-normal. Therefore, we first tested the null hypothesis $H_0 : \mu = 0$ to choose the appropriate model for estimation.

Estimation of a cost function requires data on the cost level, the output level and input prices. There are, however, no data on capital prices in the SPBNET database. An arbitrary cost function was therefore formulated without including the price of the capital input. The dependent variable used in the cost frontier was operating and maintenance costs (*COST*) or non-capital costs. Average manpower cost per employee (*MP*) was used to reflect the cost of labour. The amount of water distributed per year (*WD*) was included in the cost function as the output variable. Also included in the function was a quality variable, measured by the hours of piped water available per day (*QUALI*).[8]

In addition, some environmental variables were included in the model specification. These are variables that may be expected to affect the performance of the firm but are not entirely under its control. Their inclusion ensures that the various water operators are effectively comparable. A density variable, measured by population served per connection (*DEN*), was included because it plays an important role in defining the network infrastructure. Another variable used as a control was the annual water resources per capita (*WRS*). GDP per capita (*GDP*) and the freedom index (*FRD*) were included in an attempt to capture the extent of economic development and the quality of governance, respectively. In order to account for the effects of ownership on performance, a dummy variable (*ONS*) was included in the model, which took the value of 1 if the utility was privately owned. Table 9.5 lists the variables used in the estimation.

A translog cost function that includes the second-order and cross terms would leave the estimation with very few degrees of freedom; therefore a Cobb–Douglas specification was adopted. All the variables except the ownership dummy were logged. The procedure for estimation was as follows. An error component (EC) model was first estimated with the assumption of a truncated distribution for the inefficiency term. If the hypothesis $\mu = 0$ is rejected, this means that the assumption of the truncation distribution is correct and the results based on this model can be adopted. If μ is not significantly different from zero, an EC model assuming a half-normal distribution should be estimated instead. In order to test the robustness of the results, a technical efficiency effects (TEE) frontier was also estimated in which the inefficiency effects are expressed as a function of the ownership dummy.

Table 9.5   Variables in the stochastic cost function

Variable	Definition	Data source
COST	Operating and maintenance costs (US$)	SPBNET
WD	Water distributed per year (m³)	SPBNET
QUALI	Number of hours of water availability per day	SPBNET
MP	Manpower costs per employee (US$)	SPBNET
WRS	Water resources per capita	World Resources Institute
DEN	Population served per connection	SPBNET
GDP	GDP per capita (US$)	World Development Indicators
FRD	Freedom index	The Fraser Institute
ONS	Ownership dummy (1 = privately owned)	SPBNET

In total, 76 observations were included in the estimations, including nine private sector firms.[9] The program FRONTIER 4.1 was used to obtain the maximum likelihood estimates of the parameters and the efficiency measure. The results of the EC model with the truncation-distribution assumption showed that μ was 0.47 with a standard error of 2.56. A likelihood ratio test was performed and the results showed that the hypothesis $\mu = 0$ could not be rejected at the 10 per cent level. Consequently, the results from the model with

Table 9.6   The error component (EC) and technical efficiency effects (TEE) results

Variable	EC model (half-normal)	Variable	TEE model
Constant	7.10 (3.01) ***	Constant	7.28 (3.18)***
ln(WD)	0.44 (5.41) ***	ln(WD)	0.45 (4.96)***
ln(QUALI)	−0.17 (0.70)	ln(QUALI)	−0.23 (0.90)
ln(MP)	0.68 (10.38) ***	ln(MP)	0.69 (9.77)***
ln(WRS)	0.23 (2.18)**	ln(WRS)	0.28 (2.50)***
ln(DEN)	−0.21 (2.80) ***	ln(DEN)	−0.23 (2.60)***
ln(GDP)	−0.28 (1.71) **	ln(GDP)	−0.25 (1.53)*
ln(FRD)	−0.98 (0.64)	ln(FRD)	−0.99 (0.83)
ONS	0.45 (1.21)	δ(ONS)	0.88 (1.10)
Γ	**0.86 (9.67)**	γ	0.92 (10.64)
LR test	6.68 ***	LR test	8.68 ***
Total observations	**76**	**Total observations**	**76**

Notes:
Figures in parentheses are *t*-statistics.
*** significant at 1% level.
** significant at 5% level.
* significant at 10% level.

the half-normal assumption were adopted. Table 9.6 shows the results along with those from the TEE model.

The results from the EC model and from the TEE model are consistent. The values of γ in the two models indicate that the vast majority of residual variation is due to inefficiency effects. This is also confirmed by the generalized likelihood-ratio statistics, both exceeding the critical value at 1 per cent level obtained from Table 1 of Kodde and Palm (1986). As expected, the output variable, $\ln(WD)$, has a positive and significant effect on operating costs. So does the variable labour price, $\ln(MP)$. The density variable has a negative and significant sign, and accords with the expectation that it is more cost-efficient to serve a population located more densely. The negative and significant coefficient of $\ln(GDP)$ suggests that the cost of water distribution is lower in wealthier countries. The freedom variable seems to have negative effects on the level of costs, but the impact is not statistically significant. Contrary to our expectation, however, the quality variable results show negative, although not significant, effects and the water resources variable shows positive and significant effects (the latter finding being consistent with the relationship between efficiency scores and water resources in the earlier DEA results). Turning to the role of ownership, which is our main concern, surprisingly the coefficient of the ownership dummy (*ONS*) in the EC model is positive, suggesting that private ownership is associated with higher costs. However, the result is not statistically significant.

In order to determine the robustness of this result, the inefficiency term was expressed as a function of the ownership dummy in the TEE model. In the TEE model the efficiency error μ has a mean of m_i and $m_i = \delta x_i \cdot x_i$, which is a vector of variables that may influence the efficiency of a firm. This was taken as the ownership dummy in our estimation. The results of the estimation (Table 9.6, final column) show that the coefficient δ in the contemporaneous auxiliary regression is positive but not significant.[10] The results were consistent with the outcome from the EC model. Overall, the safest interpretation of the cost frontier results is that there are no significant differences in cost-efficiency between private and state-owned water companies in Africa.

TRANSACTION COSTS AND WATER CONCESSIONS

The studies of water privatization in developing countries undertaken, including our own, suggest that private ownership can be associated with higher performance, although it is not axiomatic that private suppliers are more efficient. Indeed, our cost function analysis is consistent with the most recent study by Estache and Rossi (2002), reviewed earlier, in finding no statistically significant difference in terms of cost performance between the private and state water sectors in developing countries. Before concluding the chapter, it is interesting to consider why privatization of water services may be problematic in lower-income economies. The answer seems to lie in a combination of the technology of water provision and the nature of the product, the costs of organizing long-term concession agreements or transaction costs, and regulatory weaknesses. It is to these issues that we now turn.

Past studies of privatization have indicated that competition is generally more important than ownership *per se* in explaining performance improvements in developing countries (e.g. Zhang et al., 2003a; Parker and Kirkpatrick, 2004). But unlike in the case of telecommunications and parts of energy supply, such as generation, where competition is feasible, competition in the market for water services is usually cost-inefficient. While there is scope for introducing some competition into billing and metering and into construction, replacement and repair work within water services, competition in the actual provision of water supplies is normally ruled out by the scale of the investment in fixed assets or network assets that are needed to deliver the product. Moreover, even where actual competition for consumers might seem feasible, for example where the boundaries of different water utilities meet, the costs of moving water down pipes is far higher than the costs of transmitting telephone calls and distributing electricity, and this places a serious limitation on the development of competition. Also, mixing water from different sources can raise complications in terms of maintaining water quality, which can be an important consideration for domestic consumers but more especially water-using industry, such as brewing and food processing.

In other words, the technology of water supply and the nature of the product, together, severely restrict the prospects for competition in the market and therefore the efficiency gains that can result from encouraging competition following privatization. This leaves rivalry under privatization mainly in the form of 'competition for the market' or competition to win the contract or concession agreement. However, here serious problems can also arise. These problems relate to the existence of pervasive transaction costs.

As already explained, water privatizations involve various types of contracts. Transaction costs arise in contracting for water services provision, in terms of the costs of arranging the agreements, including organizing the bidding process, monitoring contract performance, and enforcing the contract terms where failures are suspected (Williamson, 1985). The economics literature demonstrates that such costs are likely to be high where there are serious information asymmetries at the time of the contract agreement. These information imperfections are likely to be especially prevalent when contracts have to be negotiated to cover service provision over long periods of time because many future events that could affect the economic viability of the contract and the acceptability of the service offering are unforeseen, and may be unforseeable. Concession agreements in water are typically negotiated for 10 or 20 years or more. Inevitably, therefore, the contracts will need to permit periodic adjustment of variables such as price, volume and quality during the contract life. The contract will be incomplete in terms of specifying all of the contingencies that may trigger such adjustments and the form the renegotiation might take. This places a heavy emphasis on the skills of both government and companies when operating water concessions to ensure as far as possible that the outcome is mutually beneficial.

The usual approach in water concessions is to have a two-part bidding process. The first stage involves the initial selection of approved bidders, based on technical capacity, and then a final stage in which the winner is selected, based on criteria such as the price offered and service targets. However, the smaller the number of bidders, the greater the scope for either actual or tacit collusion when bidding, and the less effective will be the competitiveness of the bidding process. The evidence suggests that water concessions in developing countries are subject to small-numbers bidding. For example, in 2001, 18 companies expressed interest in operating a contract for Nepal in the first stage of the process, but in the final stage only two serious bidders remained (cited in Mitlin, 2002, p. 17). In Argentina, there have usually been only a small handful of applicants for water concessions, typically between two and four (Estache, 2002); the ill-fated Cochabama concession had a sole bidder. Pre-qualification criteria and risk restrict the bidding for water concessions mainly to a small number of players (McIntosh, 2003, p. 2). In an attempt to stimulate interest from more potential suppliers, concessions can include sovereign (government or donor agency) guarantees of profitability, but this introduces obvious moral-hazard risks – with profits guaranteed, what incentive exists for the concession winner to produce efficiently? Table 9.7 details the main international players for water concessions today. While there appears to be a number of players, in most bids only a few of these firms choose to become involved, often reflecting preferences regarding regional investment. In practice, this is not a market composed of large numbers of active competitors for all or even most contracts.

The literature on transaction costs demonstrates that small-numbers contracting is a source of opportunistic behaviour leading to higher transaction costs (Williamson, 1985). The result can be both adverse selection and moral hazard. Adverse selection takes the form of sub-optimal contracts at the outset, resulting from one of the contracting parties acting opportunistically to arrange especially favourable terms; while moral hazard occurs when one of the contracting parties renegotiates the terms of the contract in their favour during its lifetime. During contract renegotiation either the company or the government could be the loser, depending upon the results of the renegotiation. For example, in the concession involving Maynilad in Manila, the

Table 9.7   The main international firms involved in water concession bidding

Company	Country of origin
Acea	Italy
Aguas de Barcelona	Spain
Aguas de Portugal	Portugal
Anglian Water (parent company, ARG)	UK
Aquamundo	Germany
Bechtel	USA
International Water (parent companies Edison and Bechtel)	Italy/USA
Ondeo (parent company, Suez)	France
SAUR	France
Thames Water (parent company RWE)	UK/Germany
United Utilities	UK
Vivendi Environnement	France

Sources: Various.

company terminated the concession when it was refused a rate adjustment to which it considered it was entitled. By contrast, in Dolphin Bay, South Africa, the municipality felt that it had little alternative but to agree an unplanned price rise when the private sector supplier threatened to withdraw services (Bayliss, 2002, p. 16). By transferring operations to the private sector, government loses the internal skills and expertise that enable it to take over a failing enterprise.

Guasch (1999) concludes that 55 per cent of water concession contracts in Latin America were renegotiated significantly within a few years of being signed – in Buenos Aires prices were raised within months of the start of the water concession (Alcazar et al., 2000). But even the ability to renegotiate terms may not be sufficient to overcome investor reluctance to participate in water privatizations, thus reinforcing the small-numbers bargaining problem. Difficulties arise especially when private investors fear that there is no long-term political commitment to water privatization (Rivera, 1996). Moreover, corrupt payments to win concessions and 'cronyism' undermine the legitimacy of the privatization process; for example, in Lesotho the Highlands Water Project was associated with bribes to government officials (Bayliss, 2000, p. 14). Esguerra (2002) shows how the water concessions in Manila were backed by the Philippines' two wealthiest families with support from multinationals: 'It appears that the two companies' approach was to win the bid at all costs, and then deal with the problems of profitability later' (ibid., p. 2). They are also accused of trying to influence the subsequent regulatory process. The way in which the privatization in Buenos Aires helped promote the interests of elite groups is highlighted by Loftus and McDonald (2001, p. 198).

Studying cancelled concession contracts in developing countries, Harris et al. (2003) find that water and sewerage concessions have the second-highest incidence after toll roads. Given the existence of substantial potential 'sunk costs' in the water industry, this is not surprising. Tamayo et al. (1999, p. 91) note that the specificity of assets in the water industry is three to four times that in telecommunications and electricity. Reflecting this, water companies in Brazil have a high cost of capital compared to the electricity sector, reflecting the bigger regulatory risk (Guasch, 1999). Handley (1997) stresses the problems caused by inadequate risk management techniques in developing countries, while the preference on the part of the private sector for the state to remain responsible for the infrastructure in water contracting reflects the desire of companies to minimize their sunk costs.

Pargal (2003, p. 23), based on an econometric assessment of private investment flows and data from Latin America, concludes: 'the water sector differs materially from [telecoms, electricity and roads] . . . : private investment in water is not significantly affected by the passage of reform legislation in the sector and public expenditure is very important and only mildly substitutable for private spending'. Studies have shown that in telecommunications (Wallsten, 2001) and electricity generation (Zhang et al., 2003a, 2003b) the regulatory system put in place to monitor and control the prices and quality of services supplied by the private monopolist is important. However, transaction costs in water concessions reinforce serious weaknesses in government regulatory capacity in developing countries (Spiller and Savedoff, 1999, pp. 1–2). For example, in India there have been some local moves to attract private capital into water supply, notably in Tiruppur, Maharashtra and Gujarat. But regulatory systems are underdeveloped and in Tiruppur they are largely under the indirect control of the water operator (Teri, 2003, pp. 171–21). As Mitlin (2002, pp. 54–5) concludes on the experience in Manila:

> The experience in Manila suggests that the gains [from privatization] may be less than anticipated because the assumption that the involvement of the private sector would remove political interference from the water sector was wrong. It may be that processes and outcomes have simply become more complex because the water supply industry now has the interests of private capital in addition to a remaining level of politicisation and an acute level of need amongst the poorest citizens.

The decline in private sector infrastructure investments since 1997 is consistent with growing concerns about regulatory capacity and governance within developing countries (Harris, 2003). This is a concern that exists irrespective of the form that ownership takes. Therefore, to assess the effects of regulation on water privatization in Africa, we repeated our stochastic cost function analysis, but this time incorporating a regulatory variable as a dummy alongside the existing freedom variable (representing wider good governance in a country). The SPBNET database provides information on the existence of regulation of prices, water quality and customer services. The different regulatory indicators were combined into a composite regulation dummy to reflect the existence or lack of existence of regulation in water. Our expectation is that regulation will impact on costs, depending upon the form it takes. For example, a good regulatory regime should create more investor certainty and may reduce costs of production. Alternatively, regulation could raise costs by imposing higher and more expensive standards or by raising uncertainty for investors (usually referred to as 'regulatory risk'). The results from the new regression analysis are reported in Table 9.8. They show that the regulation dummy has a negative sign, suggesting lower costs, but it is not statistically significant. Similarly, the freedom variable is also negative and insignificant, as it was in the earlier analysis. The ownership dummy (*ONS*) remained positive but insignificant, as before (Table 9.6).

The results from this stage of the analysis were, therefore, inconclusive.[11] Regulation, both sector-specific and as reflected in the general standards of governance in a country, proved to be statistically insignificant, though there was some suggestion that they led to lower costs. Clearly, more research is

Table 9.8   Testing for the importance of regulation

Variable	EC model (half-normal)	Variable	TEE model
Constant	7.80 (3.04) ***	*Constant*	6.64 (3.14)***
ln(*WD*)	0.43 (5.25) ***	ln(*WD*)	0.50 (5.72)***
ln(*QUALI*)	–0.17 (0.72)	ln(*QUALI*)	–0.32 (1.05)
ln(*MP*)	0.69 (10.28) ***	ln(*MP*)	0.69 (10.62)***
ln(*WRS*)	0.23 (2.17)**	ln(*WRS*)	0.27 (2.56)***
ln(*DEN*)	–0.21 (2.85) ***	ln(*DEN*)	–0.23 (2.06)***
ln(*GDP*)	–0.27 (1.70) **	ln(*GDP*)	–0.26 (1.75)*
ln(*FRD*)	–0.91 (0.68)	ln(*FRD*)	–0.99 (0.89)
ONS	0.45 (1.21)	δ_1 (*ONS*)	0.93 (0.67)
Regulation	–0.62 (0.68)	δ_2 (*Regulation*)	–0.89 (0.36)
γ	0.89 (10.04)	Γ	0.92 (10.64)
LR test	6.85 **	LR test	8.68 ***
Total observations	**76**	**Total observations**	**76**

Notes: For a definition of the variables, see Table 9.6. Regulation is a dummy variable for regulation, see text; γ is the proportion of the residual variation attributable to inefficiency effects.

needed in this area. The regulation variable used was far from ideal, and future research would benefit from developing a set of superior regulatory variables – variables that more closely reflect the impact of regulation rather than simply its existence.

CONCLUSIONS

This chapter has reviewed the existing econometric evidence on the impact of water privatization in developing countries and has reported the results of a new analysis for Africa, using a range of performance measures to overcome the limitations of a single performance measure. The study has reported a range of statistical indicators and both DEA and stochastic cost frontier results. Based on the statistical indicators and the DEA, the study confirms that privatization can lead to performance gains. However, the stochastic cost frontier analysis found that, while the coefficient on the ownership variable was negative, consistent with lower costs under private ownership, the result was not statistically significant.

The chapter then considered some reasons why water privatization might prove problematic in lower-income economies, identifying potential difficulties stemming from water supply technology and the nature of the product, transaction costs and regulatory capacity. These difficulties may help explain why private ownership does not have an unequivocally positive effect on performance in water supply in earlier studies. By including a regulation dummy in the stochastic cost frontier model, we attempted to shed further light on the importance of regulation, but the result was statistically insignificant. This outcome probably reflects the crudity of the regulatory variable used, which simply measures the existence of water regulation, not its impact on the management of utilities. Under conditions of perfect competition, perfect information and complete contracts ownership do not matter (Shapiro and Willig, 1990) and the regulatory environment becomes trivial. However, none of these conditions applies to water services and it is to be expected that governance and regulatory variables will be important in determining performance before and after privatization. The challenge is to develop reliable data sets on regulation for use in econometric analysis.

Finally, it needs to be stressed that while the chapter has concentrated upon a number of performance measures, a more comprehensive study would take account of possible effects beyond those discussed. For example, we have seen that privatization tends to lead to more water metering, but what is the impact of this on water consumption and health? Around major cities in developing countries lie shanty towns populated with squatters and others without legal property rights. How are their interests served by water privatization? Water privatization usually means the involvement of a handful of major international companies; but what effect does this have in terms of developing indigenous ownership of socially important assets? Also, if privatization leads to full cost recovery in water, is this outcome compatible with poverty reduction; and what are the environmental implications of privatization? Clearly, water privatization raises a complex set of considerations that deserve fuller exploration than has been possible here because of data limitations.

NOTES

1. Data for a few utilities relate to the years 1999 or 2001. Given the closeness of the years, we treat all of the data as applying to one year, 2000, to adopt a cross-sectional analysis of performance.
2. Constant-returns-to-scale modelling in DEA always leads to lower scores compared to using a variable-returns-to-scale model with the same data, due to the additional restriction introduced.
3. The data relate to the availability of natural renewable water resources and were obtained from Earth Trends Data tables: http://earthtrends.wri.org. We would like to thank Catarina Figueira for assistance with the DEA.
4. Water resource data are at the country level. Data do not exist at the utility level and therefore the input used is not ideal. In the absence of the water resource variable as an input and also excluding the freedom variable, which is also calculated at the national level, the DEA scores showed lower overall efficiency levels but the conclusions on ownership were the same. Whereas 38 per cent of private sector utilities formed the frontier, only 13 per cent of state-owned firms did so. Whereas 63 per cent of the private companies achieved scores of 70 per cent or better, the figure fell to 21 per cent for state-owned utilities.
5. DEA provides scores relative to peers with similar operating characteristics based on an estimated efficiency frontier. The resulting scores are relative not absolute scores. Therefore, a score of 100 per cent does not imply absolute efficiency but merely efficiency compared to the other units in the analysis.
6. To assess whether the quality of service proxy might have biased the results, the DEA was undertaken using simply water distributed as the output, and number of staff and number of connections as the inputs. The result was fewer units on or close to the frontier but the overall conclusion on the role of ownership was broadly the same. Whereas 10 per cent of state-owned firms scored 100 per cent, 17 per cent of privately owned ones did so. Scores of 70 per cent or above were achieved by 17 per cent of state firms and 27 per cent of private sector firms.
7. For more details on the stochastic cost frontier, see the Appendix.
8. Again, the results using an alternative quality indicator, namely unaccounted-for water, produced similar results.
9. Because the variables used in the cost frontier and those in the DEA analysis are different, the size of the sample sets for the two methods are different, due to missing data for some of the variables.
10. A TEE model including a constant term in the inefficiency term was also estimated. The results are similar to those shown in Table 9.6.
11. A Tobit model was also used to assess the impact of the regulation variable on the DEA scores discussed earlier. The result was also statistically insignificant.

REFERENCES

Aigner, D., Loell, C. and Schmidt, P. (1977), 'Formulation and Estimation of Stochastic Frontier Production Function Models', *Journal of Econometrics*, **6** (1), pp. 21–37.

Alcazar, L., Abdala, M. and Shirley, M. (2000), 'The Buenos Aires Water Concession', World Bank Research Working Paper 2311, Washington, DC: World Bank.

Battese, G.E. and Corra, G.S. (1977), 'Estimation of a Production Frontier Model with Application to the Pastoral Zone of Eastern Australia', *Australian Journal of Agricultural Economics*, **21**, 169–79.

Battese, G.E. and Coelli, T.J. (1995), 'A Model for Technical Inefficiency Effects in a Stochastic Frontier Production Function for Panel Data', *Empirical Economics*, **20**, 325–32.

Bauer, P., Berger, A., Ferrier, G. and Humphrey, D. (1998), 'Consistency Conditions for Regulatory Analysis of Financial Institutions: A Comparison of Frontier Efficiency Methods', *Journal of Economics and Business*, **50**, 85–114.

Bayliss, K. (2000), 'The World Bank and Privatisation: A Flawed Development Tool', mimeo, London: Public Services International Research Unit, University of Greenwich.

Bayliss, K. (2002), 'Privatisation and Poverty: The Distributional Impact of Utility Privatisation', Centre on Regulation and Competition Paper No. 16, Manchester: Centre on Regulation and Competition, University of Manchester.

Brubaker, E. (2001), *The Promise of Privatization*, Toronto: Energy Probe Research Foundation.

Clarke, R.G. and Wallsten, S.J. (2002), 'Universal(ly Bad) Service: Providing Infrastructure Services to Rural and Poor Urban Consumers', Policy Research Paper 2868, Washington, DC: World Bank.

Collignon, B. and Vézina, M. (2000), 'Independent Water and Sanitation Providers in African Cities: Full Report of a Ten-Country Study', mimeo, Washington, DC: UNDP–World Bank Water and Sanitation Program.

Esguerra, J. (2002), *The Corporate Muddle of Manila's Water Concessions: How the World's Biggest and Most Successful Privatisation turned into a Failure*, London: Water Aid.

Estache, A. (2002), 'Argentina's 1990 Utilities Privatization: A Cure or a Disease?', mimeo.

Estache, A. and Kouassi, E. (2002), 'Sector Organization, Governance, and the Inefficiency of African Water Utilities', World Bank Research Working Paper 2890, Washington, DC: World Bank.

Estache, A. and Rossi, M. (1999), 'Comparing the Performance of Public and Private Water Companies in Asia and the Pacific Region: What a Stochastic Cost Frontier Shows', Policy Research Working Paper, Washington, DC: World Bank.

Estache, A. and Rossi, M. (2002), 'How Different is the Efficiency of Public and Private Water Companies?', *World Bank Economic Review*, **16** (1), 139–48.

Guasch, J.L. (1999), 'Experience from Concession Design in Latin America and Caribbean', mimeo.

Handley, P. (1997), 'A Critical Review of the Build–Operate–Transfer Privatisation Process in Asia', *Asian Journal of Public Administration*, **19** (2), 203–43.

Harris, C. (2003), 'Private Participation in Infrastructure in Developing Countries: Trends, Impact, and Policy Lessons', World Bank Working Paper No. 5, Washington, DC: World Bank.

Harris, C. et al. (2003), 'Infrastructure Projects: A Review of Cancelled Private Projects', *Public Policy for the Private Sector*, **252**, Washington, DC: World Bank.

Hulls, D. (2003), 'Water for Sale?', *Development*, 1st quarter, pp. 32–4, London: DFID.

Jalilian, H., Kirkpatrick, C. and Parker, D. (2002), 'Creating the Conditions for International Business Expansion: The Impact of Regulation on Economic Growth in Developing Countries', Discussion Paper No. 54, Manchester: Centre on Regulation and Competition, Institute for Development Policy and Management, University of Manchester.

Johnstone, N. and Wood, L. (2001), 'Introduction', in N. Johnstone and L. Wood (eds), *Private Firms and Public Water: Realising Social and Environmental Objectives in Developing Countries*, Cheltenham, UK and Northampton, MA, USA: Edward Elgar.

Kaufmann, D., Kraay, A. and Zoido-Lobatón, P. (2002), 'Governance Matters II: Updated indicators for 2000/01', Policy Research Working Paper, Washington, DC: World Bank.

Kirkpatrick, C. and Parker, D. (2004), 'Regulation, Trade Liberalisation and the Provision of Water Services in Developing Countries: An Assessment of the Impact of the General Agreement on Trade in Services (GATS)', mimeo, Manchester: Centre on Regulation and Competition, Institute for Development Policy and Management, University of Manchester.

Kodde, D.A. and Palm, F.C. (1986), 'Wald Criteria for Jointly Testing Equality and Inequality Restrictions', *Econometrica*, **54** (5), 1243–8.

Loftus, A.J. and McDonald, D.A. (2001), 'Of Liquid Dreams: A Political Ecology of Water Privatization in Buenos Aires', *Environment and Urbanization*, **13** (2), 179–99.

McIntosh, A.C. (2003), *Asian Water Supplies: Reaching the Urban Poor*, London: Asian Development Bank and International Water Association.

Megginson, W.L. and Netter, J.M. (2001), 'From State to Market: A Survey of Empirical Studies on Privatization', *Journal of Economic Literature*, **39**, June, 321–89.

Mitlin, D. (2002), 'Competition, Regulation and the Urban Poor: A Case Study of Water', Discussion Paper No. 37, Manchester: Centre on Regulation and Competition, Institute for Development Policy and Management, University of Manchester.

North, D.C. (1990), *Institutions, Institutional Change and Economic Performance*, Cambridge: Cambridge University Press.

OECD (2000), *Global Trends in Urban Water Supply and Waste Water Financing and Management: Changing Roles for the Public and Private Sectors*, Paris: OECD.

OECD (2003), 'Water Partnerships: Striking a Balance', *OECD Observer*, 7 April, Paris: OECD.

Pargal, S. (2003), 'Regulation and Private Sector Investment in Infrastructure: Evidence from Latin America', Policy Research Working Paper 3037, Washington, DC: World Bank.

Parker, D. and Kirkpatrick, C. (2004), 'Privatisation in Developing Countries: A Review of the Evidence and the Policy Lessons', *Journal of Development Studies*, **41** (4), 513–41.

Rivera, D. (1996), *Private Sector Participation in the Water Supply and Wastewater Sector: Lessons from Six Developing Countries*, Washington, DC: World Bank.

Shapiro, C. and Willig, R.D. (1990), 'Economic Rationales for the Scope of

Privatization', in E.N. Suleiman and J. Waterbury, *The Political Economy of Public Sector Reform and Privatization*, Boulder, CO: Westview Press; also reprinted in D. Parker (ed.) (2001), *Privatisation and Corporate Performance*, Cheltenham, UK and Northampton, MA, USA: Edward Elgar.

Snell, S. (1998), 'Water and Sanitation Services for the Urban Poor – Small-Scale Providers: Typology and Profiles', mimeo, Washington, DC: UNDP–World Bank Water and Sanitation Program.

Spiller, P.T. and Savedoff, W. (1999), 'Government Opportunism and the Provision of Water', in W.D. Savedoff and P.T. Spiller (eds), *Spilled Water: An Institutional Commitment to the Provision of Water Services*, Washington, DC: InterAmerican Development Bank.

Stevenson, R. (1980), 'Likelihood Functions for Generalized Stochastic Frontier Estimation', *Journal of Econometrics*, **13** (1), 57–66.

Tamayo, G., Barrantes, R., Conterno, E. and Bustamente, A. (1999), 'Reform efforts and low-level equilibrium in the Peruvian water sector', in W.D. Savedoff and P.T. Spiller (eds), *Spilled Water: An Institutional Commitment to the Provision of Water Services*, Washington, DC: InterAmerican Development Bank.

TERI (2003), 'Research Centre for Regulation and Competition: Draft Report', TERI Project Report No. 2003 RP44, New Delhi: The Energy and Resources Institute.

Wallsten, S. (2001), 'An Econometric Analysis of Telecom Competition, Privatization, and Regulation in Africa and Latin America', *Journal of Industrial Economics*, **49** (1), 1–20.

Williamson, O.E. (1985), *The Economic Institutions of Capitalism: Firms, Markets, and History*, Cambridge: Cambridge University Press.

World Bank (1995), *Bureaucrats in Business: The Economics and Politics of Government Ownership*, Oxford: Oxford University Press for the World Bank.

World Bank (2003), *Private Participation in Infrastructure: Trends in Developing Countries in 1990–2001*, Washington, DC: World Bank.

Zhang, Y.-F., Kirkpatrick, C. and Parker, D. (2003a), 'Electricity Sector Reform in Developing Countries: An Econometric Assessment of the Effects of Privatisation, Competition and Regulation', Discussion Paper No. 31, Manchester: Centre on Regulation and Competition, Institute for Development Policy and Management, University of Manchester.

Zhang, Y.-F., Kirkpatrick, C. and Parker, D. (2003b), 'Competition, Regulation and Privatisation of Electricity Generation in Developing Countries: Does the Sequencing of Reforms Matter?', mimeo, Manchester: Centre on Regulation and Competition, Institute for Development Policy and Management, University of Manchester.

APPENDIX

Data Envelopment Analysis

DEA is a non-parametric method of assessing the relative efficiency of units without the need to establish the appropriate functional form. A best-practice frontier is created by comparing each actual decision-making unit (DMU), e.g. firm, with 'best' comparable DMUs. A fundamental assumption is that if one DMU, e.g. A, can produce $X(A)$ units of output with $Y(A)$ inputs, then other DMUs should also be able to do the same if they are managed efficiently. Similarly, if producer B can supply $X(B)$ units of output with $Y(B)$ inputs, then other DMUs should be able to do the same. DMUs A, B, C etc. are then combined to form a composite or virtual DMU with composite inputs and composite outputs. For each DMU a 'best' virtual DMU is generated. If the DMU can produce more output with the same input, or the same output with less input then the original DMU is deemed *inefficient*. To generate the best virtual DMU, linear programming techniques are used. Analysing the efficiency of n producers is then a set of n linear programming problems.

The following notation applies to an input-oriented DEA. Here λ is a vector describing the percentages of other DMUs used to create the virtual DMU and λX and λY are the output and input vectors, respectively, for the DMU under consideration, and X and Y represent the virtual outputs and inputs. The aim is to minimize inefficiency, represented here by Θ. An output-oriented DEA maximizes output given the inputs through a similar procedure.

$$\min \Theta,$$
$$\text{s.t. } Y\lambda \geq Y_0,$$
$$\Theta X_0 - X\lambda \geq 0,$$
$$\Theta \text{ free, } \lambda \geq 0.$$

The Stochastic Cost Frontier

Stochastic frontiers are typically classified as production functions and cost functions. The theoretical specification of the cost function is

$$C = f(Y, P, X) \exp(\varepsilon), \tag{9A.1}$$

where C is total cost, Y is the output vector, P is a vector of input prices, X is a vector of all relevant exogenous variables needed to allow comparison across firms, and ε is the error term. In the stochastic frontier, the error term ε can be decomposed into two parts, namely μ_i and v_i. The random error, v_i, accounts for measurement error and other random factors, such as the effects of weather, strikes, etc., on the level of costs, together with the combined effects of unspecified factors in the cost function. The v_i s are usually assumed to be independent and identically distributed normal random variables with mean zero and constant variance, σ_v^2. The μ_i component represents cost inefficiency and is assumed to be distributed independently from v_i and the regressors.

Various distributions have been assumed for the inefficiency term – half-normal, gamma exponential and truncated-normal. The truncated-normal distribution is a generalization of the half-normal distribution. It is obtained by the truncation at zero of the normal distribution, with mean, μ, and variance, σ_μ^2. Estimation of the truncated-normal stochastic frontier involves the estimation of the parameter, μ, together with the other parameters of the model. A null hypothesis, $H_0 : \mu = 0$, is usually tested by conducting a Wald or a generalized likelihood-ratio test. The purpose is to test which model, the truncated-normal or the half-normal, can capture the distribution of the inefficiency term. If the null hypothesis cannot be rejected, this means that the simpler half-normal model is an adequate representation of the data. Both the half-normal and the truncated-normal distributions are modelled in either LIMDEP or FRONTIER, the two software packages used for stochastic frontier analysis.

Following the parameterization proposed by Battese and Corra (1977), σ_μ^2 and σ_v^2 are replaced with $\sigma^2 = \sigma_\mu^2 + \sigma_v^2$, $\gamma = \sigma_\mu^2/(\sigma_\mu^2 + \sigma_v^2)$. This is done with the calculation of the maximum likelihood estimates in mind. The parameter, γ, must lie between 0 and 1, with 0 indicating that the deviation from the frontier is due entirely to noise and 1 indicating that deviation is due purely to inefficiency. It can be tested whether any form of stochastic frontier production function is required at all by the following null hypothesis, $H_0 : \gamma = 0$. If the null hypothesis cannot be rejected, this indicates that σ_μ^2 is zero and hence that the inefficiency term should be removed from the model. This leaves a specification with parameters that can be consistently estimated using ordinary least squares. A one-sided generalized likelihood-ratio test can be used to test the null hypothesis. If the $H_0 : \gamma = 0$ is true, the generalized LR statistics have an asymptotic distribution, which is a mixture of chi-square distribution (Battese and Coelli, 1995). The critical value for the LR test can be obtained from Table 1 in Kodde and Palm (1986), with degrees of freedom equal to the number of restrictions involved.

Two types of models can be estimated for a cost frontier, namely the error component (EC) model and the technical efficiency effects (TEE) model. Battese and Coelli (1995) proposed a TEE model, in which technical efficiency effects are assumed to be independently distributed and non-negative random variables. For the ith firm in a sample, the technical inefficiency effect, μ_i, is obtained by truncation of the $N(m_i, \sigma_\mu^2)$ distribution, where $m_i = \delta x_i . x_i$ is vector of observable explanatory variables.

10. Why regulations matter: a small-business perspective

Judi Hudson

It is increasingly recognized that a vibrant small and medium enterprise (SME) sector holds the potential to mop up unemployment, drive growth and make a substantial contribution to the empowerment of disadvantaged groups. The importance of these roles is difficult to overstate in the South African context. It is also true to say that ten years into South Africa's democracy, the growth of the small business sector has been modest. Former minister of trade and industry Mr Alec Erwin has said that the SME contribution to GDP at 35 per cent 'should' be between 60 and 80 per cent – something which would be achievable in the next ten to 15 years (*Business Day*, 2002). According to the most recent Global Entrepreneurship Monitor (GEM) survey, South Africa lies among a group of countries with below average rates of entrepreneurship. South Africa is the only developing country in the GEM survey that is not performing on key measures of entrepreneurial activity. It is also the only one whose scores are getting worse.

This sounds like bad news. But perhaps the real question is not so much how South Africa compares internationally, but rather how it compares with its own past (Hudson, 2003a). While South Africa's rate of enterprise growth is lower than many of the small-business-driven economies of the world, there can be little doubt that it is already higher than it was 20 years ago. At that time, South Africa's small-business economy was either neglected during the apartheid era, or in the case of black-owned enterprises, actively discouraged. That is no longer the case: SMEs have increased their role as suppliers to the public sector and to larger corporations. At the same time, their share in national exports and in overall employment has become significant. In addition, while in GEM terms South Africa might appear a weaker performer in comparison to many developing countries, it has at least managed to hold its own *vis-à-vis* some developed countries.

Nevertheless, the challenges are considerable. South Africa faces the dual task of integrating itself into the global markets as a competitive economy while simultaneously overcoming internal problems created and continuously reinforced by apartheid. This chapter argues that the regulatory context will be of central importance in determining the extent to which the SME sector can help South Africa face up to these challenges.

THE LEGACY OF APARTHEID

There is no question but that entrepreneurship was blunted in South Africa by apartheid policies. Such policies contributed to the emergence of a highly dualistic economy characterized by a high-productivity (modern) and a low-productivity (informal) sector with scant interaction between them, and a division along racial lines. The apartheid era also saw the exclusion of the majority of potential entrepreneurs from proper education and access to property and/or financial resources. One commentator has suggested that, to understand where the South African economy currently stands, one needs to go even further back than the days of apartheid. According to Mhone (2001), the constrained role of SMEs is the consequence of at least three historical legacies:

- the nature of colonial development based on a model that simultaneously exploited and marginalized the majority of the labour force without absorbing them into sustainable economic activities;
- the biased way in which an import substitution strategy was implemented to the benefit of particular groups and large scale economic activities; and
- the legacy of apartheid, which resulted in unequal access to various forms of capital and opportunity in the labour market based on race, gender and age. Policies imparted a bias in favour of large-scale and capital-intensive enterprises through a wide and complex array of regulatory and supportive measures.

The apartheid legacy is linked to the structural role and status of the SME sector and partly explains the participation of various groups on the basis of race and gender. For example, in 1999, StatsSA estimated the number of entrepreneurs (self-employed persons) at about 1 630 000 or 3.7 per cent of the population. About 70 per cent of these 1.6 million entrepreneurs operate in the informal sector, 41 per cent are women – this illustrates two of the main challenges of any SME support strategy. Regarding the nature of businesses associated with particular population groups, African females had the highest incidence of informality while white males had the highest incidence of formality.

However, it should be stressed that even in the days of apartheid – where regulations discriminated specifically against the development of black businesses – there were many examples to support the view that 'you can't put a good entrepreneur down'. Entrepreneurship will out, as it were. As Kane-Berman notes,

> Richard and Marina Maponya . . . made their fortunes more than 25 years ago. Not only was this before the term 'empowerment' was coined, but they made it when the National Party government lumbered black entrepreneurs with dozens of handicaps designed to nip success in the bud. Herman Mashaba, boss of the haircare company Black Like Me, started out in a homeland nearly 17 years ago and last year opened up in London. (Kane-Berman, 2003, p. 1)

The growth of the taxi industry and spaza shops shows how the efforts of ordinary people, 'voting with their feet', created new rights in the business field despite a hostile official and legal environment. The Group Areas Act could not prevent many Indian businesses prospering, using white nominees and front companies, and attracting white customers to areas where Indians could operate legally (Hudson, 2003a).

In addition, as Berry et al. (2002) warn us,

> There is a danger in ascribing all the responsibility for the underdevelopment of SMMEs to political disenfranchisement, since the corollary to this argument is that the new economic order provides a sufficient condition for the revitalization of the SMME economy. The removal of apartheid, although necessary, has been insufficient in unraveling the full potential of the SME economy. (Ibid., p. 9)

GETTING MACROECONOMIC POLICY RIGHT – A NECESSARY BUT NOT SUFFICIENT CONDITION FOR ENTERPRISE GROWTH

Stable macroeconomic policies in the form of the growth, employment and redistribution or GEAR strategy – while an essential basis for development – have not been sufficient to encourage business growth. The rate at which jobs have been created lags well behind the number of job-seekers. Research by an economist based at the University of the Western Cape, Haroon Bhorat, shows that employment would have needed to expand more than 33 per cent since 1995 to have provided jobs for all new entrants in the job market (Hudson, 2002).

Also important are the legislative and institutional factors, together with an appropriate regulatory regime. Entrepreneurship can be hampered through deliberate policy – such as apartheid – or inadvertently through a maze of inappropriate regulations (Hudson, 2003a). A key research finding of a ten-country study, seven in Africa and three in Central Europe, by Bannock Consulting in the UK is that an appropriate regulatory and institutional environment is the single most important element in a country's economic growth strategy. Only one other factor – a country's level of available skills, especially technical skills – is anywhere near as strongly correlated with per capita economic growth (Bannock, 2002).

Education and skills strategies are inherently long term – akin to 'turning a supertanker'. Most usefully, they must be complemented with interventions to improve the regulatory and institutional environment within which business operates in the short term. While the importance of education should not be downplayed, it must be remembered that entrepreneurial success is possible even on the back of limited formal educational qualifications. In some cases, no education might be better as it is not so much education *per se* but its orientation and quality that matters. An entrepreneurial culture is not boosted in an educational environment geared to generating bureaucrats rather than calculated risk-takers. In addition, too narrow a focus on formal education obscures the important and often hidden curriculum of family experience, exposure to entrepreneurial role models and learning-by-doing/from experience (Hudson, 2003a).

Despite the strong mandate given by the South Africa's White Paper on the national strategy for the development and promotion of small business (1995), and National Small Business Act, which paved the way for public sector institution building, it is clear that much work remains to be done. Government's track record in supporting South Africa's entrepreneurs is not well regarded. TIPS (Trade and Industrial Policy Strategies) quotes a survey in 2000 showing that 57 per cent of emerging SMEs interviewed in Gauteng and 70 per cent in the Western Cape, for example, had never had contact with or even heard of any small-business support institution.[1] A World Bank survey indicated that 'no more than 20% of SMEs were aware of Khula and Ntsika programmes' (Chandra et al., 2000). There may well be exceptions to this picture, but it would be fair to say that government's 'reach' into this sector is seen to be low. There is an uneven spread in where, how and in which field services are offered. Poor coordination results in a replication of services and clustering of institutions in urban areas.[2] It must be noted that South Africa is not unique; supporting small business is difficult all over the world. Nevertheless, there is a need for a reconfiguration of policy. In particular, rather than promoting support services, government's explicit focus might usefully shift to removing the barriers that might make the support less necessary.[3]

A BETTER ENVIRONMENT FOR BUSINESS, PARTICULARLY SMALL BUSINESS

Enterprise start-ups and operation are influenced not only by markets but also by the regulatory and institutional environment established by governments.

The cumulative impact of numerous regulations and formalities originating in many areas and layers of government is to slow down business responsiveness and to discourage – not necessarily prevent – entrepreneurship. Covering 145 countries, the World Bank's *Doing Business in 2005* supports this conclusion. A time-and-motion study measuring the obstacles facing entrepreneurs performing standardized tasks, the report has three main findings:

- businesses in poor countries face much larger regulatory burdens than those in rich countries – three times the administration costs, nearly twice as many bureaucratic procedures and delays associated with them. Countries that most need entrepreneurs to create jobs and boost growth – poor countries – put the most obstacles in their way;
- overly complex regulation and weak property rights exclude the poor from doing business. With burdensome entry regulations, few businesses bother to register, opting to operate in the informal economy instead. In most poor countries 40 per cent or more of the economy is informal. Women, young and low-skilled workers are hurt the most;
- the payoffs for reform appear to be large. Businesses spend less time and money on dealing with regulations; government spends fewer resources regulating and more providing basic social services. An improved regulatory environment could increase annual economic growth in many developing countries by as much as 1.4 per cent per year. More specifically, in 2002, the Dutch government set a goal of cutting expenditures on administrative burdens by 25 per cent by 2006. Actal, an independent agency for cutting red tape, estimates that $2 billion has already been saved by conducting impact assessments before new regulations reach Parliament. The benefits of regulatory reform are likely to be greater in developing countries, which regulate even more.

The regulatory and administrative aspects of the environment in which firms operate can have a substantial impact on a country's competitiveness and capacity to create jobs, as well as on the health of the SME sector. This is for a number of reasons. In the first place, compliance costs vary with firm size, with small business suffering most. While regulations affect the private sector as a whole, they weigh most heavily on smaller firms because of their limited administrative resources, uncertain cash flows, and limited understanding of their rights in relation to, for example, tax matters. Complying with regulations can be expensive and difficult, assuming a business can work out what constitutes compliance in the first place.[4] Many small firms do not have dedicated in-house tax specialists or human resources staff. In addition to costs of lawyers and consultants there is little doubt that navigating 'red tape' requires not just time but patience and results in a fair amount of stress. A large corporation may well be able to absorb these costs; the situation is different for small enterprise. This is also the area where there is the greatest degree of non-compliance.

Examining the costs of administrative compliance in almost 8000 SMEs, an OECD report[5] found that compliance costs per employee were over five times higher for the smallest SMEs than for the largest. An American study has concluded that firms employing fewer than 20 employees face an annual regulatory bill of US$6975 per employee. This burden is 60 per cent higher than that faced by firms with more than 500 employees. A South African study found that compliance costs represent 8.3 per cent of turnover for enterprises with annual sales of less than R1 million, and 0.2 per cent of turnover for corporations with sales of R1 billion or more. Average compliance costs per person employed for firms with fewer than five employees are apparently ten times higher than for a firm with between 200 and 499 employees (SBP, 2004). The disproportionate impact of regulations on small business has a sharp significance in the South African context, where the weight of the smallest size category (micro) is overwhelming.

Of course, informal and formal entrepreneurs respond differently to the policy and regulatory environment as the former tend to ignore regulations, taxes, levies, health standards and the like. A large informal sector can be an admission that the regulatory costs imposed on business are too high and inappropriate. As de Soto states, 'Massive extralegality is not a new phenomenon; it is what always happens when governments fail to make the law coincide with the way people live and work.'[6]

As Bannock Consulting argues, even though regulations may not be enforced in the informal sector, inappropriate regulations act as a barrier to development by keeping a large proportion of the population out of the formal economy (Hudson, 2002). Somewhat unhelpfully, such regulations offer incentives to remain small and informal. Unfortunately there is a cost to be met here since there is little job security in the informal sector and jobs tend to be low paid. While entrepreneurial activity might be promoted here, this would have to be at the price of non-compliance in respect of tax and other regulations. An important additional problem with the informal sector is that firms do not grow to their efficient size, thus reducing the number of productive jobs and diminishing the opportunities for growing out of poverty. At the same time, businesses do not pay taxes, reducing the resources for the delivery of basic infrastructure.

In a revealing survey, 150 South African informal sector enterprises were recently asked whether or not officials had interfered with their operations in any way: 28 per cent said yes; 62 per cent of these had had stock confiscated or destroyed, 19 per cent had been prosecuted and fined, 17 per cent had been ordered to close or move on, 10 per cent had been asked to pay bribes. These are costs borne by these enterprises. Advantages of formalization identified were: less harassment (30 per cent); cheaper stock/inputs and credit (17 per cent); the possibility of government aid (24 per cent); and a better image for marketing and tenders. Among the perceived disadvantages to registering their businesses were taxes (38 per cent), costs in relation to rewards (22 per cent) and red tape (7 per cent) (SBP, 2004, p. 14). If regulation were simplified, entrepreneurs would find benefits in moving to the formal sector in the form of greater access to credit and the legal system. In addition, large corporations and the public sector might take them on as suppliers as enterprises need a tax certificate to tender for contracts.

Essentially, when imposed at unrealistic levels, inappropriate regulation divides the economy into formal and informal sectors and erects barriers between the two, which perpetuates the division. Somewhat unhelpfully, inappropriate regulations offer incentives to remain small and informal. Small-business consultants have suggested that rather than see the informal sector as 'unfair competition' to the formal sector, it is more useful to see it as an incubator to build skills and assets before an enterprise enters the formal sector. However, surveys conducted across Southern Africa indicate that less than 1 per cent of firms 'graduate' from the micro-enterprise seedbed and become more established enterprises employing more than ten people (Mead and Liedhold, 1998). It would be unwise to underrate the degree of economic activity and commercial spirit in the informal sector. Commenting on the implementation of reforms in Peru, economist Hernando de Soto notes:

> Some 276 000 ... entrepreneurs recorded their businesses voluntarily in new registry offices we set up to accommodate them – with no promise of tax reductions. Their underground businesses had paid no taxes at all. Four years later, tax revenues from formerly extralegal businesses totaled US $1.2 billion ... We ... cut dramatically the costs of the red tape to enroll small businesses. By 1994 Peru had the world's highest growth rate of about 13% per annum. It was a huge shock. The fact is that people do come in. This is not to say that people do not care about their tax bill ... All we had to do was make sure the costs of operating legally were below those of surviving in the extralegal sector, facilitate the paperwork for registration, make a strong effort to communicate the advantages of the programme, and then watch hundreds of thousands of entrepreneurs happily quit the underground ... Extralegal manufacturers and shopkeepers know basic arithmetic.[7]

A study conducted in Egypt concluded that the extra-legal economy employs over 8 million people (about 40 per cent of the workforce) and has assets of almost $250 billion, 30 times the market value of all companies registered on the Cairo Stock Exchange.[8]

Informal entrepreneurship has 'boomed' in South Africa with a total growth of 10.9 per cent in the period 2002–2003. Among population groups, informal enterprise growth was highest among African women at 13.9 per cent; for African men growth is 10.7 per cent.[9] This expansion of informal enterprise represents a potential resource that could be harnessed for growth and development. It suggests that attention should be paid to barriers to entry in the formal sector.[10] The potential exists for the South African economy to grow faster and more equitably if the most successful elements of the informal sector could be brought into the formal sector. Part of the challenge lies in making the process of formalizing easier so that informal enterprises do not become trapped in sub-scale activities.[11] While a degree of non-compliance is perhaps inevitable, widespread and enduring non-compliance can devalue regulatory instruments in general and diminish the credibility of the government.[12] A better strategy to promote compliance is perhaps to discard what is not useful (unnecessarily complex bureaucratic procedures) and enforceable and absorb what works.

SOME EXAMPLES OF REGULATORY DRAG

As noted earlier, external forces tend to have more impact on small businesses than on large ones. Changes in government regulations, tax laws, labour and interest rates affect a greater percentage of expenses for small businesses than they do for large corporations. 'Such limitations mean that small businesses can seldom survive mistakes or misjudgements' (Welsh and White, 1981, p. 55).

Against this backdrop, how is South Africa doing? A 2004 study suggests that South African businesses incurred regulatory compliance costs of about R79 billion, or 6.5 per cent of GDP (SBP, 2004, p. 2). According to a recent OECD survey (reproduced in Cordova-Novion and De Young, 2001), the equivalent compliance costs in Australia and New Zealand stood respectively at 3.0 per cent and 2.8 per cent of GDP.

Thus the impression is that South Africa has a high regulatory compliance burden. However, it is interesting to note that a small-scale survey in Uganda put compliance costs higher – as much as 11 per cent of GDP for all firms.[13] Naturally, in making any international comparisons, there is a need for caution. Still, it is clear that these issues need to be investigated further.

One benchmark for reflecting on the levels of regulatory compliance is the World Bank's *Doing Business in 2005* study. In this study New Zealand topped the list of countries where it was the easiest for businesses to operate, followed by the USA, Singapore, Hong Kong, Australia and Norway. Botswana and South Africa rank in the top quartile, with Botswana ahead of South Africa – the latter's relatively rigid labour market increased the regulatory burden on businesses and curtailed employment and economic growth according to the report. Other findings include:

- It takes 38 days to register a new business in South Africa – faster than Germany, and definitely quicker than Haiti, which comes last at 203 days. But *Doing Business* points out that for business entry, only two procedures – registering for statistical purposes, and for tax and social security – are necessary to fulfil the social functions of the process. Australia, New Zealand and Canada limit the process to the latter two, whereas South Africa has nine.
- It takes 58 procedures for a creditor to collect her debt in Sierra Leone but only 11 in Australia; 27 days in Tunisia but 1459 in Guatemala, according to *Doing Business*. South Africa's 26 procedures take 277 days. The fewer procedures, the lower the cost, and the shorter the time to resolve the disputes. As confidence in dispute resolution rises, entrepreneurs become more willing to enter contracts beyond their narrow circle of known business partners.
- Good bankruptcy laws allow entrepreneurs to learn from their mistakes and try again with relative ease. Bad bankruptcy laws can take the spark from a country's entrepreneurial spirit. A typical business bankruptcy might take four months in Ireland, five in Japan, but can take more than ten years in India and Brazil! South Africa's two years needs to be seen in this context – not among the worst, but leaving room for improvement.

In addition to the World Bank study, there is further in-country work that highlights some challenges in terms of the regulatory environment for doing business, particularly for South Africa's entrepreneurs. For example:

- Many South African entrepreneurs see the Skills Development Levy as 'just another tax'. Not having produced a training plan that can be recognized by their Sector Education and Training Authority (SETA), some entrepreneurs pay their levy without claiming it back.
- Particularly difficult is the South African Revenue Services' (SARS) decision that VAT should be paid on invoice rather than on receipt of payment. This has led to cash flow constraints for small businesses subcontracting to larger entities that are sluggish in paying, for example, many government departments. This change was implemented without visible consultation.
- A study by Upstart Business Strategies (Upstart Business Strategies, 2004) found that the total administrative burden per SME in terms of VAT compliance amounted to R8441 per year. According to the Upstart report, 'of the enterprises registered for VAT, approximately 498 500 are SMEs'. Upstart then notes that the total VAT-induced administrative burden for the 498 500 SMEs amounts to R4.37 billion. These

administrative burdens originate mainly from the obligation to keep records (70 per cent of the total administrative burdens) followed by the tax return (28 per cent).

- The Upstart study was followed a few months later by a survey of 1794 businesses of all sizes conducted by Markdata and published by the Small Business Project. VAT – cited in 19 per cent of responses, with other tax-related issues (PAYE and SARS together totalling 20 per cent) – emerged as the most troublesome and time-consuming regulation; labour laws were mentioned in 12 per cent of responses, and SETA and RSC levies in 11 per cent. On average the annual cost of regulatory compliance per firm was R105 174 for all sizes and sectors (SBP, 2004, p. 9).

- Studies in different geographical areas may well throw up different emphases; almost every sector of the economy has regulations specific to its type of operation. A study conducted in South Africa's Free State province in 2003, for example, identified the poor state of tourism marketing as a first group of constraints on growth, and excessive or unnecessary regulations imposed by national, provincial and local authorities upon business development which negatively affect tourism businesses, as the second. The most prominent concerns among the regulatory issues related to constraints upon businesses from signage regulations (which in the Free State province were formulated in the 1940s), labour regulations and costs for zoning applications.[14]

FUTURE PERSPECTIVES

A South African NGO recently urged in a *Headline report* that 'a growing body of research is showing that work to improve the regulatory environment for business should be a national priority' (SBP, 2004, p. 16). There is evidence to suggest that the authorities have begun to take this conclusion on board. The South African government has openly expressed its commitment to ensuring the appropriateness of regulation in order not to restrict economic activity. In the 2004 Budget Speech, for example, the Minister of Finance, Mr Trevor Manuel, said:

> Reducing the regulatory burden on [small] businesses is a key element of Government's strategy for encouraging employment creation. A working group will be established this year to review the compliance burden on small businesses.

The SARS Commissioner, Mr Pravin Gordhan, has initiated a process to identify ways to ease the tax administration burden for small businesses. He said, 'We take SMMEs seriously and want to assist them and at the same time want better compliance from them.' Government has already attempted to improve the tax system for SMEs in SA. For example, the VAT registration threshold was increased to R300 000, relieving firms below the registration threshold of the necessity of administering the tax. President Mbeki himself, in his State of the Nation speech in May 2004, spoke of the need for government to 'continue to work to reduce the cost of doing business in our economy'.

Thus the SARS initiative fits into government's broader agenda of reducing compliance burdens and removing the regulatory barriers to the advancement of the SME sector given depth and weight by President Thabo Mbeki's announcement in his State of the Nation speech. The SARS initiative is likely to be significant. Studies have shown that tax compliance costs absorb a large share of the total administrative costs of businesses. In the UK tax compliance costs – on the basis of studies available – appear to account for 40–50 per cent of all regulatory costs. Respondents to a survey conducted in New Zealand claimed that approximately 30 per cent of compliance costs are tax-related, 30 per cent employment-related and 25 per cent environment-related. The issue of reducing compliance burdens for SMEs – not just confined to tax but incorporating labour, health and safety and related business regulatory and compliance issues – is important if South Africa is to capitalize fully on its recent upsurge in entrepreneurial activity.

More broadly, while the concept of regulatory impact assessments is relatively new to South Africa, it promises to play an increasingly significant role in the formulation of policy. It fits in well with a programme by the Department of Public Service and Administration – *From red tape to smart tape* – which aims to reduce red tape more widely in the public sector. The National Treasury is currently working with the Presidency on a pilot project around building regulatory impact assessment into government processes. Thus there are bright spots in the South African context. It will, of course, take time for the impact of changes to be felt, but there clearly have been moves in the right direction.

CONCLUDING REMARKS

It will be evident from the preceding discussion that regulatory compliance costs represent a significant brake on the growth potential of the SME sector. In order to reduce this burden, three steps might usefully be taken.

* Regulation should only take place when necessary, after considering non-regulatory alternatives.
* Regulation should be conducted with a light touch, proportionate to the risk.

- Existing regulations should be simplified wherever possible. Inroads must often be made to tackle the stock of unnecessary bureaucracy that already exists – a tricky task as vested interests may protect their turf and resist the process. This points to the vital ingredient of political will, high-level political backing and leadership, all of which are essential.

It must be remembered that the regulatory environment is just one facet of the overall business climate. Also important, particularly in the South African context, are: the quality and availability of staff, crime, infrastructure, the savings rate, the impact of HIV/Aids on a business as well and the cultural attitude to entrepreneurship.[15] In addition, it is easy to overlook the role of trust and personal networks in business. While these factors undoubtedly play a role, this chapter has argued that a reduction in the administrative burden for SMEs is a vital concern.

While regulatory reform is sometimes equated with deregulation, deregulation in itself represents an insufficient principle on which to base reform.[16] The objective must be smart regulation and better enforcement of a simplified regulatory structure. At the same time there needs to be a focus on improving the quality of government. Essentially, the argument is that the regulatory burden on the private sector should be as modest as possible – mindful of the need to protect citizens and consumers from unsafe products, to preserve the environment for current and future generations, to shield employees from unfair employment practices, and to defend the public accounts from the erosion of the tax base.

NOTES

1. TIPS (2002), p. 39.
2. Ibid.
3. Such a conclusion is shared by the Bannock Consulting report. See also Hudson (2002).
4. Ibid. See also Hudson (2003b, 2003c).
5. Cordova-Novion and De Young (2001).
6. See Hudson (2001), p. 2.
7. Ibid.
8. Quoted in United Nations Commission on the Private Sector and Development (2004), p. 9.
9. See *Annual Review of Small Business in South Africa* (2004), p. 23.
10. Ibid.
11. Ibid., p. 20.
12. http://www.cabinet-office.gov.uk/regulation.
13. Quoted in SBP (2004).
14. See *Annual Review of Small Business in South Africa* (2004), p. 77.
15. See Hudson (2003d), p. 1.
16. See Hudson (2005).

REFERENCES

Annual Review of Small Business in South Africa 2003 (2004), Pretoria: Department of Trade and Industry.

Bannock, G. (2002), *Indigenous Private Sector Development and Regulation in Africa and Central Europe: A Ten Country Study*, August.

Berry, A. et al. (2003), 'The Economics of Small, Medium and Micro Enterprises', *Trade and Industrial Policy Strategies*, Pretoria: Department of Trade and Industry.

Business Day, 12 November 2002.

Chandra V. et al. (2000), *Constraints to Growth and Employment in South Africa: Evidence from Small, Medium and Micro-enterprise Firm Surveys*, Washington, DC: World Bank

Cordova-Novion, C. and De Young, C. (2001), 'The OECD PUMA Multi-Country Business Survey – Benchmarking the Regulatory and Business Environment', in C. Evans, J. Pope and J. Hasseldine (eds), *Tax Compliance Costs*, Sydney: Prospect Media.

Hudson, J. (ed.) (2001), *The Mystery of Capital: Why Capitalism Triumphs in the West and Fails Everywhere Else – A South African Conversation with Hernando de Soto*, Johannesburg Centre for Development and Enterprise.

Hudson, J. (2002), 'An Enabling Environment for Private Sector Growth: Lessons from International Experience', report, SME Alert Series, Small Business Project (SBP).

Hudson, J. (2003a), 'Debunking Myths in the South African Context', paper presented at the 48th International Council for Small Business Conference, Belfast, 18 June.

Hudson, J. (2003b), *Understanding Regulatory Impact Assessments: Key Issues from the International Experience*, SBP, January.

Hudson, J. (2003c), *A Small Business Perspective on Tax Compliance*, SBP, October.

Hudson, J. (2003d), *Is South Africa a Good Place to do Business?*, SBP, November.

Hudson, J. (2005), 'Moving Towards Smart Tape: Regulation and Small Business', *Global Entrepreneurship Monitor 2005*, Cape Town: University of Cape Town Graduate School of Business.

Kane-Berman, J. (2003), 'Empowerment Versus Entrepreneurship', *Fast Facts*, No. 3, South African Institute of Race Relations.

Mead, D.C. and Liedholm, C. (1998), 'The Dynamics of Micro and Small Enterprises in Developing Countries', *World Development*, **26**, 67–9.

Mhone, G. (2001), *Entrepreneurship in Small, Medium and Micro Enterprises in South Africa: Findings Based on the 1999 October Household Survey*, Prepared for the Ntsika Enterprise Promotion Agency

SBP (2004), *Counting the Cost of Red Tape for Business in South Africa: Headline Report*, November.

TIPS (Trade and Industrial Policy Strategies) (2002), *The Economics of SMEs*.

United Nations Commission on the Private Sector and Development (2004), *Unleashing Entrepreneurship: Making Business Work for the Poor*, Report to the Secretary-General of the United Nations, New York: United Nations Development Programme.

Upstart Business Strategies (2004), 'Value-Added Tax Act and Regional Services Councils Act-Induced Administrative Burdens for Small Businesses', presented at the Easing the Administrative Burden for Small Enterprises Workshop, Johannesburg, 18 June.

Welsh, J and White, J. (1981), 'A Small Business is Not a Little Big Business', *Harvard Business Review*, July–August, p. 55.

World Bank (2005), *Doing Business in 2005: Removing Obstacles to Growth*, Washington, DC: World Bank.

11. The changing regulatory environment and its implications for the performance of small- and medium-sized enterprises in Ghana

Ernest Aryeetey and Ama Asantewah Ahene

Significant changes in Ghana's business environment have been anticipated following the proclamation of a 'golden age of business' by the current government soon after its election in 2000. The proclamation represented the culmination of several years of economic reform, which had latterly allocated the private sector a central role as 'the engine of growth'. This has resulted in the creation of a Ministry of Private Sector Development alongside the already existing Ghana Investments Promotion Centre (GIPC) and the National Board for Small-Scale Industries (NBSSI). The main purpose of these public agencies is to develop an enhanced environment for the functioning of private enterprises, most of which are SMEs. They are expected to provide the policy framework for the operations of firms and also regulate them in a manner that provides all categories of firms with fair access to the market and public resources. While it is not very clear what the regulatory mandate of these bodies is, beyond the registration of different types of firms, they have some influence on such matters as labour recruitment, minimum wage enforcement, standards in production and location of industries.

In addition to the public agencies for regulating enterprises, there are a number of bodies that ostensibly seek to bring about self-regulation with a view to improving the operating environment for firms. These include the Association of Ghanaian Industries, Federation of Associations of Ghanaian Exporters, Private Enterprise Foundation, EMPRETEC and Ghana Association of Women Entrepreneurs. The interest of these bodies in improving such matters as access to credit for members, negotiating tax concessions for members, providing training in entrepreneurship, providing information about external markets and maintaining industry standards is quite well known. Self-regulation is basically perceived as an attempt to reduce undue government interference in the operations of businesses.

This chapter discusses the influence that public regulators and self-regulatory

237

agencies have had on the performance of SMEs in the last decade. It is recognized that the experimentation with different modes of regulation in such areas as taxes, production, standards, labour laws, location of firms and prices will have some impact on the production methods that firms choose. The chapter also addresses the evolution of regulatory environment in Ghana as well as identifing how the regulatory choices made by firms affect their performance.

The chapter is structured as follows: in Section I we discuss the scope of SME activity in Ghana. This is followed with a presentation in Section II of the institutional developments and the evolution of regulatory agencies. Here we emphasize the fact that most of the institutional developments have largely addressed the concerns of larger enterprises and these have usually been related to the issues of either attracting investments or promoting the payment of taxes. In Section III we focus on recent changes in the regulatory environment where considerable self-regulation has emerged to complement state regulation. In Section IV, we present findings on how small enterprises have responded to the new institutional developments in terms of organization and performance.

I. THE SCOPE OF SME ACTIVITY

Small- and medium-sized enterprises (SMEs) are generally perceived to be the seedbed for indigenous entrepreneurship and to generate a plenitude of small investments that would otherwise not have taken place. SMEs use mainly local resources and thus have fewer foreign exchange requirements while adapting more easily to customer requirements. Due to their small and perceived flexible nature, SMEs are expected to be able to withstand adverse economic conditions and survive where many large businesses would collapse. SMEs tend to be labour intensive, which implies lower capital costs and job creation (Anheier and Seibel, 1987; Liedholm and Mead, 1987; Schmitz, 1995). They have often been described as improving the efficiency of domestic markets and making productive use of scarce resources, and thus facilitating long-term economic growth in poor countries.

SMEs in Ghana have been acknowledged to face many obstacles in their development, and this is often linked to the absence of a clear vision of the roles in development and the obvious lack of a credible policy framework and distinct credible interventions to promote their growth and expansion (Aryeetey et al., 1994). It may be noted that local entrepreneurship was not seriously promoted in Ghana in the colonial period, and in the early 1960s, small-scale enterprises were seen as political threats. State involvement in import-substituting industries was the approach of the President of the First Republic in his bid to modernize the economy. Due to the heavy importation of raw materials and intermediate goods, the cost of development became high, resulting in pressure on the foreign exchange reserves. This led to the enactment of the Exchange Control Act in 1961. Import licensing was introduced with quantitative restrictions, high tariffs and administrative restrictions on prices. The Export Promotion Council was established in 1969 to improve exports in the economy, including non-traditional goods. This was certainly not an environment that was supportive of small enterprises.

In the 1980s the deterioration in the balance of payments led to a continuous increase in the general price level and the overvaluation of the exchange rate, which led to a reduced capacity utilization in the import-dependent large-scale manufacturing sector. As the large state sector found it difficult to support the huge labour force it employed, it began to lose some of the labour, which soon found itself in self-employment but at a very low or largely informal level. Indeed, as the economy declined, large-scale manufacturing employment stagnated. According to Steel and Webster (1990), small-scale and self-employment grew by 2.9 per cent per annum but their activities accounted for only a third of the value-added.

Also at this time, the deteriorating economic conditions led to the implementation of a Structural Adjustment Programme (SAP) and the Economic Recovery Programme (ERP), which aimed at removing distortions in the market mechanism. Under these programmes, the trade and industrial policies sought to restore incentives for the production of food and industrial raw materials and export commodities. Trade controls were removed, and a market mechanism allocated foreign exchange, while price controls were abolished. The decontrolling of interest rates, a reduction in tariffs, the abolition of import licensing and a revision of the investment code were instituted. The base of the tax structure was broadened, subsidies to public enterprises were cut and small-scale manufacturing and services were promoted. But it is important to observe that these trends have not solved the problems of the SMEs.

It is interesting that while SMEs represent over 95 per cent of enterprises in most OECD countries, and generate over half of private sector employment, the sector employs only about 15.5 per cent of the labour force in Ghana (Parker et al., 1995). We may emphasize the point, however, that despite this small number of direct employees, the number of people that depend on SMEs for their livelihoods is considered to be much higher. This is linked to the informal nature of a number of the transactions of some SMEs. In acknowledging the growth problems that SMEs in Ghana and most parts of Africa face, one may also point out that most SMEs will begin small and eventually die small, without ever having seen any expansion in terms of employment numbers and output.

It is not clear which of the problems that SMEs face are the results of specific public policies and which ones are structural. There is indeed a tendency to attempt to solve all problems with policy measures. Surveys commonly reveal that factor availability and rising costs are the most common constraints that SMEs face. Other constraints often mentioned are the lack of access to appropriate technology, the existence of inappropriate laws, regulations and rules, thus impeding the development of the sector, weak institutional capacity and lack of management skills and training.

It may be noted that the trade liberalization policies of the 1980s and even later exposed many SMEs to greater external competition than they were used to or could cope with. Aryeetey et al. (1994) identified this problem in 12.5 per cent of medium-sized enterprises in Ghana. Riedel et al. (1988) reported that tailors in Techiman, who used to make several pairs of trousers in a month, went without any orders with the coming into effect of trade liberalization. It is again reported in Aryeetey et al. (1994) that only 1.7 per cent of firms export their output, as a result of limited international marketing experience, poor quality control, product standardization and little access to international partners.

There exists a high start-up cost for small firms, including licensing and registration requirements, which impose excessive and unnecessary burdens on SMEs. The cumbersome procedure for registering and commencing business are key issues often cited in surveys. However, Aryeetey et al. (1994) found that this accounted for less than 1 per cent of their sample. Lall and Pietrobelli (2002) noted that potential investors still spend significant time fulfilling bureaucratic requirements. Other constraints on SME development include the lack of protection for property rights, which in turn limits SMEs' access to foreign technologies. Access to land, utility installation and services, and import procedures remain obstacles to the development of SMEs. The high cost of settling legal claims and excessive delays in court proceedings adversely affect SME operations. Lall and Pietrobelli (2002) find that the response of the investor community to investment promotion has been weak, as evidenced by falling foreign direct investment (FDI) inflows in the late 1990s.

The existing literature recognizes that changes in the regulatory environment affect various types of firms in different ways. Changes in tax regulation see larger firms more easily adapting than small- to medium-sized firms. Labour and product standard regulations of firms might operate in favour of larger firms and may actually have a negative impact on SMEs. Due to their lack of capacity, SMEs are less likely to deal effectively with problems concerning bureaucratic networks and complexities than larger firms. On the other hand, SMEs are also more likely to adapt to changing bureaucratic conditions by engaging in more informal approaches to problem solving. This may have its costs, though, in generating business expansion.

Despite the relatively large number of institutions that have been created over the years to oversee the development of SMEs, it is not clear what their regulatory roles were intended to be. It was always obvious that the NBSSI was expected to promote their development, but it was not obvious what the scope of its regulatory role was going to be, particularly since it has never had the means to compel SMEs to behave in any distinct manner. In a sense, the issue of regulating SMEs with a view to creating a level playing field has never been a major policy objective, except when one takes into account the intervention in the 1970s to reserve some classes of small-business activity for Ghanaians. In sum, while regulatory systems may promote competition and innovation (which are necessary to promoting industrial competitiveness, job creation and economic growth), the operating features of SMEs pose considerable difficulties when it comes to improving or changing the environment for their development.

II. INSTITUTIONAL DEVELOPMENTS AND THE EVOLUTION OF REGULATORY AGENCIES FOR SMES

Recent Initiatives

As indicated earlier, the landscape for the regulation of SMEs is quite confusing. Aside from the difficulty of identifying the regulatory functions of the public agencies in charge of them, it is now even more difficult to tell which public institutions have clear regulatory functions and which do not. Against this background, we may note that in 2001, the new President created, for the first time in the country's history, a Ministry for Private Sector Development (MPSD), and appointed a minister of cabinet rank. The main functions of the new ministry are to translate the vision of a 'golden age of business' into realizable sets of actions and to coordinate the various programmes for the development of the sector. In addition, the new ministry is expected to provide a single point where private sector operators can interface effectively with government. Thus, although not formally stated, it would appear that the primary responsibility for the indigenous private sector and SMEs has now shifted to this new ministry.

There is currently a plethora of papers that seek to guide private sector business initiatives. Policy papers issued by government in support of the sector comprise The Investment Code 1985 (PNDC Law 116), the Export and Import Act, 1995 (Act 503), the draft Integrated Industrial Policy for Increased Competitiveness (MOTI, Nov. 2000), the Draft Policy Paper on Micro and

Small Enterprise Development (May 2002), the Ghana Poverty Reduction Strategy Paper (2002–2004); and the Policies, Strategies and Action Plan (2002–2004) by the Ministry of Private Sector Development.

In addition to these, a number of 'President's Special Initiatives' (PSI) on garments, textiles and cassava starch have been established since 2001. These measures are aimed at boosting the production of these products for export. The PSI on garments and textiles is targeted at the US market, taking advantage of various protocols offered by the Africa Growth and Opportunities Act (AGOA), while the initiative on cassava starch for industrial use is aimed at EU countries. The PSI is expected to inject over US$3 billion into the economy in export revenue and provide thousands of jobs over the next five years.

Older Organizations

While new initiatives are emerging, old roles performed by older organizations have not changed. The Ministry of Trade and Industry (MOTI) still retains the primary responsibility for the indigenous private sector, consisting mostly of SMEs. In addition to this, however, various other ministries have responsibility for SME matters, including the Ministry of Finance, the Ministry of Food and Agriculture and the Ministry of Tourism. Other agencies, such as the NBSSI, Ghana Investment Promotion Centre (GIPC), Ghana Free Zones Board and Ghana Export Promotion Council, also implement programmes for the promotion of small business, even if these programmes are severely segmented.

Government has continued to expect that, with such an array of actors in the sector, significant progress would be recorded, but this has not been the case. The MOTI has never managed to exercise a strong leadership role, while NBSSI's mandate, combining policy coordination with implementation and delivery of programmes across the country for SMEs, has always been seen to be too broad, and sometimes even conflicting for an institution with minimum resources. In effect, there is hardly any coordination of efforts or real impact. Furthermore, the MOTI is generally perceived to be concerned mainly with large-scale businesses. Consequently, SMEs, which comprise the majority of the indigenous private sector, do not particularly align themselves with the ministry or believe that their peculiar needs are taken into consideration in policy matters (Aryeetey et al., 1994). Although the NBSSI is established purposely to help develop and promote the sector, it is, like most of the ministries, departments and agencies involved, not adequately resourced with funds, logistics and people to be effective. As a government agency, its structure, processes, people and conditions are seen to be anything but entrepreneurial or business-like.

Involving the Private Sector in Policy Development and Outcomes

It is important to acknowledge that major attempts have been made to involve the private sector in the development of policy, but that these initiatives have seen collaboration mainly with the larger operators, with little direct benefit to the smaller ones. In 1992, the government, in an attempt to strengthen the response of the private sector to economic reforms, undertook a number of measures, including the setting up of the Private Sector Advisory Group. As a result, the Manufacturing Industries Act, 1971 (Act 356) was abolished, and this led to the repealing of a number of price control laws. The Investment Code of 1985 (PNDC Law 116) was also enacted in an attempt to promote joint ventures between foreign and local investors, along with the Legislative Instrument on Immigrant Quotas. The latter grants automatic immigrant quotas for investors. The Ghana Investment Promotion Centre (GIPC) was established in 1994 to promote and regulate FDI. The government also set up an Investors' Advisory Council in 2001 comprising 20 local and international business leaders.

In 1995, the Free Zones Act (Act 504) was enacted with the establishment of the Ghana Free Zones Board (GFZB). The Ghana Free Zones Act gives incentives to firms exporting more than 70 per cent of their annual production and the GFZB promotes the processing and manufacturing of goods. Goods from the free zones are exempt from customs duties. Incentives for free zone companies include a ten-year tax holiday, that is, 0 per cent income tax and guaranteed 8 per cent income tax after the tax holiday. Total exemptions from dividend withholding tax and relief from double taxation for foreign investors/employees are also incentives enjoyed within the free zone. Also, no import licensing is required, 100 per cent foreign ownership is permitted and there are no restrictions on foreign exchange accounts and repatriation of profits. Most firms operating within the free zones benefit from many other incentives and preferential market access, mainly to the EU. The Free Zones Act, indeed, allows exporting firms free zone status, even outside the zone. An UNCTAD (2002) survey found that, while satisfied with free zone benefits, investors identified the need for improvement in technology, education, and credit access and tax incentives. UNCTAD (2002) concludes that 'The focus on export incentives seems to have stifled attention to the importance of technology upgrading and human resource development.'

In addition to the Free Zones Board there exists the Trade and Gateway Programme, which is inter-sectoral and aims at making Ghana the preferred business destination in West Africa. The programme involves advising such agencies as the Customs, Excise and Preventive Service (CEPS), Ghana Immigration Service (GIS), Ghana Civil Aviation Authority (GCAA), Ghana Ports and Harbours Authority (GPHA), Ghana Investment Promotion Council

(GIPC), Ghana Free Zone Board (GFZB) and the Environmental Protection Agency (EPA) to offer more courteous, friendly and business-like services devoid of bribery and corruption in order to reduce the cost of doing business in Ghana. The strategy is to attract a mass of export-oriented firms into Ghana to facilitate export-led growth.

The Export Development and Investment Fund

In aid of industrial and export services within the first quarter of 1998, the government proposed the establishment of an Export Development and Investment Fund (EDIF) in 1997, operational under the Exim Guarantee Company Scheme of the Bank of Ghana. The 1998 Budget Statement buttressed the promotion of the industrial sector by stating that specific attention would be given to the textiles/garments, wood and wood processing, food and food processing and packaging industries for support in accessing the EDIF for rehabilitation and retooling. The government also supports industries with export potential to overcome any supply-based difficulty by accessing EDIF and has rationalized the tariff regime in a bid to improve their export competitiveness.

Measures to Attract Further Foreign Direct Investment

In addition to the development of new organizations and programmes, there have been some changes in institutional arrangements intended to make Ghana more attractive. But these do not necessarily target small businesses. For example, visas for all categories of investors and tourists may now be issued on arrival at the ports of entry, while the Customs, Excise and Preventive Service at the ports has been made increasingly proactive, operating seven days per week.

In order to improve the availability of skills for foreign investors, the government now supports programmes aimed at skills training, registration and placement of job-seekers, and training and retraining of redeployees. This has resulted in a 5 per cent rise in enrolment in the various training institutes such as the National Vocational and Training Institute (NVTI) and the Opportunities Industrialisation Centres (OIC). As at the end of 1997, 65 830 out of 72 000 redeployed persons who were retrained under master craftsmen had been provided with tools and had become self-employed.

Legal Instruments, Acts in Support of Business Development

The operation of companies in Ghana is governed by the Companies Code 1963. Provisions under Act 179 allow foreign firms to register a place of business. The general public must be allowed, under this Act, to subscribe to the shares of registered foreign firms in Ghana. The Partnership Act 1962 (Act 152) and the Business Name Act, 1962 (Act 151) make provisions for partnership and business name (sole proprietorship) formation respectively in Ghana.

The Ghana Investment Promotion Centre (GIPC) Act, 1994 (Act 478) provides for international arbitration in disputes and for technology transfer agreements to be legally effective. The latter must be negotiated with the GIPC. Investment in all sectors of the economy, other than mining, petroleum, free zones and portfolio investments, cannot be established without prior approval by GIPC. Mining and petroleum sector projects have to be approved or licensed by the Minerals Commission and the Ministry of Mines and Energy respectively. The Ghana Free Zones Board administers free zone operations whilst the Ghana Stock Exchange handles portfolio investments. It is required by law for all foreign investors intending to invest in Ghana to register under Act 478 at the GIPC.

Ghana's Capital Investment Act 1963 and the 1973 Investment Decree and Investment Code already incorporated fiscal incentives for investors. The incentives comprise tax holidays in the form of five–ten-year exemptions (the amount varies by sector and is higher for rural banks and agriculture), accelerated depreciation, allowances of 5–20 per cent on plant/machinery, exemptions from import duties on machinery and equipment, investment allowances and arrangements for profit repatriation.

There are location-specific incentives which favour small start-up businesses in Ghana. While full taxes are applicable to businesses located in urban areas, those setting up in rural areas and district capitals may enjoy concessions under the Internal Revenue Act 592 (Industrial Concessions). Manufacturing industries located in regional capitals other than Accra and Tema enjoy a 2 per cent rebate, customs duty and income tax exemptions and other inducements. The Commissioner of the IRS (Internal Revenue Service) has the power to give other incentives to businesses when it is requested and deemed fit. Capital expenditure on R&D is tax deductible.

Taxation and Small Businesses

The fiscal environment has undergone significant changes since the adoption of the Economic Recovery Programme (ERP) and Structural Adjustment Programme (SAP) in the mid-1980s. Changes that have taken place have aimed at expanding and diversifying the tax base, spreading the tax burden in a fairer manner, reducing the cost of doing business by removing distortions in corporate tax and improving the revenue base of government. Administratively, the reforms are meant to make tax administration and compliance less cumbersome, to improve the record keeping of businesses, to strengthen the system for tax collection and, to some extent, to control smuggling. These changes have also shifted the focus from direct to indirect taxes.

The problem for small businesses where taxes are concerned, however, is their extreme variability and unpredictability. The Local Government Act, 1993 (Act 462) empowers all district assemblies to levy rates, tolls, poll tax and licences on businesses as well as households. According to work carried out by the NBSSI (National Board for Small-Scale Industries) concerning taxation and small-scale business operations, there is hardly any uniformity in the rates applied by districts, and the rates are seldom predictable, thus making SMEs extremely insecure. NBSSI reported that the commonest complaints during its study were the perceived notion of overburdening of taxes. UNCTAD concludes that 'income tax remittance regulations have an adverse effect on firms' working capital, since payments are made on prior assessments of profits and audits take up to four years, resulting in delayed and reduced refunds'.

The government allows businesses to write off additional plant and equipment in two years and carry forward the unutilized capital allowance indefinitely in order to minimize the profit tax on the operations of industrial establishments. The tax compliance cost (costs incurred by businesses in meeting the requirements of the tax structure) is deducted from sales before income is taxed. This includes payments to professional tax advisers, rent, air conditioning and light, additional office space, postage, telephone charges and travel to communicate with tax advisers or office as well as time costs. The self-employed are taxed according to the personal income tax schedule, which is also applied to the incomes of employees. Thirty-five per cent of profit is deducted as tax when a self-employed business becomes a limited liability company. A three-year tax holiday is granted to small-scale manufacturers.

The operational fees charged on small-scale industries depend on the type of industrial activity rather than on urban and rural rates. An example cited in the study by NBSSI is the operational fee for mining in the Wassa West District in the Western Region. This is ¢500 000 whilst the maximum fees for other industrial activities in Sekondi/Takoradi is ¢180 000, which is almost twice as much as Tamale's maximum figure of ¢100 000. The small-scale manufacturers in Ashanti and Western Regions are not charged registration fees, but those in Tamale are charged ¢2000 in addition to the operational fees. Property rates on industrial buildings are 0.75 per cent in Kumasi and 80 per cent in Tamale.

The Income Tax Law exempts the first three years' commercial income of agricultural processing activity of small-scale firms that operate as registered companies, the first five years' residential or commercial rent income from newly completed buildings, the first five years' income of developers of housing estates operating as companies and the interest and discounts on Treasury Bills and savings accounts of sole proprietors. Dividend income on receipt by the entrepreneur is taxed at 10 per cent. Businesses under the Income Tax Law are obliged to register with the IRS office nearest to the place of operation noted on the application form. Registration has to be renewed annually, and must be completed separately for each area of operation up to a maximum of five premises. Filing of income tax returns also needs to take place within specific time frames. In addition, entrepreneurs are supposed to deduct tax from employees' salaries each month and pay it to the IRS by the 15th of the following month, withhold 5 per cent from any payments made out for contract works above ¢200 000 and keep all records on their business transactions for six years before disposing of them, except if the IRS has granted permission otherwise.

The CEPS Law enjoins manufacturers to acquire licences annually for each operating premise, pay excise duty on all locally manufactured goods consumed in Ghana not later than 21 days after delivery, and pay sales tax on all goods manufactured locally. Income returns are to be filled and submitted to CEPS not later than the 10th of each following month of sales. The Income Tax Law allows the entrepreneur the right to object to and dispute any assessment of tax within 30 days after notification. Likewise the CEPS Law gives the entrepreneur the right to appeal against any decision of the commissioner of CEPS within 21 days to the Tax Tribunal.

Sole proprietors and partners enjoy Social Security Relief, which is granted in respect of contributions to the Social Security and National Insurance Trust (SSNIT) Pension Scheme for entrepreneurs. The maximum is 17.5 per cent of gross business income. There is also the Life Assurance Relief for entrepreneurs with personal life insurance policies in Ghana, which constitute a maximum of 10 per cent of annual gross business income, or the annual sum assured. Basic Personal Relief is granted to all individual taxpayers. Marriage/Responsibility Relief is given to a married man or woman or unmarried person with two or more dependants on application. Children's Education Relief is granted to cover a maximum of three children of the entrepreneur in a recognized first- to second-cycle school in Ghana.

There is an assortment of other benefits but they are little known to many small entrepreneurs. For example, entrepreneurs with aged dependants can claim ¢200 000 each for a maximum of two such old people. The Income Tax Law further makes provision for disabled entrepreneurs for a grant of 25 per cent of their business income. Also, entrepreneurs above 60 years are entitled to relief on application. Losses in any year may be deducted by entrepreneurs against the next five years' income, while accelerated depreciation allowance enables entrepreneurs to write off capital expenditure on plant within two years and five years of building. Excise duty on goods lost or damaged during removal or evaporation is remitted to entrepreneurs. Very few SMEs have shown knowledge of these facilities in surveys (NBSSI, 2002).

III. NEW FORMS OF REGULATION AND RESPONSES BY SMES

In this section, we cover both developments in the reform of taxes and the operations of new public agencies, as well as the development of self-regulation through private sector organizations.

New Trends in Tax Organization

With recent reforms in the revenue mobilization agencies, the main public institutions responsible for tax administration are the Internal Revenue Service (IRS), the VAT Service, and the Customs, Excise and Preventive Services (CEPS). Unlike in the past, the decision to offer rebates and other concessions to investors is no longer the responsibility of the Ghana Investments Promotion Centre and the Minerals Commission; these are the responsibility of Parliament. Major tax policy measures implemented over the period include personal income tax relief and the conversion of sales tax into value added tax (VAT). Import taxes have also changed significantly. With a few exceptions, all imports currently attract import duty and import VAT. The import VAT is calculated on the duty-inclusive value of the goods. In addition, excise duty is levied on some imports. A special tax of 10 per cent has been imposed on some previously zero-rated commodities (e.g. human hair, potatoes, fruit and juices, mineral water, paints, cosmetics, clothing, cooking oils etc.). There is a zero rating on VAT for pharmaceuticals, thereby ensuring a level playing field between local manufacturers of drugs and importers of drugs.

In 1995, the sales tax was converted into a value added tax (VAT) at a flat rate of 17.5 per cent. This was repealed and the sales tax was reintroduced at 15 per cent. The VAT Law was reinstated in 1998 at 10 per cent and adjusted to 12.5 per cent in 2000 (VAT Amendment Act 579). The Corporate Tax Law (2000) reduced tax rates from 35 per cent to 30 per cent and withholding tax increased from 5 per cent to 7.5 per cent. The 45 per cent Corporate Tax for Banking and Insurance in 1992 to 2000 changed to 32.5 per cent in 2003. Tax on the hotel industry is 25 per cent and Non-traditional Exports is 8 per cent. Businesses must pay VAT and indirect taxes, such as customs duties. Companies listed on the Ghana Stock Exchange are charged 30 per cent as tax. Manufacturing companies in the regional capitals outside Accra/Tema pay a 25.25 per cent tax whilst manufacturing companies outside the regional capitals pay 17.5 per cent tax.

The threshold for tax changed from ¢150 000 in 1992 to ¢210 000 in 1994, ¢318 000 in 1995, ¢600 000 in 1996–98, ¢900 000 in 1998–2000 and ¢1.2 million in 2001. There is no uniformity in the threshold for tax; it is related to the minimum wage, where a certain percentage attracts tax. With respect to VAT, in 1995, the threshold was ¢25 million. In 1998 when it was reintroduced, the threshold was raised to ¢200 million. With the amendment in 2000, the threshold was reduced to ¢100 million. The Internal Revenue Service (IRS) in Ghana has set up collection points near taxpayers in sub-districts of the various regional capitals. In the rural areas, there is field collection of taxes. The IRS introduced the self-assessment system in 2000. Whereas the sales tax was collected only at the manufacturing and importation stages, VAT is collected at all stages of production and distribution. Registered businesses now collect and pay VAT on a self-assessment basis. It is certainly more difficult for SMEs to escape VAT collection and payments.

VAT Services penalties for non-compliance with the law range from various pecuniary fines up to ¢100 million to imprisonment terms of up to five years on conviction and the compounding of offences. As regards enforcement, a number of businesses have been arraigned before the courts and sentenced under the law. In some instances, sentences have included seizure of assets of defaulting businesses. However, most of the defaulters eventually settle out of court. There are no special advantages for small firms in respect of taxes, besides the VAT thresholds.

Regulation of Exports

With the government's current orientation towards diversified exports, particular attention is paid to companies engaging in non-traditional exports (NTEs). Non-traditional exporters are taxed at 8 per cent and are exempt from some export duties. Incentives for exporters include the Export Proceeds Retention Scheme, where NTE exporters can retain 35 per cent export earnings in foreign bank accounts for related import purchases and expenses. The Custom Duty Drawbacks allows manufacturers to draw back to 100 per cent of import duty and other taxes on imported raw materials where these materials are used in export production. A manufacturer of agricultural products who exports part or all of his production can claim 40–70 per cent tax rebate of his tax liability. This scheme is called the Corporate Tax Rebate. Bonded warehousing allows manufacturers to seek a custom licence to hold imported raw materials intended for manufacturing export products in secure places without payment of duty. NTEs are exempt from export duties, and discretionary incentives can be negotiated with specific investors.

The Export and Import Act 1995 (Act 503) has eased exporting and importing procedures considerably. For instance, the requirement for full pre-payment of export proceeds before obtaining an approved A2 Form, a major constraint faced by first-time exporters, was abolished with the new legislation. The reduction in documentation has led to increased value of NTEs as a result of voluntary declaration of the commercial value of shipments. Many SMEs and private sector businesses are now engaged in NTEs, which have grown considerably over the past ten years due to the Medium Term Plan for Non-Traditional Exports, 1991–95. This programme has been jointly implemented by the Ministry of Trade and Industry (MOTI) and the Ghana Export Promotion Council to promote growth in non-traditional exports.

The Trade and Investment Programme (TIP), (1993–97) was a USAID-sponsored intervention aimed at increasing individual and national export earnings, generating employment and attracting more businesses into the exports sector by influencing official policies and bottlenecks that hinder exports and providing support services to GEPC and MOTI. Through TIP, a new Import and Exports Act was passed in 1995, which liberalized the documentation and procedures relating to export trade. In addition, there have been some other donor-funded programmes. Notable ones over the past five years include a private sector development programme funded by IDA, the Capacity Development and Utilization Programme funded by UNDP, GEDPRO funded by DFID, and a DFID-supported Challenge Fund.

Investment Code

The promulgation of the Investment Code in 1985 (PNDC Law 116) made it easier for businesses to reduce the cost of, and improve, compliance with laws and regulations. The measures in the Investment Code include an immigrant quota in respect of an approved number of expatriate employees to be engaged and a personal remittance quota for expatriate staff. For certain transactions, exchange control exemptions apply to the transfer of foreign currency out of the country. Furthermore, there exists a guarantee protecting private businesses against expropriation by the government and there is provision for the registration of all technology transfer agreements.

Changes in Labour Regulations

Labour Regulations stipulate that the prescribed minimum remuneration should be paid to any worker or group of workers and records kept. The Industrial Relations Act allows for negotiation between management and workers (or their unions) to determine wages and benefits. The Workman's Compensation Law also allows and indicates how payments should be made to injured workers.

The insurance laws of the country make it obligatory for employers to contribute 12.5 per cent, and the employee 5 per cent, of an employee's income to the social security fund of the SSNIT. This provides a pension as well as disability benefits for workers, when due.

The labour regulations prescribe that the minimum remuneration may be arrived at through negotiation between government, organized labour and employers. The International Labour Organization (ILO) Convention on Minimum Wage is applied in Ghana. The procedure for employment and firing is indicated in the labour laws as well as in collective bargaining agreements. This is, however, applied in the formal sector and not in the informal sector. When employees are to be made redundant, the Labour Decree demands that management applies to the Chief Labour Officer before carrying out such an exercise. Where employees are unionized, the law requires that the union be involved in the negotiations, whereas management must negotiate the terms with affected employees and with non-unionized employees. There is a general perception that small firms find compliance with the labour laws a lot more difficult than larger firms. The period of notice for declaring redundancy depends on the category of affected employee(s). For instance, artisans/labourers are supposed to be given at least two weeks' notice. However, where there is a collective agreement with a stipulated period above that of the Labour Decree, the former should be applied. Also, where the employee has worked for more than three years, a minimum of one month's notice should be given.

On compensation, once again, this is supposed to be the subject of negotiation between management and the local union or affected staff. If there is a collective agreement, the conditions as laid down must be followed. Furthermore, the employer must settle any accrued benefits of the employee when there is no collective agreement. Management and affected staff must negotiate the terms. In cases where individuals feel that they have been treated unfairly, they can take the case to the Commission for Human Rights and Administrative Justice.

Regulations and Standards

The Ghana Standards Board (GSB) was established in 1967 as the institution in charge of standards, metrology, testing and quality assurance. Its core activities are standards development; testing and certification services; the analysis of food, drugs and industrial raw materials; physical testing of materials, textiles, garments and paper products; calibration services, and training, consumer complaints, public awareness campaigns on labelling rules and good trade practices. Lall and Pietrobelli (2002) detail strong positive achievements by the Board, including acceptance by the EU of GSB testing and health certificates for fish exports and accreditation by the Japanese government for chemical analysis and certification of food in March 1999. Lall and Pietrobelli (2002) note that GSB has a strong reputation in Africa, and the UN Drugs Control Programme (UNDCP) chose it as a centre for the training of analysis of drugs for the African Anglophone sub-region. The Board has carried out training in ISO 9000, and is near to being certified.

However, Lall et al. (1994) find widespread lack of appreciation of standards in Ghanaian industry, and note that GSB lacks resources to prepare standards; to encourage industry to use them and to enforce standards in a meaningful way. Lall and Pietrobelli (2002) find that funding remains a major constraint, with no funding for R&D. Total revenues amount to $2.2 million (twice Ugandan revenues, but much less than other SSA countries). The government contributes 82 per cent of total revenues. As in other public agencies, salaries form a disproportionate share of the total budget (77 per cent in 1999). GSB has staff strength of 403, but this is largely administrative staff (250). The wider business community sees the technical and scientific expertise as adequate, with 49 of the professionals holding a masters degree. However, government levels of pay are insufficient to attract good graduates and motivate them to stay.

A codex committee has been set up under the Ghana Standard Board (GSB) to work exclusively on food standards in Ghana and to give clear guidelines on global food standards so as to facilitate exports. Its operations are required to be in accordance with the global international food standards being compiled by the UN Agency, the *Codex Alimentarius* Commission (CAC).

Phytosanitary regulation stipulates that exporting producers outside the EU must guarantee that the product leaving their countries is in a healthy condition. The phytosanitary certificate, without which the product may not be introduced into the EU, has to be legalized by the food inspection department of the country of origin and the product inspected with respect to insects and diseases. The certificate may not be issued more than 14 days before the date on which the product leaves the country. Some of the products that need the certificate are citrus, pears and mangoes.

The entry-price system is a price regulation set by the EU in 1995 for imported fruit and vegetables. The system replaced the reference price system, which set import duties on fruit and vegetables until 1994. This price system is the minimum price set for imported products. If a product's import price is below the entry price, a duty is imposed. Products such as tomatoes, apples, pears and cucumbers undergo the entry-price system.

The Bio-terrorism Act, 2002 requires owners, operators, or agents in charge of a domestic or foreign facility that manufactures, processes, packs or holds food for human or animal consumption in the USA to register with the US Food and Drug Administration (FDA). The law requires that the exporter must have a US agent. Also, prior notice must be given to the FDA before food is imported or offered for import into the USA no later than noon of the day before the day the food arrives at the border crossing at the US port of entry. The Ghana Standards Board enforces these regulations in Ghana.

Regulation of Credit Flows

Access to credit has been one of the main bottlenecks to SME development. It is interesting that while the financial sector reforms sought to remove all forms of non-market allocations of credit, there have been a number of interventions in the last decade that have sought to ensure that distinct groups of businesses have obtained credit. The only difference between these and earlier versions of directed credit has been that they have attempted to ensure that interest rates are not too different from market rates.

The initiatives have included the Business Assistance Fund (BAF) (1994) and the Rural Finance Project (1995), which provide both short- and long-term finance for small-scale businesses. The Export Development and Investment Fund (EDIF) was set up in 1997 but became operational in July 2001. It provides funding for exporters and their sub-contractors. There is a general perception that since the implementation of these measures is only just beginning, it might be too early to assess their impact on access to credit. In addition, there exists the Private Enterprise and Export Development project (PEED), a joint Ghana Government/World Bank project to address the financial constraints of the non-traditional export sector through a credit of US$41 million. The project granted loans of up to ¢50 million to small and micro enterprises in the manufacturing and service sectors, including returnees from abroad seeking to establish new enterprises from the Promotion of Small and Micro Enterprise Fund (PSME). This is a joint Government of Ghana/German Government facility. In the early 1990s the Fund for Small and Medium Enterprise Development (FUSMED) was supported by the IDA and provided finance to SMEs so as to increase employment, output and incomes. In 1989, the Programme of Actions to Mitigate the Social Costs of Adjustment (PAMSCAD) began to provide funds to assist SMEs.

IV.   THE REGULATORY ENVIRONMENT AND ENTERPRISE PERFORMANCE

This section presents the findings of a survey conducted in two metropolitan areas in Ghana, Accra and Tema. The study involved 200 SMEs (firms with fewer than 30 employees) using a structured questionnaire to interview entrepreneurs/owners of these firms. The firms were randomly selected using a listing of small and medium firms from the National Board for Small-Scale

Industries (NBSSI), the Association of Ghana Industries (AGI), and the Registrar General's Office. As could be expected, some of the names and locations in these lists were outdated. Consequently, other firms had to be substituted for those originally selected. Firms involved in sectors such as wood processing, food processing, garments/textiles, services and manufacturing were chosen for the survey. However, the number of firms chosen in each sector was not equal. Questions were asked concerning the operations of the firms as well as the compliance of the various regulations in the country. The regulations considered were the licensing, investment code, location, registration/reporting, labour, standards and support services. Some of the information gathered includes the ownership structure, the characteristics of the firm and entrepreneur and the operations of the firm.

Business History

The survey findings indicate that of the 200 firms interviewed, 12 firms were established between 1950 and 1970, 39 firms between 1971 and 1990 and 144 firms between 1991 and 2004. The phenomenal growth in SMEs between the 1990s and early 2000s is no surprise, as the economic reforms had taken significant hold then, with their associated benefits and side effects. For the purposes of the study, we undertook another period division to observe the growth of SMEs between 1993 and 2002, and after 2003, so as to learn what had occurred in the intervening decade. The outcome is strikingly similar to the earlier conclusions; many more firms were launched in the 1993–2002 period than the entire period preceding that decade. The evidence after 2002 also suggests a trend similar to that witnessed in the preceding decade. Figure 11.1 depicts trends in SMEs over these periods.

Figure 11.1 also depicts the pattern of firms' start-up capital. With regard to the amount of capital firms began with, over 45 out of the sample started with a capital of less than $600. It should be noted that not all firms provided answers to the question of start-up capital. Notwithstanding this shortcoming, firms that began business with a capital of less than $5600 constituted over 70 per cent of the sample.

An examination of the 200 firms by firm size reveals that 80 of them had between one and five employees when they started business; however, this declined to 14 for firms that started in 1993. The decline, though, had apparently reversed by 2003. Significantly, the majority of the firms in all three period categorizations were employing between one and 15 people. Firms employing between 16 and 30 persons were rather few; both for those considered at start-up and for the year 2003. Clearly, firms within the manufacturing sector constituted the largest share compared to the other sectors based on firm size classification. This pattern is presented in Table 11.1 and in Figure 11.1.

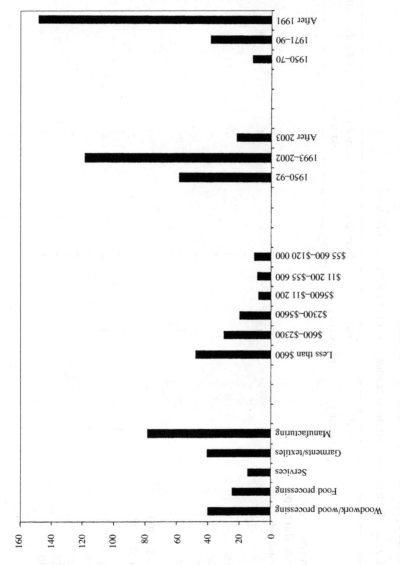

Figure 11.1 Number of firms by output classification, start-up capital and year of start of business

255

Table 11.1 Firm size according to economic activity output classification

Firm size	Wood processing	Food processing	Services	Garments/ textiles	Manufacturing	Total
Period: start-up						
Own account*	1	–	–	–	1	2
1–5	18	10	5	14	33	80
6–10	1	4	5	–	15	25
11–15	–	1	1	–	5	7
16–20	1	–	1	–	3	5
21–25	–	–	–	–	1	1
26–30	1	2	–	–	7	10
Period: 1993						
Own account	–	–	–	–	–	–
1–5	4	2	–	5	3	14
6–10	–	2	–	–	3	5
11–15	2	–	1	–	1	4
16–20	–	–	2	–	–	2
21–25	–	–	–	–	–	–
26–30	2	–	1	1	6	10

Period: 2003

Own account						
	–	–	–	–	–	–
1–5	16	6	1	18	17	58
6–10	7	4	2	5	15	33
11–15	3	–	2	2	4	11
16–20	1	1	1	–	2	5
21–25	1	–	–	–	1	3
26–30	2	2	3	1	19	27

Note: * Own account refers to one-man business.

Source: Survey data.

257

The second relatively large sector is wood processing, followed by those engaged in food processing and then by those engaged in garments/textiles. In Ghana most of manufacturing firms are located in the Accra–Tema metropolis, while most of the wood processing firms are located near their source of raw material, which is the forest zone. This explains the dominance in the sample of firms engaged in manufacturing activity.

Firm Characteristics

There were more male owners of firms than females. Thus, while the population structure of Ghana indicates that there are more females relative to males, in the enterprise field, males dominate. Generally in Ghana, it appears that women are relatively more risk averse than their male counterparts. While the males take the risk to enter into businesses with long gestation periods, women are more often seen in the buying and selling and other businesses with shorter gestation periods. This is largely a cultural phenomenon, in that women are expected to use their income on the upkeep of the home. This cultural demand means that generally most women cannot afford to establish enterprises with long-term returns.

Firms that are classified as sole proprietorships constituted about 58 per cent of the sample, whilst limited liability enterprises as well as partnership respectively constituted about 35 per cent and 7.5 per cent of those surveyed. About 60 per cent of the firms interviewed had fewer than six paid employees. Interestingly, there are more firms with limited liability status than partnerships. About 71 per cent of the sampled firms are in fact small enterprises, that is, firms with fewer than ten employees. Owners of the firms are not so eager to increase employees due to lack of funds to expand their businesses and to the limited scope of the market.

Manufacturers of wood and carvings complained about the dwindling size of the export market for their products. This was held to result largely from the 11 September 2001 disaster in the USA, the main export destination.

Other firm characteristics, especially regarding the age of firm owners and their educational attainment against the size of firms, are presented in Table 11.2. The study shows that the majority (about 48 per cent) of firm owners fall within the 30–39 and 40–49 age group categories. This is the economically active population group. Thus, SMEs are not the resting place of retirees in Ghana but are rather the destinations of adventurous young entrepreneurs with the desire to develop their own businesses and see them grow. Again, those with a minimum of secondary education are in the majority (65 per cent). This obviously indicates that the owners of SMEs are literate, with attendant favourable implications for the management and performance of their enterprises.

Table 11.2 Characteristics of firms

	Firm size classification						
	1–5	6–10	11–15	16–20	21–25	26–30	Total
Gender							
Male	74	32	10	4	6	26	152
Female	34	7	1	2	1	3	48
Legal status							
Sole proprietorship	70	30	6	4	–	5	115
Partnership	10	3	1	–	–	1	15
Limited liability	22	7	4	5	6	26	70
Age of owners*							
20–29	14	2	–	–	1	–	17
30–39	39	7	1	–	1	1	49
40–49	13	13	3	3	2	12	46
50–59	7	7	3	1	–	5	24
60 +	9	2	1	1	1	4	18
Education							
None	19	2	5	1	1	4	56
Primary	–	1	–	–	–	–	2
Middle school	7	2	1	–	–	–	11
Secondary	21	7	2	2	1	–	37
Vocational/technical	25	14	1	1	1	3	44
Tertiary	19	9	3	2	4	13	50

Note: * Some respondents were unwilling to disclose their ages.

Source: Survey data.

Whilst the start-up capital for SMEs ranges from less than $600 to about $120 000, the sources from which these amounts are raised varied considerably (Table 11.3). Some firms had more than one source of start-up capital. In spite of the varied sources that were available to firms, the main sources were own savings and borrowing from friends and relatives. It is, however, not surprising to note that only 1.5 per cent of the firms interviewed obtained their start-up capital from a local bank. The lack of access to outside sources of capital is one of the main constraints faced in establishing SMEs and was very often the first issue touched on by respondents. The opinion was frequently expressed that the banks were not friendly to the SMEs and that government intervention to rectify this situation would be welcomed.

About 29 per cent of the entrepreneurs were salaried workers in their previous occupation, 25 per cent established their businesses right from school, and 18 per cent had been apprentices in similar industries. This is depicted in Table 11.4. Being an apprentice for about three years before owning one's own enterprise is the norm for firms in the wood processing and some garments/textiles sectors. Half of the entrepreneurs had received no training at all either from the government, NGO, local or foreign firm. Very few of the firms interviewed exported their products (see Table 11.5). These firms constitute 18 per cent of the total firms surveyed and found mainly in the garments/textiles sector. Firms in the wood-processing sector gave the 11 September disaster as the cause of their falling exports.

To obtain a better understanding of the performance of firms under the new regulatory environment, we carried out a regression of performance variables, in this case, profit and growth in employment from 1993 to 2003. The profit variable is derived from the cost and sales of firms in 2003. These were regressed on cost per unit of labour, age of firm owner, age square (to examine the impact of ageing on firm performance), previous experience of firm owners, ownership structure of firms, gender and three dummies to capture the impact of the regulatory environment. The last are mainly centred on labour regulations because of measurement issues.

The regression results indicate that all the dummies for regulations were insignificant. In the first regression, reported in Table 11.6, the variables which turned out significant are cost per unit of labour and ownership (Ghanaian or non-Ghanaian). However, at the 10 per cent level of significance, previous experience and gender turned out to be significant. Though the age and age square variables are insignificant, their directions of change are rather interesting. One would expect that a younger person, though dynamic, would lack the expertise and experience to improve performance, whilst as one ages and gains more experience, one is able to bring the many years of business practice to bear on performance. But the regression shows otherwise, implying that the younger the owner of the firm, the better the performance. Previous

Table 11.3 Sources of start-up capital for firms

| | Output classification | | | | | |
	Wood processing	Food processing	Services	Garments/ textiles	Manufacturing	Total
Start-up capital						
Less than $600	18	6	2	15	7	48
$600–$2300	7	4	2	9	8	30
$2300–$5600	4	2	1	1	12	20
$5600–$11 200	–	–	1	2	5	8
$11 200–$55 600	–	–	1	2	6	9
$55 600–$120 000	–	–	1	–	10	11
Sources of capital*						
Own savings	33	21	12	36	64	166
Borrowing from friends/relatives	8	–	2	10	12	32
Loan from foreign/donor agency	–	–	–	–	4	4
Loan from local bank	–	1	–	–	2	3
Loan from money lender	–	–	–	1	–	1
Loan from supplier	1	–	–	1	1	3

Note: * Multiple responses.

Source: Survey data.

Table 11.4 Previous occupation according to age of firm owners

| | Age of respondents (firm owners) | | | | | |
	20–29	30–39	40–49	50–59	60 +	Total
Previous occupation						
Unemployed	1	5	2	–	1	9
Salaried worker	1	14	23	11	9	58
Worked with another SME	4	7	6	4	–	21
Operated another business	1	3	9	4	4	21
Studying*	13	23	6	6	2	50
Apprentice	10	25	1	–	1	37
Barrister-at-Law	–	–	1	–	–	1
Farmer	–	–	–	–	1	1
Trader	–	1	–	–	1	2

Note: * This refers to persons who completed education and afterwards started a business.

Source: Survey data.

Table 11.5 Export performance

| | Output classification | | | | | |
	Wood processing	Food processing	Services	Garments/ textiles	Manufacturing	Total
Exporting						
Yes	8	5	1	14	9	37
No	37	21	16	23	66	163

Source: Survey data.

experience is significant at the 10 per cent level and suggests that owners of firms who had worked previously in the same or similar economic sector are more likely to perform better and increase employment. The gender variable suggests that male firm owners are more likely to bring about improved performance than female firm owners. The signs of all the dummies for regulation indicate that firms that comply with these regulations are more likely to have a decline in performance compared with those firms that do not comply. This makes intuitive sense since compliance comes with a greater cost to firm owners. Surprisingly, the sign for ownership is negative, which seems to suggest that firms owned and operated by Ghanaians are less likely to have improved performance compared to firms with a non-Ghanaian ownership.

In the second regression, reported in Table 11.7, per unit labour cost, PULC, and ownership turn out to be the only significant variables. Quite interestingly, the signs for all the regulation dummies with the exception of the minimum wage compliance have changed from the first regression as well as

Table 11.6   Measuring firm performance I

Dependent variable: employment growth

	Coefficient	T-statistic	Prob. value
Constant	1.016	1.019	0.321
PULC	0.666	3.870	0.001
Age	−1.491	−1.018	0.321
Age square	1.573	1.071	0.297
Previous experience	0.328	1.774	0.091
Ownership	−0.387	−2.111	0.048
Min. wage compliance	−0.099	−0.539	0.596
SSNIT contributions	−0.046	−0.190	0.851
Labour registration	−0.035	−0.165	0.871
Gender	0.278	1.811	0.085
$R^2 = 0.648$	Adj. $R^2 = 0.490$	F = 4.099	Prob. = 0.004

Note: Employment growth is measured as the percentage change in firm employment levels between 1993 and 2003. PULC refers to cost per unit of labour. Ownership is a dummy variable: 1 if enterprise is Ghanaian owned, and 0 otherwise. Previous experience is a binary variable, measured as 1 if owner has previous experience, and 0 otherwise. Min. wage compliance is dummy variable with 1 if firm complies with minimum wage law when paying labour, and 0 otherwise. SSNIT contributions is a dummy where 1 measures firm paying workers' social security contributions and 0 otherwise. Labour registration is a dummy for workers registering with labour office: 1 if workers are registered, and 0 otherwise. Gender is a dummy with 1 if male and 0 if female.

Table 11.7   Measuring firm performance II

Dependent variable: firm profit

	Coefficient	T-statistic	Prob. value
Constant	−2.782	−0.909	0.365
PULC	0.766	13.282	0.000
Age	0.010	0.025	0.980
Age square	−0.024	−0.064	0.949
Previous experience	−0.010	−0.178	0.859
Ownership	0.192	3.231	0.002
Min. wage compliance	−0.049	−0.792	0.430
SSNIT contributions	0.084	1.105	0.271
Labour registration	0.093	1.468	0.145
Gender	0.012	0.208	0.836
$R^2 = 0.651$	Adj. $R^2 = 0.625$	F = 25.120	Prob. = 0.000

Note: All the variables are as previously defined. Firm profit is measured as the difference between total sales in 2003 and total cost for the same period.

the signs for age, age square, previous experience and ownership. In this case, we could conclude that SMEs have largely been unaffected negatively by the regulatory environment, but rather improved their profits.

Out of the 200 sampled, 24 firms complained of registration procedures. With regard to the impact of registration procedure on output, very few, indeed only five firms saw the registration procedure as being detrimental to output. Similarly, a very small number (three) complained of these procedures either as lowering productivity or as being a waste of time. Not surprisingly many more firms (11) noted delays in the processes of setting up a business as a major factor affecting output and performance. The percentage of respondents that considered there were undue delays in setting up firms was approximately 46 per cent.

In general, firms did not perceive the need to acquire licences as affecting their output. With regard to the acquisition of land, the general observation is that the processes for acquiring land did not lower productivity. Neither were they considered a waste of time and nor did they lead to a reduction in output. However, a significant proportion of firms, 35 per cent, noted that the process of acquiring land delayed the setting up of businesses, as well as hindering their ability to expand their firms when the need arose.

Similarly, the survey revealed output as being unaffected by the property rights structure under the current regulatory framework. What actually emerged is the apparent lack of awareness among SMEs of the property rights framework. This certainly calls for more awareness raising by the regulatory bodies.

The survey revealed that most firms (about 65 per cent – reported in Table 11.8) obtain their licenses from the Registrar General's Office, whilst about 27 per cent obtained theirs from the Ghana Standards Board. The Environmental Protection Agency is the next most important institution from which SMEs obtain licences. Other institutions that firms are more likely to obtain their licences from include the metropolitan authorities. When it came to the issue of renewal of licences, firms renewed them on a yearly basis.

With respect to compliance, all categories of firms by size appear not to comply with regulations relating to labour. In the most important aspects of regulations, a maximum of 32 per cent of firms surveyed complied with the requirements for SSNIT contributions. For the minimum wage regulations the equivalent figure was 29 per cent. As is depicted in Table 11.9, firms that employ ten persons or fewer and those that employ between 26 and 30 persons were more likely to comply than other size categories.

When we consider the benefits and support services that SMEs are supposed to receive from the regulatory institutions, most firms are rather at a disadvantage. In fact, many firms are unaware of the benefits structure the exists within the new regulatory framework. With the exception of the AMA and the GNTFC, which occasionally organizes grand sales, exhibitions and trade fairs – mainly to promote and provide markets for businesses (SMEs included) – the other regulatory institutions provide very little support for SMEs (see Table 11.9). The SMEs, however, complained that the fairs organized by the GNTFC were too expensive and held no special attractions for them.

CONCLUSIONS

This chapter has discussed the influence that public regulators and self-regulatory agencies have had on the performance of SMEs in the last decade. The chapter has addressed the evolution of the regulatory environment in Ghana as well as identifing how the regulatory choices made by firms affect their performance. While different modes of regulation in such areas as taxes, production, standards, labour laws, location of firms and prices may have some impact on the production methods that firms choose, these effects have not been strong. There are certainly other reasons for the slow growth of enterprises.

The results of the survey involving 200 firms in this study indicated, among other issues, that most entrepreneurs, because of distrust, refuse to go into partnerships and also lack the enthusiasm to expand businesses due to limited

Table 11.8 Regulations according to the current number of paid employees

	Firm size classification						Total
	1–5	6–10	11–15	16–20	21–25	26–30	
Licensing Agency							
Registrar General's Office							
Yes	52	31	10	6	6	24	129
No	39	4	1	–	–	5	49
Ghana Investment Centre							
Yes	3	–	1	1	–	7	12
No	88	35	10	5	6	22	166
Ghana Standards Board							
Yes	12	12	6	4	1	20	55
No	86	24	6	2	5	12	135
Environmental Protection Agency							
Yes	3	5	2	3	2	11	26
No	89	31	9	3	5	18	155
Others*							
Yes	16	4	–	–	1	4	25

Note: * Others include all other agencies, e.g. state, local, district and metropolitan bodies that SMEs are obliged to report to.

Source: Survey data.

267

Table 11.9 *Regulations: compliance, benefits and support services*

	Firm size classification						
	1–5	6–10	11–15	16–20	21–25	26–30	Total
Compliance							
Labour registration	3	5	2	1	2	12	25
SSNIT contribution	12	16	4	2	4	26	64
Minimum wage	18	12	4	4	4	15	57
Benefits							
Duty drawback	–	–	1	–	–	5	6
Investment Code	–	1	–	1	–	6	8
Reduction in income tax	–	–	–	–	–	–	–
Support services							
GIC	–	1	–	1	–	7	9
NBSSI	2	1	–	1	–	2	6
AGI	1	1	1	2	–	4	9
GNCC	1	–	–	–	–	1	2
GNTFC	6	4	–	2	–	2	14
GEPC	3	1	1	1	–	2	8
GEA	–	–	–	1	–	4	5
AMA	20	10	1	2	3	6	42

Note: GIC is Ghana Investment Centre, NBSSI is National Board for Small Scale Industries, AGI is Association of Ghana Industries, GNCC is Ghana National Chamber of Commerce, GNTFC is Ghana National Trade Fair Company, GEPC is Ghana Export Promotion Centre, GEA is Ghana Employers Association, and AMA is Accra Metropolitan Authority.

268

Table 11.10 Major regulatory constraints of SMEs

	Firm size classification						
	1–5	6–10	11–15	16–20	21–25	26–30	Total
Registration	6	3	4	1	3	6	23
Licence acquisition	5	2	–	–	1	3	11
Access to land	18	11	3	2	–	6	40
Lack of protection of property rights	1	1	–	1	–	2	5
Utilities	3	7	1	1	–	2	14
Others	15	2	1	–	–	2	22

Note: * Others consist of financial capital (82%) and marketing (18%).

access to funds and markets. This usually restricts the growth of most businesses in the country and raises further questions for future research. Such questions would include the issue of whether regulations in favour of increasing market access to SMEs would promote their growth. Another key question concerns the superior performance of foreign-owned businesses compared with local ones. Another key conundrum to be thrown up by the survey relates to the observation that there exists little ambition for growth among businesses. This is related to the low level of entrepreneurship qualities. Business owners appear to be apparently content with easy and undemanding management arrangements, which go hand in hand with the avoidance of regulations.

Most SMEs are apparently unaware of the entire array of regulatory arrangements in place. They have little interaction with the responsible bodies. The survey showed high non-compliance with regulations, notably in the field of labour regulations (SSNIT contributions and minimum wage compliance). The assessment of the major constraints faced by SMEs suggests that access to land represents a major obstacle faced by firms. Regulations that may sometimes trouble firms concern those relating to registration, licence acquisition, property rights and utilities as well as those that block access to capital. Business support services are not seen to be operating in favour of the larger firms, especially in promoting products at fairs and in improving credit access. In sum, the environment faced by SMEs is not conducive to their aspiring to larger scales of production or more sophisticated forms of organization.

REFERENCES

Anheier, H.K. and Seibel, H.D. (1987), 'Small Scale Industries and Economic Development in Ghana', *Business Behaviour and Strategies in Informal Sector Economies*, Saarbrucken, Germany: Verlag Breitenbech.
Aryeetey, E., Baah-Nuakoh, A., Duggleby, T., Hettige, H. and Steel, W.F. (1994), 'Supply and Demand for Finance of Small Scale Enterprises in Ghana', World Bank Discussion Paper No. 251.
Lall, S. and Pietrobelli, G. (2002), *Failing to Compete: Technology Development and Technology Systems in Africa*, Cheltenham, UK and Northampton, MA, USA: Edward Elgar.
Lall, S., Navaretti, G.B. Teitel, S. and Wignaraja, G. (1994), *Technology and Enterprise Development: Ghana under Structural Adjustment*, New York: St Martin's Press.
Liedholm, C. and Mead, D. (1987), 'Small Scale Industries in Developing Countries: Empirical Evidence and Policy Implications', International Development Paper No. 9, Dept of Agricultural Economics, Michigan State University, East Lansing, MI, USA.
Parker, R.L., Riopelle, R. and Steel, W.F. (1995), 'Small Enterprises Adjusting to Liberalisation in Five African Countries', World Bank Discussion Paper No. 271, African Technical Department Series.
Riedel, J. et al. (1988), *Small-Scale Manufacturing and Repair Activities in the Urban*

Area of Techiman/Ghana, IFO-Institute for Economic Research, Africa Studies No. 115, Munich: Weltforum Verlag.

Schmitz, H. (1995), 'Collective Efficiency: Growth Path for Small Scale Industry', *The Journal of Development Studies*, **31** (4), 529–66.

Steel, W.F. and Webster, L. (1990), 'Ghana's Small Enterprise Sector: Survey of Adjustment Response & Constraints', Industry Series Paper No. 41, World Bank, Industry and Energy Department, Washington, DC.

UNCTAD (2002), *Investment Policy Review: Ghana*, Geneva: United Nations Conference on Trade and Development.

12. Regulating for competition: the case of Telkom in South Africa

Oludele A. Akinboade and Fungai Sibanda

South Africa's telecommunications (telecoms) giant, Telkom, achieved corporate status in October 1991 under the then Department of Posts and Telecommunications. It remained under state ownership until May 1997 when it was partially privatized through the sell-off of a 30 per cent equity stake to the Thintana Communications consortium comprising Telekom Malaysia Berhad and SBC Communications of the USA. However, government remained the majority shareholder with a 70 per cent stake. This stake has since been reduced to 38 per cent. In 1997 the government undertook a policy of managed liberalization of the telecommunications industry.

In 1997 Telkom was issued with an exclusivity licence, granting it the privilege of being the country's only public switched telecommunications service provider for the coming five years. However, this privilege came with a number of responsibilities. Telkom was set a number of targets to achieve within the five-year exclusivity period, with the possibility of extending it to six years should the targets be met. Key licence targets included the roll-out of 2.69 million new access lines, a further 120 000 payphones and the replacement of more than a million non-digital lines as well as achieving quality-of-service targets that included improving the rate of fault repairs and service activation and eliminating the waiting list. Heavy financial implications would ensue for not meeting these targets.

During this period, a number of regulatory measures were undertaken that brought about drastic changes in the telecoms environment. The entry of mobile operators posed a major competitive challenge to Telkom for the first time. The regulatory institutions were merged into a single authority in July 2000. Telkom's exclusivity expired in May 2002, and the entry of a second network operator (SNO) has been imminent. Evidence elsewhere indicates that incumbent firms will adopt strategies to maintain their dominance in the market in the face of pending competition. An effective and proper regulatory regime is imperative in dealing with such eventualities. Such strategies may involve engaging in anti-competitive conduct in a bid to limit competition and increasing tariffs in order to enhance profitability as much as possible before the entry of a rival.

This chapter seeks to analyse the telecoms market from a regulatory policy (including competition policy) perspective. It will highlight the challenges faced by regulators during the transition from regulation to competition and propose possible solutions to some of the challenges. It will also evaluate Telkom's conduct and performance over the past few years.

The next section gives an overview of the telecoms regulatory environment. Section II discusses the telecoms market structure and the competition issues arising from the policy directive of the Department of Communications as contained in the draft Convergence Bill, 2003 (the Bill) and the Telecommunications Act No. 103 of 1996, as amended (the Act). In Section III, possible solutions to the competition problems identified in Section II are discussed. Section IV looks at the regulatory challenges posed by convergence, and Section V discusses Telkom's performance in terms of identified indicators. The chapter ends with a concluding section.

I. THE REGULATORY REGIME

Since the early 1990s, Telkom has been aware of impending deregulation of the sector. There is a general belief that competition in any sector is a driver for innovation, leading to new and better product offerings, that it provides greater product choice and promotes cost efficiency resulting in low consumer prices. However, in network industries dominated by large incumbents, the nature of competition that can obtain depends to a large extent on the type and effectiveness of regulation during the transition to liberalization and after. Most important of all is ensuring a level playing field among all participants post liberalization.

A major initiative was undertaken by the South African government in the setting up of a converged regulator as a means of ensuring economic, social and technical regulation. It was seen as important that such a structure be in place before other forms of telecoms convergence can occur. In South Africa, the process of regulatory convergence was completed in July 2000 when the then Independent Broadcasting Authority (IBA) in charge of broadcasting regulation was merged with the telecommunications regulator of the time, the South African Telecommunications Agency (SATRA), to form the new regulator, the Independent Communications Authority of South Africa (ICASA), responsible for both broadcasting and telecommunications regulation. ICASA was established in terms of the Act of the same name (2000) to regulate the telecoms and broadcasting industry. The national Department of Communications is the policy making body whilst the Act grants the Minister of Communications (the Minister) certain powers over the sector. The telecoms sector is also subject to general competition laws governing the wider economy. The Competition Commission of South Africa (the Commission) is responsible for competition regulation. In terms of its mandate, ICASA, among other things, grants licences in the telecoms and broadcasting industries and sets the terms and conditions of every licence granted.[1] ICASA also makes rules and regulations that govern the two sectors as well as monitoring the activities of licensees to enforce compliance with these rules and regulations.

The advantages of a merged regulatory structure can be summarized as follows:

1. In a converged environment, services that were traditionally separate, such as voice, data and broadcasting transmission, may be indistinguishable. It would be difficult for two separate regulators to deal with such overlaps.
2. From licensing, regulation enforcement and dispute resolution perspectives, it is much easier for industry to deal with one authority and it is easier for that one authority to coordinate its tasks.
3. A merged entity removes the duplication of services and frees up public resources for other uses.
4. There is one government department responsible for the broadcasting and telecoms sectors. It is also logical to have a single regulator in the sector.
5. International best practice points to consolidated regulatory structures.
6. Merged regulators offer the sector an opportunity to benefit from economies of regulation.

The OECD (2004) identifies the following different angles from which the need for regulation can be viewed:

- Competition regulation: it is necessary to protect the competitive environment by monitoring and investigating anti-competitive conduct and assessing mergers.
- Economic regulation: tariff regulation should encourage efficiency and cost-related pricing. In the absence of regulation, monopolists might charge excessively.
- Access regulation: where essential facilities are concerned, access by competitors must be monitored to ensure non-discriminatory, fair and equal access.
- Technical regulation: this type of regulation is necessary to assure compliance with quality, safety, privacy and environmental standards.

Whereas economic and access regulation depend on the structure of the market, the pace of deregulation and technological advancement, competition and technical regulation will always be a necessary part of economic activity. These functions raise the age-old question of regulatory jurisdiction; that is, who is best suited to deal with which type of regulation? The following are possible approaches that are used in different jurisdictions in managing the relations between regulators and competition authorities:

(a) Competition authorities can be granted all sectoral regulatory functions for a particular sector or sectors.
(b) Competition law enforcement can be separated from sector-specific regulation, so that the competition authorities adjudicate all competition issues while the regulator deals with all other regulatory matters.
(c) The competition authorities can have concurrent jurisdiction with the sector regulator on competition issues.
(d) The sector regulator can retain exclusive jurisdiction over competition issues in its sector.

It is generally accepted that technical regulation cannot reside within a competition agency. Another general observation is that technical and economic regulation are better combined and dealt with by one agency, preferably a sector regulator (OECD, 2004). Whilst it is clear from government policy[2] that competition authorities in South Africa should undertake competition regulation, there is still a great deal of new legislation that mandates sector regulators to deal with competition matters.

Although the Competition Act provides for memoranda of agreement to be entered into with regulators authorized to deal with competition matters, the Competition Commission believes that this was meant as a temporary measure until such time that new legislation would come into being or amendments were to be effected to such sector legislation. The concurrent jurisdiction model has its own pitfalls. These include forum shopping, double jeopardy, inter-organizational conflict, forbearance,[3] etc.

The draft Convergence Bill takes a step in the right direction by clearly demarcating specific roles for the regulator and the competition authorities. The Commission believes that competition matters are best dealt with by competition authorities, whereas the sector regulator is best placed to deal with sector-specific technical and economic regulation. This doesn't preclude the possibility and desirability of some kind of working arrangement and information disclosure agreement between the agencies. Role separation is the model advocated for in the Bill. Whereas the competition authorities are equipped to investigate and prosecute players for anti-competitive behaviour and to assess merger applications, ICASA should be left to deal with issues such as:

- Licensing for entry
- Regulating tariffs where there is limited or no competition
- Setting guidelines for interconnection agreements and pricing
- Setting guidelines for facilities leasing
- Regulating access to essential facilities
- Resolving disputes between players and between players and their customers
- Determining number portability and allocation issues
- Regulating frequency allocation
- Ensuring a level playing field between state-owned and private operators
- Determining universal service obligations.

II. THE TELECOMS MARKET STRUCTURE AND COMPETITION ISSUES

The telecoms market can be divided into various sub-markets including fixed telephony, mobile telephony, value-added services, paging, wireless data services, network provision, Internet and satellite communications. Telkom, by virtue of its market position, is active in most of these segments and faces competition in some segments from other operators or service providers. The discussion will now focus on some of these market segments and highlight the competition issues therein.

Fixed-line Market

The belief that fixed-line telephony is a natural monopoly, coupled with the view that telecommunications is a basic service to which everyone is entitled, resulted in monopolistic government-owned telecoms companies that have forever been shielded from the vagaries of competition through legislation and regulation. This has been the structure of the telecoms market worldwide, South Africa included. It is for this reason that there is currently only one player in this market, even though Telkom's exclusivity period expired in May 2002, thereby technically opening the way for the licensing of a second network operator (SNO). Unfortunately there have been delays on this front. Telkom therefore continues to reap the benefits of being the sole supplier in this market. Although there is provision for assessing the need for a third network operator in the future, that is likely to remain on the back burner for a long time to come. Until the full operation of the SNO, the industry and consumers have to contend with a vertically integrated monopolist.

The fixed-line telephone market can be subdivided into local-access and long-distance markets. The latter can be divided further into national and international segments. Although there are companies with the necessary infrastructure and capabilities[4] to enter some of these segments and offer meaningful competition to the incumbent, current legislation forbids them from doing so. The contestability of the local-access market is affected by a tendency to exhibit natural monopoly features. Duplication of resources at the local level is not economically feasible. There is general consensus that competition at the local level will take time to develop. Thus new entrants into the fixed telephony market would require interconnection.

Competition Issues

A vertically integrated monopolist has an incentive to keep out, or limit, competition as much as possible. The telecoms industry is dominated by bottleneck facilities. For a facility to be a bottleneck, or essential, it must be difficult for third parties to offer a service to consumers without access to the specific facility (Cowie and Marsden, 1998). It must also not be economically feasible to duplicate the facility. Thus, incumbent firms would want to deny access to services that are in competition with theirs. Alternatively, where access is granted, it may be on discriminatory and unfair terms.

Regulators around the world have developed a common approach of mandating incumbents to provide third-party access to essential facilities. However, the 'essential facilities doctrine', as it is commonly called, has the potential to be abused or manipulated by new entrants who wish to avoid investing in key infrastructure. This puts regulators in the very difficult position of having to determine how far to go in terms of declaring a particular facility essential and therefore regulating its access. Essential facilities can also result in a 'chilling effect' on innovation. In other words, firms would be wary of investing in certain projects or cautious to innovate for fear of having their facilities declared essential. A counter-argument is that since most incumbents are former (or presently) state-owned enterprises, most of their infrastructure is government funded and therefore should be available to the public, including competitors. It is thus crucial for regulators to make balanced judgements on these issues. It is also necessary for them to ensure a competitive landscape.

The following are some of the areas in which it is possible for incumbents to ward off competition through anti-competitive actions:

- **Network effects/externalities** Liebowitz and Margolis (1997) define network effects as a change in the benefit, or surplus, that an agent derives from a good when the number of other agents consuming the same kind of good changes. It is the additional value derived from being able to interact with other users of the product. The utility to subscribers of joining a particular network increases with an increase in the total number of subscribers belonging to the network. Therefore large networks tend to dominate markets, especially those that first entered the market. Rules requiring compulsory interconnection are very important as they ensure that customers joining a particular network have access to customers of other networks, thus reducing the anti-competitive impact of network effects.

- **Interconnection charges** The need for interconnection can be used as a platform for raising the rivals' costs. Interconnection is necessary when a call originates or terminates at a competitor's network. In such instances an interconnection fee is charged to route and terminate the call. Because in most instances incumbent firms have more customers than new entrants, high interconnection charges will benefit the incumbent. Interconnection prices can act as a barrier to entry for potential entrants. When it comes to negotiations on such charges, incumbents also have more bargaining power by virtue of being the network owners. None the less, it would appear that, globally, mobile phones have high interconnection fees relative to fixed-line operators. Since there are generally more mobile than fixed-line subscribers in South Africa, and other countries, it makes business sense for mobile termination fees to be high, because this will translate into high revenues for mobile operators. The Bill obliges network service licensees to interconnect on fair terms and for the sector regulator, the Independent Communications Authority of South Africa (ICASA), to set guidelines and regulations for interconnection and to resolve disputes that may arise. The common competition concerns arising from interconnection relate to excessive pricing and the denial of access to the incumbent's facilities.
- **Discrimination and predatory pricing** A network operator with monopoly power in local access may discriminate in favour of its long-distance or international telephone service. Alternatively, the incumbent may charge high prices for its monopoly services and low or predatory prices where it faces actual or potential competition.
- **Bundling** Access to a monopolist's network may be subject to the purchase of a bundle of services that are not needed by a customer who is a competitor. This could be another way of raising the rivals' costs or raising barriers to entry. A requirement to unbundle could therefore help lower barriers to entry and protect new entrants from anti-competitive tying arrangements.
- **Cross subsidization** Most telecoms companies operate in many different markets and they may charge high prices where they are dominant and use the revenues to subsidize low prices where they face

competition. New entrants may then find it difficult to match the incumbent's low prices in areas where it may be easier to enter the market.

- **Quality of service**   Price is not the only element that can be manipulated by incumbent firms. There is also the likelihood of offering a poor-quality service by, for instance, delaying interconnection. This is done so as to make the overall service of a competitor look inferior in the eyes of consumers.

The Second Network Operator

An important question regarding the imminent entry of the second network operator is what impact it would have on the fixed-line market. There are two possibilities: a *de facto* duopoly or effective competition. Rather than engage in a price war, as has been the case in the South African airlines market, the new entrant might adopt a strategy of following the market leader and thus avoid head-on competition. The competition authorities would frown upon this kind of strategy, although a major defect in the current competition legislation is that it does not recognize the anti-competitive effects of collective dominance or complex monopolies like other jurisdictions. However, since the SNO already owns key telecoms infrastructure, value-added network service (VANS) providers would welcome the opportunity to choose with whom to interconnect or from whom to lease facilities. This might be the trigger for competition. Thus from an infrastructure viewpoint the SNO has the ability to provide some form of competition to Telkom.

The process of licensing the SNO has been dogged by controversy, with two failed bids already. However, the Minister went ahead and appointed two of the second-round bidders that were rejected by ICASA. These have been partnered with an empowerment company and two government-owned entities to form the SNO. However, the empowerment partner instituted legal proceedings contesting the constitution of the SNO.

The latest proposed structure of the SNO as announced by the Minister[5] would be as follows:

(i)   A new company, SepCo, will be incorporated which will hold 51 per cent of the equity share capital of the SNO.

(ii)   Control of SepCo will be held by a new financial investor, which will have a 51 per cent shareholding in SepCo. WIP Investments Nine (Proprietary) Limited trading as CommuniTel and Two Telecom Consortium (Proprietary) Limited will each hold 24.5 per cent of SepCo.

(iii)   Transtel and Esitel will together hold 30 per cent of the equity share capital of the SNO.

(iv) Nexus will hold 19 per cent of the equity share capital of the SNO.
(v)   The new financial investor will control the board of SepCo.
(vi) SepCo will control the board of the SNO.

It remains to be seen whether this structure will be acceptable to all the SNO partners.

Evidence from other countries suggests that the second network operator is more likely to target the profitable business sector, rather than the residential sector (Hodge and Theopold, 2001). There is therefore room for strong competition for business customers. Moreover, because of government's share holding in the SNO, it is also likely to target the government departments. However, realizing these threats, the incumbent is 'locking in' certain key corporate clients by negotiating long-term contracts (*Engineering News*, 2004). Projections are that the new SNO might capture about 20 per cent of the market at the most, with 10–15 per cent being a realistic forecast (*Sunday Times*, 2003). To the extent that the SNO services residential customers, competition might be limited. The regulation of Telkom might therefore still be necessary. The Act provides for a third network operator licence to be granted, but only after May 2005 (Department of Communications, 2001).

The Mobile Market

Although there are currently three players, with two clear market leaders, there is provision in the Telecommunications Act for the Minister to license a fourth operator in the future, after careful assessment of the environment. Such a licence could only be granted after December 2003 (Department of Communications, 2001). It is not clear what the optimal number of players in this market is. However, current players have an incentive to limit this number and maintain the status quo. Estimates put the current number of subscribers in this market at close to 16 million and the saturation level at around 21 million (*Engineering News*, 2004). Whilst the fixed-line market has been stagnant or declining in the recent past, the mobile sector has been expanding at a phenomenal rate. The entry of mobile services provided Telkom with some form of competition. For a great number of people mobile phones have become a viable substitute for fixed-line phones whilst for some the two are used as complements. Factors that would influence consumers to substitute their fixed-line phone in favour of a mobile one include lower prices, improved network coverage and quality of service, and richer mobile phone functionality. Those using the two as complements are influenced by factors such as the reliability and cost of service of fixed-line services. Competition within this sector has resulted in innovative ways, not only technologically, but also in the areas of marketing and billing. The introduction of third-generation (3G) technology promises rapid transmission of data through mobile phones. This will enable mobile firms to make even further inroads into the broader converged telecoms market. A *Sunday Times* survey (2003) observes that increased competition and tight margins mean that mobile operators will always be looking at ways of enhancing their technology and streamlining their operations to reduce costs.

Competition Issues

Interconnection

Mobile termination charges appear to be way above cost in many countries around the world[6] where there is a huge differential between fixed-line and mobile termination charges. In South Africa mobile termination rates are 5.2 times higher than those of fixed-lines (Gillwald and Kane, 2003). The often-cited argument is that the two exhibit different cost structures. Also, because the mobile market is perceived to be more competitive, operators argue that competition would constrain their pricing behaviour. As a result, excessive pricing allegations would be unfounded, and calls for regulation unjustified. Currently, Vodacom handles about 60 per cent of the mobile traffic. Any attempt, through regulation or other means, to reduce call termination charges would impact negatively on Vodacom's revenues, while favouring those networks with fewer subscribers.

Least-cost routing

A new development in the South African market is that of least-cost routing firms (LCRs). The Pretoria High Court ruled in December 2003 that least-cost routing is not illegal. LCRs thrive on the fixed–mobile substitution. At the international level, LCRs offer a callback service to avoid high prices. To the extent that competitive prices would obtain as a result of the SNO entry, LCRs might not be an important factor in the future value chain. This is an important development that is likely to put pressure on Telkom's pricing policy.

Value-added Network Services

The first value-added network service (VANS) licences were issued in 1993 (Hodge and Theopold, 2001). Since then the sector has managed to attract a large number of players, including up to 200 Internet service providers (ISPs). The economies of scale in this segment are not as large as in fixed or mobile markets, thus permitting a large number of players. The number of Internet users has grown from around 100 000 in 1994 to approximately 3.7 million in 2003 (Goldstuck Report, 2004). However, the current restrictive regulatory environment hampers full competition and the benefits of convergence. VANS do not own infrastructure and neither are they allowed to do so. They are required to provide their services through Telkom-owned facilities, or through those of the SNO in the future. This policy is a clear protection of the fixed-line operators at the expense of efficient service and low prices to consumers. It is also a step backwards from convergence. The restrictive policy is based on the belief that in order to attract investment and be able to ensure a fair return on investment for the SNO and to secure a market for Telkom's infrastructure, some form of protection is required. This raises many competition concerns, especially where a vertically integrated incumbent like Telkom as a network provider is also active through subsidiaries in the value-adding segment; that is, it competes downstream with the VANS. Common anti-competitive conduct includes predatory pricing, access refusal, price discrimination, poor service and excessive interconnection charges.

Other Competition Issues

There are disagreements within the industry as to Telkom's exercise of market power in voice services and the degree of encroachment into exclusive terrain. Telkom has accused the VANS of offering services which by 'regulation' should be offered exclusively by the licensed fixed-line operator. Voice services include Voiceover Internet Protocol (VoIP). Due to its exclusivity over voice, Telkom is able to offer a bundled package consisting of voice, data and value-added services, whereas the VANS can only offer value-added services. This gives Telkom a competitive advantage. The VANS counter-accuse Telkom of denying them access to telecoms facilities, which, in terms of the Act, it is obliged to provide since the VANS are not permitted to do so. Where facilities are granted, the cost is very high, which prohibits fair competition. They also accuse Telkom of leveraging its market power through anti-competitive conduct downstream where it competes with the VANS. This relates primarily to predatory pricing. These accusations have been tested at every possible legal institution governing the sector including ICASA, the Competition Commission and the courts. Although the sector has great potential for growth, the legal wrangling coupled with numerous restrictions on VANS has had a dampening effect on innovation, investment and growth. According to Gillwald and Kane (2003), the VANS sector shrunk from 5.5 million in 1999 to 4.9 million in 2002.

Private Telecommunications Networks

Telkom has exclusivity over telecoms facilities and voice services. As a result, there is no facilities-based competition and the only voice service competition is from mobile operators. Value-added service providers can only lease facilities from Telkom and the SNO; they may not obtain voice services from anyone other than Telkom and the SNO, notwithstanding the fact that there are other players who can offer the same service.

Telkom owns the country's undersea cable connecting South Africa with parts of Africa, Europe and the Far East. There are concerns that access to this infrastructure may be offered at high prices and on unfair terms and conditions to competitors. However, Eskom Enterprises and Transtel both have existing communications infrastructure that can only be used for their internal business purposes. They are not permitted to provide a service to third parties. However, since they form part of the licensed SNO, their infrastructure will be used in future to provide a public switched telecommunications service within the licence conditions of the SNO. This also raises the question of whether such firms are being denied the full benefits of convergence or not: do they have the capacity and economies of scope to offer voice services and to service the international telephony market?

In terms of the Telecommunications Act of 1996, as amended, Sentech holds a licence to provide an international telecoms gateway service enabling it to operate as a carrier of carriers. However, the licence is conditional upon Sentech facilitating international calls for mobile phone operators, but not to third parties. Sentech is also licensed to offer a multimedia service, but cannot offer a voice service.

III.   POSSIBLE REMEDIES

Market Structure

Vertical separation

Many of the problems in the telecoms sector are rooted in the structure of the industry. Specifically, the vertical integration of incumbents is the source of most of the anti-competitive behaviour. In certain jurisdictions, vertically separating the incumbent has been seen as a panacea. The idea is that a vertically separated operator has no incentive to discriminate or deny access to an essential facility (Geradin and Kerf, 2003). This is the route that was taken in the USA with the breakdown of AT&T. However, vertical separation is not always the best solution since it may result in a loss of economies of scale and scope. Also the cost of breaking up a monopoly like Telkom might outweigh any potential benefits flowing from the measure (Hodge and Theopold, 2001). As things stand in the South African context, this might not be a viable option.

Another form of vertical separation could involve prohibiting network providers from participating in certain downstream segments like the VANS market. The same economies of scope argument can be used against this option.

Licensing

The number of licences issued for, say, fixed-line network operators will determine the amount of competition in this market. However, the number of players in a market is not a definite predictor of the level of competition. A market with three players might have more effective competition than one with say five or more players. What counts is the intensity of competition rather than the number of competitors.

Licensing requirements giving exclusivity to incumbents raise artificial barriers to entry to certain segments of the market. A more appropriate measure could involve removing Telkom's exclusive rights over voice services and telecoms facilities. This might increase competition in these segments. A case in point is the restrictions on Sentech's licence conditions and those of other private network operators like Eskom Enterprises and Transtel. A refinement of the regulations to lift these restrictions would allow Sentech to offer VoIP. VANS could also be allowed to offer VoIP in addition to the data service they offer, as well as being permitted to set up their own infrastructure in competition with fixed network operators. The current restrictions are seen as attempting to protect the fixed-line market for the benefit of both the incumbent and the new entrant/s. The amended Telecommunications Act simply extends these restrictions and the Bill is silent on them. As a result, there is still no indication as to when these restrictions will be lifted for VANS to take advantage of a convergent environment. A relaxation of the licence conditions will usher in facilities-based competition.

Market Conduct

Network access

According to the OECD (2004), as a result of deregulation in the past two decades, the regulation of terms and conditions under which competing firms have access to essential facilities provided by rivals has become the single most important issue facing utility regulators, an issue which is both theoretically complex and inherently controversial. New entrants require access to existing facilities. It is the sector regulator's role to ensure that access to essential facilities is granted on non-discriminatory terms and at reasonable rates. Even where new entrants own facilities, interconnection with the incumbent may still be necessary. Farrell (1997) notes that the right of entrants to share the incumbent's network facilitates the growth of competition. However, he contends that rules to deregulate this are necessary so that sharing does not become a long-term solution, but rather should be a stepping-stone to facilities-based competition.

Interconnection

As already alluded to, the need to interconnect can be used to disadvantage competitors. Regulators should ensure that new entrants are empowered to negotiate on an equal footing with the incumbent. Although the Bill allows industry players to negotiate interconnection rates, where agreement cannot be reached, ICASA is obliged to intervene. It is in the best interests of industry to avoid regulatory intervention by setting competitive rates. In the UK, call termination charges are subject to regulation (Oftel, 2003). This forces players to adopt efficient technologies that would reduce the cost of interconnection.

Unbundling

In order to facilitate fair competition, the regulator should adopt rules obliging the incumbent to provide network elements to competitors on an unbundled basis under rates, terms and conditions that are fair and non-discriminatory (Federal Communications Commission, 1999).

Number portability

The ability of customers to change service providers without a need to change their numbers will be an important factor that will increase the ability of tele-com service providers to compete. The cost of switching from one operator to another can be high in the absence of number portability, especially for businesses that have to notify customers and suppliers and change their letter heads and so on. Although it is an expensive operation, number portability is crucial for competition (De Wet, 2001). Lack of it can be a constraining factor, giving the incumbent a competitive advantage. The Bill requires ICASA to provide regulations regarding number portability. Since mobile services have become a viable alternative to traditional fixed-line service for a large number of consumers, mobile-to-fixed number portability would ensure that consumers have an unprecedented degree of flexibility and convenience in cutting the cord on their landlines without incurring switching costs.

Tariffs

Monopoly services should be regulated to avoid excessive pricing and the exploitation of consumers.

IV. TOWARDS CONVERGENCE

Convergence: An Overview

In the past the legislative and regulatory frameworks around the globe were prone to limit the full exploitation of the benefits brought about by advances in information and communications technology. From the advent of the computer, to the creation of the World Wide Web, to the proliferation of mobile phones and a host of other communication gadgets, operators and consumers have been restricted in terms of exploiting opportunities offered by technological development. In South Africa, for instance, operators have had to hold a separate licence for each type of technology they use. Such restrictions, coupled with the structure of the market, have resulted in limited competition in telecoms. The move towards convergence, if properly managed, promises to set the stage for unlimited market entry, increased competition and enhanced welfare benefits for consumers. At the same time, operating in a converged environment calls upon the regulatory institutions to develop rules and regulations that will ensure a level playing field between incumbents and new entrants, while guarding against market consolidation and anti-competitive behaviour.

According to Katz and Woroch (1998), convergence in telecoms refers to the ability to deliver voice, video and data services using a single integrated infrastructure. Thus, in a converged world, telecoms users are able to, among other things, transmit content over the telecoms and IT infrastructure, handle telephone calls over the Internet or TV, get Internet access through TV, transmit data over mobile phones, access multimedia applications over the mobile network, advance mobility of usage and high speed communication and distribute content over broadband to different devices (Shy, 2000; Ngcaba, 2003). For this to happen, it is paramount for information technology, computing, broadcasting and telecoms systems to be integrated.

The draft Convergence Bill, 2003 (the Bill) aims, among other things, at the promotion of competition, encouraging investment and innovation in the communications sector and ensuring an environment of open, fair and equal access (Department of Communications, 2003). In terms of the Bill, communications licences will no longer be granted on the basis of a specific technology used. Instead, players will be able to compete within a broader telecoms market. Service, as opposed to type of technology used, is what matters in an environment of convergence (*Dataweek*, 2004).

The challenge facing regulators and policy makers in the telecoms sector, as in other sectors, is how to ensure that the incumbent network operator does not undermine the objectives of liberalization and convergence by, for instance, erecting artificial barriers to entry. At the same time, liberalization should not disadvantage the incumbent by, say, placing obligations from which new entrants are exempt. Whatever the policy approach, what is clear is that the transition from a regulated to a competitive environment with convergence can never be a smooth one; hence the need for a proper regulatory regime.

Moreover, convergence encourages the adoption of complex business models that blur the traditional market boundaries, as we know them. This poses major challenges from a regulatory perspective. For instance, the relevant product market for fixed telephony, as defined today, might change in a few years' time and is different from how it was defined in the past. To this end, properly structured, well-resourced and independent regulatory institutions are paramount, not only to keep abreast of developments in the sector, but also to make firm and credible decisions that can stand up to the strictest scrutiny.

Regulatory Challenges in a Converged Environment

Market definition
The art of correctly defining a relevant market is paramount in competition policy. First, market definition is useful in determining the level of concentration in a particular market for merger evaluation purposes. Horizontal mergers in highly concentrated markets are likely to be blocked or approved subject to divestiture or other conditions. Second, market definition is crucial in determining whether a firm is dominant in the market and therefore prohibited from certain conduct. A rule of thumb among competition agencies is to define the market as narrowly as possible, both from a product and geographic perspective, whereas players have an incentive to broaden the relevant market in order to dilute their market shares.

Significant complementarities in demand that characterize telecoms services add to the difficulty of defining relevant markets. Telecoms services often include a collection of complementary components that are bundled together as part of an overall service. Deciding whether individual elements of a service belong in the same market or whether they form different markets can be a daunting task.

With convergence, traditionally separate markets may now form part of the same product or geographic market. Thus convergence results in a great many overlaps between markets, thereby making the art of defining the relevant market an elusive one. For instance, are mobile and fixed telephony in the same market? Are they substitutes or complements? If they are part of the same market, Vodacom may be a dominant player, if the number of subscribers is a defining factor. However, if they form separate markets, Telkom is dominant in the fixed-line market. Market definition can make or break a case. According to the International Telecommunications Union (2002), large corporations that are able to offer a bundle of services compete with smaller players who compete with other networks. Also, users can access the Internet through dial-up access, an integrated services digital network (ISDN), an asymmetric digital subscriber line (ADSL) or a cable TV connection. In terms of Internet access, these technologies can form part of the same market, whereas when looked at from a different angle they might form different markets.

From a geographic viewpoint, the Internet and interconnection points permit the geographic market of players to extend beyond traditional boundaries. A service provider based in the USA may be competing with local South African service providers. However, closer scrutiny may reveal different market conditions and regulatory features that would put the two in different geographic markets even though they may be offering the same service.

Consolidation

Whereas the conventional natural monopoly theory is premised on the idea of exploiting the economies of scale inherent in network industries, convergence offers opportunities for firms to reap economies of scope by allowing a player in one market to offer services in another market without a major reconfiguration of its business offering. Thus, with convergence, we might witness a new wave of vertical and horizontal mergers as firms take advantage of economies of scale and scope.

Where competition has been introduced it is the duty of the competition authorities and sector regulators to ensure that such competition is cultivated and maintained. Mergers and acquisitions that would result in high concentration levels which could lead to an abuse of dominance should not be allowed, and nor should licence applications that may result in anti-competitive cross-ownerships. Cowie and Marsden (1998) warn of the real danger of creating super-monopolies through convergence. This view is shared by Gillwald (2003), who contends that licensing and ownership rules are crucial in avoiding concentration and market dominance that accompany the trend towards convergence.

Deregulation versus Re-regulation

While the industry moves towards greater deregulation and convergence, it is necessary that proper regulations are put in place to prevent the abuse of market power by incumbents in those segments of the market that are not contestable, like the local loop. This necessitates regulation of elements such as tariffs and the quality and level of service. New entrants might also need some protection until they are established. This would require that restrictions be placed, say, on the number of entrants in a particular market segment, on cross-ownerships and on the entry of incumbents into certain markets. However, placing restrictions on what firms can or cannot do raises the question of why is it necessary to regulate in a converged environment, because firms should be able to enter any market by virtue of the economies of scope inherent in that market.

V. TELKOM'S PERFORMANCE

Universal Access

One of the key mandates of the regulatory authority is the prompting of universal service and access by means of licence requirements. A second responsibility is to ensure that licensees contribute to the Universal Service Fund. Between 1997 and 2002 Telkom made a capital investment of R48 billion to enhance the capacity and functionality of an ageing network that needed considerable modernization, rehabilitation (digitization) and mass expansion to areas not served under the apartheid government (Kekana, 2003). An important development regarding access to telecoms services brought about by the amendment of the Telecommunications Act in 2001 is the provision allowing small businesses to apply on invitation by the Minister of Communications for licences to provide services and facilities to under-serviced areas with a teledensity of less than 5 per cent. Section 40 of the Act requires that the Under-serviced Area Licensee (USAL) provide telecoms services, including Voiceover Internet Protocol (VoIP), fixed–mobile services and public pay telephones.

Access to telecoms services in South Africa has been racially and regionally unequal. According to White (2003), whites residing in urban areas tend to have much better access to telecoms facilities than blacks. In rural areas the gap between blacks and whites is even higher.

The attainment of social objectives plays an important role in deciding how to regulate the telecoms market. Since rapid infrastructure roll-out to previously underserviced areas is critical to the promotion of universal service and economic empowerment and since these areas are generally either low income or rural, the feeling has been that full-blown competition in fixed-line services would not serve the objectives best. The reasoning is that:

- new entrants would target the more lucrative and easily established business and long-distance markets first and not seek to roll out in these underserviced areas,
- competition in these markets would squeeze the profitability of Telkom and so limit its own ability to roll out in these unprofitable areas; and
- the option of contributions to a universal service fund was not desirable until basic exchange infrastructure was in place in some areas to which low-income households could be more cheaply connected.

The targets set for Telkom in its five-year exclusive licence included rolling out 2.69 million new lines, of which two-thirds will be in underserviced areas and for priority customers. It was estimated that this would require capital investment in the region of R53 billion.

Roll-out Targets

The specific roll-out targets set for Telkom were relatively tough, with the expansion in new lines expected to rise from 340 000 in 1998 to 665 000 in 2002 (Hodge and Theopold, 2001). The only part of local access network that is not covered by the exclusivity agreement is customer premises equipment (CPE), which was opened to full competition immediately on passing the Act. Telkom would win an extra year of exclusivity if by the end of the fourth year it had achieved a roll-out of 90 per cent of its cumulative five-year total line target and 80 per cent of its five-year underserviced line target. This would be granted if Telkom accepts a new five-year total of 3 million new lines and a proportionate increase in its underserviced line target. There were financial penalties for failing to reach these targets. Telkom would pay penalties of R450 per line for the first 100 000 and R900 per line for each extra line missed. If it missed priority customer targets the penalty per unit would be R4500, schools R900, public payphones R2250 and villages R1125.

On the face of it, Telkom has performed quite well, improving telecommunications access since 1996. Thousands of new lines have been installed and the network is almost fully digitized. Times for installation and for remedying faults have dramatically reduced. Telkom is also more efficient, as shown by the number of fixed telephone lines per employee increasing from 75 in 1997 to 149 in 2004 in Table 12.7 below. This represents considerable improvement in employee efficiency. Fixed-line access grew by 1.6 per cent between 1997 and 2004, while the penetration rate increased by 0.4 per cent only over the same period (see Table 12.1).

Initial roll-out targets were met until 2000/2001, when Telkom made a business decision to clamp down on bad debt and enforce strict settlement of

Table 12.1   Telekom's access and penetration rate

	1997	1998	1999	2000	2003	2004	CAGR % change 1997–2004
Fixed-line access ('000)	4258	4650	5080	5490	4844	4821	1.6
Fixed-line penetration rate (%)	10.1	10.8	11.8	12.8	10.7	10.4	0.4

Source: Telkom *Annual Reports* (various years).

accounts (Telkom, *Annual Report*, 2001). This resulted in mass disconnections of about 1.1 million lines in 2001 and a decrease in the number of active fixed-lines of 575 000 despite a roll-out of more than 630 000 new lines. In 2002 a further 606 000 lines were disconnected as 675 000 new lines were being rolled out. These massive disconnections compromised the objective of improving universal access even under conditions in which thousands of new lines were being rolled out. Hodge (2003) estimates the cost of wasted investment in disconnected lines at R17 billion.

Table 12.2 shows that Telkom's subscriber base grew from about 4.2 million in 1996 to about 4.8 million in 2003, whilst the figure for Africa is 13 million in 1996 and 24 million in 2003. While Telkom's subscriber base grew by a meagre 14 per cent between 1996 and 2003, that of Africa grew by almost 85 per cent during the same period. The local mobile phone sector subscriber base, on the other hand, grew by a whopping 18 times and that of Africa increased 45 times, as shown in Table 12.3. This paints a bleak picture for the future growth of the fixed network. In order to forge ahead in the market, Telkom has to compete aggressively with mobile operators and the SNO in the near future on price and service quality.

Telkom's Quality of Service

Telkom's quality of service is regulated under the terms of Condition 6.1 and Schedule B of its main licence. These lay down improvements to be achieved, in the period before effective competition, in respect of numbers of customer fault reports, time taken for fault repair, serviceability of public payphones, time taken to provide exchange lines and numbers of customers waiting for service.

To date, Telkom has, as required, eliminated the old waiting list. However, Telkom did not meet all of the targets for each relevant financial year. For the year 1997/98 it incurred service quality penalties of R3.3 million in respect of speed of fault repair and provision of service to business customers, and a roll-out penalty of R299 700 in respect of roll-out to schools. For the year 1998/99 Telkom incurred a service quality penalty of R299 700 in respect of speed of fault repair for residential customers.

The general perception is that Telkom's quality of service is steadily improving, but perhaps not as rapidly as might be the case if it were subject to effective competition.[7] This would further support the case for moving as rapidly as possible to competition, while maintaining measures of consumer protection, particularly for residential customers, until competition becomes effective.

Better incentive effects and a more directly favourable impact on customers are achieved by including service guarantees in individual customer contracts.

Table 12.2 *Telkom's subscriber base*

	Main fixed lines ('000)			Subscribers per 100 inhabitants		
	1996	2003	CAGR (%)	1996	2003	CAGR (%)
Subscribers	4 258.6	4 844.0	1.7	10.56	10.66	0.0
All Africa	13 411.4	24 711.9	10.5	1.92	3.01	7.1

Source: Elaborated from ITU (2004) data.

Table 12.3 *Telkom's mobile phone subscriber base*

	Subscribers ('000)			Subscribers per 100 inhabitants			% Total telephone subscribers (2003)
	1996	2003	CAGR (%)	2001	2003	CAGR (%)	
Subscribers	953	16 860	209	24.21	36.36	6.3	77.7
All Africa	1 150.8	50 803.2	5395	3.21	6.16	11.5	67.3

Source: Elaborated from ITU (2004) data.

These are preferably accompanied by the acceptance of limited liability. Customers who suffer the effects of failure to provide service to the guaranteed levels receive compensation and limited redress for any consequential loss. This provides powerful internal incentives, at minimal cost, for the company to improve its service performance and improves its relationship with its customers. At the same time, regulatory intervention is minimized.

Further useful incentives to the company and benefits to customers can be achieved by requiring the company to publish its main quality-of-service statistics on a regular basis. These statistics, which can usefully be published on a regional basis, should relate to key parameters that are of particular interest to customers, such as time to provide service, speed of fault repair, calls lost due to network failure, response time for directory inquiries, and so on.

Tariffs

Telkom's tariffs have been regulated by ICASA since 1997 as part of the new licence conditions. Before that, tariffs were approved by the relevant Minister. Products are classified as either basket (volume 1) or non-basket (volume 2). Volume 1 products are those that are provided by Telkom only and are not subject to competition. These include line installation and rental, domestic and international call charges and ISDN services. Non-basket services are those that can be provided in competition with other service providers, such as premise equipment. ICASA employs a price cap form of regulation (generally known as CPI-X) as provided for under the Act and in Telkom's licence conditions. The regulation conditions point out explicitly that Telkom's average increase in revenue through tariff adjustments for basket-related services is limited to CPI less 1.5 per cent. However, Telkom may increase some individual basket services by up to CPI + 5 per cent, and still not fall foul of the regulations.

Traditionally, long-distance and international calls have been priced at very high levels. Revenues so obtained would then be used to subsidize local calls and telephone line rentals, which were priced below cost. In anticipation of competition, Telkom embarked on a tariff rebalancing drive aimed at ensuring that prices were cost based. Tariff-rebalancing is also aimed at achieving an appropriate ratio between local and international call charges as well as simplifying the pricing structure. For instance, in 2002, the actual price per minute of a local call increased by 23.9 per cent whereas that of a long-distance call decreased by 12 per cent.[8]

Table 12.4 shows that the ratio of long-distance to local calls has been declining since the tariff-rebalancing exercise. Experimenting with tariff rebalancing started in 1995 but became fully implemented from 1997. Falling international and long-distance call charges does not suggest that these calls

Table 12.4   Telkom's long-distance to local call ratio

Year	1997	1998	1999	2000	2001	2002	2003	2004
Ratio	13.2	9.2	7.7	6.9	5.8	2.7	2.7	2.6

Source: Telkom *Annual Reports* (several years).

are any cheaper, comparatively speaking. A research report by NUS Consulting comparing call costs between 14 countries, including Australia, the UK, the USA, Germany and SA, found that although Telkom reduced its international call costs, it still has the most expensive international call tariffs at 125.4 US cents. Telkom also fared worst in the local calls, moving from fifth- to second-most expensive, with the cost rising by 2 per cent to 14.2 US cents per three-minute call. Telkom's call charges rose from being 59 per cent of the average consumer's combined telephone and ISP bill in 1993, to 85 per cent of the bill by 2003.[9] Telkom has, however, criticized the report, saying that it compared them with developed countries whereas a more appropriate survey comparing Telkom with its peers in the emerging markets rated them favourably. The importance of telecoms costs in business and social development cannot be overemphasized.

International voice traffic volumes constitute about 11 per cent of Telkom's revenues. The Online Publishers Association, whose members include the SABC, Media 24 and MWeb, claim that business pays up to 13 times more for Internet charges in South Africa than in the UK,[10] despite receiving an inferior service. The high costs are growth inhibiting since most businesses operate via the net. Not only that; South Africa is said to be losing out as a hub for the call centre industry to countries like India, which have competitive telecoms prices. According to Melody (2003), Telkom's unjustifiably high prices are preventing consumers and service providers from having sufficient access to its network.

Residential Tariffs

It appears that deregulation is yet to result in the bringing down of the cost of access to telecommunications in South Africa. During its days as a public monopoly Telkom subsidized local call rates with revenues generated from long-distance and international calls. Following the company's partial privatization, Telkom embarked on a process of rate rebalancing to bring their tariffs in line with their cost. While international tariffs have fallen and the rebalancing of local and long-distance rates was achieved, this was accompanied by dramatic increases in the cost of local calls and a rezoning of long-distance rates.

The general expectation by telecoms users is that improvements in technology, new services, market liberalization and increased productivity would reduce the cost and therefore the prices of telecoms services. In many countries, fixed-line operators reduced connection charges, subscription and usage rates largely because they came under pressure from mobile phone operators and/or the second national carrier.

However, in South Africa local call prices have been increasing annually by substantial margins. Table 12.5 shows that the cost of a three-minute call at peak time increased by more than four times between 1997 and 2004. The greatest increases were recorded during the three-year period 2001 to 2004, when the cost more than doubled. Between 1997 and 2001 local call charges increased moderately, averaging 16 per cent before recording a sharp increase of 64 per cent in 2002. Although residential telephone connection charges were kept constant between 1999 and 2001, they have been on an upward path ever since. Monthly subscription fees were reduced in 2001 but have also been increasing since then. The two actions were aimed at encouraging subscription to the network. Taken together, between 1997 and 2004 Telkom increased residential connection charges by 175 per cent, residential monthly subscription fees by 35 per cent and the cost of a three-minute call at peak time by more than four times. These price hikes have resulted in massive disconnections, thereby reversing the benefits of the roll-out exercise. A massive 60 per cent of Telkom's disconnections are due to non-payment, while the other 40 per cent are customer initiated, driven by factors such as:

- Customer no longer needs the service
- Migration to prepaid service
- Migration to mobile telephony
- Affordability
- Physical relocation
- Death.

Business Tariffs

In South Africa, businesses pay the same connection and usage charges as residential fixed-line telephone users. Businesses, however, pay a higher subscription fee than residential users. During 1996–2000, the trend has been a general escalation in Telkom business tariffs to take advantage of the general businesses' price-inelasticity of demand.

Profitability

Although the financial performance of Telkom improved markedly from the

Table 12.5 Telkom's residential tariff rates

Year	1997	1998	1999	2000	2001	2002	2003	2004
Residential telephone connection charge	R170	R207.77	R210	R210	R210	R240	R268.95	R274.35
Residential monthly phone subscription charge	R60.9	R68.2	R75.7	R83.3	R62.7	R70	R76.2	R81.9
Cost of a local 3-minute call (peak)	35¢	45¢	50¢	58¢	64¢	105¢	120¢	148.5¢

Source: Telkom *Annual Reports* (several years).

Table 12.6 Telkom's financial performance, 1993–2004 (million Rand)

	1993	1994	1995	1996	1997	1998	1999	2000	2001	2002	2003	2004
O/P	2986	2474	2636	3040	4437	4286	3436	3908	4984	4191	6514	9088
N/P	411	760	845	1209	1950	2475	2333	1617	1360	1221	1630	4523
E/S (¢)	7.0	19.5	255.0	343.0	482.0	461.0	418.8	290.2	244.1	219.2	292.6	812.0

Note:
O/P – operating profit.
N/P – net profit.
E/S – earnings per share.

Source: Telkom *Annual Reports* (several years).

mid-1990s in terms of revenues, partial privatization of the utility somewhat surprisingly coincided with a fall in profitability (see Table 12.6). This trend has been reversed in 2004. Net profits during the early 2000s have been lower in comparison with the financial performance in the late 1990s. The lower profitability is partly due to retrenchment costs as Telkom has been shedding staff, with a 20 per cent and 8 per cent decline in employees in the 1999/2000 and 2003/04 financial years respectively.

Telkom announced its best results ever in 2004, with net profits of over R4 billion and a year-on-year increase in earnings per share of 177 per cent. Fixed-line operating cost reductions of R536 million and cash flow of R4 billion have allowed for debt reduction of about R3.5 billion and a 90¢ per share dividend. The granting of an exclusivity period was also meant to help raise the market value of Telkom, allowing for a better price on the equity sale. The stock price has more than doubled since the public offering in March 2003. Despite Telkom's rosy financial record, only about 30 per cent of households remain connected to the fixed network.

Productivity (see Table 12.7)

Telkom has cut the number of its employees by almost 50 per cent since 1993, declining from a high of about 62 000 employees in 1993 to about 32 000 in 2004. The total number of job cuts during this period averages 30 000. About 3000 employees lost their jobs in 2004 alone. Since the exclusivity period, Telkom has cut its labour force by almost 44 per cent. Telkom has contended that only a small percentage of the retrenchments are forced, that is, employees had no choice in the matter. Although this has contributed to Telkom's productivity as measured by the number of employees per service line, the figure of 149 employees per line for the financial year ending 31 March 2004 is still far from the international benchmark of 250 employees per line. With retrenchments being an unpopular means of achieving this target, Telkom will instead have to increase the number of service lines. This is also a major challenge, seeing that most people now substitute their land lines for mobile phones. Moving ahead, new strategies of luring back subscribers to the fixed-line network must be sought. None the less, employee productivity increased significantly as fixed telephone lines per employee rose by more than 12 per cent per annum between 1997 and 2004.

Improvements in employees per line over the entire period correspond with improvements in revenues per employee and revenues per line. The roll-out programme saw a peak of 5.5 million lines installed in 2000. However, due to disconnections, this figure has been dropping ever since. Unless countermeasures are adopted, the situation could revert to that of the early 1990s. Although not shown in Table 12.7, Telkom's operating costs have been rising

Table 12.7 Telkom's productivity indicators

	1993	1994	1995	1996	1997	1998	1999	2000	2001	2002	2003	2004
TL (R'000)	3458	3594	3773	3926	4259	4645	5075	5493	4962	4924	4844	4821
Em	61991	61255	59896	57501	57496	57813	60613	49128	43758	39444	35361	32358
TL/Em	56	59	63	69	75	82	83	112	113	125	137	149
R/TL (R)	2231	2546	2799	3204	3574	3878	4079	3859	4287	4722	4987	5169
R/Em (R'000)	124	149	181	222	284	349	374	489	605	693	n/a	n/a

Note:
TL – telephone lines.
Em – employees.
TL/Em – telephone lines per employee.
R/TL – revenue per telephone line.
R/Em – revenue per employee.

Source: Telkom *Annual Reports* (several years).

by an average of 2.5 per cent per annum between 1997 and 2003. Operating costs per line increased from R2652 in 1997 to R3189 in 2003 (Telkom, 2003). A major portion of these costs reflects one-off payments such as retrenchment costs that are actually due to decisions that will increase productivity in the medium term.

CONCLUSIONS

Whilst liberalization promises exciting opportunities for new entrants and incumbents, the regulatory environment seems to contain many restrictions that will make it difficult for potential entrants to compete on an equal footing with the incumbent. There are possible solutions that could eliminate these restrictions. However, this calls for a balance to be struck between managed liberalization, which is the way government is choosing to go, and a fully open landscape, where players will be free to enter any market segment and compete with each other on an equal footing. The move towards competition also calls for prudent regulation. The Bill proposes major changes to the way ICASA will be funded in the future, which will impact (it is hoped positively) on its ability to attract and retain experienced professionals with specialized skills. The role separation between ICASA and the competition agencies is another welcome development.

Although, according to the Minister, the liberalization process was part of the implementation of government policy aimed at the reduction of telecoms costs by introducing competition, providing choice and increasing access to telecoms infrastructure and services to the public,[11] the restrictive regulatory environment has impeded the realization of these aims. Effective competition has not been possible and the result of this is that the incumbent operator has entrenched its monopoly position. The barring of competition in international and long-distance calls has allowed Telkom to continue generating profits from these market segments to support the expenses of increased service provision. However, many new lines being installed by Telkom in order to meet roll-out targets have been rapidly disconnected due to customers' inability to pay. As such, gains from privatization in terms of wider service provision have been lower than expected.

Telkom's competitors (in other market segments) and customers alike have awaited with eagerness the licensing of the SNO, the adoption of the Convergence Bill and the loosening of the regulatory system. These three measures are thought of as necessary in ensuring the full benefits of low telecoms prices, better service quality and enhanced product choice. It is unfortunate that rapid gains in Telkom's productivity (as measured by its number of employees per line, the amount of revenue per line, falling operating costs and impressive profitability levels) have not been distributed to customers in the form of lower tariffs. This is unlikely to change unless drastic measures are taken to remove the regulatory stranglehold on the sector.

NOTES

1. Types of licences include frequency licence, telecom services licences and broadcasting licences.
2. As enshrined in the Department of Public Enterprises policy document (2000): 'An accelerated agenda towards the restructuring of state owned enterprises: A policy framework'.
3. Where a regulator withdraws its jurisdiction on a matter in favour of another regulator, players might see this as an abdication of responsibility.
4. For example Eskom Enterprises, Transtel and Sentech (although the first two now form part of the SNO).
5. Decision of Dr Ivy Matsepe-Casaburri on the granting of a licence to the second national operator. Ministry of Communications, 26 August 2004.
6. A study by the UK Competition Commission put the figure at 30–40 per cent above cost.
7. See Telkom, *Annual Report 1999/2000* (p. 73).
8. Telkom, *Annual report* 2002.
9. 'Telecoms report slams Telkom', http://www.itweb.co.za/sections/telecoms/2004.
10. L. Stones, 'Telkom fees, service "stifle growth" ', *Business Day*, 19 August 2004.
11. Decision of Dr Ivy Matsepe-Casaburri on the granting of a licence to the second national operator. Ministry of Communications, 26 August 2004.

REFERENCES

Cowie, C. and Marsden, C.T. (1998), 'Convergence, Competition and Regulation', *International Journal of Communication law and Policy*, IJCPLP Web-Doc 6-1-4.

Dataweek (2004), 'It is No Longer Equipment, It is All About Service', June www.dataweek.co.za.

Department of Communications (2001), 'Telecommunications Amendment Act 2001', *Government Gazette*, No. 22889.

Department of Communications (2003), 'Draft Convergence Bill, 2003', *Government Gazette*, No. 25806.

De Wet, P. (2001), 'Telkom Likely to Oppose Sentech License', www.itweb.co.za.

Engineering News (2004), 'Telecommunications'.

Farrell, J. (1997), 'Prospects for Deregulation in Telecommunications', speech given at Federal Communications Commission.

Federal Communications Commission (1999), 'Connecting the Globe. A Regulator's Guide to Building a Global Information Community', www.fcc.gov/connectglobe/.

Geradin, D. and Kerf, M. (2003), *Controlling Market Power in Telecommunications: Antitrust vs. Sector Specific Regulation*, Oxford: Oxford University Press.

Gillwald, A. (2003), 'National Convergence Policy in a Global World. Preparing South Africa for Next Generation Networks, Services and Regulation', LINK public policy seminar series.

Gillwald, A. and Kane, S. (2003), *South African Telecommunications Sector Performance Review*, LINK Centre, University of the Witwatersrand.

Goldstuck Report (2004), *Internet Access in South Africa, 2004*, World Wide Worx.

Hodge, J. (2003), 'Extending Ownership in Telecommunications in South Africa. Policy, Performance and Future Options', TIPS Working Paper.

Hodge, J. and Theopold, N. (2001), 'Competition and Regulation in the Telecommunications Industry in South Africa', paper prepared for the Competition Commission, School of Economics, University of Cape Town.

International Telecommunications Union (2004), *Main Telephone Lines, Cellular Subscribers, Subscribers per 100 People*, Geneva: International Telecommunications Union.

International Telecommunications Union (ITU) (2002), 'Competition Policy in Telecommunications: Background Paper', Workshop on Competition Policy in Telecommunications, Document: CPT/04, Geneva: International Telecommunications Union.

Katz, M.L. and Woroch, G.L. (1998), 'Symposium Introduction: Convergence, Competition and Regulation', Compilation of papers given at the Bridging Digital Technologies and Regulatory Paradigms Conference at the University of California, Berkeley, 27 and 28 June 1997.

Kekana, N. (Group Executive, Telkom) (2003), 'Not So – We Have Given Voice to Many South Africans', *Sunday Times*, 7 December.

Liebowitz, S.J. and Margolis, S.E. (1997), 'Network Effects (Externalities)', mimeo, Management School, University of Texas at Dallas, Texas and Department of Economics, North Carolina State University, North Carolina.

Melody, W. (2003), 'Telkom Blocks the Information Highway', *This Day*, 1 December.

Ngcaba, A. (2003), *Convergence Policy Process – A Pre-Briefing for Stakeholders*, Department of Communications (SA).

Oftel (2003), *Review of Mobile Wholesale Voice Call Termination Markets: EU Market Review*, London: Oftel, 15 May.

Organisation for Economic Co-operation and Development (OECD) (2004), 'Relationship between Regulators and Competition Authorities', *Competition Law and Policy*. CD-Rom.

Shy, O. (2000), 'Digital Convergence, Competition and Antitrust Law', mimeo, Department of Economics, University of Haifa, Israel.

Sunday Times (2003), 'Future Looks Bright for SA's Telecoms Industry. Survey: Telecommunications', 18 May. www.suntimes.co.za/2003/05/18/business/survey06.asp.

TelkomSA Limited (various), *Group Annual Report*, Pretoria.

White J. (2003), *An Introduction to Telecommunications Liberalization and Regulation in South Africa*, www.iimahd.ernet.in/ctps/Justine-India-Conf-Paper.pdf.

Index